KING OF FANG AND CLAW

THE COMPLETE PULP MAGAZINE ADVENTURES

Zar, the lion, struggled to escape the landslide that he had created, dug in deep as with an ominous rumble the whole face of the bank came crashing downward.

THE COMPLETE PULP MAGAZINE ADVENTURES

BY
BOB BYRD

COVERS BY
J.W. SCOTT

ILLUSTRATIONS BY
L.F. BJORKLUND
EARL MAYAN

INTRODUCTION BY
WILL MURRAY

BOSTON
ALTUS PRESS
2008

TABLE OF
CONTENTS

INTRODUCTION

IT'S NOT DIFFICULT to reconstruct the motivation behind publisher Martin Goodman deciding to publish *Ka-Zar* in 1936. His three-year-old pulp publishing house was a bottom-of-the-barrel operation all through the Great Depression. The big trend at the time was hero pulps—The Shadow, Doc Savage and the like.

Goodman was a follower, not a trend-setter. He never ventured into traditional hero territory. He stuck with safe genres like Western and detective tales. But one of the most successful protagonists ever to emerge from the pulp jungle was Edgar Rice Burroughs' Tarzan of the Apes. Created in 1912, Tarzan stands as a true original, and as personified by Johnny Weismuller, he was capturing a new generation of movie-goers in a series of MGM Tarzan films then breaking box-office records. *Ka-Zar* was timed for release to coincide with two major Tarzan events. The 19th Tarzan novel, *Tarzan's Quest*, was released in hardcover on September 1, two months before the November premiere of *Tarzan Escapes*, the third in the MGM series. Goodman intended to capitalize on all that free publicity.

Ka-Zar was an August or September release. The August 1936 issue of *The Kable News-Gram* carried this painfully discreet promotional blurb:

> "*Ka-Zar* is more than a fiction magazine. It is the old, never-ending, yet most thrilling of all stories, the fight of man against wild nature. *Ka-Zar* has the stuff, and we invite you to

prove it to yourself."

No other pulp house had ever devoted an entire magazine to a Tarzan knockoff. Goodman was about to enter a brave new world of imitations. Would readers flock to a new Jungle King? Was there an audience for other Tarzans? Would he be sued?

Beyond that, easy speculation becomes difficult. The first issue of *Ka-Zar* hit U. S. newsstands with a John W. Scott cover, a lead novel whose title was slightly different within as without, and an author no one had ever heard of.

The identity of Bob Byrd remains as much a mystery today as it was 70 years ago in 1936.

As far as anyone can research, it appeared only four times: on the three Ka-Zar novels, and on *Scourge of the Sky Hellions,* a 1938 lead novel in Goodman's *American Sky Devils.* This infrequent use suggests a personal pen name, not a house name. But one of the heroes of the day was Admiral Richard E. Byrd, explorer of the South Pole. To the people of the 1930s, the surname Byrd was evocative of adventure.

So the house name theory can't be discounted.

Often clues to lead-novel writers can be found in the back pages of the magazine in question. Anatole Feldman and Beech Allen were prominent bylines in the first two issues. In reality, they were Anatole France Feldman and Hedwig C. Langer, husband and wife. A Chicago writer, Feldman was one of the more prolific pulpsters in the days when gangster pulps were booming. He was responsible for the notorious hoodlum-hero "Big Nose" Serrano, who ran in Harold Hersey's *Gangster Stories,* and elsewhere. The Depression killed that whole sub-genre. Feldman, his wife and fellow pulp writer Wallace R. Bamber were the backers of the ill-fated *Far East Adventure Stories* in 1931. After that, Feldman—who also wrote as Tony Field and other variations on his name—drifted over to Standard Magazines, where he ghosted some of the earliest installments of the Phantom Detective series and contributed exotic fiction to *Thrilling Adventures.*

If Martin Goodman were searching for a seasoned pulp writer to pen lead novels set in a foreign clime, Tony Feldman was an excellent bet.

Another possibility is Robert O. Erisman, a prolific writer who also edited Goodman's pulp chain. He might have been Bob Byrd. He may be Robert O. Kenyon, a byline that ultimately became a house name.

Lastly, a Robert L. Byrd had one story in an issue of *World Adventurers* in 1934. Was he a real person? Unknown. But it's possible. Could these two Byrds be one and the same? No one knows.

Adding to the intrigue, *King of Fang and Claw* was reprinted by Wright & Brown of London circa 1937.

But beyond that, Bob Byrd remains an enigma.

As for Ka-Zar himself, he was a credible variation on the Tarzan theme. Rather than an Ape Man, Ka-Zar was raised as a brother to lions. His name meant Brother to Zar the Lion. Otherwise, the formula was essentially the same. White orphan grows up to become the defacto King of the African jungle. The details may be discovered in the pages that follow. As a gesture in the direction of originality, Ka-Zar is a blond. Tarzan was classically dark-haired.

One can easily imagine Goodman and his collaborators at Manvis Publishing—the division of Newsstand Publications' Red Circle imprint which published *Ka-Zar*—juggling and rejuggling the syllables in Tarzan until they arrived at a combination Goodman's lawyer would clear. (For the record, it's pronounced "KAY Sar.") The rest was mining familiar folk ore.

Ka-Zar was ostensibly a bi-monthly. But Goodman was no stickler for publicaton schedules. He released the second issue with a January 1937 cover date—three months after the first. That should have made the magazine a quarterly. Yet he waited until sales figures were in on both before releasing issue 3, dated June. Hedging his bets, Goodman retitled it *Ka-Zar the Great.*

Sales did not improve enough to continue.

Although Ka-Zar faded from the pulp scene in 1937, Martin Goodman refused to let him die. When he launched Timely Comics in 1939, Goodman revived Ka-Zar in comics form. The origin novel was adapted in *Marvel Comics* #1 by artist Ben Thompson. New stories of Ka-Zar continued in the renamed *Marvel Mystery Comics*. "Adventures of Ka-Zar" was strictly a back-of-the-book feature and never achieved the fame of Timely headliners like the Human Torch or Sub-Mariner, fading away early in 1942. Some of these strips carried the legend, "Ka-Zar Created by Bob Byrd," further deepening the mystery behind his creator. Why credit a house name not used on the strip itself?

In 1954, Goodman launched *Jungle Action*, a comic book featuring Lo-Zar, a renaming of Ka-Zar. Like Ka-Zar, he was a blond-haired jungle man. Zar the lion was nowhere to be found, however. Don Rico and Joe Maneely did the strip. *Jungle Action* lasted only a year. Goodman's timing was poor. Over at Fiction House, they were folding their *Jungle Stories* pulp after a successful 15 year run showcasing their own Tarzan knockoff, Ki-Gor.

Flash forward a decade. As Marvel Comics, Timely is resurgent in the 1960s. Again, Goodman decided to revive Ka-Zar. He instructed his editor and head writer Stan Lee to bring him back. Lee couldn't immediately find a solo spot for the forgotten jungle lord in any of Marvel's magazines, so he and artist Jack Kirby reinvented him for an early issue of *The X-Men* in 1965. This time he was Kevin Plunder, orphan son of the English lord who discovered a lost world of prehistoric dinosaurs and primitive humans beneath the South Pole called the Savage Land.

Clearly, this milieu was inspired by Edgar Rice Burroughs' subterreanean realm called Pellucidar, which Tarzan once explored. Lee and Kirby replaced Zar the lion with Zabu the sabre-tooth tiger. This time, Ka-Zar caught on.

Before long, Ka-Zar was a popular guest star in the Marvel Universe. Forty years later, he's still around. These three novels are the foundation stones for the legend of Ka-Zar. Tarzan has since gone in to immortality among American folk heroes, leaving his many imitators forgotten today.

Somehow, Ka-Zar refuses to perish.

Will Murray
2007

BOOK I

KING OF FANG AND CLAW

KA-ZAR, Primitive white youth of the jungle, son of the Lion, fights the lustful treasure hunters of the outside world.

CHAPTER I

HEART OF DARKNESS

THE CONGO—HEART OF darkest Africa—two degrees south of the Equator.

Abruptly the sun was blotted out and a sudden deluge descended from the heavens. It fell steadily in a silver sheet for five minutes, then as abruptly stopped. It was the first rain, marking the beginning of the rainy season.

The brassy sun showed its molten face again, hotter than before. From the floor of the primeval jungle a miasmic mist steamed slowly upward. The air was sullen, brooding, oppressive.

From a thousand giant trees, matted and festooned with an impenetrable tangle of vines, the lemurs scolded querulously at one another. Vividly plumed birds screamed hoarsely as they flitted from tree to tree. And the beasts of the earth snarled and spat at each other as they wrangled over their kill.

Darkest Africa, where Nature had been prodigal and profligate. She had peopled this, her richest land, with a myriad of living things—plant, beast, bird and fish. And then, as if regretting her generosity, she had pitted the one against the other. Let the Law be that of Claw and Fang; let the strong survive.

Suddenly, above the teeming noises of earth and air, a mighty roar reverberated between the trees. As if blasted by an evil curse the jungle was hushed.

Then, a moment later, with a majestic stride a mighty lion pushed through the brush and stepped into a small, open clearing that bordered a lake of cerulean blue.

Zar the Mighty paused a moment on the edge of the clearing. Slowly, disdainfully he swung his massive head from side to side as he surveyed his domain. His tawny mane was ruffed; his tufted tail switched nervously from side to side.

Again he tilted back his head. Again the rumbling bass note of his defiance filled the clearing. But there was no one who dared answer his challenge.

Zar snorted contemptuously, lashed his tail once more and proceeded slowly down to the water's edge. This respectful silence that greeted his coming was fitting to his might and dignity. For wasn't he Zar the Mighty—Lord of the Jungle?

He drank, long and deeply. But minutes before he had his fill his head snapped up. A snarl rumbled in his throat; his leather lungs expanded and the talons of his fore-paws arched.

From high over head came an angry, droning buzz that grew louder, more insistent with every moment's passing. Zar threw back his head and looked up between the trees. What fool of a bird was this who dared challenge the might of his claw and fang?

And then he saw it, first as a speck looming out of the south. It advanced rapidly, with incredible speed, flying low; and the roar of its coming put even Zar's stentorian bellow to shame.

THIS WAS NOT Pindar the Eagle or Kru come to the vulture's feast. Zar had never seen such a bird before—one with such an incredible spread of wing—one that screamed its defiance as it flew like an arrow.

However, he felt no fear in its presence. His muscles simply bulged in anger.

From slitted, amber eyes he watched the strange bird as it soared above the clearing. It cleared the far side, then suddenly, without warning, a jet of black smoke belched forth from its side.

Zar's snarl rose on a higher note. He held his ground but crouched low. What trick was this? What strange method of attack from this strange bird?

Then, still watching, he saw the winged thing stagger in mid-air, pivot around on its mighty spread of shining wings and glide down for the clearing where he stood.

Zar ruled the jungle because of his cunning as well as his strength. Confronted by the unknown for the first time in his life, he decided to stalk this new enemy. With one bound he cleared the shore of the lake; with another he was crouched low in the tangle of brush that bordered the clearing.

Above him he heard a rushing roar of air that made him think of the times when the jungle trees bent to the storm's fury. And high above this sound came an eerie wail that grated down the long length of his supple spine.

Crouching low he looked up. The bird was swooping down headed straight for him. Smoke still jetted from its belly. It was clearing the trees now at the far side. He watched with a fascination tempered by awe. Then abruptly he tensed. One wing of this new, fantastic creature had carelessly brushed the outflung arm of a tree. There was a tearing, rending noise; the wing sheered off and the bird reeled.

Zar knew then that it was wounded and his lips bared back from his fangs. With a quiet, implacable intentness he watched the stricken thing spin to earth, crash on its one good wing and beak, bounce high into the air again, then settle down to earth with a dull thud.

Caution still ruled Zar the Mighty. This might be some ruse or trick with which he was unfamiliar. He decided to wait a moment before making his charge.

His amber eyes glinting warily, he watched. There was a stir of hurried activity about the stricken bird. Then some strange beast, the like of which Zar had never seen before, jumped from the belley of the mammoth of the skies. It walked erect on two feet like N'Guru, the gorilla.

But some instinct told Zar that this was not N'Guru, the only living thing in the jungle that dared challenge his reign. This strange beast was smaller than N'Guru, puny in comparison. Its face was white and hairless and its body was covered with something that was neither skin, fur nor feather.

The short hair stirred at the base of Zar's skull. His lips pulled back from his long, yellow teeth. A growl started deep in his throat but died still-born.

For, for the first time in his life, Zar was moved by an alien emotion—an emotion he found hard to understand. With a rising anger he realized that it was fear—fear of that ridiculous, puny, two-legged creature with the sickly-white skin.

His tail beat a savage tattoo on the earth. In his cunning, animal brain he tried to reason himself free from the shameful thing that clutched his heart. Wasn't he Zar the Mighty? One blow from his saber-tipped claws would rip the strange beast from throat to belly.

But the nameless fear held him still. It was beyond his simple, elemental reasoning. It was instinctive, deep-rooted, instilled in all animal kind since the first man climbed down from the trees and walked erect on two feet.

And with the coming of fear to Zar's *heart*, came hate—hate for this two-legged creature who stilled the battle-cry in his throat. He snarled in frustrated fury, turned from the clearing and plunged deep into the jungle growth.

CHAPTER II

THE JUNGLE TALKS

J **OHN RAND WAS** not aware of the long, bleeding gash in his forearm as he staggered from the wreckage of his plane. His only thought was for the other two who had crashed with him. With a desperate energy he tore at the shattered rear cockpit.

"Constance!" he called hoarsely. "David!"

A thin wail answered him, spurred him frantically on. A moment later he grasped a curly-headed, three-year-old boy and pulled him from the tangle of wood and metal. The child whimpered, more from fright than from pain. There was a swelling lump on his forehead, a long scratch down one cheek.

"Don't cry, son," begged Rand. "We're safely on land, now."

Swiftly he ran his hands over the sturdy little body and was relieved to find that the youngster had received no more than a bad shaking up. Then he jumped back to the plane in search of his wife.

He found her lying with her soft blonde hair pillowed against the crash pad, the heart-shaped oval of her face pallid and her eyes closed. With an ache in his heart he lifted her tenderly from the wreckage and lowered her to the ground beside the plane.

"Constance!" he called huskily. "You're not hurt?"

He raised her head. Her eyelids fluttered, opened. He repeated his anxious question.

Constance Rand's eyes were clouded with pain but she smiled nevertheless when she saw her son staring at her from round, surprised eyes. She reached out, ran tender fingers through his touseled hair in a swift caress. Then she looked up at her husband, still smiling.

"You know, John," she said coolly. "I thought it was the end. I prayed."

John Rand grinned down at her. "And lo! Your prayer was answered. Here we are, all safe and…" A twinge of pain crossed the girl's face. "Hello! You're hurt," continued Rand, suddenly sober.

"Terribly careless of me," said Constance. "But I'm afraid I am. My leg."

"Here—let's have a look," said Rand. Drawing his pocket-knife he hastily slit the left leg of her khaki breeches. Just below the knee the flesh was bruised and swollen. As gently as possible his fingers probed the injured area. And a moment later his face grew grave.

Watching him with anxious eyes, the girl saw. "Is it…" she began tentatively.

Rand nodded his head. "Yes—it's broken," he admitted reluctantly.

With a little sigh Constance sank back. "I was afraid of that," she said.

"Mummy hurt?" asked young David brightly.

Constance nodded and Rand managed a wry grin.

"Cheer up, darling. It's a simple break. We'll have you all mended and about in a short time."

Snatching his helmet from his head, he despatched the youngster to fill it with water from the lake. Then picking up his wife he settled her comfortably in the shadow of the plane's fuselage and began a crude but efficient job of resetting the broken bone.

A small medical kit had been part of the ship's equipment when it had taken off from Johannesburg that morning. But it was a painful ordeal at best. It was sheer nerve alone that kept Constance from crying out. Once—and only once—twin tears squeezed from the corners of her eyelids and coursed in the crystalline drops down her pale cheeks. She concentrated on her set teeth and clenched her tiny fists so tightly that her nails cut into her palms.

IT WAS NOT until the last splint and bandage was set firmly in place that her mind once more was free to consider their surroundings. Then her heart-felt relief that David had been unhurt in the crash and that her husband had escaped with a minor cut or two, gave way to new fears and doubts. She bathed the swollen lump on her son's forehead as Rand stayed the bleeding of his own arm. It was a curious monkey, who peering down at them and scolding them for their unwarranted intrusion, made her realize the wildness of their landing place.

"John," she asked evenly, "just what part of Africa did you choose to crack up in? Where are we?"

Rand tried to make his voice as casual as hers. "Oh, somewhere in the Belgian Congo," he replied with a shrug.

Constance's arms crept about the youngster in a protecting gesture, drew him close to her. "The Congo," she breathed. "The heart of the jungle." Then: "How long will it take us—how far is it—to—to civilization?"

John Rand could not find it in his heart to answer her question, to tell her how many hundred miles of almost impassable wilderness lay between them and the nearest outpost of the white man. Instead, without looking up, he replied easily: "We don't have to worry about that, darling. When we don't show up in Cairo they'll send a flock of planes out to search for us. One will be along any day now."

And then, as if to mock this calm assurance, somewhere deep in the jungle the mighty Zar vented his rage in a thunderous roar. Young David cocked his head and listened in wide-eyed curiosity. But a low cry broke from his mother's lips. She tightened her grip about the boy.

"John," she said, trying hard to hide the catch in her voice, "if it wasn't for you—I'd be afraid."

Rand leaned over and kissed her swiftly. "You're a brick, Connie. I've gotten you into this mess and I'll get you out." Then he straightened up to his full height. He was a young man, bronzed by the African sun, with wide shoulders and lean hips and muscles of whipcord and steel. The roar of the jungle lord was a challenge and he accepted it.

"Keep your nerve up, Connie," he said easily. "We'll be out of this in a few days. Till then, I have a rifle, two automatics and plenty of cartridges in the plane. We won't go hungry and nothing shall harm you. In a few days you'll be sitting on the verandah of Sheppard's Hotel in Cairo, telling all your friends about your thrilling sojourn in the Congo."

She touched his hand in a fleeting caress. "All right, John," she smiled up at him. "I'll be good. If only I hadn't hurt my leg, I could help you. Now, David and I will simply have to watch you labor."

"That'll be help enough," he answered.

Had he been alone in this predicament, with its promise of danger and excitement, John Rand might have actually enjoyed the experience. It was not the first time in his adventurous career that he had had to call upon his ingenuity and resourcefulness to survive. He had earned the self-confidence which now possessed him.

Hunting through the tangled debris that had been the plane he salvaged their luggage. He regretted that he had taken no such item as an axe with him but he had a stout knife and it would have to serve his purpose. Armed with it, he slashed boughs from the trees that fringed the clearing, tore great lengths from the tough lianas that hung in loops from the branches down to the jungle floor. The plane would never leave the earth again; it was wrecked beyond all repair. So he put the shattered parts to better use.

By the time the sweltering day had drawn to a close he had erected a makeshift but comfortable lean-to under the protecting wing of the plane.

The setting sun lingered a moment atop a distant mountain peak that thrust a jagged cone, sheer and forbidding in the western sky. Its last slanting rays bathed the clearing and the lake beyond in molten gold. Mauve shadows crept out from under the dense trees of the surrounding forest. Then the sun dropped down behind the peak and the deepening shadows encroached upon the makeshift camp.

In front of the shelter, Rand built a roaring fire. From the cot of leafy branches that he had prepared for her, Constance watched him from soft eyes. Like all emotions of childhood, David's first fear had been short-lived. Now he was enchanted with this strange, new environment. With fascinated eyes he watched the birds make their last brilliant flights across the clearing and come to roost in the tops of the giant trees. A scampering monkey made him clap his hands in delight.

Whistling cheerfully, Rand prepared a meal from the scant provisions that they had carried in the plane. A tin of biscuit, bars of chocolate and powdered milk. The latter he mixed with water from the lake and heated in battered tin cups over the fire.

Night comes suddenly in the jungle. The magnificent sunset was followed by a brief twilight while they ate. When Rand went to rinse out the cups at the shore of the lake, a chill wind blew in across the waters. It rustled the leaves of the trees and awakened other noises and murmurs in the forest depths. An incessant chattering rose above the low hum of myriad insects. Some creature—bird or animal, he did not know—occasionally emitted a plaintive wail.

He came back to find David curled up in his mother's arms, peacefully asleep. Getting coats and a tarpaulin from the wreckage of the plane, he covered them both. Then with his rifle across his knees, he sat down with his back against the open end of the shelter, prepared for an all-night vigil.

For a while husband and wife conversed in low tones, careful lest they wake the sleeping youngster. Beyond the circle of light cast by the fire, the jungle was a wall of impenetrable blackness. Once greenish eyes winked back at them. Rand threw another handful of brush on the blaze and the eyes vanished. With soothing words he reassured his helpless wife.

Whether her confidence in him banished her nameless fears, or whether the terrific strain of the day's events had taken its toll at last, he did not know. But the blessed sleep that claimed David stole over Constance at last. And John Rand remained alone at his post on vigilant guard.

At first the myriad noises of the night held his entire attention. Unseen life stirred in the tree-tops. Strange rustlings sounded around the wreckage of the plane. Once, far out on the lake, there was a mighty splash. Twice during the night, deep in the jungle a panther screamed. Both times David cried out and both times Constance awoke to quiet him with a tender hand and murmured words of comfort.

The stars, though of dazzling brilliance, seemed very far away and cold. Gradually the various sounds of the jungle grew more familiar in Rand's ears and his mind strayed back to the events leading up to their disastrous crash.

CHAPTER III

MAROONED

A **HIGH-SPIRITED YOUNG** Yank, John Rand had roamed the world in search of adventure and fortune. He had found them both. The Gods had indeed been kind to him.

In a romantic two-weeks' interlude between his fortune seeking expeditions, he had wooed and won the gentle Constance and had spirited her away from under the very nose of the stern headmistress of a fashionable French finishing school. Neither of them had ever regretted the elopement.

Constance had brought her share of luck with her, for shortly after their marriage, Rand had stumbled on a rich diamond field in the Transvaal and wealth had become theirs. And with the birth of their son a year later, their home on the outskirts of Johannesburg had become a paradise indeed.

Now looking into the glowing heart of the fire in the depths of the jungle, Rand wondered at the strange trick Fate had played on him. In his adventuresome youth he had learned many things and the art of flying an airplane had been not the least of them. For his own pleasure, when the income from the diamond field permitted him to satisfy all his desires, he had purchased and maintained the plane that now lay in ruins behind him.

And when Constance had received the telegram two days before, that her father was seriously ill in Cairo, he had immediately suggested that they make the trip to his bedside in the plane. That their course would lay over thousands of miles of wild and dangerous territory, they had never considered for a moment.

Rand sighed. If it had been himself alone who had crashed, he would not have minded. But Constance and his son complicated the situation.

He shrugged philosophically. They would be there a couple of days at the most. A rescue ship would surely come in search of them—probably it was on its way already. He would be ready for it. In the morning he would prepare a great signal fire in the center of the clearing, ready to be lit at the first sound of an approaching plane. It was fortunate indeed that they had crashed in the clearing instead of in the heart of the thick jungle. A rescue ship could make a safe landing and easily take off.

The fire died down to glowing embers. He caught himself nodding, prodded the blaze to life again and added more brush. Slowly the stars wheeled their majestic course across the heavens and the hours passed. Then at long last the impenetrable blackness slowly lightened to a murky gray, the first herald of the coming day. Rand stirred, rose and stretched and greeted the booming sunrise with a smile.

Young David pushed back the tarpaulin with chubby hands, sat up and looked about him with wondering eyes. Rand placed a finger to his lips, lifted the youngster across the still form of his mother and led him down to the lake.

To a three-year-old, to whom the common-place features of every-day life are still a mystery and a delight, the heart of the African jungle is hardly more startling. David was enchanted. To him, the Dark Continent was a place of dazzling sunshine and brilliant color; of pleasing smells and intriguing noises.

The night life of the jungle had died with the dawn to yield place to the equally noisy life of day. A flight of long-tailed, scarlet birds wafted across the lake and came to rest in a squawking group in the tree-tops. Slender, spidery monkeys trooped through the branches and peered curiously down at the strange invaders of their domain. One, bolder than the rest, cautiously approached the tail of the plane. With a gleeful whoop, David ran to catch it.

Rand smiled at the comical mixture of surprise and disappointment on his face when the monkey scurried agilely off, mocking the youngster over his shoulder as he went.

WHEN THEY CAME back to the lean-to to prepare breakfast they found Constance awake. Her leg was setting nicely and bothered her little. Rand adjusted the splints, served breakfast and then set to work to prepare the signal fire. He warned his wife that yet another day might pass before rescue came, but the sight of the towering brushpile and the wet tarpaulin lying beside it, ready to blanket the smoke and send it up in signal puffs, cheered her greatly.

She made no complaint, though Rand knew that her broken leg gave her constant pain. The loaded rifle was set against the lean-to and young David warned of dire results if he should touch it. An automatic was strapped to Rand's belt and thus prepared for whatever the day might bring, he set to work to make their shelter yet more comfortable and safe.

To the youngster, this task was delightful play. Despite his happy conviction that he was being of great assistance, he was constantly underfoot. He picked up his father's knife, dropped it and the sharp blade missed his foot by inches. He stumbled over a gnarled root and the rush of his fall blew a shower of sparks from the fire a scant foot away. Ten minutes later, while making faces at himself in the mirror of the lake he fell into the water and was thoroughly drenched. After that episode he was seated beside his mother and requested to remain there.

The day wore on, hot and sultry, with a sudden deluge in mid-afternoon. A few minutes later the torrid sun turned the damp floor of the jungle to a steaming mist. Always Rand and his wife listened, ears strained, for the sound of an approaching motor.

The sun wheeled its long arc across the heavens and headed down towards the distant mountain peak that rose up to meet it. At last they touched, quivering in a shimmer of heat and a riotous sunset flared its vivid colors over the land. And then, in the brief hush of silence with which the jungle paid tribute to the sun's glory, they heard the sound for which they had been waiting.

The jungle had humming noises of its own. But the distant drone of a powerful motor floated unmistakably across the still air. Rand leaped at once to his waiting pile of brush. With hands that trembled slightly in their eagerness he scratched a match and set it ablaze. Then, after a moment, he seized the damp tarpaulin and blanketed the flames.

The drone of the approaching plane grew steadily louder. Whipping back the tarpaulin, Rand set a great puff of black smoke skyward. Then hastily he blanketed the fire again, to repeat the operation.

The last slanting rays of the sun picked out a glinting speck in the sky and turned it to shining gold. It grew slowly larger until it resembled a giant, iridescent dragon fly soaring far above the earth.

"John!" called Constance anxiously. "He's going to miss us. He's bearing north instead of west!"

Rand flung a hasty glance upward. He whipped up a last cloud of smoke from his fire, then clutching the tarpaulin, he raced down to the shore of the lake.

The plane loomed larger now but its nose was not pointed directly for the clearing. And it was riding high—much higher than Rand would have wished. With a sinking feeling at the pit of his stomach, he realized that from where the unknown pilot rode in his cockpit, the wreckage of Rand's ship was hidden by the towering trees and the clearing itself was scarcely visible.

Swiftly he splashed out into the lake until the water rose above his waist and waved the tarpaulin over his head. But the plane held to its steady course and did not falter.

THOUGH HE KNEW the pilot could not hear him, he cried out hoarsely. He flapped the heavy tarpaulin until his arms ached.

But neither the rising column of smoke from the clearing nor his wildly gesticulating figure were seen. The motor of the ship in the air rose to a high crescendo, then diminished again as it continued on.

Not until it had become a vanishing dot in the blue did John Rand's arms drop. Wearily he plodded back to his wife and child. Constance made a manful effort to conceal her bitter disappointment. She smiled, a little tremulously.

"Well, it looks as though we've failed to thumb a ride."

Rand dropped the tarpaulin and sank down beside her. "Pooh! This is a main highway. Busy traffic. There'll be another along in a moment." Then, more soberly, he went on. "He'll be back—probably tomorrow. It was the sunset. If he had come an hour earlier, he'd have spotted me at the edge of the lake. Or if he'd come an hour later, he'd have seen the light of the fire. Better luck next time."

But in the most important aspect of this optimistic prediction, Rand was wrong. True, the plane came again on the next day—and one the day after that. But each time it was farther from their lonely camp. The last time it appeared, it was but a dim speck far towards the horizon.

Helplessly they watched it vanish from their sight and no amount of forced good humor could hide the ache in their hearts.

Then three days passed and though they strained eyes and ears, the ship did not come again Reluctantly they had to voice the dismal conclusion that their would-be rescuers had given them up to the jungle.

Constance consoled herself with the thought that as soon as her leg had mended, they would begin the long over-land trek that would carry them out of the wilderness. Her husband would not deprive her of this meager consolation but he realized that until the long rainy season was ended—and it had just set in, in earnest—they must remain in their lonely outpost.

They were both astounded and in a measure glad, to hear

young David declare that he liked the jungle and had no desire to leave it. The fact that he was thoroughly enjoying their enforced sojourn in the wilds lightened their own burden.

CHAPTER IV

THE JUNGLE TAKES ITS TOLL

IT WAS EXACTLY a week since the mighty Zar had watched the strange bird come swooping down to rest in the clearing. Now curiosity stirred again in his mind. For a long while he hesitated, remembering the alien emotion he had felt for the first time at the sight of the grotesque, two legged creature. Then impelled by a fascination he could not resist, he headed for the camp.

He had not travelled far when he came to an abrupt halt. His head came up and sniffed the air with flaring nostrils. The tip of his tail twitched when his nose told him that N'Jaga, the leopard, was already stalking in the same direction.

Zar's amber eyes gleamed with resentment. One peremptory roar to announce his coming—and N'Jaga would reluctantly relinquish the trail to his mighty overlord. A growl started deep in his throat, then died.

Zar's pride ruled the jungle but it did not rule his own cunning brain. Let N'Jaga stalk this strange prey. He would be content to wait—to watch—to learn.

His huge paws trod the jungle floor as silently as pads of velvet. His tawny body wove easily through the dense, tangled undergrowth, barely disturbing a leaf in his passing.

From the branches of a tall tree Nono, the monkey, saw him. Safe in the swaying tree top, he shrilled a warning to the jungle folk. Zar glanced up from slitted eyes, snarled and went on. A terrified bush rat scurried across his path and dived squealing into the brush. Zar ignored the little creature with studied disdain.

The unfamiliar scent of man came first to warn him that he was nearing his destination. Treading yet more carefully, he wormed his way through a dense tangle and at last reached a point that gave him a broad view of the clearing.

The stricken bird still lay where it had fallen. From a queer shelter beneath its outspread wing a fascinating sound—Constance's voice—issued occasionally. Zar tilted his majestic head to one side and listened. Before the shelter the two-legged creature squatted on his haunches, busily engaged with something. And wonder of wonders, six feet away from him a smaller creature—undoubtedly the cub of the larger one—gamboled about.

Zar's keen eyes missed no detail of the scene. Thirty yards off to his left he made out the form of N'Jaga, lying crouched on his belly, his spotted shape barely distinguishable in the dense brush, his small eyes riveted on the group in the cleating. Zar was content to lie still and watch, only the very tip of his tail moving.

The strange cub continued to scurry about. His movements carried him farther and farther away from his busy father—closer and closer to the spot where N'Jaga lay like a motionless statue. Zar sensed what would happen, but he did not stir. The cub was not his. No such emotion as pity had ever stirred his stout heart. Life is cheap in the jungle and no vestige of regret marks a creature's passing.

So he watched N'Jaga tense his springy muscles, saw the stupid cub linger a fatal moment near the edge of the jungle. N'Jaga could wait no longer for the toothsome tid-bit to come even closer to his lair. With an ear-splitting scream he sprang, his sleek, spotted body hurtling out of the undergrowth.

Even as his first bound covered half the distance between him and the startled cub, a cry of terror rang out from the shelter under the wing.

"John—David! Quick!" It floated across the clearing on a quivering note.

Quicker than the lightning strikes the two-legged creature snatched up a long stick that lay near him, jumped up and pointed the stick at the bounding N'Jaga.

There was a roar and a pale flash, then a puff of smoke wafted from the end of the stick. N'Jaga halted in midstride, screamed. Zar saw a streak of bright crimson appear on his spotted hide as he whirled to face this new menace.

THE TWO-LEGGED CREATURE did not run. The stick pointed at N'Jaga again. And for the first time, the leopard felt the strange fear that the wiser Zar had sensed a week before. Crouching, his tail lashing, he hesitated. And then, instead of charging in fury at the father of the cub, he suddenly wheeled around and vanished like a yellow streak.

The salty tang of blood came faintly to Zar's nostrils. Silent as a great shadow he bellied backwards. And while N'Jaga crept off to some quiet spot to nurse his wound, Zar glided back into the jungle fastness.

The scene that he had just witnessed was engraved indelibly on his memory. The stick had been pointed at N'Jaga. There had been a roar and a flash of fire. And N'Jaga had limped as he fled from the encounter. Zar had been wise, indeed, when he had been content to lie hidden and watch. His instinctive hatred for this two-legged creature was not lessened. But now it was tempered by a deep respect.

When the leopard had vanished, John Rand hurried to young David, snatched him up and carried him back to his anxious mother. To his amazement, his son looked at him from reproachful eyes.

"You hurt him," he accused. "You hurt him, daddy. Now he won't come back—never—never."

In silence, Rand looked at his child. When the huge leopard, with its jaws agape, had leaped at him, David had not shown even the slightest, instinctive fear.

Rand recalled the youngster's delight in the monkeys and birds and lizards with which the clearing abounded. And now a strange thought flitted through his mind. It was so elusive that he could not quite grasp it; but had he been able to do so, he would have realized that to young David the beasts of the jungle were companions and friends. Something within the child responded to them and he knew them, trusted and loved them.

Instead of trying to answer his son's accusation, he patted the youngster's head and for the rest of the day, he was a very thoughtful man.

And so, with death ever at their elbows, Rand and his family continued to survive in the heart of the African wilderness. Roots, berries, strange fruits and the game which was always plentiful fed them. Every day parts of the wrecked plane were added to the original lean-to, until they were housed in a safe and comfortable dwelling. Water and fuel were within easy reach. David's skin bronzed until in the tattered remnants of his clothing he resembled a sturdy young savage. And while his parents became merely reconciled to their strange environment, he fell more and more under its spell.

Boredom never exised there, for constant dangers kept them ever on the alert. There was the time when David's restless feet took him too close to a slender, emerald-green snake, sunning itself on a tangle of roots. The reptile hissed a sibilant warning and then uncoiled with the suddenness of a broken spring. Swift as it struck, John Rand was a fraction of a second faster. He knocked the youngster sprawling as he leaped forward and the snake buried its dripping fangs in the tough leather of his high boots. Snatching the automatic from his hip, he fired three times in rapid succession and the snake threshed wildly in its death throes.

Again David reproached his father and no graphic description of the reptile's deadliness could change the boy's attitude. He mourned the passing of a fellow denizen of the wild.

They heard the distant trumpeting of an elephant herd and one day Rand, hunting in the jungle depths for game, was startled by a loud crashing through the lower branches of the trees. The sound was made by a tribe of great apes on their migration to new feeding grounds and twice he caught glimpses of dark, flat-nosed faces peering through the leafy boughs.

At night great cats prowled on padded feet around their dwelling. They could hear the sniffing of curious and hungry beasts and the loaded rifle was never far beyond Rand's reach.

OFTEN THEY LAID awake far into the night while in low voice Constance made plans for the day when she would be able to travel. To please her, Rand discussed in detail their possible routes, the equipment they would need and the minimum amount of provision they could carry. But he was grateful for the darkness that hid his face from hers, while she talked of Cairo, of friends in far-off London, and in Johannesburg.

For she was mending slowly—very slowly. And though the broken bones were knitting at last, she was growing wan and weak. Knowing the courage and the will within her slender body, he blamed it on the enervating climate. The damp, steaming miasma seemed to sap all strength from her. She grew thin and violet shadows made hollows under her eyes.

His fears for her were justified. The day came when she complained of a racking headache. And soon she was consumed by a raging fever.

Rand was dismayed. He had seen the ravages of mysterious tropical maladies before. He dosed her from the quinine supply of the medical kit that he had carefully guarded. But her weakened body did not respond. Shaken by alternate spells of burning fever and chills that made her tremble from head to foot, she grew steadily worse. Rand stayed constantly by her side and David listened wide-eyed when his mother began to ramble incoherently about the home that she had left.

Late one night, after a fitful, restless sleep, she woke to find her husband still keeping vigil beside her. She smiled up at him.

"Faithful John," she murmured.

Her voice was low and husky, but sane. Rand placed a cool hand on her fevered brow. "You're better," he said eagerly. "You know, I think you've passed the crisis."

Constance smiled again but shook her head. A strange soft light glowed in her deep-set eyes. "No, John. I—I'm going to die—very soon."

An expression of anguish crossed his face, then he forced a laugh from his lips. "Nonsense." He leaned over and pressed his face to hers. "You're not going to die. You can't leave me—I need you," he said huskily.

She stroked his bearded cheek with tender fingers. "I don't want to leave you. It's God's will. I'm not afraid—for myself." She slipped the wedding ring from her wasted finger on to his. "My dearest possession. I want you to wear it for me, John, always," she said softly.

Rand felt of the smooth, gold band. Though he could not read the inscription engraved on the inside of it, he knew it by heart: *"From John Rand to Constance Dean."*

Constance went on, her voice sinking to a whisper, so weak that it was barely audible. It seemed to Rand's straining eyes as though a shadow flitted across her face. "John," she managed feebly, "you'll take good care of David—won't you?"

"With my life," he answered.

She smiled weakly up at him. "I knew you'd say that." Her straying fingers sought and found his. With the contented sigh of a tired child going to sleep, she closed her eyes.

CHAPTER V

THE END OF THE RAINS

JOHN RAND NEVER knew that the hyena and jackal were prowling outside his rude shelter; never knew when the stealthy approach of Zar sent them slinking into the brush.

If he had known, he would not have cared.

Morbidly he toyed with the idea of ending it all, there by the side of his wife. He was tired, weary. Life held no meaning for him, had no purpose now that Constance was gone.

Then the cry of his son calling out in his sleep for a mother who would never answer again, brought him back to sanity. If not for himself, he had to live for David. It was enough that he had the death of his wife on his hands. The boy must live. For Constance's sake. It was her dying wish. The boy's name had been the last to pass her lips before a merciful God had taken her from her sufferings to the eternal peace of heaven.

That thought—that conviction—fortified Rand, eased the poignant pain of his grief. He would live for his son, dedicate his life to the boy. For in him the flesh and blood of Constance were resurrected.

For the first time in many years John Rand prayed—prayed to the God, who in his infinite wisdom had created man as well as the savage beasts that roamed the jungle. His words were humble, penitent. He asked nothing for himself; only for the strength, the courage and the cunning to survive for his son and to eventually win back with him to civilization.

Rand did not sleep that night and it was not until the first pale light of dawn lit up the east that he stirred from the side of his wife. He had much to do.

First was the heart breaking task of fashioning a coffin from the fabric wings of the plane. It was crude at the very best, no more than a canvas covering for the lovely body. But he could not bring himself to commit his wife to the raw earth, uncovered.

David watched him from wide, scared eyes as he worked. "Mummy sick?" he asked in a small, hushed voice.

Rand turned to him, placed a gentle hand on his touseled head. "No, son," he answered softly. "Mummy is sick no longer. All her troubles are over. She has gone to heaven. God has taken her from us."

Little David smiled happily at the mention of the Deity. "God is good," he said, expressing the fundamental philosophy behind all true religion. "He won't let mummy cry any more."

Rand swept up the youngster in his arms and crushed him to his breast. Emotion gripped him and it was a moment before he could speak. "Amen to that, son," he cried reverently. "Yes, God is good. Mummy will cry no more."

David was satisfied with that and scampered cheerily about the clearing while his father labored over the grave. For a shovel he had nothing better than the jagged end of a shattered spar from the plane, but the ground was soft from the rains and his labor was one of love.

By noon his work was done. Calling David to him, he made his way slowly to the lean-to. There, with tender arms he picked up the shrouded body and with his son following after him, started back for the shallow grave.

Never had the heart of darkest Africa witnessed such a strange funeral procession. The jungle seemed to have stopped breathing while it watched.

Before the raw hole in the ground, Rand crushed his wife to him, while his lips moved in prayer. Then, reverently, he lowered his burden to its final, earthly resting place. He had fashioned a pillow of wild flowers for Constance's head; and now with David at his side they dropped orchids into the open grave.

Rand dropped down to his knees. "Pray, son," he said in a choked voice.

DAVID KNELT DOWN beside him and pressed the palms of his hands together as his mother had taught him. From wide eyes he looked trustingly into the blue of heaven: "I know you'll take care of mummy, God. And thank you."

There was such a simple, all-embracing faith behind the words that Rand felt sure that God had heard. He felt better.

"Amen," he said.

Slowly he filled in the grave and together with his son piled rocks over the little mound. From parts of the shattered propeller a cross was fashioned and placed at the head of the grave. And thus ended the saddest task it had ever been John Rand's misfortune to perform.

It was not until the following morning that Rand felt the full shock of his loss. He could not believe that Constance had gone from him forever, that never again would her eyes smile into his.

For the next week he brooded for long hours over her grave, heaping it high with jungle flowers, while all unheeded his son chased gaudy-winged butterflies around the clearing.

It was only the urgent demands of David's body that brought him out of his reveries. And then only long enough to satisfy the youngster's need for food.

Night brought him no surcease. Cradling the boy in his arms he would throw himself on the rude couch in the lean-to and in vain woo sleep.

One night prowling jackals about the grave sent him leaping from the shelter. Snatching a glowing brand from the low burning fire he charged into the night. He was consumed by an insensate, unreasonable fury. Not that! Anything but that! The thought of Constance's body despoiled by noisome beasts horrified him—became an obsession that haunted him.

The next day he heaped more stones upon the grave.

The rainy season was in full sway by now. Intermittently throughout the day and night the clearing was drenched by heavy deluges. They came sudden, without warning, as if some celestial gardener had opened a valve in heaven.

And then, two weeks after Constance had died, David fell sick. He had caught some strange jungle fever that sent up his temperature to perilous heights.

The boy's illness was the one thing that could have moved Rand from his lethargy, brought him back to reality and to his responsibilities to his son. For the first time he realized how he had neglected those responsibilities; how, in his selfish sorrow he had violated the last promise he had made to Constance.

His heart turned sick as he listened to the boy's childish prattle in delirium. If David died... but he did not dare think of that.

For three days and nights, with no more than a moment's snatched sleep, he nursed the youngster. No mother could have shown more care, more tenderness or patience. And then, on the morning of the fourth day, the fever was gone as suddenly as it had come. Sane-eyed, David smiled up into his father's face and asked for food.

The supply of powdered milk had long since been used. Now, with a prayer of thanks on his lips, Rand stirred up the fire, picked up the rifle, patted the boy reassuringly on the head and crept cautiously from the lean-to.

Deep in a cane-brake he took up his post by the side of a game trail that led down to the edge of the lake. A leopard passed before the sights of his gun, drank its fill from the lake and departed, unmolested. The hyena, jackal and wild pig also drank their fill and went their way.

Then Rand tensed and his finger tightened on the rifle. An antelope with a fawn at her flank minced gingerly down the trail. The female's head was back and her velvet nostrils quivered as she sniffed the air.

Some sense of smell or sound, or perhaps a combination of both, flashed a warning of danger to her brain. She whinnied the alarm to her young—her haunches tensed for a spring....

RELUCTANTLY, EVEN THOUGH it was for his son, John Rand squeezed the trigger of his rifle. The mother antelope bounded forward for a sheer twenty feet, but the bay fawn did not follow after her. As if its slender, dainty legs had suddenly turned to water, it crumpled in the center of the trail.

And from deep in the jungle, challenging the crack of the rifle, came Zar's rumbling roar. Many times he had watched the two-legged creature of the clearing with the strange, shiny stick in his hand. Many times he had seen him point that stick at some wild thing of the jungle. The stick would bark. And as night followed day, the animal it was pointed at would drop.

Zar could not understand the magic of this, but he feared. And because he feared he hated. The two-legged creature that looked like N'Guru, could deal death at a distance!

Zar roared again and from a side trail stalked Rand as he carried the fawn back to the lean-to.

That day and the day after, David gained strength on strong meat broth. By the end of the week he was himself.

Though the episode had turned out happily enough, it brought Rand to a fuller realization of the dangers that confronted himself and his son. Not only must they be eternally on guard for prowling beasts, but they had a more insidious enemy to face. One that was unseen—that struck silently, without warning—fever!

He was increasingly anxious to win back to civilization. But the fact that the rainy season was then at its height made the attempt impracticable if not impossible. If he had been alone he might have ventured it with the chances fifty-fifty that he won through. But with David, the long trek would be out of the question.

Much as he hated the enforced delay, caution dictated that course. And there were other deciding factors. By the time the rainy season came to an end, David would be months older. In the comparative safety of their camp he would become hardened, jungle wise, immune to tropical fevers, against their long trek through the trackless wilderness.

And then there was the added consolation that while they waited, he would be near Constance's grave.

In short, Rand resigned himself to three months of waiting. He determined, however, that at the first sign of a let-up in the rains, they would set forth.

In preparation for that day he studied for long hours the large map of the Dark Continent that had been tacked to the dashboard of his plane. As close as he could calculate, he had cracked up some two degrees south of the equator, between the 25th and 28th meridians, east.

Approximately two hundred miles to the east lay Lake Kivu. From there it would be comparatively easy to travel down the Ruizi River to Lake Tanganyika, the furtherest outpost of the white man. If, on the other hand, he went west, he should reach the Congo River within a hundred miles; and from thence, another trek of a hundred miles paralleling the stream due north should bring him to a tiny Belgian settlement.

There was little to choose between either course. Each offered the same danger of savage man and savage beast to every heart-breaking mile. Rand decided to wait the moment of his departure before making his decision.

The days dragged slowly by into weeks; the weeks into months. He took the enforced delay with a stoic calm and marveled at the sturdy muscles developed in the legs of his son—at the affinity the youngster had developed with the forbidding jungle.

David knew where the sweetest smelling flowers bloomed for Constance's grave; where the most luscious fruit ripened to satisfy their appetites. He made friends with the smaller animals, imitated the raucous cries of birds and strode the jungle trails as unafraid as Zar, before the coming of man.

As the rainy season dragged towards a close at last, Rand

made his simple preparations for the long trek. He was increasingly sparing of the bullets for the rifle, hunting only for the necessity of food. And of each kill, a portion was dried to be taken along on the journey.

CHAPTER VI

THE STORM

THE RAINS HAD decreased now, from a steady, twenty-four hour drumming to two heavy downpours—one in the early morning, the other at eventide. Rand's spirits picked up at the early prospect of taking the trail. The impenetrable jungle wall that surrounded the little clearing was a challenge to him—to his strength, courage and fortitude—and eagerly he accepted it.

Not that he minimized the dangers that would confront him and his son, but he had faith in himself, confidence in his ability to win through. Somehow he had the feeling that the spirit of his dead wife would watch over them, guide their faltering steps back to safety.

His heart was heavy at the thought of abandoning Constance's grave to the jungle, but he was fortified by the knowledge that she would have had it so. Mentally he made the resolution that once he returned his son to civilization, he would immediately form an expedition and head once more back for the clearing that had been his home for the past six months. He would disinter Constance's body then and bring it back with him for proper burial in the neat, trim cemeteries of her homeland.

The day came at last when Rand spoke of his hopes and plans to his son. It was towards sunset and the day had been marked by but one brief shower in the early morning.

"Well, son," he began in a cheery voice, "tomorrow we start for home."

"Home?" echoed David with a puzzled frown.

"Yes. Back to civilization. Back to the land of people—white people. Street cars, electric lights, trains," elaborated Rand enthusiastically.

"What's that?" asked David, still puzzled.

Rand smiled wryly to himself. In six short months—though they were comparatively a long span in the youngster's life—his son had completely forgotten everything he had once known of civilization. The most common words of civilized society conjured up no corresponding association in his mind. Such was the blessing of boyhood. An experience that might have blighted a more mature mind had left him untouched. He had taken the hardships and dangers of their enforced sojourn in the wilds as the natural manner of life. More, he had enjoyed it. And if his sturdy brown body was any evidence, he had thrived on it.

The terror and tragedy that had attended their exile had left him untouched. He was a little animal, as quick and animated as the monkeys that sported in the trees; as natural and untrammeled by the restricting influences of civilization as ever man had been before.

Rand envied him his simple acceptance of his mother's death; his easy forgetfulness of sorrow and grief.

"Yes, son," he began again, "tomorrow we start for home. Don't you remember? The house we lived in before we came here?"

David shook his head. His face was serious and frowning. "Where's that?" he demanded.

Rand flung his arm to the south. "Way, way off in there, beyond the lake," he answered. "A long way—a hard way. You'll get tired—we'll both get tired," he corrected. "And maybe we'll be hungry. But you'll take it like a man, eh, son?"

YOUNG DAVID FELT no elation at the prospect of leaving his beloved clearing. But at this last appeal of his father—man to man—he responded. "I'll take it like a man, dad," he repeated.

Rand clapped him fondly on the shoulder. "I knew you would."

David's brows screwed up in concentration and he thought for a moment. "We leave mummy here?" he asked at last.

A momentary shadow passed over Rand's face. "Yes, son, for a little while. But we'll come back for her." He cupped his boy's palm in his right hand, picked up the rifle in his left. "Come, we'll say good-bye to mummy for a little while. We'll leave some flowers on her grave."

They left the lean-to and slowly, hand in hand, walked across the clearing towards the little mound at the far side. They had tended it faithfully every day and it was covered with a blanket of hibiscus.

The grave held little significance for David's immature mind and the placing of flowers upon it was but a pleasant ritual that had to do with the gathering of wild, sweet smelling blooms.

Rand placed his offering on the grave, then bowed his head in prayer. For a long time he communed with his wife—so long that he failed to note the bank of ominous black clouds that were massing in the west. He wasn't aware that the sun had taken on a peculiarly brassy glare—that the myriad tongues of the jungle were stilled. Not a breath stirred, not a leaf rippled. The birds and monkeys had fallen strangely silent and all life seemed suspended as if waiting with bated breath for the stroke of doom.

The first intimation of danger that Rand had was a sudden soughing high in the tree tops above him. He looked up quickly in alarm. Not a tree stirred as yet and as he watched, the bank of black clouds in the west rolled across the sky as if poured from an inkpot, blotting out the sun.

Then, with a sudden blast, the storm broke. The wind screamed on a high, off-key wail. In perfect unison the towering trees of the jungle groaned and keeled far over. Jagged bolts of vivid purple rent the heaven and flashed luridly from sky to earth. With the first flash of lightning the rain came. It descended in a blinding, driving sheet as solid as a wall.

In the first second of the storm's fury Rand and his son were drenched. The screaming wind snatched their breath away and the air was filled with hurtling limbs and branches torn from the trees. All about them the mammoth baobab trees plunged and fell, smitten by the jagged bolts from above.

Rand swept young David to his arm and plunged for the shelter of the tall trees that bordered the clearing.

"It's all right, son," he shouted in David's ear, above the fury of the storm. "This will be over in a few minutes. It's the last twister of the rainy season—and the worst."

David did not answer. He was too fascinated by the storm.

They crouched there together on the edge of the clearing, lashed by the wind and the rain. The intermittent flashes of light lit up their faces with brilliant purple. Then, a second later, a sizzling bolt directly above them blinded them completely. The roaring clap of thunder that followed it immediately was equally as effective in deafening them.

If it had not been for these two factors, Rand would have known that the giant baobab tree, under which they had sought shelter, had been smitten—would have known that even with the lightning's flare it was crashing down on them.

Too late he realized their peril. It was the crash of the smaller trees about them, splintered like match wood by the fall of the towering baobab, that first told him of imminent peril. He glanced up once hastily and his heart constricted in his throat. The mammoth trunk of the tree was plunging straight down for them.

HE ACTED INSTINCTIVELY in the emergency. With a mighty thrust he flung David from him, clear of the path of the crashing destruction, then leaped far to one side. He succeeded in escaping the solid bole of the tree, which would have crushed the life from his body. But an outflung branch of the toppling giant crashed into the back of his head and sent him spinning drunkenly forward.

A bomb exploded inside his skull. He staggered wildly, dropped his rifle, flung out his arms to regain his balance, failed and plunged face down to the jungle floor.

How long he lay there, John Rand never knew. Slowly, painfully he crawled back to consciousness. He was first aware of an angry rumbling in his ears which he confused with the fury of the storm that had been raging. A moment before? It seemed so to him. In reality it was a matter of hours.

And the rumble was not thunder. It was Zar's voice, venting his hate, as he lashed his tail in the brush twenty yards from the clearing.

Rand was next conscious of something tugging at his shirt and an insistent small voice drilling into his ears.

"Get up, daddy. Get up! I'm hungry."

He opened his eyes and stared blinking up into the small, tired face of his son. The storm had long since died out. From the vast dome of heaven a million winking stars looked down on the small jungle clearing.

"Daddy sleep?" asked David.

Rand brushed a hand across his eyes, staggered up to his feet. "Why, yes, I must have been, son." Zar's roar, so close at hand that he could almost feel the hot breath of it, brought him back to the reality of the moment. He stooped down swiftly, snatched up his rifle from the ground, then clasped David's hand firmly in his own. "Come on, son," he urged. "We got to get out of this."

Swiftly he made his way back to the lean-to. And a few minutes later, as if nothing out of the ordinary had happened that day—as if he had never planned to start the long trek back to civilization on the morrow—he stirred up the camp fire and went casually about the routine business of preparing the night's meal.

"We're going home tomorrow?" asked David when the meal was over.

Rand looked at him with puzzled eyes. "Home, son?" he

echoed. Then he threw out his arm in a wide gesture that took in the rude lean-to, the clearing and the encroaching jungle beyond. "Why this is home, son," he said patiently. "This clearing, here, in the jungle. Where your mother is."

David smiled up at him. "I'm glad," he said simply.

Rand threw a protecting arm around his sturdy shoulder, returned the smile. "Of course you are, son."

CHAPTER VII

ZAR THE MIGHTY

JOHN RAND NEVER recovered mentally from the blow that the falling jungle giant had struck him. Though rational in every other respect, to the end of his days he labored under the delusion that the jungle was his home. He liked to believe that this tract of wilderness belonged to him and since no one was there to refute him, the notion grew until it became an absolute conviction.

The outward manifestations of civilization fell rapidly from him. His beard became a luxuriant growth that Zar the lion might have envied. His supply of ammunition became exhausted and in its place he managed to fashion ingenious weapons from the remains of the plane. Together he and David survived—and thrived.

At the age of eight, David was a husky lad, already destined to become taller and mightier than his powerful father. Some latent impulse had made John Rand teach his son to read and write. With the aid of a charred stick, blackened by fire, David had reluctantly learned his A B C's. But even such simple schooling was not to his liking.

Clad simply in a soft hide draped about his loins, equipped with a crude but efficient knife, a long bow, a quiver of arrows and a stout spear fashioned by his father, he preferred to roam the forest. He could swim like Nyassa the fish, climb with all the agility of Nono the monkey. With any of his weapons he could strike as swiftly as Sinassa the big snake. He knew now why his father had fired at N'Jaga the leopard and why he had killed the emerald green reptile. He accepted the code of the jungle. Kill only when necessary—for food, or for one's own life.

He had been only three on that fateful day when their plane had crashed to the clearing. All details of his life before that day faded swiftly from his memory. And they were never recalled, for John Rand never mentioned them. David never learned of other white men, of big ships that sailed the seas, of speeding trains and crowded cities. Such things were buried in John Rand's past and such words never crossed his lips.

Only the lonely grave of Constance remained as a symbol of what had been. It became part of John Rand's obsession to linger near that hallowed spot, to spend long brooding hours there and to protect it from the ravages of weather and prowling beast.

Occasionally the sight of the grave brought a puzzled look to David's eyes. He would screw up his face and try to grasp a memory that eluded him. But in the end he gave up the effort and the vague thoughts came no more to plague him.

The early kinship that he had felt for the animals had grown with the years. He had met and made friends with many of them. They talked with him and soon he began to understand them. He learned, with strange guttural sounds, to imitate their language and from that day a new and happier life opened up before him.

Nono, the little monkey, was his constant companion. He would snatch things when David was not looking, scamper up into the topmost branches and taunt his friend. When David shook his fist and laughed, Nono would toss sticks at him. Then, in a sudden change of mood, he would scramble down again, swing lightly up onto David's shoulder and cling to the boy's neck with spidery hands.

No longer was the lad a helpless youngster who needed constant looking after. Wise in the ways of the jungle, David went off alone on long expeditions into the forest. He had his first sight of Trajah, the elephant, and wondered what it would be like to climb upon that towering gray back and ride in state through the jungle. Some day, he vowed, Trajah would also become his friend and his desire would be gratified. He met Quog, the wild pig, and stayed that beast's startled flight with a guttural call. While swimming in the lake, he was in turn startled by a great beast that rose snorting from the shallows. And so he made the acquaintance of Wal-lah, the hippopotamus.

ON MANY OF these trips Nono accompanied him, sometimes riding on his shoulder, sometimes swinging through the vines and branches that overhung the jungle floor. And several times, though he did not know it, he had another companion. A flitting, tawny shape kept pace with him, silent as a shadow. Zar, the lion, had never forgotten the stick that spurted flame and roared. Neither had he forgotten his first instinctive knowledge that these strange two-legged creatures somehow menaced his jungle supremacy.

Still patient and watchful, biding his time, Zar had watched the cub grow to be big and strong. Some day, he sensed, the issue must be decided. No rival must stand before him.

Sha, the lioness, his regal mate, was less cautious. Twice David had seen her, once departing gorged from a kill, another at twilight when she drank from the edge of the lake. Remembering the charge of N'Jaga, he realized that here was a still more formidable enemy. He fingered his crude weapons—and wondered.

But the gods of the jungle were nothing if not capricious. And the outcome of the first meeting between Zar and David was a surprising one.

It had been a hot, sultry day. There was meat at the camp to last them several days and a fire already prepared against the coming night. John Rand was busy fashioning a new spear. Young David, footloose and fancy-free, had wandered deep into the jungle in the hope of finding Trajah the elephant.

His search had been unsuccessful. The sun dropped more swiftly toward the waiting mountain peak. A belated butterfly, large as a saucer and shimmering as a sapphire, floated across his path. A floating speck in the cloudless sky brought David's eyes upward. It circled downward in a tight spiral, grew larger as it descended. Then with wings slanted back Kru, the buzzard, dropped like a plummet toward the earth.

Curiously David veered off and made for the spot where Kru had landed. And a few moments later his arrival sent the ungainly bird flapping up from a carcass. The kill had been a small antelope and it was still fresh. Great chunks had been taken from one shoulder and haunch. And around the spot, the damp jungle floor was marked with the impressions of huge paws.

David dropped down to one knee and examined them. The pupils of his eyes, dilated and a strange tingling stirred at the nape of his neck. For the impressions had been made by a lion pair, and the larger, those of the male, were of monstrous size. Zar and his mate were in the vicinity.

David rose, cast a glance over his shoulder at the setting sun for his direction, and then proceeded, more cautiously now, toward the distant camp.

Twilight fell as he reached a swamp that he must traverse and he took to the lower branches of the trees. A good fifteen feet above the treacherous mire he traveled swiftly and safely, swinging from bough to bough as Nono had taught him, occasionally flying far through the air to catch the next stout limb.

Jacaru the crocodile slithered through the morass below him. Bats wheeled, ghost-like, past his head. In the dim light, sky, trees and underbrush were of a monotonous grayness. And the spell of the twilight, before the night came with its noisy life, lay like a hush over the land.

Then suddenly the stillness was rent by a mighty roar. And even before its echoes had died away, it came again. David crouched on a swaying limb and listened. He knew that blood-curdling sound—he had heard it many times before. Only the deep-throated bellow of Zar could wake such echoes in the jungle. But this time, there was a new note in the stentorian call. David's keen ears told him that and more. He would have sworn it—that note was fear.

THE ROAR HAD come from a spot not far before him. Without further hesitation, he redoubled his speed through the trees. And a moment later he halted in amazement.

For once the wise monarch of the jungle had erred—he had made a fatal misstep. Something far more treacherous than any living creature, had him in its grasp. Zar the mighty floundered in a patch of quicksand. And with each struggle to gain the safety of the bank, his massive tawny body sank lower into the slimy depths.

David took in the scene with one swift, all-inclusive glance. On the bank, strange whines issuing from her throat, crouched Sha. Helpless, she watched the death struggles of her fallen lord, but she dared not venture toward him. All around the quicksand was solid, grass-tufted land. But Zar was up to his haunches now and he could not hope to gain it. Even in the murky light David could see the hopeless light in the lion's amber eyes—and he could not resist the forlorn appeal.

He dropped lightly down from the tree. Zar's struggles ceased for a moment as his head swung in that direction. Sha growled, her tail lashed and she tensed her muscles for a spring.

But the desperate need of his situation did something strange to Zar's brain. Whether he realized that no enemy would come to attack him now, already doomed as he was, or whether the low words that David called out to him conveyed an unmistakable note of friendliness, will never be known. But Zar growled a peremptory command at his mate and she subsided again, whining.

David worked swiftly. With his knife he slashed desperately at boughs and brush, seized a great armful of the fallen branches and thrust them out across the morass toward the helpless lion. Exerting all his magnificent strength, Zar drew his right forepaw free of the clinging sands. Digging into the boughs, he drew himself slowly forward.

But as his tremendous weight shifted upon them, the tangle of boughs sank slowly but surely into the quicksand. Hastily David slashed down more, added them as fast as he could work to Zar's sinking foothold.

It was a matter of minutes in actual time, but it seemed eternity to the strange trio. Inch by inch Zar drew his tiring body from the quagmire that seemed reluctant to lose its prey. But David saw that they were cheating Death of its hold and he redoubled his efforts. And at last the lord of the jungle crawled across the settling boughs and gained the bank.

For a long moment in the dying twilight they faced each other across the quagmire. Sha nuzzled her master's draggled mane. From glowing eyes Zar surveyed the man cub as he stood, straddle-legged and breathing heavily, beneath the tree from which he had dropped.

And there a strange pact of truce was made. Zar growled— a low, rumbling note that held no enmity. David gave guttural answer to show that he understood. And then as night fell, the great beast turned and with his mate at his side, stalked silently into the jungle.

CHAPTER VIII

AN ARROW STARTS A FEUD

A WEEK HAD passed since David's rescue of Zar and the truce between him and the lion. The sun had been up an hour and David and his father were exploring the swamp-lands in search of straight branches of the acaya tree to be hardened in a slow burning fire into arrows.

Their search had taken them farther from the clearing than usual. David was in the act of indicating a likely tree with an outstretched arm, when suddenly his head snapped back. His nostrils twitched. His sense of smell keen as that of N'Jaga had picked up the pungent odor of smoke.

He knew that their own camp fire had been put out before they had left the lean-to. And even if that had not been the case, they were too far from the clearing for the scent of smoke to reach them.

Tilting back his head he scanned the tops of the trees towering above them.

Rand noted the rapt expression of his face and wonderingly followed the direction of his son's gaze. Keen as his own senses had been attuned to the jungle, they could not rival the youngster's. He, himself, had sensed no warning of danger. The face of the impenetrable jungle appeared the same to him as always—its sights, smells and sounds.

And then simultaneously they both saw it—a thin spiral of smoke that curled above the tree-tops. Young David made a guttural sound in his throat. Rand gripped the butt of his long spear with a fierce grip. He was assailed by a hundred conflicting emotions, none of which he could quite analyze. The sight of that smoke, from a campfire he knew was not his own, stirred dim memories in the back of his clouded brain. He frowned in his concentration as he tried to bring them to light but they eluded his mental grasp.

Then they were gone and Rand was clear eyed once more. The only emotion aroused in him by the sight of that smoke, was one of danger—one of outrage. Someone was encroaching on his kingdom—someone had stumbled perilously close to Constance's grave.

He made a warning signal of silence to the boy—a signal that was not needed—then lowering his spear to the ready, moved forward cautiously. He slipped between the boles of the giant trees without making a sound. And David followed, stepping where he stepped. Not a twig snapped beneath their feet; no leaf stirred at their passing. Zar could not have stalked his quarry more stealthily, more warily.

Long before their eyes could tell them anything, their ears warned them that whatever it was they were approaching, there were four of them. Outside of his father, David had seen no other man for years. The dim remembrance of his soft faced mother was something that came to trouble him only in dreams. The possibility that there were other two-legged creatures like himself, had never occurred to him.

His thumb and forefinger held a long arrow taut against the string of his bow. He was prepared to see N'Guru and his tribe going through their strange rituals; or Chaka and his family of great apes dancing around a jungle drum. But he was not prepared for the sight that met his eyes a few moments later when they came to a slight opening in the trees, made by the gurgling passage of a small stream.

His father held up his hand in warning. They froze, shadows in the shadowy forest. Concealed behind the pendant foliage of a tree they peered into the clearing.

In the center was a small fire that sent a plume of smoke lazily upward. Near it was a strange shelter that resembled somewhat the lean-to in which he and his father lived. But it was not these things that held David's rapt attention. Squatted on his haunches before the fire, stirring something in a pot, was a man—a man like himself or his father—except for the fact that he was black. He was naked, save for a ragged cloth around his middle.

TWO MORE BLACKS were scooping up gravel from the bed of the stream in shallow pans. And standing over them, watching their labor, was still another man. But this one was white—and fat. He had a strange, domed covering on his head; strange wrappings encased his legs. And instead of the skin of the leopard or antelope, his body was covered with tight-fitting wrappings.

David studied these strange men, the first he had any knowledge of ever having seen, with curious attention. His breast seethed with a welter of emotions he could not analyze. His first impulse was to run forward and greet them. But he had been schooled too long in the jungle to act rashly.

True, the men before him seemed harmless. There was not a weapon in slight. The revolver strapped to the white man's belt meant nothing to him. But he had long since learned that even the most harmless appearing animal has defenses and when attacked or surprised can prove dangerous.

With a sign that his son should stay where he was, Rand grasped his spear firmly in his hand and stepped out into the clearing. David watched him go from narrowed eyes and some instinct told him to keep the arrow fitted to the bow.

His father had covered half the distance to the stream before his coming was discovered. The black crouching over the fire looked up, saw the bearded giant striding across the narrow glade, cried out and toppled backward.

At the shrill cry of alarm the white man at the stream whirled, made a lightning movement towards his hip and, watching,

David was surprised to see something bright and shiny flash in his hand. He, David, sensed that it was a weapon and the string of his bow became taut.

The two blacks at the stream crouched back; the white man took up a defensive attitude. A thrill of pride coursed through David's veins as he saw that his father never faltered. Looking neither to the right or left Rand made straight for the waiting trio at the water's edge.

Though he could not make out the words, David knew when they began to talk. His father's arm flung out in a wide gesture that embraced the jungle about them, then pointed commandingly to the east.

The fat white man answered. His father spoke again. Then they were both talking at once and from their animated gestures David knew that their words were spoken in anger.

Then, as he watched, the white man snatched one of the pans from the blacks and held it up for Rand's inspection. He talked rapidly, gesticulated wildly.

But John Rand was not impressed. With a sudden movement he dashed the pan to the ground and pointed again to the east.

No words were necessary to tell David that it was an order to leave. The white stranger listened in sullen silence—then he saw his father turn slowly on his heel and start back towards where he was hidden in the brush. He was proud of his father's arrogance in turning his back on an enemy; but even more surprised at his carelessness.

He became doubly watchful and a moment later he was thankful that he had. His father had taken but three strides from the stream when the fat stranger slowly raised the shining rod in his hand and pointed it at his back.

SOME DIM MEMORY of the past, when his father had pointed a shining stick at N'Jaga, galvanized David into action. His bow bent deep. The shaft of the arrow nestled against his ear for a fleeting moment, then sped forward.

John Rand was aware of a sudden humming beside his ear,

then of a startled, guttural curse behind him. He whirled around. The face of the stranger was contorted in agony. Protruding from his upper right arm an arrow still quivered. His hand hung limp at his side and blood ran crazily between his fingers. And now those fingers slowly relaxed and opened and a heavy automatic revolver trickled from them to clatter metallically to the ground.

John Rand laughed shortly, swept his arm around at the jungle once more, turned again on his heel and walked back to where his son lay hidden in the brush. But if David had seen the devils of hate leering out of the stranger's eyes, he would have fitted another arrow to his bow. And it would have found the fat white man's throat, instead of his upper arm.

Rand joined his son, expressed his thanks in the silent grip of his hand on David's arm and nodded his head towards the depths of the forest. As silently as they had come they faded into the murky depths.

Rand was more than usually silent that day, as he wrestled with the vague, disturbing thoughts in his brain. No word passed between him and his son concerning the incidents that had occurred that morning. It was not until after their evening meal that he brought up the subject.

For the past hour he had given particular attention to his weapons and now, satisfied that they were ready for any emergency, he spoke.

"This jungle is sacred to your mother, who lies buried here," he said grimly. "Remember that, son. It is ours—and no other man must be allowed to profane it. We shall keep it for ourselves—and for her."

David knew nothing of the faraway King who, according to the laws of the white man, counted their lonely wilderness amongst his possessions. He listened solemnly to his father's words, understood the trust imposed upon him and nodded gravely.

CHAPTER IX

MURDER IN THE JUNGLE

THE WHITE MAN whose arm had known the bite of David's arrow, had other ideas. Seated before his fire, he cursed one of the blacks for his clumsiness when the fellow changed the dressing on his wound. Another managed to be busy at a safer distance.

Paul DeKraft, with a heart as greasy as the rolls of fat that covered his body, had a past as black as one of his natives and a future a little less promising. He was known and hated from the gaols of Sydney to the dives of Suez; from the gambling dens of Canton to the breakwater of Cape Town. He had committed every crime on the statutes of the white man's law. And only his sly and cunning brain had saved his neck from the gallows.

Right now he was in the grip of a sullen rage that the natives knew and feared. He vented his indignation on the nearest and, though the black could understand only a word or two, he poured forth his tirade, highly spiced with profanity. He knotted his fist in his black beard.

"Emeralds, Bouala. Emeralds—that's what we've stumbled on in this God-forsaken stream. Emeralds worth a King's ransom." With a vicious, back-handed blow he sent the unfortunate Bouala spinning.

The black crashed to the ground, rubbed his cheek and said dutifully: "Emeralds. Yes, Inkosi."

DeKraft jumped to his feet. "And some half-crazy hermit

thinks he can order me away from here, does he? Throws them on the ground as though they were pebbles. And then expects me to forget all about them. Hah!"

Bouala rolled over, but not quickly enough. DeKraft's heavy boot lashed out and brought a wail of agony as it landed. Then a soft footfall sounded in the darkness beyond the firelight and DeKraft's head snapped in that direction. Bouala took advantage of the moment and crawled painfully away.

The form of the third native advanced into the glow.

"Well, Mubangi?" said DeKraft.

"They sleep, Inkosi," answered the newcomer. "The crazy one and a boy."

DeKraft took a step toward him, his fists clenched. "You did not look—you were afraid to go near. There are others—other men." He raised his right fist in a threatening gesture.

Mubangi fell back. "I saw, Inkosi," he protested. "The man and the boy. No others."

DeKraft hesitated. His eyes were gleaming slits in the firelight. "They have guns?"

The native shook his head. "Mubangi saw no guns," he answered.

DeKraft fingered the crude bandage that encircled his aching arm. "Excellent," he murmured. "That will make it easier—much easier."

Then sinking down before the fire, he made plans that boded no good for John Rand and his son.

David, also, slept little that night. The day had been an eventful one, indeed. The sight of other men had started a long train of fancy in his brain. He wondered where they came from. Closing his eyes he recalled the strange garments of the white leader. He remembered the significant gestures that had passed between the latter and his father. He remembered, too, that John Rand had ordered them to leave his wilderness domain.

Before the dawn he rose, careful not to disturb his father, and slipped out into the clearing. Plunging into the jungle, he headed for the other camp.

The motive that sent him to spy upon the invaders was compounded of many things. For one thing, if the men were to return from whence they came, he might never see them again. And he would like to observe them while he could. For another, the white leader had attempted the life of his father. David was glad that he had been watchful then and he meant to keep his eyes on the stranger until he had gone well beyond the borders of their wilderness home.

THE PEBBLES THAT John Rand had flung from the other's hand, he did not consider. To him, even more than to his father, they were just that—pebbles and no more. Nono occasionally picked up things that took his eye—bright colored feathers, smooth sticks, bits of shining rock. But that was because Nono was a monkey, and silly.

The grayness that precedes the dawn had lightened the jungle when David cautiously approached the camp. Parting a tangle of creepers, he peered out from his cover. The dying embers of a fire smouldered before the tent. No sound issued from within.

Were they sleeping? He cocked his head to one side and strained his ears. But the silence was profound. Raising his head, he sniffed of the damp air.

No scent of man carried to him. He looked puzzled. Had they departed already on their long journey? Strange that they should have left their possessions behind them. Unless John Rand's warning and David's arrow had instilled such a fear in their hearts that they had fled in haste.

Pushing through the vines, David cautiously approached the tent. It was empty, right enough. Curiously he fingered the stuff of which it was made before he ventured inside. There he examined the various things that belonged to the strange white man. A canvas cot puzzled him for long moments before he realized its use. He poked into a kit of eating utensils, peered into a box of cartridges, found a bottle of Holland gin.

The first two items he could make nothing of. Examining

the latter, he accidentally pulled the cork. To him, the colorless liquid within was water. He raised the bottle to his lips and took a long swallow.

An agony of fire consumed his throat. The rare phenomenon of tears came to his eyes. The bottle slipped from his nerveless fingers and spilled over, as he spat to rid himself of the terrible stuff.

The lesson was well-learned and he tasted nothing more. He found a circular, shining disc and when he looked at it, he was astounded to see his own face look back at him. The reflection was far more clear than any he had seen in the smooth waters of the lake. He was fascinated by the mirror and would have taken it then and there, but he remembered Nono's penchant for glittering things and with a rueful smile at such foolishness he laid it down again.

Leaving the tent, he headed back for his own camp. He would tell his father about the many and wonderful things that the strangers had left behind them. Perhaps his father would be able to tell him what they were and what they were used for.

Elated with his discovery, he moved along the jungle trail, swinging through the forest with an easy, deceivingly fast stride. The first tinge of dawn was flaming in the east; about him the jungle stirred, whispered and came to life.

There was a care-free, abandoned song in David's heart as he neared the clearing. Then abruptly a staccato crack pulled him up in mid-stride. The song in his heart died. He sensed danger and fitted an arrow to his bow.

For a moment the explosive sound puzzled him. It was not the roar of any jungle beast, he knew, yet it was vaguely familiar. Then with sudden clarity he remembered—his mind flashed back to that distant day when his father had shot the bounding N'Jaga. A sound like the one he had just heard had accompanied the proceeding.

And hard on this realization, a second shot came from the direction of the clearing.

David waited for no more. He bounded forward. Thoughts of his father gave an added speed to his legs. He broke through the jungle wall into the clearing and for once he threw caution to the winds.

One swift glance told him that the lean-to was being consumed by billowing flames. No one was in sight. With an agonized heart he jumped forward, at the thought that his father had been trapped in the burning shelter. Then a dark object, crawling along the ground a few feet from the lean-to, caught his eye.

With a decided shock he realized that it was his father and from Rand's slow, tortured movements it was obvious that he was wounded.

DAVID SPED TO him, dropped down beside him on the ground. "Father!" he cried. "What happened?" Then he saw that the front of Rand's chest was stained an ugly red.

At the sound of his son's voice, John Rand collapsed. Tenderly David lifted his head from the ground, stared down anxiously at his drawn face.

"You're hurt. Badly. What happened?" he whispered urgently.

With an effort, Rand forced open his eyes. A flood of relief passed over his face as he recognized his son; then the relief was followed swiftly by a look of apprehension. Weakly he grasped the boy's arm; his lips worked feverishly but no words came.

David sensed from the expression of his face and from his tense attitude that he was trying to transmit a warning. A warning against what? If he had seen the naked black even then sneaking around a corner of the burning lean-to, he would have known.

His head close to his father's lips, he was still trying to interpret the latter's mumbled words when something sharp pricked him at the base of his spine.

He straightened slowly, pivoted even more slowly on the

point of the spear in the black's hand. He recognized the native at once as one of the men he had seen at the camp of the fat white man.

With his fists clenched impotently at his sides, he glared at the native. He knew what that spear was, pricking now into his belly, and coolly he calculated his chances against it. But before he could act, the black called out and to his surprise the fat white man followed by two other natives, came on the run from the far side of the burning shelter. And in the fat white man's hand was a long, shining stick.

It was all very clear to David, then, what had happened. This fat, two-legged creature had wounded his father—with the stick. He—David—was consumed by an all-embracing hate and his fingers crept to the knife tucked in his belt.

He ignored the spear still pricking his middle and confronted the white man. "Fat-Face has wounded my father," he said coolly. "And for that, Fat-Face shall die."

Paul DeKraft rocked back on his heels and gave vent to a raucous laugh. "Spunky, eh? But you're wrong, kid. It's the other way around. I'm going to kill you, see? I don't want no witness to this little scene this morning—and dead men tell no tales." He laughed again. "I don't know who you or your father are—daffy, both of you—but you're in my way. It's the only way out, kid."

David only half understood the meaning of his words. He only knew that Fat-Face had wounded his father and now intended to kill him. In his arrogant youth he laughed at the idea. Coolly he measured the fat man from narrowed eyes and knew that he was his master.

But he had completely forgotten the speed of the death lurking in the shiny stick.

Slowly he drew out his knife. The rifle whipped up.

There could have been only one possible outcome of the affair a moment later—David's death—if Fate had not intervened.

All unknown to the parties concerned, there had been another spectator to the grim drama. Crouched on the fringe of the clearing, his slitted amber eyes, watching them, lay Zar. If David had forgotten the terrible destruction of the fire stick, not so the lion. And now this one was pointed at the man-cub, the creature who had rescued him from the quicksands.

A low growl rumbled in Zar's throat. Then with a mighty roar, he leaped into the clearing. At the first note of his challenge, the native with the spear stepped hastily back.

DeKraft whirled. A lion, bigger than any he had ever seen, was plunging straight for him. Hastily he raised the rifle; hastily he fired. Too hastily—he realized bitterly a moment later. He saw his bullet kick up a cloud of dust by the side of the lion's head, saw the jungle lord, jaws agape, loom ever larger before him.

DeKraft knew that he would not have time to reload before the sabre claws and dripping fangs of the lion sank deep into his flesh. Death touched at his craven heart. With one coordinated movement he grasped his native spearman and threw the screaming black straight into the path of the charging lion.

WAITING FOR NO more, he turned on his heel and fled across the clearing on the heels of the other two.

The black spearman went down before Zar's charge like a sack of straw. There was a lightning movement from the lion's forepaw and the unfortunate black lay disemboweled.

Satisfied with his work thus far, Zar propped his forefeet on the native's chest and threw back his head. The roar of the male lion who has made his kill rumbled through the forest.

Crashing heavily through the undergrowth, ever further away from the clearing, DeKraft heard and wiped the sweat from his brow. Then a smile curled at his greasy fat lips. True, he had failed to kill the brat of the mad jungle hermit. But he had every confidence that the lion would take care of that oversight. He was well content.

Once Zar had proclaimed his might over the dead native,

he swung his majestic head slowly about and surveyed the clearing. It was deserted save for the man-cub and his father. The bearded one lay prone on the ground and Zar knew that he was wounded.

He roared once to say that he had fulfilled his obligation and that there was nothing more for him to do. Then slowly, his tufted tail switching from side to side, he walked to the edge of the clearing with majestic stride and disappeared.

John Rand had fainted from loss of blood at the moment that Zar had charged. He regained consciousness a few minutes later, with David leaning over him, forcing cool water between his lips.

With an effort he swung his head and looked about the clearing.

David understood his unspoken question. "Gone," he said tersely. "Zar killed one of the blacks and scared the others off."

Rand smiled feebly. "Zar the lion, eh—your friend?"

David nodded. "Drink now, father," he ordered.

But John Rand knew that he was beyond all aid. "No use, son," he said. "Too late. I'm dying…. I'm going to join your mother."

His eyes closed and David's heart was swept by an anguish of sorrow. His world seemed to be crumbling about him and he could not speak. After a moment his father's eyes fluttered open again.

With fast-ebbing strength, Rand tugged at the narrow gold band on his little finger. He succeeded in removing it at last and with a trembling hand, slipped the loop onto one of David's fingers.

"Your mother's wedding ring," he gasped. "Keep it—to re-member her by." He spoke through a breaking bubble of blood. "And David—boy, bury me by her side in the clearing. She was—she was an angel."

For the last time John Rand looked into the eyes of his son and smiled. Then his chin dropped forward on his chest and with the simple conviction that he would join Constance in the Great Beyond, he died.

CHAPTER X

KA-ZAR, BROTHER OF ZAR

THE DEATH OF his father marked a definite turning point in David's life. He had just turned thirteen at the time and in those few minutes late that afternoon, as he stood with bowed head at the fresh-filled grave, he definitely made the transition from boyhood to manhood.

He was on his own now, alone in the heart of a vast and savage wilderness. The responsibilities to survive—the effort, the brain and the brawn and the cunning, devolved squarely upon his shoulders. No longer would his father make decisions for him; no longer would his father step to the front when danger was near. He was the master of his fate.

In most respects he was admirably equipped to survive against the terrible odds against him. In stature he was a man full grown, with a body superb and flawless. His muscles were as supple as N'Jaga's and he was as quick to strike as Zar when danger threatened. His eyes were as keen as those of Pindar, who sighted his prey from a mile in the sky. And save for the antelope, no thing that stalked the jungle had a keener sense of smell or hearing than he.

The jungle and the beasts that lived in it, he knew like the palm of his hand. He could swing swiftly through the trees like the apes; or with his nose close to the ground he was as sure on the trail as Sha, mistress of the mighty Zar.

All these things were in David's favor. But whether he had the savage heart to kill without regret, was yet to be proved.

Save in one respect. Fat-Face!

Hate clouded his vision as he stepped from the grave with Zar at his side. His judgments had never been schooled by contacts with civilization. His emotions had been completely decivilized by ten years in the jungle fastness. Of the things that belonged to civilized society he had no standard of comparison.

The fat white man had killed his father, brutally and without reason. Therefore there would be an undying feud between him and the white man and all the white man's tribe.

Until the blazing sun sank down behind the volcanic cone in the west, he hovered near the twin graves of his parents, the only humans he had ever known and loved. Manfully, mutely he struggled with his grief, blind to the life that flowed about him unruffled, unconcerned as if murder had not been committed in the clearing a few hours before.

And ever by his side strode Zar, watchful, wary, lest N'Jaga take advantage of the moment and strike the man-cub in his hour of blind grief.

In his simple heart Zar had some vague understanding of the emotion that filled the man-cub. He expressed his sympathy with an occasional rumble in his throat, at which times David would run the hard knuckles of his fist from the top of the lion's skull to the tip of his blunt nose.

The twilight fell and still David lingered near the graves. The lean-to that had been the only home he remembered, was now but a heap of ashes. He recalled the tent at the other camp. It was doubtless there, intact. But something deep within him rebelled at the thought of occupying the home of the hated white man.

Zar sensed his uncertainty. With a low, guttural call, the lion walked toward the fringe of the jungle. Six paces away he stopped, looked back over his shoulder. Slowly David walked up to join him. But when he reached the lion's side, Zar moved off yet another half dozen paces.

Then David realized that Zar was leading him somewhere. He hesitated but a moment. The clearing held nothing but memories for him now. He made a whining sound to show that he understood, then keeping pace with his tawny friend, he followed him into the jungle.

THEY TRAVELED SWIFTLY and silently through the gathering darkness. But their journey was a long one and the moon was well up over the tree-tops when they reached their objective.

Screened as it was by bushes and an overhanging tree, David did not see the entrance to the cave until they were directly before it. A narrow space between two huge boulders, the opening appeared only as a blacker patch in the shadows. David had often searched for the lair of Zar and his mate and been unable to find it. Now, he came as an invited guest.

Zar halted, emitted a low growl. In answer, a tawny shape appeared in the opening.

When she saw the tall form beside her mate, Sha pulled back her lips and spat. Again Zar growled, deeper this time, and Sha subsided. Without another sound she moved backward into the shadows.

Zar stood still and looked at David. And the latter, knowing that he was expected to do so, dropped to all fours and crawled into the cave. The soft pad of Zar's footfalls followed him.

The rising moon sent its glow deeper into the opening and lightened the dark interior of the lions' lair to a drab grayness. Lying on the rocky floor, her narrowed eyes fastened unblinkingly on David, Sha again voiced her resentment. The female is indeed more savage than the male. By the very duties Nature has imposed upon her, she is more selfish, more wary and more jealous. The coming of this strange man-cub to her sacred home, roused instant antagonism within her.

Zar growled his displeasure at her attitude. And David, quickly learning the meaning of the various inflections of their language, joined the conclave.

At length a pact was made between them. Sha reluctantly

agreed to accept David as a comrade, but he sensed that it would be a long time before the last vestige of suspicion would be entirely erased from her mind. Zar, on the other hand, showed the full measure of his gratitude for the time that the boy had saved his life. He accepted David as a blood brother, a relationship that each solemnly understood would be broken only by death itself. And in the language that would henceforth be his own, David was given a new name. From now on he would be known as Ka-Zar, brother of Zar the Mighty.

With the new name, began a new life. Ka-Zar soon lost the few vestiges of civilization that had survived his stay in the jungle. Now he became but another beast, pitting his superior intelligence against the reign of claw and fang. The language of his dead father, he relegated to a dim corner of his memory. Each day he became more proficient in the guttural speech of the animals. He walked where Zar walked, drank where the lion drank and together they shared their kill. And side by side they slept in the cave that Zar had made his home.

The denizens of the jungle soon accepted him and his strange union with the lion. There were those who loved him and those who hated him. But love or hate, there was none who denied him the respect which was his due. This latter was true, at least, among those who lived in the vicinity. Since he had joined the lion, he had not seen Trajah the elephant, whose pilgrimages took him on long journeys. Nor Chaka and his tribe of great apes, also wanderers. Nor N'Guru the gorilla, whose haunt was the dense forest that covered the distant mountain peak.

THOUGH KA-ZAR HAD chosen the lion's cave in preference to the tent of DeKraft, he had not forgotten the belongings left by the white man. One day the reflection of his own face in a placid stream reminded him of the glittering mirror. The more he thought of it, the more he wanted it. And though he had not the faintest idea what good it might do him, he determined to visit the camp again and find it.

To reach a decision was to carry it out. He set off at once

with his long, loping stride toward the distant spot. And at last, after an uneventful journey, he came to the stream where DeKraft had washed out the pebbles.

Profligate Nature had been at work. A tangle of brush and vines had closed in about the tent. Dampness and mould had rotted its fabric until it sagged, a shapeless, ugly, gray growth.

Some distance away, in the direction of his old home, Ka-Zar heard the crashing of branches. It told him that Chaka and his tribe of great apes were once more passing through the vicinity.

From inside the tent, too came a sound—the muffled stir of something moving about. Ka-Zar's eyes narrowed; he fingered the knife at his belt, that he had always kept keen and shining. That tent and all that was within it, was rightfully his. And he had no intention of letting anyone else despoil it.

Softly he crept forward, raised the sagging flap.

A huge, hairy ape stood with his back to the entrance. In one hand he clutched the precious mirror and it was evident, from his pose, that he was held fascinated by his own reflection within it.

As low rage possessed Ka-Zar, filling his deep lungs, he roared the mighty challenge of Zar.

Clutching the mirror, the ape whirled. From sullen, red-rimmed eyes he stared back at the strange two-legged creature in the opening of the tent. The roar of the lion, coming from this queer hairless animal, evidenfly puzzled him. But he showed no fear.

In the guttural language of the jungle, Ka-Zar demanded the mirror.

The ape's shoulders stooped over in a crouch. His broad nostrils flared. "Bardak found it," he answered.

Swiftly Ka-Zar measured his challenger. He did not know that Bardak, though of full growth, was young and the trouble maker of his tribe. But he could see that the ape equalled his own height and that Bardak's mighty chest and long arms were far more powerful than his own.

The realization came to him that here, in this small space, his weapons would do him no good. Out in the open, with the spear or the bow and arrows that his father had taught him to make and use, he would stand a chance. Caution told him to wait until the advantage was his. But despite his better judgment, Ka-Zar could not find it in his heart to evade the ape's challenge.

Drawing his knife, he repeated his demand for the mirror. And in answer, Bardak thumped upon his broad chest and gave vent to the bellowing war-cry of the apes.

It was too late to back down now. With the shining blade clutched tightly in his fist, Ka-Zar edged forward. Bardak flung the mirror upon the mouldering cot and stretching forth his long arms, came to meet him.

Instinct told Ka-Zar that once in the grasp of those terrible arms, he would be crushed and mangled. Side-stepping the ape's shambling rush, he staked all on a sudden powerful stab at the beast's unprotected side.

But Bardak's clumsiness was deceptive. Even as the sharp blade pricked his side, one hairy hand shot out and closed about Ka-Zar's wrist.

THE APE'S FINGERS were like bands of steel. They tightened, and an agony of fire shot up Ka-Zar's arm. The gleaming blade slipped from his paralyzed hand and thudded to the ground. He braced himself as Bardak pulled him forward.

A momentary wave of awful hopelessness swept over him. Weaponless, in the cruel grip of the big ape, he faced a terrible death.

And then the spirit of his dead father came to his rescue. He recalled the tricks that he had learned on the occasions they had wrestled with each other. Suddenly he let his arm and body go limp. Then, in the instant while Bardak was bewildered by this unexpected lack of resistance, he broke free, grasped Bardak's long left arm in two hands and twisted it to a position between the ape's shoulder blades.

He was behind Bardak now and safe for the moment. And instead of the ape clutching his wrist, it was he who twisted the arm of the ape. With all the strength of his powerful young body he forced Bardak's hand up towards his thick neck.

In his battles with other members of his tribe, Bardak had known only the method of straining an opponent to his broad chest and crushing him there. He could use his teeth, too, but now he could only gnash them in helpless rage. This arm lock baffled him and he did not know how to break it.

Ka-Zar hung grimly on, pressing his advantage. He strained his powerful muscles until his heart and lungs threatened to burst. Slowly but inexorably, the ape's arm went up... up... up....

A liquid fire of agony ran down the length of Bardak's arm. His shoulder flamed with pain and a roar of rage tore from his lips.

Ka-Zar knew then that he had won. Another wrench—and Bardak the troublemaker would be crippled forever.

There was no reason for him to hesitate then. Mercy has no place in the wilderness. A foe vanquished is an enemy—and an enemy is slain. But something deep within Ka-Zar's heart stayed him and hardly understanding why, he rose above the laws of the jungle.

"Ka-Zar is your master," he panted in Bardak's ear.

And with a painful croak Bardak answered: "Ka-Zar is my master."

Releasing his hold, Ka-Zar took a long step backward. "Ka-Zar gives you your life. Go!"

The ape glared at him from red-rimmed eyes. Then nursing his throbbing arm, he shuffled from the tent.

Ka-Zar realized full well that he had spared a life—and gained a bitter enemy. But he knew that Bardak had no heart for further punishment just then. Dismissing the ape from his mind, he turned his attention to the matter that had brought him there.

First he recovered his knife, thrust it once more into his belt. The mirror followed it. DeKraft's other possessions held no meaning for him. He left them there. Let Bardak come back for them—if he dared.

Then, eager to tell Zar how he had mastered the ape, he set out once more for the cave.

CHAPTER XI

TRAJAH THE ELEPHANT

ZAR HEARD HIS tale in silence and then displayed his disapproval of the man-cub's foolish act of pity with a rumbling grunt. From her corner of the cave Sha spat disdainfully. But Ka-Zar only smiled. Such was the glory of his strength that he could afford to be magnanimous. Bardak dead and the tale of his passing would be forgotten with him. Alive, he was an ever present testimony, to his, Ka-Zar's, might.

The days passed into weeks, the weeks into months. Ka-Zar roamed the jungle with Zar at his side. Wallah the hippopotamus greeted them as they drank together in the first flush of dawn. Coiled on a hot rock, Sinassa the snake watched them from unblinking eyes as they rested themselves in the heat of mid day. And at eventide, Dikki the jackal slunk on their trail to gorge himself on their kill when they had had their fill.

Nothing transpired to disturb the serene flow of Ka-Zar's days. He made weekly pilgrimages to the little clearing by the lake that had been his home for his first ten years in the jungle. But by now the acute grief he had felt at his father's death had mellowed into a gentle melancholy. He had learned that it is the one inevitable rule of the jungle that all things must die. However, the realization of that fundamental truth in no way lessened his hate of the fat white man. The vow he had sworn over his father's grave was still in force.

Not that he had the slightest idea of the symbolism behind the gesture—but because his father had taught him to do so—he would gather flowers from the grassy floor of the glade and adorn the twin graves with them. The simple act gave him a strange, inexplicable pleasure.

However, even with the passage of months, Sha never fully accepted him as one of her own. Her attitude towards him was one of surly toleration and she gave him to understand that if it had not been for Zar, her master, she would have none of him. In addition to her instinctive fear and hate of the man cub, her emotions were now tinged with jealousy.

Ka-Zar understood Sha's feminine psychology and was secretly amused by it. But of late, the lioness, as she kept closer and closer to the cave, became more sullen, spiteful and unapproachable.

She became heavy of limb, her movements slow. And every night Zar would bring to her the tenderest quarter of a fresh kill.

It was early one morning at the beginning of the rainy season that Zar suggested to Ka-Zar that they absent themselves from the cave for a day or two.

The man cub understood and was glad. He growled his approval. He had never forgotten his early desire to make friends with Trajah the elephant. Here was an opportunity and he suggested to Zar that they go in search of the great gray beast and his herd.

Zar was familiar with the regular pilgrimages of the elephants. He knew where Trajah could be found and he readily agreed to lead Ka-Zar in that direction.

Glad to get away from Sha, who had been most surly and unfriendly of late, they set off. Their bellies were full and though several times they caught sight of easy quarry, they pressed steadily on.

They stopped once to drink their fill from a winding stream. Soon the rains would swell it to a rushing torrent. But now its rocky bed made for easier traveling than the dense undergrowth that crowded the jungle. They followed it.

A few minutes later, while still traversing the narrow ravine, they heard a loud crashing ahead of them. As they pulled up short, the trumpeting of a mighty elephant echoed through the air.

Zar snarled a single command. "Flee!"

Dumfounded, Ka-Zar watched the lord of the jungle make a single long leap, then scramble up the rocky side of the ravine. Ka-Zar could not believe his eyes nor his ears. Zar, ruler of the wilderness, and his proud brother—flee from a beast? It was incredible, unbelievable!

FROM THE SAFETY of the high, sheer bank Zar urgently repeated his warning. But before Ka-Zar could move, a great gray shape appeared at the head of the ravine.

The elephant was one of Trajah's herd. Though not quite as large or as powerful as the mighty leader, this one was nevertheless an enormous beast. His huge ears waved, fan-like, on either side of his head. His trunk weaved slowly from side to side. A sinister, reddish gleam shone from his little eyes and a strange, musk-like smell wafted down wind to Ka-Zar's nostrils.

Ka-Zar had never seen those gleaming tusks impale a living creature, tearing out its vitals. He had never seen that snaky trunk wind about a victim, then shatter bone and flesh against a boulder or a tree trunk. He had never seen those huge feet trample a beaten enemy until only bloody pulp remained.

But instinct warned him vaguely of some such dire fate. And instantly he gauged the distance between the swaying beast and a towering daboukra tree whose immense bole rose up from the stream bed off to his right.

The elephant's piggish little eyes fastened on the strange two-legged creature in his path. Red flames of hate flared up in their depths. Flinging back his head, he trumpeted a shrill challenge. Then with tusks gleaming, he charged forward.

With incredible speed Ka-Zar dashed for the daboukra. Hand over hand, like Nono the monkey, he climbed swiftly up its smooth bole. He gained the lower branches just in time. The elephant's tusks missed him by scant inches. Hurriedly he climbed upward.

Below him, the elephant squealed his rage. He capered awkwardly for a moment about the trunk of the tree. Then setting his front feet firmly on the rocky ground, he braced his massive forehead against the bole of the daboukra and pushed.

High up in the tree Ka-Zar clung to his perch. The topmost branches quivered, swayed far over. Slowly but surely the elephant increased the pressure.

It seemed impossible that the immense jungle giant in which Ka-Zar had taken refuge could be so shaken by a living beast. But that great gray shape below him was the most powerful creature that existed. The daboukra quivered along its entire length and when it cracked a series of staccato warnings, Ka-Zar realized that he was not safe.

Flattened until he was scarcely visible on the opposite bank of the ravine, Zar watched the titanic struggle. Ka-Zar clung to his thrashing perch and glanced swiftly around. There were many towering trees about him, but the distance between him and the nearest was just too great for him to negotiate.

With insane determination, squealing and grunting, the elephant continued his assault. A violent shudder racked the daboukra from topmost branch to root. It swayed far over, poised for a moment at a perilous angle and then with a grinding noise, headed in a great arc for the ground.

Ka-Zar had timed its fall to a fraction of a second. At just the right moment he let go his hold and with the impetus given him by the toppling daboukra, described a long parabola through the air. His outstretched arms caught the branches of the nearest tree and the sudden break in his flight almost tore him from his hold. He crashed against a limb with a force that knocked him breathless, but hung desperately on.

Recovering swiftly, he swung himself upward. Now he was on the outer fringe of the massed jungle and traveling swiftly through the leafy passages, he circled around to a point where he could gain the other bank and rejoin Zar.

THE ELEPHANT TRUMPETED his frustrated rage. Then seeing that his victim had successfully escaped him, he suddenly wheeled and went plunging blindly off down the ravine.

Ka-Zar lay by the lion's side and recovered his breath. His narrow escape from death made him very thoughtful. He considered the matter in silence.

Here, then, was a beast who violated the code of the jungle. Trajah and his tribe did not eat meat, so that it was not for food that the elephant had tried to kill him. Neither was there a feud between them, an old score of vengeance to be settled. And the only other kill sanctioned by the jungle code—to slay in self defense—was out of the question in this case. The mighty elephant had no fear of this puny two-legged creature.

Why, then, had the great beast been so fiendishly intent upon stamping out his life? Ka-Zar was still pondering the matter when another crashing brought him up to a crouch. Together he and Zar peered over the edge of the bank.

In the same direction from which the other had come, a towering gray form appeared at the head of the ravine. Slowly, majestically it moved down the stream bed and Ka-Zar recognized Trajah himself. In his wake came his herd, crowding down the narrow ravine. Several of the females paused to drink and Trajah waited patiently beside them.

Ka-Zar jumped to his feet. His lungs expanded and he growled a greeting.

The heads of the herd swung up to look at him. Trajah surveyed him with the same majestic calm.

"I am Ka-Zar, brother of Zar," announced Ka-Zar.

Trajah acknowledged the introduction.

"We come in peace," went on Ka-Zar. "How is it, then, that one tried to slay me?"

A distant trumpeting sounded far down the stream. Trajah flapped a lazy ear. "That one was Tupat," he answered. "The madness has come upon him."

It was strange, after Ka-Zar's recent encounter with the enraged beast, how docile these huge gray monsters were. He realized that he had nothing to fear from them. Sliding down the steep bank, he walked boldly up to the great leader.

"Madness?" he repeated. He shook his head. He did not know that in one respect, his own father had gone mad. He did not know what it meant to lose one's senses.

Zar, though, had encountered mad elephants before. That was why he, the lord of the jungle, had recognized the strange note in Tupat's trumpeting and had sought refuge high up on the bank. Now he came down and stood beside his brother.

And so Ka-Zar learned how occasionally the strange madness descends upon a great gray beast and starts him tearing off into the jungle, uprooting giant trees and slaying all in his path. Sometimes, in his red blindness, he plunges over a cliff and dies. Usually the spell is short and, recovering, he rejoins his herd.

Trajah and his tribe were now following the rampaging Tupat. Slowly, for even they feared a brother when the killing lust was upon him. They would keep well behind him and soon he would quiet down and rejoin them.

Ka-Zar realized as he studied Trajah, that the elephant leader was possessed of a keen brain. And Trajah, in turn, seemed to know that this strange brother of the lion was not the silly, helpless creature that he looked. Zar and Ka-Zar lingered awhile with the herd. And when at last they departed on their homeward journey, Ka-Zar had made another, and valuable, friend.

THEY WERE BOTH tired and spent when at last they reached the cave. But Zar soon received the great satisfaction of knowing that in his absence he had become the father of two sturdy, clawing sons.

Ka-Zar was equally delighted. In an attempt to see them he peered into the cave and received a blow that sent him spinning backward. He picked himself up and rubbed himself ruefully. Sha's paw had lashed out with incredible speed and it was fortunate indeed that her claws had been sheathed.

Limping, he rejoined Zar, who had been wiser than he in not venturing too near. And that night they both stretched out before the entrance to the cave, to guard the tawny cubs that had come to bless the royal pair.

CHAPTER XII

BARDAK THE TROUBLEMAKER

THE ONE KINK in the mental psychology of Bardak the great ape was that he remembered the unpleasant things in life, rather than the pleasant ones. And since the ascendancy of Ka-Zar in the jungle, the unpleasant scores he had to settle had increased rapidly.

Bardak was young, headstrong and willful. He was in the first flush of his full strength and the blood was hot in his veins.

With a bitterness that made him pound his great chest, he recalled the short-lived delight that he had experienced by making faces at himself in the circle of bright glass he had found in the camp of the Oman. And with a bitterness even greater, he recalled his battle with Ka-Zar, when the latter had taken the reflecting glass from him.

It was like pouring oil on Bardak's angry temper to realize that Ka-Zar had shown mercy. Though he had been bested in fair fight—though he had been completely at the mercy of the lion-man, Ka-Zar had spared his life.

The humiliation of his defeat ate deep into Bardak's soul. But that was not the worst of it. Ganya, the most desirable of the unattached females in the tribe and the one he courted, mocked him at every opportunity, taunted him that the puny Ka-Zar had bested him in battle.

Bardak would chase her through the trees, vowing that he would snap her neck like a twig when he caught her. And when Ganya fled to the topmost branches, where his greater weight would not permit him to follow, he would vent his wrath by strutting across the jungle floor and boasting of the dire things he would do when next again he met Ka-Zar.

Wise old Chaka, leader of the tribe, counseled caution. But Bardak would have none of it. In the courting season his masculine ego had been slighted and in the eyes of Ganya he had been made to appear ridiculous.

As far as Bardak could see, there was only one way to restore himself in the eyes of the apes—and especially Ganya. He must produce that wonderful bit of glass he had told them about, boast that he had taken it from Ka-Zar. And to this end he began to scheme in his cunning brain.

For two days he concealed himself high in the tree that overlooked Zar's cave. Carefully he noted the comings and goings of Zar and Ka-Zar. For the simple reason that he never saw the lion-man make faces at himself in the bit of glass, he was sure that he did not carry it on his person. And by the same process of elemental reasoning he arrived at the conclusion that the mirror was in the cave.

The certainty of this simplified Bardak's problem. He could gain possession of the mirror without again running foul of Ka-Zar. Only Sha and her two cubs, who seldom wandered far from the cave, stood between him and the possession of the thing that would restore him to respect in the eyes of Ganya.

And when he had that bit of glass he would tell Chaka what an old, timid, fool he was. Bardak thumped his chest. Some day he would challenge Chaka for leadership of the tribe. But first he had to get that bit of shining glass.

Bardak was blessed with at least one virtue—that of patience. For two days he clung to the branches of the tree that overlooked the cave, without showing himself. And early on the morning of the third day his patience was rewarded.

With the rising sun Zar and Ka-Zar emerged from the mouth of the lair and disappeared silently into the jungle. A few moments later Sha, followed by Zoro and Sulani, her two cubs, left the cave to sun themselves in the hot rays that slanted through the trees.

BARDAK WATCHED THEM with small red eyes, grimaced. He determined that if Sha strayed away but a scant few feet from the cave, he would enter it and make his search.

And then chance favored his bold plan. An impudent, unwary aingu bounded across the shallow clearing almost directly beneath Sha's nose. If it had not been for her cubs, Sha would have feigned sleep at this show of lese majeste. But it was high time, she decided, that the sons of the mighty Zar had their first lesson in the hunt.

With a snarl, she arched her back and sprang after the fleeing aingu. The rodent dove precipitately into the tangled undergrowth at the far side of the glade. And once the scent was in her nostrils, Sha could not resist the chase. She followed after the aingu, leaving her cubs and the mouth of the cave unguarded.

Bardak saw his opportunity and he took it. Dropping a sheer twenty feet, from limb to limb, he reached the ground before the leaves of the brush had settled back into place after Sha's passing. He ran with long, ungainly strides, propelling himself forward by the knuckles of his hands.

He paused a moment at the mouth of the cave, glanced once swiftly about him, then stooping, crawled through the narrow opening.

Only on rare, ritual occasions were Bardak and his tribe meat eaters. Now the strong blood-tang odor of the cave flared his nostrils wide, made his own blood quicken. He moved forward cautiously, feeling the sides of the tunnel-like passage as he went.

He was stirred by a twinge of fear. If Sha or her mate should return, he would be trapped. For a moment he considered beating a hasty retreat but the thought of Ganya drove him on.

He reached the cave proper a moment later, stood erect and glanced swiftly about him. Bones littered the floor. At one corner of the far side the stones of the floor were worn smooth, marking the spot where Zar and Sha lay down to rest. Opposite this was a rude bed of dried branches and moss, not unlike the couch that Bardak himself slept on.

He crossed to it swiftly and a moment later his sense of smell confirmed what his cunning brain had told him. This was where Ka-Zar slept—this, in all probability, was where the bit of shining glass was hidden.

With unholy enthusiasm at his destructiveness, Bardak attacked the litter with feet and hands. A minute later it lay strewn about the four corners of the cave. From the floor he picked up a long stick of wood that glittered at one end. He examined it curiously a moment, incautiously touched the shining tip, felt a prick on one finger and saw the red blood ooze from his skin. With a grunt he dropped the spear and continued his search. But to his bitter disappointment, the mirror was not there.

After risking so much he had failed. The thick veins in Bardak's throat swelled with anger. Then a short roar from Sha, muffled by distance and the walls of the cave, reminded him of the danger of his position. He beat a hasty retreat down the short tunnel that led to the mouth of the cave and emerged into the glade just as Sha broke clear of the jungle wall on the far side. At his feet the lion cubs tumbled over one another.

Sha saw him immediately, screamed and leaped forward. In answer Bardak pulled back his lips and gnashed his teeth together. He had started his spring for the lowest branch of the tree that hung over the cave, when some mad impulse seized him.

If he had failed to retrieve the bit of shining glass, he would not return to the tribe empty-handed. He would bring back with him a greater trophy—a living token of his fearless courage. With one long arm he swept up Zoro, the nearest of the lion cubs, and leaped for the limb. Agilely he swung himself up and Sha's frantic lunge a split second later missed his hindquarters by a matter of inches.

With the clawing cub pressed tight to his chest, Bardak climbed swiftly to the upper branches of the tree. Here, from this safe retreat he snarled down at the lioness beneath him, while Sha wore herself out in impotent lunges at the overhanging branches above her.

The jungle echoed and re-echoed to her snarls of rage. And a moment later, drifting in on the wind came two answering roars—one from Zar, the other from Ka-Zar.

Bardak heard and was afraid. However, he did not relinquish his prize. With Zoro clutched firmly to him he swung off through the trees and from the ground below Sha followed his progress, making the day hideous with her screams.

ZAR AND KA-ZAR were some miles from the cave when Sha's first roar of rage silenced the jungle tongues. They sent their answer echoing back, then plunged swiftly through the tangled growth for the glade. A moment later Sha's cry of rage drifted to them, crowded with overtones of trouble. The mane on Zar's neck ruffed out and a snarl trembled in his throat. Ka-Zar gripped his knife tighter and increased his long stride.

In an undeviating line they made straight for their objective and the lesser creatures of the jungle scurried to make room for their passing. Halfway to the cave, the direction from whence came Sha's call changed. Zar answered her and followed after Ka-Zar as he turned off abruptly to the right.

They cleared the narrow end of the swamp in three strides, forded a swift-running stream and guided by Sha's cries, pressed steadily forward. It was plain to them that she, too, was on the trail and the course they were following was shrewdly calculated to intercept hers. They also knew by the note of baffled rage in her voice that something out of the ordinary had taken place.

A few minutes later her cries became stationary and breaking through a dense tangle of matted lianas, they found her lunging at the lower branches of a tree that towered above her. Her ears lay back flat against her skull and flecks of foam dripped from her bared fangs.

Zar leaped to the side of his mate, nuzzled her. Sha shook him off impatiently, spoke in staccato growls: "Bardak the ape—he has stolen Zoro and taken to the trees."

As one the heads of Zar and Ka-Zar snapped back. From high up in the branches of the surrounding trees Chaka and his tribe glared down at them. Chattering in their midst, holding the clawing lion cub in one hand and pounding his chest with the other, was Bardak.

Zar bellowed in futile rage. "Come down, Bardak! Or you and your tribe will pay for this!"

Bardak's only answer was to hold out the squealing Zoro still further, dangling it over the perilous heights.

Zar addressed Chaka: "The cub. You are the chief of your tribe. The cub—or war to the death between us."

But Chaka was concerned only with keeping the peace among his own people. In matters between the apes, he exercised his authority. The lion cub, however, was not his affair and he told Zar so.

The lord of the jungle trembled from regal mane to lashing tail, in the grip of a terrible rage. He gave vent to a roar that sent smaller animals scurrying to cover for miles around. But the apes in the trees only looked back at him unmoved and Bardak chuckled. For the mighty Zar was helpless in his fury— he could do nothing and they knew it.

Off to their right was the swift-flowing stream that coursed past Zar's cave, further down. Here it ran between high, rocky banks, strewn with great boulders. An immense oulangi tree thrust its head high into the sky above it.

With one arm wrapped around the terrified cub, Bardak made for it. Ka-Zar realized his intention and raced toward the bank. Snarling, Zar and his mate followed, while the other apes watched in stony silence from their perches.

High, high up in the oulangi, Bardak climbed with his prey. Ka-Zar could have followed but he knew that before he could reach the ape, he would be too late. Instead he tried to stop Bardak with a warning.

"Ka-Zar is your master," he called.

THE APE PULLED his lips back from his fangs in a hideous grin. "Then let Ka-Zar save his brother," he retorted, indicating the whimpering Zoro.

"Ka-Zar showed you…" Ka-Zar stopped. There was no word for 'mercy' in the language of the jungle. Instead, he finished: "This time Bardak will die."

But the ape refused to be cheated of his vengeance. Still farther he climbed up into the giant tree, up, up, until he reached the topmost branches that would not hold his weight. Then slowly he edged out along a swaying limb.

Now Zar and Sha saw what he intended and their roars made the very ground quake. The vengeful ape meant to hurl their cub from the tree, crushing out his life against the rocks below. Already, to them, Zoro's death was inevitable. But they reckoned without their strange blood-brother.

For Ka-Zar had arms. His eyes were riveted on the ape. He saw Bardak hurl the tawny little body downward and judging the arc as the cub hurtled earthward, he leaped out among the boulders.

A breathless silence held them all. Ka-Zar's eye was keen and his arms powerful. He braced his body as Zoro spun toward him. The cub landed in his outstretched arms with such force that he staggered perilously a moment before regaining his balance.

The impact knocked the breath from Zoro's body but he was not injured and a moment later Ka-Zar climbed up the bank and tossed him gently toward his bewildered parents.

With strange, whimpering cries, Sha licked her trembling cub. But up in the tree Bardak, cheated by the miracle, chattered his frustration.

The ape's rage was matched by the black fury in Ka-Zar's heart. Now that the cub was safely out of the way, he could go up after the troublemaker. Whipping out his knife, he placed it between his teeth. Then with a mighty leap he gained the lowest branch of the oulangi and started upward.

Bardak saw him coming and crouched on his limb, grimacing hideously. Fear was in his heart and had there been no witnesses, he might possibly have fled. But now his whole tribe, with Ganya among them, was watching. He could face death, but not disgrace.

If the odds had been against Ka-Zar during their first encounter in the tent, they were still greater against him now. The mad light of panic flared in the ape's red eyes and made him far more formidable than if he had been cockily confident. And remembering the terrible agony that Ka-Zar had inflicted upon him before, Bardak was doubly cautious now. He had the advantage, too, for Ka-Zar must climb up to meet him.

The fight would be in the tree top. For though Chaka and his tribe were more at home on the ground, twin deaths in the shape of Zar and Sha waited eagerly down there now.

Ka-Zar glanced over his shoulder as he climbed. Chaka and the other apes still sat motionless and he realized that, even as the stealing of the cub had been strictly Bardak's affair, so too, this coming battle did not concern them.

Far overhead wheeled Kru the vulture. His sharp eyes had made out the strange gathering of these big beasts and now he sailed on motionless wings watching Ka-Zar and the ape. There would be a kill and he waited patiently for death to come to one of them.

Ka-Zar's brain told him that he must, somehow, get past his enemy—get above him. He was close to where the ape crouched, now. Circling the huge bole of the tree, he swung himself up on the opposite side.

Bardak's intelligence was dulled by the rage and fear that possessed him as he watched the two-legged creature reach his level. His clawing hands reached out, but at that instant Ka-Zar whipped the knife from between his teeth. The shining blade glinted in the sun.

BARDAK'S EXPERIENCE WITH the spear he had found in the cave was still fresh in his memory. Here was another shining thing and it, too, would cut him. Instinctively he drew back and Ka-Zar, taking advantage of the moment, leaped up to a higher branch.

It swayed perilously under his sudden weight. Cautiously, still clutching the knife, he edged out along it over the crouching form of the ape. As he went, the limb cracked along its length in staccato warning.

Gathering his muscles, Ka-Zar prepared himself for the leap. And as the branch gave way, he dropped down full upon the back of his enemy.

Bardak squealed wildly. But before he could recover from his startled amazement, Ka-Zar's left arm slid around under his chin and snapped back his head. Then the hand that held the gleaming blade described a swift arc through the air and the sharp knife buried itself to the hilt at the base of Bardak's throat.

The ape's scream was stilled abruptly. Ka-Zar jerked the knife free and a jet of crimson blood spurted in its wake. He had just time to catch a new hand-hold among the branches as the huge, hairy body collapsed.

There was a series of crashes as Bardak's lifeless body plunged down through the leafy branches of the oulangi. Then, turning over once in mid-air it landed spread-eagled on the boulders of the bank below. Bardak had met the very fate that he had intended for the helpless cub of Zar.

Kru spiraled slowly downward as Ka-Zar tilted back his head and sent the roar of the jungle lord echoing and re-echoing through the forest. Then sheathing his dripping blade, he dropped swiftly down through the tree.

The kill had been accomplished so swiftly that Chaka and his comrades hardly realized what had happened. Not till Bardak's body struck the rocks, never to move again, did they realize that one of their number had met his doom at the hands of this strange two-legged creature. By the time Ka-Zar came striding over toward them, they were muttering among themselves.

He halted below them and looked up at Chaka. "I am Ka-Zar, brother of Zar," he declared arrogantly. "Who molests my brothers—dies."

The mutter of the apes grew louder. Several showed their fangs. Then as one, they looked at their leader.

Chaka considered the weak-looking, yet formidable creature who dared to issue this ultimatum. Chaka was powerful, far more powerful than the troublesome Bardak had been. He felt no fear of this strange Ka-Zar.

But he was ruler of his tribe by virtue of wisdom as well as brawn; of cunning as well as courage.

"Bardak was unruly," he temporized.

Again the apes muttered angrily, but Chaka stilled them with a guttural syllable. "Bardak is dead," he told Ka-Zar. "Bardak forgotten. Chaka goes."

The apes knew their leader too well to question his courage. His decision quenched the last smouldering embers of resentment among them. And at his signal they moved off slowly through the trees.

As Ka-Zar stood watching them go, a tawny shape moved silently up behind him. Something moist, then soft fur, brushed lightly against the hand that hung at his side. He looked down to see the amber eyes of Sha glowing up at him. And a great peace came to his heart as he realized that at last her suspicions were gone—that she accepted him.

CHAPTER XIII

TRAJAH COMES FOR HELP

WITH THE TRUCE between him and Sha cemented at last into an eternal friendship, a new era of happiness dawned for Ka-Zar. Graciously the lioness permitted him to play with her cubs and he found endless delight in frolicking with them. He spent long hours in the hot sunshine before the cave, while Sha lay in the entrance watching. He cuffed them gently in mock battles, sent them spinning when both leaped upon him at once. He laughed at their absurd imitations of Zar's mighty roar and when the day came that one first flattened on his belly, stalked an imaginary kill and leaped upon it, he reported their progress as proudly as Zar might have done.

But the Fates that ruled the destiny of this lonely wilderness had started something, on that long-ago day when they had sent the crippled airplane spinning down into the clearing. That momentous event had brought a chain of others in its wake. And the addition of this strange man-cub to the jungle folk had a profound effect upon all subsequent happenings.

A month after the death of Bardak, Ka-Zar was awakened one night by the loud trumpeting of an elephant. Zar stirred beside him, growled low. Ka-Zar raised himself to one elbow.

The trumpeting came again, nearer this time, and the man-cub rose. "It is Trajah," he said. "I will go."

He crawled swiftly out of the cave. It was just light enough for him to see the huge form of the elephant leader coming toward him. And as he advanced to meet the gray beast, Nono chattered down at him from a tree.

The elephant came to a halt when they met and began a restless swaying. Ka-Zar did not need to ask the reason for the unexpected summons. He sensed that there was trouble afoot in the jungle. But he was not prepared for the startling nature of that trouble.

"Your brothers," said Trajah. "They have taken Tuta, a female of my herd."

"My brothers?" Ka-Zar thought of Zar and Sha, lying back there in the cave with the sleeping cubs. For a moment he was sorely puzzled, then suddenly he understood. Men! Trajah meant men—the Oman!

Eagerly he tried to learn more. But the language of the jungle is limited. Some things, however, he could understand without being told. Apparently Trajah had come for his help, thinking that he might be more able to cope with his own kind. But why the Oman had taken Tuta, and why Tuta was unable to get away from them, he could not figure out. After his own experience with the mad Tupat, he knew the titanic strength of the elephant.

"Where are these brothers of mine?" he asked.

"Two days journey from the cave," answered Trajah.

"Wait," said Ka-Zar. "I will go with you."

Crawling back into the cave, he gathered up his weapons. Zar questioned him with a single low growl that ended on a rising inflection.

"I go with Trajah," he answered. "On a long journey." Then leaving the cave again, he rejoined the waiting elephant.

Nono dropped down onto his shoulder and he tried to brush him off. The monkey, however, only clung the tighter. With a shrug, Ka-Zar allowed him to remain.

With Trajah in the lead, the party traveled south, following the edge of the great lake—on whose shores John Rand had so unexpectedly landed. They reached its southerly end and there their progress was halted by a wide river that was the outlet of the lake. Ka-Zar was a powerful swimmer but as he gauged the distance he must cross and the rush of the sweeping current, he hesitated.

Trajah saw his doubt. Winding his long trunk about Ka-Zar's body, he raised the man-cub, swung him through the air and deposited him high on his own broad back. Nono wrapped both arms around Ka-Zar's neck and uttered shrill squeaks, compounded of delight and fear.

And thus, Ka-Zar's boyish wish—to ride on the great elephant—was gratified at last. He clung to his precarious perch as Trajah strode straight into the river. When the waters swirled up about his shoulders, the elephant struck out with a mighty stroke.

The current was swift and when at last Trajah labored up the opposite bank, they were a mile farther downstream. When they plunged into the jungle once more, Nono again took to the trees. But Ka-Zar laid very flat on his friend's broad back, lest the branch of a tree should brush him off in their passing.

TOWARDS SUNSET OF the second day, they paused on the brow of a high hill. From his point of vantage on the top of the elephant's back, a panorama lay before Ka-Zar that held him breathless.

For him, memory began vaguely with the days when he and his parents had lived in the lean-to. All before that had been long since blotted from his mind. Except for the breaks made by small clearings, by lake and stream, he knew nothing but dense jungle. And quite naturally, if he thought about it at all, he thought that the great forest was endless.

Now, for the first time, he saw where it ended. And beyond its outer fringes stretched a great, grassy plain. It extended far to the distant horizon, flat as the surface of the lake. A hot wind came in puffs across it, rippling the tall grass in undulating waves of gray-green and mauve. Ka-Zar's eyes, keen as those of Pindar the eagle, made out enormous herds of strange beasts moving slowly across the level expanse.

While he was marveling at the wondrous sight, Trajah raised his head and trumpeted loudly. And from somewhere in the distance, came an answering call.

"Tuta," Trajah said.

Ka-Zar knew, then, that they were near the end of their journey. And though, as yet, he had no idea what they would do when they got there, he cautioned silence.

"You, too," he called to Nono. "Let us have no more of your silly chatter."

Nono grimaced back at him, but thenceforth maintained a dutiful silence. Trajah moved down the side of the hill into the thinning fringe of the forest. Several times Ka-Zar caught further glimpses of strange beasts that roamed the plain. Once a band of zebras, bizarre in their black and white stripes, galloped past. Another time he stared in amazement at a big, ungainly creature with a tremendously long neck—the giraffe. And later, he saw a familiar tawny shape slink through the tall grass.

Ka-Zar first saw the rising thread of smoke that wafted from the camp fire. Then he heard the faint sounds of the men, busy with their preparations for the evening meal. He called a low note into Trajah's ear and when the elephant halted, slid agilely to the ground.

"Wait here," he commanded.

Leaping up into the nearest tree, he swung from bough to bough, with Nono following his progress on higher branches. Swiftly and silently they gained the outermost fringes of the forest.

The plain was a vast oven of blistering heat by day and so these men had pitched their tents in the shade of a great baobab. Now, high in this tree, Ka-Zar and Nono looked down on the encampment directly beneath them.

Several black men were busy before the fire. Three tents, similar to the one DeKraft had used, opened toward the plain. Ka-Zar passed them over with a glance, then stared in fascination at the array of cumbersome objects behind them.

He had never seen a cage before. In a way, these strange shelters reminded him of the lean-to. But he could see no opening in them and in each one was a jungle beast.

Nono squeaked when he saw that one held about eight frightened members of his long-tailed tribe. Ka-Zar stilled him with a warning growl. There was a brother of N'Jaga, stirring restlessly in his confined quarters. Beside him, Quog the wild pig squealed in rage. A big, long-legged stork stood with his head on his breast in profound melancholy. And beyond them Tuta stood swaying in the long grass, her head swung in the direction from which Trajah had last called her and her gaze yearning.

KA-ZAR TOSSED BACK his long hair and his brows knitted in a frown. She was not confined in one of the strange shelters. Why did she stay there, then?

"Go back to Trajah," he whispered to Nono. "Tell him to call again."

The monkey sped nimbly off and Ka-Zar turned again to watch Tuta intently. The hush that comes with the sunset had fallen over plain and forest. A moment later it was shattered by the trumpeting of the elephant—strident, commanding, pleading.

Tuta's head came up. With an answering cry, she lunged forward, only to pull up with a sudden jerk. And then, as she thrashed against the bonds that held her, Ka-Zar saw them. The swaying grasses revealed the stout ropes that bound each of her feet to stakes set firmly into the ground. All Tuta's strength could not break them.

The opening flap of the center tent billowed outward and a white man stepped into Ka-Zar's view. He was not DeKraft, for he was tall and slender and his hair was the color of N'Jaga's glistening coat. He snatched up a long rifle that leaned against the front of the tent and turned to peer into the dense jungle whence Trajah's call had come.

With his eyes watchful, but a little half smile playing at the corners of his lips, he addressed the unseen elephant. Up in the tree, Ka-Zar heard his voice.

"Back again, eh?" he said in clear English. "Sorry, old boy. But she can't join you. There's a new home waiting for her—far away—in a nice zoo."

It was a long time since Ka-Zar had heard his own tongue. He understood everything but the last word of the white man's speech. His voice had been pleasant but though its tone seemed to convey no threat, Ka-Zar scowled. The jungle was Tuta's home. And somehow, some way, he would see that she returned safely to Trajah and the rest of the herd.

In a different language the white man flung a command at the blacks who had paused to stare. Then, as they busied themselves at their work again, he strolled over to inspect Tuta's hobbles. She plunged and squealed again at his approach. Keeping at a safe distance, he circled about her. Then apparently satisfied that she was firmly held captive, he strode back to his tent and disappeared.

Ka-Zar studied the camp intently, then left.

CHAPTER XIV

JUNGLE MYSTERY

SILENT AS THE deepening shadows, Ka-Zar made his way back to the waiting elephant. He did not know man-made rope but it resembled the tough lianas that hung in festoons from the lower branches of the jungle trees. Now he understood why Trajah had been unable to free this hapless member of his tribe and had come to him for aid. And he knew that his gleaming knife would be able to accomplish what all the elephant's mighty strength could not do.

"Tuta will be free," he told Trajah.

The elephant tossed his trunk to show his pleasure. He took an eager step forward in the direction of the camp.

Ka-Zar barred his path on straddled legs. "Not now. We must wait until night comes. Then—" he drew his knife from his belt, tested its gleaming blade on his finger—"then I will steal into the camp."

Reluctantly Trajah agreed.

"We will not hurt the Oman," continued Ka-Zar. "I think they meant Tuta no harm. There is another matter, too. Other jungle brothers are held captive in the camp. We must help them, also."

Nono jumped up and down, happy to think that his forlorn brothers would also be freed. Tugging at Ka-Zar's arm, he begged to be allowed to help.

They waited, while the dusk deepened. Since the Oman had fire-sticks, they knew it would be fatal to attempt the rescue of the jungle beasts until the two-legged creatures had retired for the night. Not until the camp was quiet would they venture forth.

Ka-Zar warned the elephant that he must be content to wait where he was. If he moved in the direction of the camp, the noise of his coming would surely arouse the men.

With the rising of the moon, Ka-Zar and Nono returned to their vantage point in the big baobab. The wind had changed and their scent was carried to the captives in the cages. The leopard's head whipped up. The monkeys began a nervous jabbering, Ka-Zar risked a low, guttural call, commanding them to silence.

A black, scrubbing the cooking pot with handfuls of grass, heard him. But never dreaming that such a sound could have issued from a human throat, he continued with his work.

Ka-Zar's life in the jungle had given him a patience that matched his courage. Several times the men passed directly beneath him but not the faintest sound told them that something was watching them from the baobab.

The moon rose higher—an enormous orange ball that crept up, slowly from the horizon. It turned gradually to silver and its rays bathed the vast plain with a mystic, bluish light. The camp fire was piled high for the night and finally the last black crawled into a tent and vanished.

Ka-Zar had learned to be more than cautious. Ten minutes later his low note of warning floated softly from the tree. Then, with Nono, he swung down through the leafy branches and dropped lightly to the ground. First he circled each tent, his footfalls making no noise in the tall grass. He located each man within by the sound of his breathing and from the regularity of that breathing knew that they were all asleep.

Not until then did he rejoin Nono, who was crouching on top of the cage that held his brothers. For breathless minutes he explored the unfamiliar contrivance, seeking some way to open it. At last he managed to unfasten small ropes that held a sliding panel on one end of the cage.

Threatening the silly creatures with dire punishment, indeed, if they made a sound, he drew the panel carefully upward. The excited monkeys jammed at the opening, squeezed through and with Nono joyfully leaping ahead of them, scampered for the trees.

THE BIG STORK came next. Evidently it had been a prisoner for quite some time, for when Ka-Zar opened the door of his pen, he stepped out and looked about him in bewilderment. At last he realized that he was free. With a flap of his long wings he soared into the air and headed out over the plain.

Swiftly and silently Ka-Zar went on with his task. Quog made a straight rush into the darkened forest. The leopard lingered long enough to growl an acknowledgment to his strange rescuer, cast a baleful eye at the motionless tents and then vanished like a blacker shadow into the darkness of the night.

Tuta stirred restlessly at Ka-Zar's approach. He had to risk another warning to quiet her. Then with the sharp blade of his knife he sawed at each rope in turn until she was free. Fearful lest she should arouse the camp before they were well away, he led her quite some distance along the edge of the grassy plain. Not until he was sure that they were out of earshot of the sleeping men, did he plunge once more into the jungle and take her by a circuitous route back to where Trajah patiently awaited them.

STEVE HARDY, BIG game hunter and wild animal collector, turned over on his cot. He woke suddenly from a fitful sleep and wondered what it was that had awakened him. Hitchihg himself up onto one elbow, he listened. No strange sound disturbed the stillness.

Still he felt uneasy. And finally it dawned upon him that it was the very silence that bothered him. Never had the camp been so still. Of the specimens that he had collected, there were several who complained about their captivity—all through the nights.

Pushing aside the mosquito netting that draped his bed, he thrust his feet into his boots. He picked up the flashlight that always lay within easy reach and got his rifle on the way out of the tent.

He did not need to click on the button of the flash. The moon bathed the camp with brilliant light, throwing the tents and the animal cages into sharp relief. And Steve Hardy was astounded to learn that the big leopard, his most magnificent specimen, was no longer behind bars.

Uneasily he glanced about him and to his dismay he quickly learned that the others had vanished likewise, while he had slept. He shouted and a moment later he was joined by his retinue of Ankwalla blacks, all instantly wide awake.

Quickly he pointed to the empty cages, hurling questions at them in their native tongue. But they were as baffled as he and as they thought about it, more and more terrified. Huddling at his heels, they followed him from cage to cage.

Hardy was beside himself with rage. The arduous labor of months, undone in a single night! His Ankwalla boys would not have done this—there would have been no reason for it. Surely no inquisitive monkey could have pried into camp and accidentally freed all his animals. The sliding doors were too heavy for a monkey to have lifted. The bull elephant that had called to the cow from the jungle—an elephant does not unfasten ropes… elephant… elephant…

Suddenly Hardy looked up. His elephant, too, was gone!

The natives jabbered excitedly as they raced after him to the spot where Tuta had been tethered. Hardy dropped to one knee, picked up the rope still fastened to one of the stakes. And the bright moonlight revealed the startling fact that it had not been torn, but neatly cut in two!

Slowly he rose to his feet. An oath died still-born on his lips. Common sense told him that a man, armed with a knife had cut that strand of rope. But as far as he knew, no man—white or black—was within a thousand miles of his lonely outpost.

Why, in God's name, he asked himself, would any man release all his animals and vanish again? A madman? Madness would not have protected him against the ferocity of that huge leopard. He gazed about him, half-expecting to see a mangled lifeless corpse. But only alternate patches of shadow and brilliant moonlight marked the grass around the camp.

From deep in the jungle came the trumpet call of two elephants. And then, not far from his lonely camp, another challenging sound echoed out of the wilderness. It was the deep-throated, mighty bellow of a lion. It was, though Hardy did not know it, the triumphant call of Ka-Zar, brother of Zar, lord of the jungle.

While Hardy meditated, baffled and angry, on the mysterious evil that had visited him, his Ankwalla boys held a whispered conclave. Then headed by his gun boy, they marched up to where he stood.

THEIR LEADER EXPLAINED that for some reason, the all-powerful gods of the jungle were angry. The spiriting away of the animals had been a warning to them all. Unless Hardy and the rest departed at once, they, too, would vanish as mysteriously and as silently as the beasts.

In vain Hardy argued with them. He had come many thousands of miles and had spent a considerable amount of money organizing this expedition. They must patiently begin their labors all over again. But he could not explain the startling events of the night and they would not listen to him. What dire fate awaited them when the jungle gods should spirit them away, they could only guess at darkly. But depart the Ankwallas would, and Steve Hardy, perforce, must go with them.

CHAPTER XV

MARK OF THE LEOPARD

THE NEWS OF Ka-Zar's exploit in freeing the jungle beasts from the traps of the Oman, traveled swiftly through the forest. As one who had witnessed the miracle, Nono the monkey bragged loudly to Sinassa the snake. And in turn, Sinassa passed on the tale to Wal-lah the hippopotamus, with fresh embellishments. With each telling of the tale, the fame and prowess of the man-cub grew, until all the jungle accepted him, at last, as a friend.

That is, all but one. N'Jaga, whose spotted flank still bore the scar of John Rand's bullet and who limped slightly as a result of it, could not forget his hate. If anything, it was fanned to new heights as he scornfully listened to the jungle creatures sing the praise of Ka-Zar.

Next to Zar the lion, N'Jaga had been feared and respected in the jungle. And now, with a bitter intensity he resented the intrusion of the man-cub who had usurped his place in the jungle scale. He felt that he had lost caste, that the only way to regain it was to prove his mastery over Ka-Zar.

And to this end, N'Jaga sulked many long hours in the forest, devising ways and means to dispose of his enemy. He was too wise to seek an open conflict with the man-cub. Though he scorned the puny strength of Ka-Zar in contrast to the might of his own supple limbs, he yet feared the two-legged creature for his tricks and for the cruel weapons he wielded with his hands.

N'Jaga early decided that the basis of his campaign should be cunning. And after much deliberation, he hit upon a plan that offered every prospect of success.

A hundred times, from a discreet distance, he had stalked Ka-Zar along the jungle trails. He knew that invariably every day the man-cub went down to the lake, to swim there a long time and to gossip with Wal-lah. Before entering the water he would strip himself of the skin that covered him. But more important than this was the fact that he would leave his weapons on the shore of the lake.

N'Jaga ran a dripping tongue over his jowls as he matured his plans.

It was late in the afternoon of the following day that Ka-Zar swung swiftly through the trees to the shore of the lake. He dropped lightly to the narrow strip of sand that formed the beach and shouted a greeting to Jacaru who floated motionless in the shallows like a log.

Ka-Zar was hot and tired from a long hunt with Zar and he tingled at the prospect of plunging his naked body in the cool waters of the lake. He stripped swiftly and as the cunning N'Jaga had known he would, carelessly dropped his knife to the sands.

With a long springy stride he leaped out to the end of a log that projected far into the lake, poised there a moment, then dove cleanly into the water. He swam under the surface for a long distance, came up puffing and snorting by the side of Wal-lah far out in the water.

For a few moments they talked, then with a long easy stroke, Ka-Zar struck out for the distant shore of the lake, which was still bathed in dappled sunshine. He reached the far side at last. His favorite spot was a deep pool close in to shore. A giant baobab tree, smitten by a bolt during some ancient storm, hung far over it and made an excellent perch for diving.

But first he had to pay his respects to the nimble Nyassa. Vainly he tried to capture the fish, but with consummate ease she eluded his darting fingers.

TIRING OF THE sport at last, he rose to the surface, rolled on his back, relaxed completely and floated. For a few minutes he studied the outlines of the clouds drifting high in the heaven and imagined that he could see in their ever-shifting shapes, the faces of the different jungle beasts.

Then a furtive movement along the trunk of the baobab, a few feet above his head, caught his eye. Instead of seeing the fancied faces of the jungle beasts in the clouds—Ka-Zar saw a very real one, in the flesh.

It was N'Jaga on the trunk above him, poised for a spring. The spotted haunches of the leopard were tensed back, his rump was raised and the talon-like claws of his forepaws were arched.

From malignant green eyes he glared down at Ka-Zar.

Fascinated, hypnotized, Ka-Zar stared back. He knew that he had been trapped; knew that N'Jaga had cunningly awaited this opportunity before striking.

Then silently, without a sound, the leopard sprang. All the pent-up hate of his dark heart propelled his body forward. But even while he was in mid-air, Ka-Zar rolled his body over.

Instead of gouging out his eyes and slashing his face to ribbons, N'Jaga's claws sank deep into the man-cub's back.

Ka-Zar was conscious of streaks of liquid fire tearing across his spine. Pain, greater than any he had ever known before, consumed his body. Like a stone he sank beneath the weight of the beast whose talons still clung to the flesh of his back. Desperately, by a sheer effort of will he fought off the numbing fog that settled on his brain. Every sense of self-preservation rose to his defense.

But unarmed, he was helpless against the superior weight and strength of the leopard. Hard as his hands were, they were no match for the fangs and claws of N'Jaga.

And then Ka-Zar's brain—the thing that set him apart and above the beasts—came to his rescue. It was futile, he knew, a losing, hopeless battle, to try to fight N'Jaga on such unequal terms. To come to the surface meant death. His only salvation lay in sinking ever deeper to the bottom of the lake.

Jungle cats have an aversion to water and it was a measure of N'Jaga's hate that he had plunged into the lake to destroy his enemy.

Ka-Zar knew this and prepared to act. The leopard was still clinging to his back and from all indications was content to stay there. But the man-cub thought differently. With a sudden movement he shot up both his arms and encircled N'Jaga's head that loomed up above his own. His fingers locked together in an unbreakable grip and exerting his every ounce of strength he applied pressure to the cat's neck until N'Jaga's head was pressed close to his own.

Together they sank towards the bottom until Ka-Zar thought that his lungs must burst; until N'Jaga could stand the pressure no longer. A fear, that in fulfilling his vengeance, he, too, must die, stirred in his brain. His claws ripped from Ka-Zar's back. Wildly he struggled to break the hold on his neck—to reach the surface—and air.

Then the strangling hold around his throat relaxed. True, he desired the death of Ka-Zar greatly but he desired his own life more. He pushed down on the water with his large padded paws and propelled himself towards the surface. He knew that the man-cub was sorely wounded and he doubted whether he would ever rise to the surface again.

He was content. N'Jaga had won.

The leopard was right—in at least one respect. He had indeed been the victor in this first conflict with the man-cub. And when he reached the shore of the lake he screamed his triumph to the listening ears of the jungle.

BUT SO PREOCCUPIED was he in proclaiming his might, that he failed entirely to see the torn and mangled thing rose slowly to the surface of the lake and clutch weakly at a low-hanging limb of the baobab.

If N'Jaga had not under-estimated the stamina and endurance of his enemy, he might have tarried there by the shore and finished his work at his leisure. For Ka-Zar was too spent, too weak from loss of blood to offer further resistance.

But the leopard's heart was full of vain glory and without a backward glance at the lake, he stalked off into the forest, proclaiming his kill.

It was a long time before Ka-Zar gathered sufficient strength to work his way to shore. A still longer time before he skirted the lake to retrieve his loin cloth and knife. Fever consumed his body and his limbs were like water beneath him. His brain was numb but the lesson he had learned from his encounter with N'Jaga gave him a grim, if bitter, satisfaction.

It was this—never again, no matter what the circumstances, would he be caught without his knife. And the bare knife was clutched in his hand when he stumbled at last into the cave.

For days Ka-Zar lay helpless and sick in the cave. For days Zar and Sha stood guard over him, tending his wounds the only way they could—by licking them.

At long last the fever left his body and a skeleton of his former self, he struggled to his feet. In celebration of the event Zar brought fresh-killed antelope quarter to the cave, and fruits fresh gathered by Nono the monkey.

Ka-Zar ate, drank and slept again. And from that time on his recovery was rapid. But ever after he bore the mark of N'Jaga upon his back.

CHAPTER XVI

RETURN OF THE OMAN

WHEN PAUL DEKRAFT had fled from the jungle clearing, with the sound of Zar's roar echoing in his ears, he had taken with him two secrets. First, the grim details of the death of the mad jungle hermit; second, the location of the richest emerald beds it had ever been his good fortune to stumble across.

The first dark secret slipped readily from his mind. It was not the first time that he had killed nor would it be his last. But the second was forever with him, a shining promise of a vast fortune to be looted by him alone.

The lure of those emeralds, to be picked up by handfuls from the bed of that jungle stream, spurred him on to herculean efforts. He worked, robbed and plotted murder to accumulate a stake to take him once more to the heart of the Belgian Congo.

And now, after five long years, at the end of another rainy season he was leading a large party into the heart of the wilderness over which Zar and Ka-Zar had ruled for so long.

The expedition consisted of a score of blacks and one white man—Ed Kivlin. He was a renegade like DeKraft and if he was not as villainous as the Hollander, it was only because DeKraft had lived some few years more than he and had served a longer apprenticeship to the devil.

DeKraft had not taken him along out of the open generosity of his heart. He had been motivated by far baser and more practical reasons. It was simply that Kivlin had a few hundred dollars—and he needed them. For food, shovels, guns and ammunition, but mostly ammunition.

And all the time there was a little idea in the back of his head that perchance a little accident would befall his benefactor. No matter how it came about—before the fang and claw of some jungle beast or from a bullet from his own gun—he was convinced and determined that Eddie Kivlin would not come out of the jungle with him.

Once he had made his alliance with Kivlin and the dollars, DeKraft started to assemble his party. But to his disgust and impatience, he found that as soon as he mentioned the Congo as his destination, the native blacks shunned him as if he carried the plague.

Strange tales, weird, wonderful and unholy, had drifted down from the Congo. They had first been brought back to civilization by a great white hunter and his camp followers. The tales had to do with a jungle god, the protector of all wild things, who was incensed at man for molesting the beasts of the forest.

Hadn't this god, who spoke with the voice of the lion, liberated a season's catch of the great white hunter? Hadn't he slashed the ropes that held the mighty elephant; broken open the cage that held a huge leopard?

The tale grew with the telling and DeKraft was forced to deceit and trickery to assemble the natives he needed. It was not until the party was a month's march from the nearest white outpost or native village that he told the blacks their real destination.

Then unarmed, without food, it was too late for them to turn back. DeKraft laughed long and raucously over what he considered the good joke he had played on them.

The natives listened to him in silence and with hate in their hearts. Sullenly they struggled on with the party but with each mile they penetrated deeper into the Congo, the greater became their superstitious fears.

It was at the end of a long, hot day when DeKraft triumphantly led his party at last into the small glade he had quitted so precipitately five years before.

HE LOOKED ABOUT him with greedy eyes. Nothing had changed, except that the vines and brush had crept in from the forest and made a dense growth that covered the clearing. The last, tattered remains of his tent still remained where he had abandoned it. The stream still rushed by, innocently tumbling over a fortune in uncut emeralds.

He pounded Kivlin enthusiastically on the back, threw his arm wide. "So help me, Eddie," he said, "here we are! A fortune—there in the stream—ready to be picked up by the handfuls."

Kivlin grinned wolfishly, took a long pull from a bottle of square-face gin and wiped his mouth with the back of his hand. "We didn't get here any too soon for me," he answered. "And as far as a fortune goes, I could use one."

"Plenty for both of us—plenty for both," said DeKraft heartily. Then he turned hurriedly away to hide the crafty gleam in his eyes.

He issued a string of terse orders to his bearers. Under the lash of his tongue and the persuasive power of his heavy fist, they hurried about the business of making camp. With long knives the undergrowth was cleared away. Tents were pitched; the supplies and ammunition stored away. A half hour after their arrival a thin plume of smoke went up from their fire to announce their coming to the jungle beasts.

It is significant that both DeKraft and Kivlin slept little and lightly that night and in both their hands were heavy automatics. True, the blacks were sullen and surly, but it was not for fear of them that they crept into their respective cots thus armed.

The thoughts of each were the same. A fortune! Why share it? Each in his own way planned towards the same end.

However, despite their mutual distrust and treachery, the first night passed uneventfully.

KA-ZAR WAS A two-days-march distant from the cave when DeKraft pitched his camp in the clearing. He was on one of his frequent pilgrimages to the feeding grounds of Trajah and he was all unaware that his old enemy, Fat-Face, had returned to his domain; all unaware of the trouble that was brewing for him in the jungle he had so long ruled with Zar.

His first intimation that some serious mischief was afoot came three days later. It was night and he was listening to Trajah's account of distant lands that the elephant had seen on his long migrations.

Trajah was in the midst of some strange and fascinating tales when abruptly, from far off, came the stentorian roar of a lion. Ka-Zar's head snapped up and his eyes narrowed. The elephant's large ears flapped slowly at right angles to his head.

"Zar calls," said Ka-Zar.

"The lion calls to his brother," echoed Trajah gravely.

A vague, disturbing premonition stirred in Ka-Zar's brain. Swiftly he threw back his head, expanded his leather lungs and a moment later the forest shook as he sent the lion's call echoing back to Zar.

Three times more Ka-Zar repeated his roar, then without a sound the massive form of Zar materialized out of the brush. With Trajah lumbering at his side, Ka-Zar stepped eagerly forward to meet him.

He rumbled a warm greeting deep in his throat, then before Zar could answer it, asked what had brought his brother on his trail.

In a few swift grunts and snarls Zar told him. Many two-legged creatures like himself—many Oman—white and black—had come to the glade by the stream that babbled over many stones. They had brought fire sticks with them. There was much death. There was trouble brewing in the forest of Ka-Zar and it would be wise for Ka-Zar, brother of Zar, to return.

The white man's adage that the elephant never forgets, is based on sound fact. He never forgives an injury and he never forgets a friend. To his distant dying day, Trajah would carry always with him the memory of that time when Ka-Zar had rescued Tuta from her strange captivity.

Now trouble had come again to the jungle and there was no question whether the elephant would stand by his friends. Knowing Ka-Zar's delight in riding upon his lofty back, Trajah waited for no more. His trunk snaked out, wound about Ka-Zar's body and lifted him easily up to his favorite perch. Then with Zar gliding swiftly along in the lead, they began their long journey back to the cave.

Ka-Zar was troubled with vague apprehensions of what might already have occurred during his absence. And when at last they reached their home, he found that his fears were well founded.

In the trees around the cave mouth squatted Chaka and his apes, waiting for his return. He slid down from the elephant's back and walked forward as the big leader swung down from his perch and came shambling over to meet him.

Chaka's manner conveyed neither open hostility nor full-hearted friendship. He grunted a greeting, then cocked his head on one side and surveyed Ka-Zar gravely from head to foot. It was plain to see that he nursed suspicions, but was reserving a decision.

"Your two-legged brothers have returned," he announced. "And death comes with them."

Ka-Zar brushed back a lock of his long hair and scowled. "They are not my brothers," he growled. "I belong to the tribe of Zar."

Chaka thrust forward a pendulous lower lip, scratched thoughtfully at one ear. "You are a two-legged creature," he said slowly.

KA-ZAR REALIZED THAT words were futile. His actions must speak for him. "Death speaks from their fire-sticks?" he asked.

"Two moons ago," answered Chaka, "Dakar saw something that glittered and went to examine it. The Oman cried out and one of them pointed at Dakar with a fire-stick. It spoke with the voice of thunder and Dakar died." A mournful sound rose from the apes squatting in the trees, corroborating his words. "Yesterday," Chaka continued, "Babba, a female, wandered foolishly too near their home. A fire-stick spoke swiftly, many times, and Babba died from many wounds."

At this recital of their loss, the apes in the trees set up an angry muttering. One called to Chaka. "Let us go and kill these Oman."

Others took up the cry of vengeance. Chaka hesitated, looked to Ka-Zar.

The brother of Zar shook his head. "Do not try," he warned. "The fire-stick strikes like the lightning and before you could kill, many more would join Dakar and Babba in the Great Sleep." His eyes narrowed and he fingered the knife at his belt. "I have driven these Oman from the jungle before and I will do it again. Keep well away from their home while I go see what can be done."

Zar and Trajah would willingly have accompanied him. But he told them that he desired to go alone and leaving his friends and the muttering apes to await his return, he set out at once for the camp.

His ears quickly told him that the men had made their home where DeKraft's old tent still mouldered. When he approached the spot, Nono saw him from his vantage point in the upper branches of a tall tree. The little monkey, fearful and yet overcome by an insatiable curiosity, could not tear himself away from the scene of so much activity.

Ka-Zar, too, took to the trees. He reached one that gave him a clear view of the camp in the clearing and then, flattened along a stout limb and so screened by the dense foliage that he was invisible from below, he watched.

The fact that the men had come to this very spot brought back once more all the terrible memory of that day when his father had been killed. And with it revived the deep seated desire to wreak vengeance upon the fat, black-bearded man.

He saw many black men busy before the tents. One took a

steaming kettle from sticks that held it suspended above the fire, carried it a little apart and set it down to cool. A white man suddenly appeared from the fringe of the forest, on the opposite side of the clearing. Ka-Zar stiffened.

A long fire-stick hung loosely from the crook of the man's arm. His head was covered by something that looked like a bloated, white mushroom. He took it off, revealing a thatch of hair, the color of the flaming sunset. Then he looked towards one of the tents and called out: "Hey, Dutch!"

In answer, a bulky form pushed out from the tent. Ka-Zar saw a swarthy face, an untidy black beard, a bulging belly. A low growl rumbled deep in his throat and the hair at the base of his skull prickled. His usual caution was drowned by the deep, undying hatred that suddenly flamed up within him. There stood the slayer of his father—and he had to fight the impulse to snatch his knife, scream the kill of the lion and drop down from the tree to confront his old enemy.

For a long moment the battle raged within him, then wisdom conquered. Every nerve in his body taut, he lay on the branch and glared his hatred from slitted, tawny eyes.

THE TWO MEN stood for a moment, conversing in low tones. A clumsy, bristly gray creature wandered out from the forest into the clearing. Quag, brother of Quog the wild pig, paid no heed to his strange new surroundings. He was headed for the stream to slake his thirst and on his way, he nosed for the berries and succulent roots that comprised his diet.

The cooling kettle was directly in his path. Carelessly he nudged it with his snout. It tipped over, spilling its savoury contents on the ground.

One of the blacks shouted. DeKraft looked up, saw at a glance what had happened. With a torrent of oaths he snatched the rifle from Kivlin's arm, whipped it to his shoulder and blazed at the clumsy pig who had spoiled his dinner.

There was a stab of flame, an echoing roar. The hapless Quag squealed once in shrill agony, then pitched forward, never to move again.

His needless death, the wanton cruelty with which DeKraft had taken a jungle life, added fuel to the flame of Ka-Zar's wrath. Again he had to battle the impulse to challenge the vicious Fat-Face, who had shattered the peace of the forest.

With a low growl, telling Nono to follow, he edged lithely back along the limb, turned and headed towards the cave. When he was well out of ear-shot from the camp, he sent the monkey off on a strange errand.

"Go! Find all the big beasts of the jungle and tell them to go to Zar's cave. I will wait for them there. Make haste, silly one."

While Nono obediently set off, he continued on his way to rejoin his friends and the troubled apes. They greeted him with expectant gaze but he merely went to sit on a great boulder and there silently pondered his problem.

CHAPTER XVII

OUTCAST

K **A-ZAR HAD CHOSEN** a swift courier. In ones, in twos, in large groups, the animals came to learn the reason for his summons. Keeping well to their own kind, they gathered in the vicinity of the lion's lair, waiting for Ka-Zar to speak.

It was well into the afternoon when the last arrived. N'Jaga, with several of his spotted tribe, stalked out of the forest and warily joined the gathering.

Ka-Zar stood up on the rock and surveyed the motley collection of beasts that inhabited his wilderness domain. Chaka and his great apes still squatted on the lower branches of the trees. Nono and his long-tailed friends scurried about above them. Zar and Sha stood side by side, a regal pair, before the door of their home. Trajah swayed restlessly in his place. Quog and his grunting people moved about, champing their tusks nervously.

N'Jaga and the leopards crouched to one side, their gleaming eyes shifting swiftly at every movement. Even Sinassa the great snake had come. He stretched, coiled about a strong limb, and watched the gathering from unblinking, beady little eyes. And far overhead Kru the vulture, thinking that this meeting of the bigger jungle animals would provide him with such a feast as he had never seen, wheeled around on motionless wings.

All eyes turned to focus on the figure of Ka-Zar, dominating and arrogant, astride the rock. A hush fell upon them and flinging back his regal head, he shattered the silence with the mighty roar of the lion. Respectfully they listened as it echoed and re-echoed through the leafy fastness. Only N'Jaga's tail twitched and his lips pulled back a trifle from his teeth.

His face dark with passion, Ka-Zar launched into his speech.

"Jungle brothers," he began, "Ka-Zar, brother of Zar the mighty, called you here. Trouble has come to our home, great trouble. Oman have come again to molest us—to hurt us—to kill us."

He flung his arms out in a sweeping gesture. "The Oman are evil. Unlike us, they slay for no reason. Chaka will tell you that two of his tribe died before their terrible fire-sticks. Other beasts have perished, also. This very afternoon I saw Quag, brother of Quog, die because he had foolishly blundered into their clearing."

He turned his head to stare for a long moment in the direction of the distant camp, his jaw set at a grim angle and his eyes boding no good to the marauders who had come to violate the sanctity of his wilderness.

He turned again to his strange audience. "I, Ka-Zar, brother of Zar, shall drive them out. But now I give you all warning. Nothing can stand before the fire-sticks of the Oman and live. Let all the animals keep well away from the clearing. Let no more lives be needlessly taken. When the time comes, I will summon you and together we will have our vengeance."

He folded his arms and looked about the gathering of beasts. At once they set up a subdued muttering, growling, chattering and grunting among themselves.

N'Jaga rose to his feet, fell into a crouch. He snarled. "Ka-Zar is no lion," he growled. "Ka-Zar is of the Oman. N'Jaga does not trust him."

The beasts listened to his words, then fell to a more excited chattering. Ka-Zar knew that N'Jaga had voiced the suspicion that already lurked in the minds of Chaka and his apes. He could see that Chaka was swayed by N'Jaga's words. Glancing about the assemblage, he saw quickly that the seeds of mistrust had fallen upon fertile ground. The other beasts wavered, but already N'Jaga had gained an advantage.

The cunning leopard knew, and pressed it. "We have claws and fangs," he spat. "Why do we permit ourselves to be slain by these weak, hairless creatures—the Oman? Let us kill this one and then go to slay the others."

NONO AND HIS friends chattered shrilly up in the branches. Chaka dropped to the ground and with his tribe at his heels, lumbered forward. His threatening attitude decided the rest. Ranging themselves around N'Jaga and his snarling cousins, they flung their defiance at the man-cub.

Ka-Zar knew that his life hung in the balance. His knife, his bow and arrows, his deadly spear could not help him now. Alone, in single combat with any denizen of the jungle, they would give him a fighting chance. But let all these beasts charge him at once and he was doomed.

Yet arrogantly, boldly, he stepped down from the rock and strode up to confront them. Without a moment's hesitation, Zar and Sha ranged up at his side and Zar's deep-throated challenge rumbled from his mighty throat. Then Trajah the elephant moved majestically forward and took up a position on his other side. With a blasting trumpet, he defied any creature to approach them.

The hatred for this two-legged creature that N'Jaga had nursed so long in his breast, urged him to spring. But the sight of Ka-Zar's powerful allies stayed him. For a long moment he crouched, tail lashing, and the terrible slaughter for which Kru waited on motionless wings, hung on his decision. A pregnant silence held them all.

Then suddenly N'Jaga spat, wheeled around and quickly disappeared into the jungle.

The other beasts had worked themselves up to a pitch of emotion that robbed them of all independent thought. N'Jaga's flight set them an example. And with squeals, grunts, growls of frustrated rage, they scattered and were swallowed up by the forest. Only Nono and the monkeys remained, to hurl gibes after the departing beasts from the safety of their branches high in the trees.

Ka-Zar was left alone with his friends and with the bitter realization that he was held an outcast—a traitor—by his own people. Slowly he turned and walked soberly back to the cave. Flinging himself down before the entrance, he returned again to his problem, now doubly important and doubly difficult.

He could count only on the lions, on Trajah and the monkeys for any assistance. All the other beasts, even if they did not dare to attack him, would wait in judgment. To regain his supremacy over them and to bring peace once more to his land, he must settle the matter of DeKraft once and for all.

The task would not be an easy one, he knew. Against the white man's weapons he was powerless. And though he lay for a long time, his head pillowed in the crook of his arm, inspiration would not come.

At length he rose. The sun was descending the downward curve of its arc. The shadows of the trees grew longer. Trajah was resting from his long journey. Sha had returned to her cubs and Zar was off on the spoor of a kill. Nono's cousins had dispersed, but the little monkey came and climbed up to his favorite place on Ka-Zar's broad shoulder.

On the long hope that another visit to DeKraft's camp might bring him the inspiration he so sorely needed, Ka-Zar set off in that direction again. And soon, from the big tree, he and Nono were once more looking down upon the activities of the men.

Most of the blacks were still busy at their labors in the stream. Three hovered about the fire, getting ready the evening meal. The two white men—Fat-Face and the owner of the burnished copper hair—were seated at the far side of the clearing, watching the natives work and conversing in low tones.

One of the blacks at the stream walked over toward them, bearing a pan that held several pebbles. Both white men reached for it together, exchanged a veiled glance—then the red-haired one allowed DeKraft to take it. Together they bent their heads over the pan as the native returned to his work.

KA-ZAR COULD HEAR their voices, but he could not make out their words. Gliding like a shadow down the tree, he circled about the clearing and then stole softly towards where they were sitting. Not a leaf stirred at his passing; not a twig crackled under his feet. A scant few yards behind them, so flat against the bole of a tree that he seemed to become part of it, he listened. Their conversation was carried on in the language of his dead father and he had no difficulty following their words.

"Emeralds," DeKraft's voice came floating back to him. "A bloody fortune. And these crazy niggers damn near kept us from getting them."

The other joined him in a laugh. "What do you suppose," he asked, "was behind their yarn about an angry jungle god? Something must have put the wind up them, once."

DeKraft snorted. "Bah! You ain't seen no jungle god yet, have you? And what if you did? I never saw a god go up against a high-powered rifle. Hah, hah!" He slapped his knee and roared. "In the city or in the jungle, I never yet seen anything that a bullet wouldn't finish."

"You said it," agreed the red-headed one. "Well, if no jungle god shows up, these niggers will soon forget they were afraid." He rose, stretched. "Come on, Dutch. Laballa's got chow ready."

DeKraft climbed to his feet and they strolled over towards the fire.

Ka-Zar relaxed a trifle and his eyes were very thoughtful. The conversation of the men had been very slangy and several of the words were unfamiliar to him. City, for instance. And god. Niggers, he gathered, meant the blacks.

So the blacks were afraid of something, eh? And because of that fear, they had almost prevented Fat-Face and the other from coming into the jungle. Perhaps, then, they might be able to make the white ones leave the jungle. That is, if their fear became great enough.

A little half-smile twitched the corners of Ka-Zar's lips. He would see what he could do about that little matter.

Patiently he watched and waited for his opportunity. Laballa tended to the wants of the white leaders. The natives at the stream ceased their labors and gathered about their own food kettles, a respectful distance away.

Laballa fed the fire from a diminishing heap of brush. DeKraft called out a guttural command and in response, one of the blacks left off eating. He and Laballa picked up their spears and long knives and headed into the jungle.

The sun was setting and already mauve shadows darkened the floor of the forest. Ka-Zar knew that the two blacks had been sent for wood and it was obvious that they did not relish the prospect.

Instantly he took to the trees and swinging agilely from branch to branch, moved off to follow them. Nono leaped agilely before him and soon they came to where the natives had stopped. One slashed at low boughs and dry, dead brush, anxious to finish their task. The other stood, spear clutched in one hand and long knife in the other, and peered into the gloomy forest about them.

Neither looked up into the trees that towered high above them, but if they had, they would have seen nothing. In the dim half-light, the naked bronzed form of Ka-Zar had melted into one with the shadowy leaves and branches.

Ka-Zar waited until a moment when only the dull thud of the knife sounded in the stillness. Then with all the might that he could summon, he bellowed forth the deep bass roar of the lion.

FOR A MOMENT the cry echoed through the still air and below him the two natives stood immobile as ebony statues, literally paralyzed with fear. Then suddenly the invisible bonds that held them, snapped. Shrieking in terror, they raced pell mell for the camp.

Fear lent wings to their feet and though Ka-Zar swung swiftly in their wake, by the time he reached his vantage point they had already poured out their breathless story.

The two white men were on their feet. There was a black scowl on DeKraft's swarthy face. The other natives huddled about their terror-stricken companions, their hands clapped to their mouths.

Unfortunately, most of the ensuing hubbub of conversation was carried on in the tongue of the blacks, which Ka-Zar did not understand. But the gestures of the men made a lot of it clear to him.

DeKraft stretched forth his arm and pointed imperiously toward the forest from whence the pair had so suddenly returned. A volley of commands crackled from his lips and Ka-Zar knew that he was ordering them to return for the wood.

But the two natives shook their heads and did not budge. Their eyes rolled, their arms waved, they chattered back at him.

DeKraft's face turned slowly to a choleric purple. Forgetting himself in his rage, he bellowed at them in English.

"Sure, I know damn well there's lions around here. But don't try to tell me about one being way up in the top of a tree. Why—you cowardly, lying…"

He stepped forward, his fist lashed out with the lightning speed of N'Jaga's spring. There was a dull smack as it struck the jaw of Laballa and sent him toppling over backward into the arms of his companions.

Snatching a gun from his hip, DeKraft faced the blacks, moving its muzzle in a slow, fan-like arc. Muttering, they fell back. But though he again pointed imperiously at the jungle, backing up the order with a significant gesture of the gun, not one of the natives stirred.

Ka-Zar, well satisfied with his work, left DeKraft still trying with threats and curses to drive out the fear that was in the hearts of his men. He, himself, had had no rest since Zar had come to find him. Now, confident that a few hours sleep would revive both his tired body and his weary mind, he headed back toward the cave.

CHAPTER XVIII

FLOWERS ON A GRAVE

DAWN FOUND HIM standing over the graves of his parents. He communed a moment with their spirits in silence and deep in his heart, renewed his vow that he would wreak vengeance on his father's slayer. Then, fortified for whatever the day might bring, he started again for the camp of the white men.

He was still some distance from it, when a crashing noise off to his left pulled him up short in mid-stride. He cocked his head to one side and listened. Most animals make little noise in their travels through the jungle. This was not the sound made by Chaka and his apes, nor Trajah, nor that of Quog and his herd passing through the brush. Only one other creature would move so clumsily—a man.

With a prayer in his heart that it might be his hated enemy, Fat-Face, Ka-Zar swung up into the trees and headed swiftly toward the noise. He could not know that the Fates still turned their faces from him; that it was not Fat-Face but Kivlin, grown yet more greedy because of his good fortune who had ventured along the course of the stream in search of more emeralds.

He could not know either, that Zar, anxious and eager to aid him, had also set out for the camp. The lion's keen nostrils had caught the scent of the hated Oman and disobeying his brother's orders he lay in wait for the foolish two-legged creature who blundered toward him.

Kivlin was not jungle-wise. Not intending to share his find, if he made one, he had left the camp without telling DeKraft.

And so it was that instead of carrying a rifle, he was armed only with the heavy caliber automatic thrust in the holster at his belt. Zar, crouching behind a clump of brush at the side of the stream, saw him appear—but saw no fire-stick.

Kivlin bent over, picked up a pebble, turned it over in his fingers and then threw it away in disgust. He straightened up—and was instantly petrified with terror.

Directly in his path loomed an enormous tawny shape. To Kivlin's startled eyes, Zar appeared as huge as Trajah. The lion's shaggy mane was ruffed out into a black fringe. His fangs were bared from glistening teeth. His slitted eyes gleamed and the tuft at the tip of his tail switched angrily.

Kivlin tried to scream, but could make no sound. His numbed brain urged him to run, to bolt for his life. But his legs would not move.

A low, terrifying growl rumbled from Zar's throat. He crouched and his rippling muscles tensed for the spring. And Kivlin, coming to life in that desperate moment, flashed for his gun.

It came up in his clenched right fist, glinting ominously in the sun, and its barrel pointed full at the snarling lion. But in the split second before his finger squeezed the trigger, something thudded lightly to the ground behind him.

The sharp blade of a knife bit into the back of his neck and a warning voice hissed in his ear: "Kill the lion—and you die, also!"

Never was a man in more terrible predicament. Never had anyone such a horrible choice. Never was double jeopardy made yet more awful by such mystery.

Kivlin's nerves could stand no more. And when the voice at his ear changed suddenly to an animal growl, he wilted. His face turned ghastly and clammy beads of perspiration broke out over his body. He felt that he was going mad.

In a daze, he heard the lion growl back, then reluctantly move off to one side and watch whatever was behind the haft of that knife. Kivlin soon learned what that was. A long arm snaked around under his chin, closed like a vise about his neck. A bronzed hand shot out, wrenched the automatic from his grasp and sent it spinning into the brush.

KIVLIN'S REELING SENSES told him that he was in the grip of a man and almost mechanically, he struggled frantically to free himself. Despite all his strength, he might have been a two-year-old. For the arms that held him were massive, with muscles like bands of flexible steel.

Kivlin was hardly conscious that the lion remained where he was. A sudden violent wrench spun him around, but one hand stayed at the nape of his neck, holding him powerless. And for the first time, seeing his captor, he realized why his struggles had been so futile.

He was staring at a tremendous, bronze giant, naked save for the skin of an animal wound about his loins. A mass of black hair whipped back from the giant's head and his amber eyes held his own with a piercing intensity that transfixed him like the point of a spear.

Kivlin found his voice at last. "Who—who are you?" he croaked.

"I am Ka-Zar," answered the bronze giant, in English that had a strange, guttural tone. "Ka-Zar, brother of Zar, the lion." He pointed to the huge beast, watching them.

Kivlin shook his head as though to awaken himself from some evil nightmare. "What are you going to do with me?"

Ka-Zar fingered his gleaming knife. "I should," he answered, "help Zar finish what he had begun."

Kivlin's face turned yet more ashen. Into his eyes came the blank look of utter despair.

Ka-Zar scowled. "But, no. Your death would avail me nothing. I will give you one more chance for your miserable life." He pointed towards the camp whence Kivlin had come. "Go back. Tell Fat-Face I warn him. Leave the jungle, you and your black brothers, at once. Unless you do, you shall all die."

He shook Kivlin once and the hapless man thought that his neck had broken. Then suddenly he released his hold and stepped back.

Zar growled a mighty protest when he realized that Ka-Zar had again shown mercy to an enemy. The sound was all that Kivlin needed to set his legs in motion. Casting fearful eyes back over his shoulder, he raced madly back the way he had come. His last glance showed him Zar and Ka-Zar, standing side by side, watching his flight. Then a bend in the stream cut them off abruptly from his view and as though the devil were at his heels, he sprinted on towards the camp.

IT WAS HIGH noon. The tropical sun beat down on the little clearing that sheltered DeKraft's camp with a fierce intentness. But despite the heat, DeKraft was forcing his natives. From the bank of the stream he towered over them, a heavy bull whip in his hand. When one faltered, the stinging bite of the lash and a savage curse would drive him on again.

To DeKraft, any life but his own was cheap. Especially those of the blacks. With a fortune to be panned out of the river he could see no sense in delaying for petty, humanitarian scruples. Even as he lashed his blacks with the whip, he, himself was driven on by greed.

The horde of emeralds was increasing. He mused regretfully that he had cut Kivlin into the venture. He had been a fool. The find had been his in the first place and he was rightfully entitled to the profits.

He fingered the automatic holstered at his hip and smiled knowingly to himself. He had lots of time. They were a thousand miles from the nearest white man and the white man's law. What happened in that jungle wildness, no one would ever know.

The sound of running footsteps across the clearing snapped his head erect. It was his guilty conscience and his own evil thoughts that made him half pull the automatic from his belt. He whirled. Kivlin was plunging across the glade towards him as if pursued by every jungle demon the blacks had ever believed in.

DeKraft's eyes were quick to note the absence of the gun at Kivlin's belt and he slipped his own gun back into its holster.

Panting, wild-eyed and ashen of face Kivlin pulled up before him.

"What's eating you?" growled DeKraft. "You look as if you've seen a ghost."

Kivlin swallowed at his agitated Adam's apple and with frightened eyes looked swiftly around the clearing. "So help me," he said, "I have."

DeKraft spat disgustedly. "Either the heat's got you or you're drunk. Go back to your tent and sleep it off."

Kivlin shook his head. "I haven't had a drink all morning." He swallowed again, wet his lips. "I could use one now, though. I tell you I saw him. Him and the biggest lion God ever made."

"Saw who?" demanded DeKraft sharply.

Kivlin looked at him from wide scared eyes. "So help me, I don't know. A big tall savage—a white man from the looks of him and he spoke English. Naked as the day he was born."

DeKraft's eyes narrowed and he leaped forward. With a gnarled fist he grabbed his partner by the slack of his coat and lifted him half off his feet. "You're mad or drunk, damn you! There's no white man here. I found these emeralds and they're mine. No man can take them away from me."

Realizing that something out of the ordinary had taken place, the blacks quit their work and listened attentively. Though they could not follow the swift interchange of words between the two white men, they understood enough to sharpen their fears and apprehensions.

Kivlin struggled helplessly in DeKraft's grasp. "I tell you I saw him," he whined. "Took my gun away from me, he did. Talked to that bloody beast of a lion and the lion understood. It's got me, I tell you. It ain't natural!"

A vague, disturbing theory began to form in DeKraft's brain.

Then he noted that the blacks had ceased work and were whispering furtively to one another. How much of the conversation they had heard and understood, he did not know. But whatever it was, it was too much. This crazy story of Kivlin's if it got about, would be enough to blow his camp to hell.

WITH AN OATH he sprang down to the edge of the stream, brandishing his whip. He played it about him indiscriminately for a moment and the muttering natives protestingly resumed their labors. With a last warning of the evil that would befall them if they stopped work again, DeKraft returned to Kivlin.

"You've started something with your fool talk," he said savagely. "Let's get out of here." With a violent shove he propelled Kivlin forward and they made for their tent.

There in the comparative seclusion of the shelter, Kivlin told his tale, finishing with the warning that Ka-Zar had given him.

DeKraft sat for a long time in silence when the story was done. In the space of a moment his brain bridged five long years of time to another day in the jungle and to another clearing no more than three miles removed from the one he was then in. There had been a burning lean-to—a dying man on the ground with two bullets in his chest—and a cub of a kid standing against the point of a native spear.

DeKraft remembered the details of that scene clearly. He had been on the point of murdering the kid when the lion had charged. He had fired, missed and fled with the roar of the lion in his ears. Was it possible that the kid hadn't been killed? Was it possible that he had formed some strange, unbelievable pact with the lion?

DeKraft's camp stool crashed to the ground as he rose swiftly. By God! He would find out. He examined his automatic carefully; he picked up a rifle and examined that with equal thoroughness.

"Where you going?" asked Kivlin.

"You stay here," answered DeKraft as he started for the flap of the tent. "And keep your mouth shut. I'm going to lay your jungle god low."

PREPARED FOR ANY emergency, DeKraft made his way cautiously through the jungle and came at last to the clearing that had been occupied by the mad hermit he had murdered five years before. Though nothing untoward had happened during his short trek, his nerves were shaky and on edge as he stood at the fringe of the encroaching forest and surveyed the small glade.

He was not bothered by the ghosts of the dead past. What worried him more were the possibilities of the immediate present and future.

Cautiously he looked about. The clearing had not changed. The charred remnants of the lean-to, overgrown with jungle grass, still stood in the center of the glade. There was not one sign of life or occupancy about the place and his spirits rose.

Kivlin was mad, he mused. The heat had gotten him, probably.

Then with rifle ready, he stepped forward to make a closer inspection of his surroundings. He had taken but two cautious strides when he stopped abruptly. For there at his very feet were two low mounds of earth and stone. They were unmistakably graves.

It was not this, so much, that startled DeKraft out of his newfound assurance. It was the fact that both graves were covered with flowers—flowers that were fresh—flowers that had been picked no more than a few hours before!

DeKraft retreated hurriedly back to the protecting shelter of the encircling trees. And he was a very thoughtful and troubled man as he made his way cautiously back to his camp.

CHAPTER XIX

GREED AND DEATH

ALL THROUGHOUT THAT day, concealed in the tall branches of the trees that hemmed in the clearing, Ka-Zar kept a watchful eye on DeKraft's camp. He had been a witness to the scene between Kivlin and the Hollander by the stream; had seen DeKraft leave the clearing a few moments later, armed with a long, shining fire-stick.

For a moment he had been tempted to follow him, but decided to remain behind and watch the clearing instead. It was obvious to him that the black men were ill at ease, apprehensive about something. Ka-Zar sensed their hate for Fat-Face and felt that it was only their fear of the white man's gun and whip that kept them at their work.

For the first time an alien sentiment stirred at his heart. Though he did not know it, it was pity.

But he dismissed the feeling with a shrug. He had troubles of his own—and serious ones. With each hour that Fat-Face and his men stayed in the jungle, his own position became more difficult. Fanned by the evil tongue of N'Jaga, old fears, hates and enmities were being stirred up against him. True, he knew that Zar and Trajah would stand beside him no matter what happened, but he had serious doubts of the outcome if the jungle denizens openly revolted against him.

He was suspected and though he was embittered to think that the animals believed he would betray them, he could understand the justice of their attitude. After all, these invading two-legged creatures who had come, bringing destruction with them, were his blood brothers.

Ka-Zar smiled bitterly at that. His blood brothers! And one of them—Fat-Face—had killed his father!

No! Even though they both walked erect on two legs, there was no kinship between him and the white man. For hadn't he, Ka-Zar, sworn a mighty oath over the grave of his father—that Fat-Face should die at his hands.

Ka-Zar was proud. There was nothing but scorn in his heart for DeKraft. Even though his enemy went forever armed with the fire-stick, he felt no fear of him. It would have been the simplest thing in the world for him to have killed DeKraft—if that would have been an end of things.

But Ka-Zar knew that it would not be. There was the other white man and the blacks. He could not kill them all. And so long as they stayed in the forest with their fire-sticks, no jungle beast was safe.

Analyzing his problem, he arrived at three conclusions. First, by some means he had to capture the Oman's weapons; next, he had to make them leave the land over which Zar had ruled for so long. And lastly, when the first two objectives had been accomplished, he would kill the fat-faced one.

From his tree he saw DeKraft return, speak animatedly with Kivlin for a few minutes, then make a long oration to the black men.

The work of the camp proceeded throughout the day. Evening came, the fires were built and the evening meal prepared and eaten.

Then as the shadows fell, Ka-Zar saw DeKraft enter one of the tents and emerge a moment later carrying four of the fire-sticks. He spoke again for a long time to his blacks, then passed out the weapons to the four most sturdy ones.

Watching from narrowed eyes, high in his tree, Ka-Zar saw the four natives thus armed begin a slow pacing, one on either side of the camp. He had seen Sha pace like that before the mouth of the cave which sheltered her cubs, when danger was near. And he knew that the four natives were on guard.

Against what? Himself, probably. He smiled at the futility of it. Let the four blacks pace themselves weary. He was not interested in them. He was interested in the tent from which Fat-Face had emerged with the four fire-sticks. For he reasoned, and rightly, if the strange shelter had held four of the Oman's weapons it would probably hold more.

NOT A SOUND, not one false cry of alarm disturbed the quiet serenity of that night. The four natives paced steadily the lengths of their beats and in his tent DeKraft dreamed of untold wealth in an untroubled sleep.

He was up early with the rising sun. Rolling out of his cot he stepped to the door of his tent and glanced out. The sight of the four guards still tramping stolidly back and forth brought a grin to his thick lips.

"Jungle god!" he snorted with vast disgust. "By God, I'll fix him with a dose of lead and I'll fix those blacks at the first sign of monkey-business. It's the kid, all right, grown up. Show him a couple of guns and he stays away. Smart lad."

DeKraft threw himself into his clothes, splashed a handful of water into his face but did a far more thorough job of washing his gullet from the bottle of gin.

Well pleased with himself and with the night's strategy, he swaggered out of the tent. The clearing was flooded with golden light by now and there was a general stir of activity through the camp.

Feeling that there was no longer any need for the guards, DeKraft took the rifles from them and started with the guns for the tent that housed his supplies. He pushed through the flap, then stopped in speechless amazement. For a moment he could not believe the evidence of his eyes. Again he swept the interior of the tent. But there was no mistake about it. His stock of rifles had vanished and along with them his ammunition.

DeKraft was stunned and speechless for a moment. His first

thought was that the blacks had stolen the weapons—either as a protection against the jungle gods they feared, or what was worse—for a contemplated uprising.

Then he shook his head. He had instilled the fear of death into them too long, for that. The natives would not have dared to violate the tent.

Kivlin? No. Kivlin feared him as much as the blacks did.

There was only one other answer. The brat. DeKraft cursed bitterly though impotently for a few minutes. Then a cunning idea occurred to him. The incident of the stolen guns was the excuse he had been waiting for.

He stepped out of the tent and his loud bellow echoed across the clearing. In his hand he still clutched one of the rifles he had taken from the guards. The blacks looked up from their work and trembled in fear. A moment later, his eyes still puffy with sleep, Kivlin stumbled out of his tent, clutching an automatic in his hand. He raced across the clearing to where DeKraft still stood by the looted tent.

"What's the matter? What happened?" he asked breathlessly.

DeKraft eyed him from cunning, pig-like eyes; his hairy hands worked at his sides.

"That's a nice question from you—you little rat!" he answered.

The concentrated venom in his voice was like a slap in Kivlin's face. He stepped back and half raised the automatic in his hand in a defensive movement.

"What's eating you?" he growled. "What's happened? Why are you calling me a rat?"

"Smart guy, eh?" sneered DeKraft, playing his role to perfection. "Playing dumb, eh? Yeah, dumb like a fox!"

"You're nuts," growled Kivlin. "I don't know what you're talking about."

"Oh, no? Then take a look in the tent and see for yourself."

PUZZLED, KIVLIN HOLSTERED his automatic, looked suspiciously at DeKraft, then stepped past him and entered the tent. DeKraft followed hard on his heels.

"The guns—the ammunition—they're gone!" exclaimed Kivlin, a moment later.

DeKraft laughed. "You're telling me? Of course they're gone and you're the rat that took them. It's a double-cross but you can't get away with it, Kivlin."

For a long moment the two men stood toe to toe, glaring into each other's eyes. Kivlin suspected treachery but it never dawned on him that it had been Ka-Zar who had rifled the tent the preceding night, and who had buried forever their precious guns and bullets in the bottomless quicksands of the swamp.

"You lie in your teeth," he said at last. "If there's any double-cross, you're behind it. You've been planning it all along. I knew. I've seen it in your eyes…."

And then Kivlin saw something else in DeKraft's pig eyes— something that put the fear of God in his heart. He took a long step back, snatched at his automatic.

But before he could whip it out of its holster, DeKraft had jerked up the barrel of the rifle and prodded it deep into his navel.

Kivlin's heart turned sick at what he saw in the Hollander's eyes. Twin pulses pounded in his throat and his mouth was suddenly hot and dry.

"Don't, Dutch—for God's sake, don't," he pleaded frantically. "You can have the emeralds—all of them—honest—all of them—don't—*don't*.…"

The final word was blasted from his mouth by a reverberating explosion. DeKraft had shot and the muzzle of the rifle had been tight against Kivlin's ribs.

Kivlin swayed drunkenly on his feet for a moment, then went down slowly, joint by joint, as if he didn't want to die. DeKraft watched him from cold, implacable eyes, then when his erstwhile partner was prone on the ground he kicked at his ribs with a heavy boot.

"You poor fool," he said contemptuously. "You never had a chance. I never intended you to have one."

With the satisfaction of an honest man who has seen a job well done, he left the tent.

CHAPTER XX

NONO, THE WISE ONE

CONCEALED IN HIS tree, Ka-Zar had seen DeKraft's agitation on discovering his looted tent. He had heard him bellow in rage, seen the other white man run over to him and then the two had disappeared into the tent. A few minutes later the shot had crashed out and only Fat-Face had emerged.

Ka-Zar knew then what had happened and he was filled with a fierce joy. The red-headed one had not taken his warning— and he had died. And it was just as well that it had been at the hands of the evil Fat-Face.

Later that day, Ka-Zar saw DeKraft drive the muttering blacks in the digging of a shallow hole. The body of the red-headed one was pitched unceremoniously into it and a few handfuls of earth shoveled in on him.

Throughout the brutal performance DeKraft had to lash his natives with tongue and whip. Momentarily they were becoming more surly, trembling on the borderline of revolt. They had been tricked in the first place and now they were convinced that some evil spirit hovered onminously over the camp.

Ka-Zar saw all these things and smiled to himself. One white man had already been disposed of. It would take little more of his manipulations to scatter the blacks in terror and send them fleeing through the jungle for the land from whence they had come. And then alone with Fat-Face, he would settle his score.

With the intention of returning again to the camp when the shades of night had fallen, Ka-Zar swung off swiftly through the trees in the direction of the cave.

Along the way he passed over N'Jaga. The leopard stopped, threw up his head and spat disdainfully. Ka-Zar had not forgotten the defeat he had suffered at N'Jaga's hands when he had been caught unaware in the lake, nor the trouble the leopard was stirring up against him. He fingered the haft of his knife.

For a moment he was tempted to descend from the tree and once and for all settle the feud that had burned between him and the leopard, ever since he could remember. But after a moment's consideration he changed his mind. Tempting as the opportunity was, he had to forego it. For if by any chance N'Jaga succeeded in killing him, there would be no one to drive the Oman from the jungle.

N'Jaga saw his hesitation and attributed it to fear. He snarled up a taunting challenge.

"Later, N'Jaga," called down Ka-Zar. "And sharpen your claws against the day we meet again."

N'Jaga snarled once more in answer and Ka-Zar swung off through the trees.

He found Zar and Trajah close to the cave and told them how he had stolen the fire-sticks and the little pieces of stone that weighed so much in the palm of the hand. He had disposed of them all in the swamp. He recounted, too, how the red-headed one had died; and then elaborated on his plans for the night.

Zar and Trajah heard him out patiently, expressed their pleasure at the good news he brought. Then the lion spoke from his store of wisdom.

"Beware of N'Jaga and treachery. The jungle beasts are restless today."

Ka-Zar stood up to the full of his majestic height. "Ka-Zar is the brother of Zar," he said simply. "He knows no fear."

Then he walked over to a fresh kill that Sha had dragged in a few minutes before, cut off a generous portion of the animal's flank, squatted on his haunches and ate.

HE SLEPT THAT day until the long shadows began to creep into the mouth of the cave. Then he rose, went to the stream to drink his fill, but did not eat. He preferred to have a lean belly for the night's work.

Into his belt he slipped his keenest knife and thus armed, he emerged from the cave again. He growled a few words to Zar, who was pacing restlessly before the lair, trumpeted a low farewell to Trajah and with a mighty leap swung himself up into the nearest tree. With a long, gliding swing from limb to limb he proceeded leisurely towards the camp of the Oman.

He had traveled but a short distance, however, when from an obscure branch above him Nono dropped down, landed on his shoulder and threw spidery arms around his neck.

Ka-Zar stopped and gently cuffed the monkey. "Not tonight, silly one. Go back. Tonight Ka-Zar goes into the camp of the Oman to see what mischief he can do."

Nono chattered, scolded, pleaded and begged to accompany him, but Ka-Zar was firm. Still scolding, his long tail drooping mournfully, the monkey watched the brother of the lion swing swiftly off through the trees.

HIGH IN A tree, unseen, unheard, Ka-Zar watched the activities at DeKraft's camp come to an end. One by one the fires were banked for the night and in little huddled groups the blacks crept off to their shelters. As on the previous night, the four guards with their fire-sticks paced nervously the length of their posts.

The moon was setting behind the rim of the jungle when DeKraft emerged from his tent. He made a last tour of inspection around the clearing, barked a few words at the natives on guard, then returned to his tent.

Watching, Ka-Zar saw the interior of the shelter light up. For a few minutes the grotesque shadow of Fat-Face, as he moved about, was silhouetted against the walls of the tent. Then the light was snuffed out and silence reigned over the clearing, save for the muffled tread of the four men on guard.

With the patience of the great cats, Ka-Zar kept to the high branches of his tree, never moving. Only his eyes were alert as he took in every detail of the camp. He knew that the blacks were nervous and apprehensive and would be aroused at the slightest noise. He knew that Fat-Face slept with a fire-stick within easy reach.

Let them be deceived by the quiet; let them fall into deep, untroubled slumber. Then he would act.

The bats had ceased their blind wheeling about when at last he stirred. Silent as Sinassa, agile as Nono, he dropped swiftly from limb to limb to the ground. He withdrew the keen-bladed knife from his belt and crouching low, moved forward silently. His objective was the tent he had looted the night before. If he found more fire-sticks there, he would dispose of them as he had the others. If not, there was other work for him to do.

Moving like a blacker shadow in the shadowy night, he skirted the clearing and made his way swiftly to the rear of the supply tent. He paused here a moment, disturbed by a vague sense of danger. He threw up his head, sniffed the air and listened. The muffled tread of the black guards came to him with uninterrupted regularity. There was no other alien sound to break the alive stillness of the night.

It was through his nose that he scented danger. He sniffed the air again. The peculiar odor of the Oman was strong in his nostrils. Then he shrugged. It was only natural that it should be so, for wasn't he even then standing by one of the shelters in which the Oman had lived?

Grasping the haft of his knife tighter, he knelt down, lifted up the bottom of the tent and silently slipped inside.

He was still on his hand and knees, just in the act of rising, when suddenly a dazzling beam of light flashed in his eyes and blinded him.

Ka-Zar had never seen a flash-light before, had not the slightest conception of their construction or their use. The phenomena of this strange light startled and baffled him. Some magic of the Oman, no doubt, like that of their fire-sticks.

He straightened up slowly, tense, wary, every nerve and muscle on edge. The beam of light rose with him, still centered full in his eyes. It was impossible to see into it or beyond it. For a moment he stood there irresolute, undecided whether to charge blindly forward or to retreat. Then, with startling abruptness his decision was made for him. The light dropped from his eyes to his throat. And when his vision focused again a moment later, he saw his old enemy, Fat-Face, standing no more than three feet in front of him. In one hand he held a small tube from which the stream of light shot out—in the other a short fire-stick that was pointed directly at his heart.

Ka-Zar realized that he had fallen into a trap. And he realized, also, that Fat-Face intended to kill him, even as he would have done if the situation had been reversed.

NO THOUGHT OF begging for his life entered his head. He was too proud for that and he knew that it would avail him naught. For Fat-Face was as ruthlessly cruel as N'Jaga. From past observation he knew the terrible killing power of the short fire-stick but there was no avoiding it. Coolly he calculated his chances against it. Even if he must die he would try to take Fat-Face with him on the Long Sleep.

Then for the first time DeKraft spoke. "Caught, eh, like any dummy in a trap. The old man's brat grown up! So you're the jungle god who's been scaring hell out of my blacks. By heaven, that's rich!"

His lips curled and he spat at Ka-Zar's feet. The rolls of fat along his stomach quivered in secret mirth.

"Only Janko, the hyena laughs," said Ka-Zar evenly. "Because he is afraid."

DeKraft's eyes narrowed and he hefted the gun in his hand. "Afraid of what?" he snarled.

"Of Ka-Zar, brother of the lion. Kill, Fat-Face, while you have a chance."

DeKraft leered at him and shook his head. "Not yet, you man-ape. Plenty of time for that later. First I'm going to show those niggers what they've been afraid of. Then I'm going to show 'em how easy it is to kill you—how easy it is to kill their evil jungle spirit. That'll hold 'em in their place."

Still keeping his gun leveled at Ka-Zar, he threw back his head and roared until the camp awoke with a hundred confused noises. Two of the guards rushed into the tent and stared, speechless with wonder at the bronzed giant of a man, lit up by their master's flash-light.

DeKraft snapped them out of their awe with a string of profanity. Then he spoke to them in their native tongue. "Fetch rope, Bwala. Quick, you dog. And tell your men that I have captured their jungle god. He will never bother them again."

With loud wails the two blacks rushed from the tent. Ka-Zar heard the excited babble of their voices and though he could not understand their strange words, he knew that they were spreading the news of his capture.

There was a great stir and confusion out in the clearing. Many tongues spoke at once, then a voice was raised in a mournful, wailing chant. A moment later the steady, ominous beat of a tom-tom sounded in the jungle clearing.

Ka-Zar's heart picked up a faster beat at the savage rhythm.

"Those devils mean to raise hell tonight," said DeKraft darkly.

Not understanding the meaning of his words, Ka-Zar did not answer. Then, with a shrill buzz of excited talk, the pack of natives had congregated about the entrance to the tent. With head cocked to one side, DeKraft listened to them and what he heard brought a satanic smile to his lips.

A moment later the flap of the tent parted and Aorangi, the chief of the blacks entered. He was flanked on either side by two others who carried lengths of stout rope in their hands. The trio eyed Ka-Zar with frightened glances, then Aorangi addressed himself lengthily to DeKraft.

The burden of his talk was to the effect that the blacks demanded that he give up the evil spirit of the jungle into their hands. They would make a sacrifice of him to the benevolent god of the forest, that their expedition might be blessed and protected from harm.

Fat-Face listened attentively and the more he heard, the more pleased he became. Death at his hands would be comparatively swift and painless. At the hands of the black devils, aroused to a feverish hysterical pitch by their superstitious fears, death would be an agonizingly slow process.

WHEN AORANGI HAD finished, DeKraft nodded. He spoke a few words in the native dialect and the two blacks that had accompanied Aorangi jumped to Ka-Zar's side. Swiftly they wrenched his hands behind his back, tied them securely.

In stolid silence Ka-Zar had listened to Aorangi's long dissertation. He had not understood one word of it but from the ugly sneer on DeKraft's face, he knew that they were planning his death. He was not afraid, he did not fear death but along with every other animal in the jungle, the will to survive was strong in him.

If he had been Chaka or Diki the jackal or even the wise Zar he might have made a futile break for liberty then. But despite his kinship to the beasts, Ka-Zar was something more than an animal. He had the brain of a man and he knew that it meant instant death from the fire-stick if he made his stand then.

The tying of the rope about his hands indicated to him that he was not to be killed immediately—that he was being made prisoner. An opportunity to escape might come later.

But his hopes were short lived. His hands tied, the two blacks propelled him out of the tent. His appearance was greeted by wild cries and wails from the assembled natives and the tom-tom took up a faster, more savage beat.

No time was wasted. Surrounded by a savage, snarling horde, each man armed with spear or knife, Ka-Zar was rushed across the clearing. Still holding his automatic, DeKraft followed after him, an evil grin on his lips. He was going to relish this—the niggers were going to put on a swell show for him.

A towering tree stood at the edge of the glade on the far side. Beneath it, the seething mob came to a halt. There was a few minutes of excited talk, then Aorangi raised his spear and commanded silence. He spoke authoritatively for a moment and at the conclusion of his words a fiendish howl rose from the lips of the blacks.

The skin prickled at the base of Ka-Zar's skull and his lips pulled back from his teeth. So these were the Oman—the two-legged creatures—his supposed brothers! Bah! He would have none of them. In their howling and gnashing of teeth they reminded him of a pack of jackals—cowards at heart, fearful to attack when alone but snarling and ferocious when the pack had a helpless quarry at bay.

Ka-Zar had no further time then to make his observation on the nature of the black man. He was seized roughly by a dozen hands; the bonds that held him were cut. He struggled desperately for a moment but the sheer weight of numbers overpowered him. Swiftly his arms were wrenched around the bole of the tree and his wrists tied together once more.

He had been made captive, even as Tuta the elephant. He tested the rope that held him. His muscles knotted and swelled and the veins stood out on his forehead. But the rope was strong and cunningly tied. Even as Tuta the elephant, all his magnificent strength could not break his bonds.

Then at a signal from Aorangi, the tom-tom commenced its maddening rhythm once more. With savage howls the blacks took up their wailing chant again and brandishing their spears and knives began a slow snake dance around their captive.

At the height of the confusion, Ka-Zar felt something light land upon his shoulder. Then Nono's spidery arms encircled his neck and the little monkey's excited chatter rang in his ear.

He shook his head, smiled in the darkness at the faithfulness of the little beast. "Flee, silly one," he urged. "There is nothing you can do."

Nono whimpered, clung the tighter to his neck.

To save him from the death that awaited him, Ka-Zar spoke sharply. "Go, silly one," he ordered. "Ka-Zar orders it."

STILL CHATTERING, NONO untwined his arms and reluctantly climbed up into the tree.

Ka-Zar sighed a little sigh when he was gone, then gave his attention to what was going on around him. Faster and faster became the rhythm of the tom-tom—faster and faster danced the blacks. Their naked bodies glistened with sweat as they leaped high into the air; their features became distorted, bestial as the steady beat of the tom-tom worked them up to a fanatical pitch.

All their ignorance, their dark fears and superstitions were being expressed in the dance. With their mad gyrations the heart of darkest Africa had come to life. A human sacrifice was to be made that the jungle gods might he appeased.

Ka-Zar watched the ever increasing tempo of the dance with an ever-increasing hate. The insidious beat of the tom-tom got into his own brain, did something strange and inexplicable to him. His blood pounded through his veins, his eyes became hot, his mouth dry.

He was moved by a terrible urge to kill. And he knew that the same urge motivated the black men dancing about him—the urge to kill him—Ka-Zar.

With a maniacal fury he strained at his bonds until his head fell exhausted on his mighty chest.

Then sanity returned. The simple dignity of his untrammeled soul asserted itself. He ceased struggling, his head came up and proud as Zar, he faced his death unafraid.

Aorangi, leading the ritual dance saw and in his savage mind, somehow understood. With a loud cry he suddenly darted in from the circle of wildly dancing blacks. His long spear flashed out like the darting tongue of Sinassa and Ka-Zar was aware of a sharp pain in his side, followed by the sensation of hot flowing blood.

Once the first blow had been struck, once the first blood had been let, the other blacks followed suit. Once, during each mad circuit of the captive, each black would dart forward and back again. And each time Ka-Zar would feel the sharp bite of their blades.

With a cunningness beyond belief an ear was nicked, a cheek, an arm, a leg. Ka-Zar understood, then, their dark intentions. His was to be no swift, merciful death. He was to die slowly, painfully from a thousand wounds.

His lips set in a fixed smile. He made no sign of pain, no cry of mercy. Only he strained forward on his bonds to meet the cut of the spear heads as they flashed in at him.

How long the dance would last—how long it would be before he lost consciousness from loss of blood, Ka-Zar did not know. He resigned himself to death and if he had any regrets at his passing, it was that he could not say a last farewell to Zar, Sha and the cubs.

He was occupied with these thoughts, when for the second time that night, something from the limbs of the tree above him, dropped lightly onto his shoulder and again Nono clung to his neck. He was deeply touched by the loyalty of the little animal but he knew that the monkey only courted swift death if he stayed there.

"Go, Nono! Flee!" he ordered. "There is nothing you can do for Ka-Zar, silly one."

Nono's lips snuggled close to his ear and the monkey chattered excitedly. "Nono is a silly one no longer. Did he not see Ka-Zar with his knife free Tuta from the strong vine that held her. A strong vine now holds Ka-Zar—so. I have brought your knife from the cave."

A swift surge of exultation swept through Ka-Zar's heart. "You are wiser than Ka-Zar, Nono," he whispered. "Ka-Zar never thought of that. Quick. Cut the vine that holds me."

Chattering in his excitement, Nono swung around from Ka-Zar's neck to the back of the tree. Hanging head down by his tail from a low limb, he grasped the heavy knife in the slender fingers of his two hands and began to saw at the rope that held his friend's wrists. He was clumsy, he was awkward, he was slow. He cut as much of Ka-Zar's flesh as he did of the rope.

BUT KA-ZAR DID not mind that, did not know it in fact. All he was aware of was that the ritual dance was reaching its climax and that the bonds that held him were giving.

Patiently, laboriously Nono sawed away. Exerting his last ounce of strength Ka-Zar strained at the rope—felt it give, part—then fall away from his wrists. He was free. A moment later Nono pressed the haft of the knife in his hand. The cool feel of it sent the strength rushing through him in waves. He was free and armed and he knew that he would not die that night.

Motionless, his hands still behind the tree, he waited until Nono had swung to safety above him. Then slowly, cautiously he brought his hands forward and the haft of the knife dug deep into his palm.

The circle of dancing blacks about him was narrowing. Their unholy cries made the night hideous.

Tense in every nerve and muscle, his superb body braced back against the tree, Ka-Zar awaited his chance. He ignored the spear thrusts of the crew of lesser blacks and waited till that moment when Aorangi darted in to strike with dripping spear.

Then his left arm snaked out as swiftly as Sinassa strikes. He grasped Aorangi's spear a foot below the point and yanked it savagely to him.

The black was too startled, too amazed to let go. Before he knew what had happened he had been catapulted into Ka-Zar's arms. There was the swift glint of moonlight off cold steel as Ka-Zar's right arm rose and descended in a swift arc.

Then, even as Aorangi's lifeless body was slumping to the ground before the popping eyes of the blacks, Ka-Zar threw back his head and the mighty roar of the lion who has made his kill rumbled from his lips.

To the natives, they had witnessed a miracle. For some mysterious reason they could not understand, their intended sacrifice to the jungle god had not been acceptable. He had turned against them. Speaking with the voice of the lion from the mouth of their captive, he had slain their chief.

With wild howls they fell back, their frenzy of blood lust of a moment before, changed into a frenzy of fear and panic. In their anxiety to escape they knocked wildly into DeKraft who was as equally as surprised as they. There was a moment of utter confusion and chaos. And by the time DeKraft had regained his wits and had fought his way through the milling pack, gun in hand—Ka-Zar had disappeared.

A blind rage consumed DeKraft. With the mad idea of pursuing his prisoner into the jungle he turned and shouted hoarsely at his fleeing blacks. But the natives were pursued by a fear greater than that of the white man's wrath. They scattered wildly in all directions.

DeKraft realized then, for the first time, the utter panic that had seized them. He knew that it would be impossible to hold them there in the jungle; that by the morning the last man of them would be many miles away.

He went berserk. Snapping up his automatic he fired blindly into the backs of the fleeing natives. From the far side of the clearing a gun answered him—then another and another.

SAFE IN THE jungle fastness, with Nono perched triumphantly on his shoulder, Ka-Zar listened to the talk of the fire-sticks at the camp of the Oman. The shooting lasted for a long time, then died out. A brooding quiet fell over the jungle.

Proud of his one achievement that night, Nono leaped from Ka-Zar's shoulder to the nearest tree and started gaily on his second adventure.

He was back a few minutes later and made his report. Those of the black Oman who were not dead, had fled; the camp was deserted. And on the morrow there would be much work for Kru and his brothers to do.

Ka-Zar scratched the top of the monkey's head. "It is good, O wise one," he said with a smile. "And now Ka-Zar goes to tend his wounds and sleep. On the morrow we shall find many bright things for you to play with in the camp of the Oman."

CHAPTER XXI

KA-ZAR THE MIGHTY

KA-ZAR HAD ONLY one regret in the knowledge that the Oman had fled the jungle. Bitterly he realized that he had failed to slay Fat-Face. And though peace lay once more over the land, there was none in his heart.

The rising sun found him, with Nono swinging gaily along over his head, approaching DeKraft's deserted camp. There were several things that drew him there. He coveted the shining spears, far finer than his own, and the long knives that the natives had used. He hoped that they had left some in their haste. And if by any chance some of the fire-sticks were still there, he meant to destroy them before they could do any more harm. Nono, or one of Chaka's apes, might find them and curiosity might well prove fatal. Ka-Zar wanted no more tragedy among his people.

While Nono squatted in a tree at the edge of the clearing, he strode into the silent camp. It was evident that its occupants had left in haste. Kettles were overturned. The pans with which the blacks had been busy at the stream, lay strewn on the bank. Only ashes remained of the fires.

Before one of the tents lay a crumpled blanket, with a varied assortment of objects lying upon and about it. Evidently some one had snatched up things at random, gathered them into the blanket to carry them off and when they spilled out, fled without stopping to collect them again. Ka-Zar stooped down to see what they were.

A damp, strong wind blew in from the lake, carrying with it the scent of distant flowers and the sweetish odor of rushes. Otherwise Ka-Zar's keen nostrils would have noticed that the smell of man, always unpleasant to him, still lingered strongly in the vicinity.

When his panic-stricken blacks had left, Paul DeKraft had been possessed by the blackest rage he had ever known. Once more he had a fortune within his grasp—once more his dreams of riches were shattered. First the crazy hermit, now the hermit's even crazier son.

DeKraft's warped soul and evil mind could not stand this second blow. A madness seized him—not the flaring outburst of fury that had made him fire at the blacks, but a scheming, smouldering hate. Like Ka-Zar, he also would know no peace until he had his vengeance.

So all through the long night he had lain hidden in the brush on the fringe of the clearing, a rifle clutched in his hand. Little red devils of hate had glinted in his eyes when he saw the tall figure of Ka-Zar stride into the glade. Lovingly his hands caressed the shining barrel of the gun, but he waited until the advantage was all his own.

When Ka-Zar stooped down over the contents of the blanket, he crept silently forth from his cover. Rising to his feet, he lifted the rifle and with a wolfish grin showing yellow teeth through his beard, aimed its muzzle at the broad bronze back squarely before him.

Up in the tree, Nono did not see him. He was playing with something, utterly absorbed. He turned it this way and that, watching the sun leap from it in arrows of light.

And then, just as DeKraft's finger was squeezing the trigger, one of the blinding arrows of light flashed full into his eyes. The gun went off with a reverberating crash and the bullet sprayed leaves from a nearby tree.

Nono screamed and clutched the mirror he had been playing with. Ka-Zar whirled as he leaped to his feet.

Not twenty feet from him stood Fat-Face. In his pudgy hands was clutched the smoking rifle. His eyes were squeezed shut, as though a needle of flame had scorched them. And as he opened them again, Ka-Zar sprang like a great cat.

DeKraft was knocked flat on his back by Ka-Zar's charge. Before he could regain his breath, fingers of steel dug deep into his throat. The rifle was wrenched from his hand—and he was helpless.

THERE WAS NO mercy in the tawny eyes that gleamed down at him. If there had been, DeKraft could not have uttered the words to beg it. He was hauled roughly to his feet, shaken until his eyes popped out.

"Your fire-stick failed you," growled Ka-Zar, transferring his grip to the back of DeKraft's thick neck. "You were meant to die by my hand."

DeKraft gulped in great, hungry mouthfuls of air and gradually his face lost its purple color. "Something blinded me," he panted, "or I would have got you."

Ka-Zar looked puzzled for a moment. Up in the tree Nono, now wildly excited, danced and chattered in the branches. Glancing up, Ka-Zar saw his most prized possession, the mirror, clutched in the monkey's hand.

"Nono," he called sharply. "Mischievous one, you have stolen Ka-Zar's shining-stone."

Nono hung his head. "When Nono went last night to the cave for Ka-Zar's knife," he admitted sullenly. Reluctantly he dropped down from the tree to Ka-Zar's back and returned the mirror.

DeKraft scowled. "That's what did it—that's what blinded me. The mirror. I'd like to get my hands around that monk's silly neck for a minute."

Ka-Zar looked at the bit of shining glass that had saved his life. Then carefully he tucked it into his belt.

Disdainfully he surveyed his captive's bulging paunch and flabby body. He took his hand from DeKraft's neck.

"I could kill you with my bare hands," he said scornfully. "Try to escape me and I will."

Into DeKraft's scheming mind stole a new hope. One look at the magnificent body of the bronze giant told him that he had meant what he said. Though no bonds held him, DeKraft knew better than to make a break just then. But the mere fact that he was not already dead, meant that he might yet get a chance to turn the tables on this naked savage. The little red flames danced in his eyes again and he half-closed his lids to hide them.

Ka-Zar picked up the rifle from where he had thrown it, grasped it by the barrel and quickly smashed it against a rock.

It broke like a matchstick and DeKraft, watching, felt his confidence evaporate a trifle as he realized the strength of those powerful arms.

Ka-Zar turned to Nono and in the language of the jungle, issued a command. "Tell all the beasts that Ka-Zar has captured the leader of the Oman. Tell them to come at once to Zar's cave."

The little monkey jumped up and down, then scampered off into the forest. And Ka-Zar started Fat-Face on his journey toward his final judgment.

"Trained monkey, eh?" said DeKraft, as they stumbled along. "Kivlin—poor Kivlin," he amended with a wry grin, "told me you talked to the animals, but I didn't really believe him until I saw it myself."

"The animals are my people," answered Ka-Zar. "Of course I talk to them."

"Where are you taking me?" asked DeKraft.

"To the cave of my brother Zar, the lion."

To Ka-Zar the answer was a simple one. To DeKraft, it came like a thunderbolt. He stopped in midstride. The crafty gleam in his eyes was wiped out by a dreadful fear. His swarthy face turned a sickly saffron.

"A lion!" he croaked. "You are mad! He'll kill us both!"

KA-ZAR SURVEYED HIS fat, trembling form with scorn. "Zar is my brother. He will not kill you, unless I tell him to."

If DeKraft had known what was in store for him, the last thread of his sanity would have snapped then and there. As it was, he felt his senses reeling. With his last coherent thought he tried desperately to reason with this crazy giant.

Pawing at the front of his shirt, he pulled out a small pouch, opened it with trembling fingers and spilled a handful of great pebbles out onto his palm. For the first time in his life, his fear was so much greater than his greed that he was willing to share his fortune.

He thrust his shaking hand toward Ka-Zar. "Look," he said hoarsely. "Emeralds—a bloody fortune in emeralds. We can be rich—you crazy fool! Help me pan them from the stream and then we'll clear out together—leave this damn wilderness forever."

It was DeKraft's trump card—his last ace-in-the-hole. He had never yet seen the man who would not do anything for riches.

Ka-Zar gazed down at the pebbles that had brought so much misfortune to him and his people. His amber eyes glowed. Then with a low growl, he struck at DeKraft's hand and sent the accursed stones scattering to the ground.

By the time they approached the cave, Fat-Face was reduced to a muttering, shambling wreck. He had never learned to control his emotions. Now they swept over him in successive waves, exhausting him mentally and physically. Rage—for the precious emeralds that he had gathered were gone, scattered on the jungle floor. Greed—for the stream still babbled over countless others, just waiting to be looted. Fear—for if this madman did not slay him, the waiting lion would.

By the time he reached the cave and saw not only the lion but a towering elephant move toward him, he could only gaze back at them in numb horror.

Dazedly he heard his strange captor hold a guttural, growling conversation with the two beasts. Then stumbling, in silence, he allowed Ka-Zar to lead him up onto the big boulder. Weakly he sank onto the rock, while the bronze giant stood straddle-legged over him.

In answer to Nono's startling news, the animals came swiftly to the meeting place. Ka-Zar warned Fat-Face not to move or speak. But the warning was unnecessary. DeKraft could not have stirred or uttered a word. His quivering bulk shrank perceptibly each time a beast emerged from the forest. All greeted the sight of hated Om with bellows or snarls of rage. All would have leaped upon him, save for Ka-Zar's repeated warning.

They milled restlessly about while others continued to drift in from the jungle. And if DeKraft had entertained any hope that he might escape from the bronze madman, the last vestige of it was gone now. He was completely hemmed in by savage beasts, who looked at him hungrily from gleaming eyes and licked their chops. Ugly apes, snarling leopards, grunting pigs, a watchful elephant, a monstrous snake, mighty lions—one move, and he would be torn to pieces.

At last Ka-Zar addressed the gathering and the snarls and growls died to a murmur. Flinging back his head he stood, a magnificent and imposing figure, towering above the huddled form of the white man.

"N'Jaga has told you," he began, casting a glance at the leopard who crouched sullenly at the fringe of the gathering, "that the Oman are my brothers. You believed. Now their leader is my captive." He looked down at Fat-Face and the murmur swelled for a moment to a concerted roar of rage.

"This Om," continued Ka-Zar, "has taken the lives of many of our jungle people. He must pay for them with his own."

A chorus of approval greeted these words and there was a note of eagerness in it that penetrated DeKraft's consciousness and made him shudder.

"But before this is done," Ka-Zar continued his guttural speech, "we have something to decide among us. N'Jaga has given me a challenge. I will answer it."

He turned to Nono. "Go into the cave. Bring me a knife."

The monkey scampered into the den. While he was gone, the animals chattered excitedly among themselves. They turned to stare curiously when Nono reappeared a moment later, carrying a shining knife which he handed to Ka-Zar.

A hush fell upon the gathering. They had seen that knife bite deep into a kill and they had a great respect for it.

Ka-Zar prodded Fat-Face none too gently with his foot. "Get up," he commanded in English.

Obediently DeKraft crawled to his feet. He was a pathetic figure now. All his bravado was gone. His beard was draggled, his swarthy face beaded with sweat. And his eyes were empty of all but black despair.

FOR A MOMENT he stared at the knife. His eyes widened as Ka-Zar silently held it towards him, haft first. Unbelieving, like one in a trance, he reached out and took it. Dazedly he turned it over and over in his fingers.

Ka-Zar turned back to face the expectant beasts. "Without their weapons the Oman are defenseless. But now this Om is armed. Who among you, will face him in single combat?"

The beasts muttered amongst themselves but none spoke up. Ka-Zar waited until it was evident that no one dared to face the Om with his knife. Then he strode up to confront the surly N'Jaga.

"You talked boldly of slaying," he said. "Here is your chance. Kill this Om now and we will all acknowledge you lord of the jungle."

But N'Jaga, spitting and snarling, only bared his teeth and glared his hatred.

"Come," insisted Ka-Zar. "Whichever one of us slays this Om—he shall be king of the wilderness. Do you agree?"

Eagerly the assemblage assented. N'Jaga, too, reluctantly agreed for his fear was greater than his hate. He, himself, refused to accept the challenge.

"Let Ka-Zar kill," he growled. "If he does, I acknowledge him my master."

That was all Ka-Zar wanted. He turned to Fat-Face. "Come down," he called in English. "We shall fight, with knives. No beast will interfere. You shall have your chance to kill me."

DeKraft hesitated a moment, then as the animals fell back, leaving a cleared space in their midst, he stepped warily down from the rock. He saw Ka-Zar take a crude but deadly knife from his belt, similar to the one he clutched in his hand.

A last vestige of that indefinable something which puts man in a class apart from the beasts, returned to him. He realized that this was to be a fight to the death and that even if he won, his own life was surely forfeit. But here was an opportunity to kill the madman who had shattered all his dreams of untold wealth. And already resigned to his own fate, he determined that the bronze giant would die with him.

The old light of cunning crept back into his eyes. Clutching the knife, he edged warily forward, circling for an opening.

A hush fell upon the jungle, a hush so profound that even the sighing wind did not stir the leaves. It was a weird, unreal scene. A spectacle as terrible as any ever staged in the old Roman arena. Only here the situation was fantastically reversed. The galleries of the natural amphitheatre were filled with silent, watching beasts. And before them, settling an old score with deadly steel, two men faced each other.

Fat-Face darted suddenly in and his gleaming blade licked hungrily out at the apex of Ka-Zar's mighty ribs. But even as its point drew crimson, a bronze hand closed about DeKraft's wrist. His bulky figure was spun violently about, jerked back and clasped against a broad chest. Ka-Zar's right hand described a short, glinting arc through the air. Then it struck downward and his knife buried itself to the hilt in the quivering flesh at the base of DeKraft's throat.

The blade emerged again, dripping fluid scarlet. Ka-Zar

stepped back, releasing his hold.

DeKraft died on his feet. His knees buckled and his flabby body crumpled to the ground.

The leaves of the surrounding trees shivered and rustled softly, as though disturbed by the passing of his departing spirit. Then Ka-Zar placed one foot on the body of his slain enemy and tossing back his regal head, roared forth the mighty cry of the lion's kill.

STILL HOLDING THE gory blade, Ka-Zar strode over to N'Jaga. "You saw?" he demanded.

"I saw," growled N'Jaga.

"I am your master?" asked Ka-Zar arrogantly.

N'Jaga wriggled uncomfortably; his slitted eyes glowed. "Ka-Zar is my master," he acknowledged sullenly.

He rose and with such dignity as he could summon, stalked off into the forest. Silently his cousins followed.

Satisfied, Ka-Zar walked slowly to where Zar stood before the mouth of the cave. Standing by the side of the lion he turned and confronted the animals once more.

"Ka-Zar boasted before," he said clearly. "Zar still rules the jungle. And Ka-Zar is proud to be his brother. Let no one distrust me again. I am mighty, but I am just. Go your ways in peace."

A chorus of acclamation greeted his speech. Then scattering, the animals went off to resume the life that the coming of the Oman had so briefly but violently interrupted. Ka-Zar was left with his friends and the body of his slain enemy.

Overhead Kru the vulture spiraled slowly down from a sky of clearest azure. A troop of birds gleamed for an instant like a living rainbow as they crossed the path of the sun. And peace settled down once more over the jungle—for a while, at least.

BOOK II

ROAR OF
THE JUNGLE

*KA-ZAR, the white youth, fights
the Rajah of the Congo and his
savage warriors to rescue the
golden-haired Belgian girl.*

CHAPTER I

THE MAN WHO WAS BLIND

THE LAW OF the jungle is simple. In the bones of the dead it is proclaimed in every clearing, along every trail, by the side of every water-hole. Let the strong survive! Let the weak beware lest they perish before their might!

Cruel, ruthless; yes. Yet it is the voice of Darkest Africa that speaks. Life is cheap in the heart of the Belgian Congo.

N'Jaga the leopard lived by the law and gloried in it. With each kill that fell before the might of his claws, the hate in his heart increased.

N'Jaga left an easy trail to read across the miasmic jungle floor. His left foreleg was shorter than his right. He walked with a limp. And because of that limp, acquired years before in his first combat with man, a devil smouldered continually beneath his supple, spotted hide.

Man, to N'Jaga, was something to be feared; but something to be hated even more. According to the leopard's code, two-legged creatures—be they black or white—were to be slain on sight; mangled, disemboweled, then disdainfully tossed aside for Kru the vulture and his feathered brothers to feast upon.

And on this particular morning, the hated scent of man was strong in N'Jaga's nostrils. Belly flat to the ground, tail switching, eyes slitted, he wormed his way through the dense tangle of undergrowth towards a small clearing that bordered a rapidly coursing stream.

With the sinuous grace of Sinassa the Snake, his flattened

head parted the last screen of protecting foliage. Instantly the steel muscles of his body tensed like coiled springs. His haunches arched; the short hairs, at the base of his skull bristled up on end. Something that was a combination of hiss, snarl and spit started in his throat and was still-born. Twin streams of saliva drooled down from his bared fangs.

For, before him in the clearing was a man—one of the feared but even more hated Oman. Red lights flicked in N'Jaga's green eyes. The lashing of his tail suddenly ceased. No detail of his victim did he miss. The Om was white. He was leaning against the bole of a towering daboukra tree, as if wounded or exhausted. But more important than this, was the fact that he carried no dreaded fire-stick in his hand.

It had been a fire-stick that had caused N'Jaga's limp. He

associated them with the hated Oman. They were both evil. But here before him was a species of his ancient enemy— unarmed, helpless—his rightful prey.

The blood ran hot in N'Jaga's veins, pounded dully beneath his flat skull. But the lust that was upon him did not dull his cunning. Craftily, from the store of knowledge gained from a thousand previous kills, he judged the distance between him and the two-legged creature. His haunches gathered up beneath him, his forelegs tensed; the talons of his paws arched like hooks of steel.

And then, in that split second before he sprang, the white man moved—lurched, to be more exact. He staggered clear of the tree, his arms held gropingly before him. He stumbled a few paces to the right, tripped, regained his balance, tottered off to the left and blundered foolishly and heavily into the trunk

of a tree.

HE HUNG ON there, swayed a moment, groaned and cursed.

N'Jaga had never seen a two-legged creature move so erratically before. His fear of them and their ways was strong in his heart. He sensed a trap and with a muted snarl, subsided into the tangle of undergrowth.

From unblinking, red-filmed eyes he watched the Om—saw his stagger, lurch and fall; saw him climb drunkenly to his feet, only to crash once more into tree or boulder.

Swiftly the fear of a trap died in N'Jaga's heart. He became impatient for the kill. He tensed—a scream curdled in his throat—he sprang.

But quicker than the flashing, spotted body of the leopard, a second form leaped out into the clearing and took up a position of defiance between N'Jaga and his intended prey. And louder, more challenging, more commanding than the scream of the leopard, came the stentorian roar of the lion from the lips of the new arrival.

The lion's roar! The mighty roar of Zar, lord of the jungle!

But it was Ka-Zar, Brother of the Lion, who stood on straddled legs in the center of the clearing and defied N'Jaga to advance on penalty of death.

Of all the two-legged creatures that lived, N'Jaga hated most the one that stood before him now. Many times in the dim past their trails had crossed. In the beginning N'Jaga had contested the right of way. But bitter defeat in battle had caused him to concede the superior might of this lion-man, who with Zar ruled the forest.

With a whining snarl of frustration, N'Jaga flattened his belly to the ground and lashed his tail in impotent fury.

Bronzed by the African sun, muscled like a primeval god, the scanty antelope skin around his loins serving but to emphasize his superb body, Ka-Zar fingered the knife at his belt and confronted the leopard. He tossed back his head and the regal mane of black hair that fell to his shoulders caught and reflected the diamond-bright rays of, the sun.

Noises rumbled in his throat-deep, guttural, animal noises. He spoke in the language of the jungle beasts and his finely-chiseled lips curled in scorn.

"N'Jaga picks his prey well. The antelope is too fleet for him—the jumping-hare too nimble—the lion too strong. He chooses one of the Oman who is already stricken."

For answer, N'Jaga bared his teeth in a snarl. For a moment his hate overpowered his fear. A blind lust urged him to spring on this taunting two-legged creature who had humbled his pride in the dust many times before. There were old scores, old wounds and deep between them. Let them be settled once and for all!

Then his old fear reasserted itself, made him cautious. His tail whipped savagely and his slitted eyes probed both sides of the clearing for the best way of retreat.

Ka-Zar saw the furtive movement and interpreted it correctly.

"The Om is under my protection," he said arrogantly. "Who touches him, defies Ka-Zar also."

N'Jaga writhed under the scorn that glowed in Ka-Zar's amber eyes. The stricken Om was already forgotten—he was only a side issue in this battle of wills and courage. N'Jaga's dark heart again urged him to leap on this naked, two-legged creature who taunted him.

But that was not N'Jaga's way. Some day, his scheming brain promised him, they would meet again—some day when the advantage would be all his.

He spat, then turned abruptly and glided like a malevolent shadow toward the underbrush at the edge of the clearing.

WHEN THE FINAL leaf had settled into place behind the leopard's retreating back, Ka-Zar turned swiftly and in three long strides crossed the clearing.

The white man had crumpled to the ground. He lay on his

face, the fingers of his outflung hands dug deep into the moist earth. His soiled and travel-worn clothes were torn to tatters and the flesh of his back, showing beneath the rents in his shirt, had been torn by a thousand clutching thorns and brambles. The sores had festered and a myriad of crawling insects swarmed over them.

Ka-Zar had never seen such a pitiable object before. Strange and conflicting emotions surged in his breast—the same conflicting emotions that had always disturbed him on the infrequent times he had stood in the presence of an Om.

He nourished no love for man. It had been a man who had killed his father—who had brought death and trouble to his jungle fastness. But in the end that man had died at his hands.

In the dim past, over the twin graves of his parents, he had sworn a blood feud against the tribe of two-legged creatures. By this alone, by the simple, elemental code of the jungle, that lump of helpless flesh at his feet was an enemy.

But unthinking, unreasoning, deep in Ka-Zar's consciousness he sensed his kinship to the stricken white man at his feet. And the one thing that raised him far and above the jungle beasts that he ruled, motivated him now. Mercy.

He knelt down. With fingers that were surprisingly gentle, despite their strength, he turned the white man over. For a long moment he looked down into a worn and haggard face. Despite its extreme emaciation, accentuated by the stubble of beard on the chin, Ka-Zar sensed that the features were not cruel.

So decivilized was he, that that was his only standard of judgment. Either an animal was cruel like N'Jaga, or he killed only that he might survive.

The man's eyes were closed. His lips were parted and his breathing labored. Wise in the ways of the jungle, where death is swift and frequent, Ka-Zar knew that the Om did not have long to live. Again motivated by the strange feeling of mercy, he crossed to the bank of the stream, knelt down and sucked up a large mouthful of water. Returning to the white man, he squirted the liquid into the latter's open mouth.

The Om stirred, groaned. Then his eyelids fluttered, opened wide.

Bending over him, Ka-Zar stared down into two red and empty sockets; The man was not simply blind. No. The eyes themselves had been gouged out from his skull with some sharp instrument. The terrible wounds were still raw and unhealed and from his knowledge, Ka-Zar knew that they had been inflicted within the last few days.

And he knew more. No savage beast of the jungle had inflicted such wanton cruelty. Those wounds were made by man, upon man, with cunning malice.

Again his hate of the two-legged tribe welled up within him. Of all the animals that he knew, the Oman were the only ones who warred upon one another—who killed and maimed from the sheer lust of cruelty.

IF HE HAD stumbled across some jungle beast in a similar condition, Ka-Zar would have immediately dispatched him from his misery. Now he fingered the halt of his knife for a moment, hesitated. The uneasy kinship he felt towards the white man stayed his merciful hand. And too, he was curious as to what beast had caused those terrible wounds.

The Om stirred again. His lips moved and his words came in a whisper.

"So you've caught me again, eh, Sarput? All right, you devil, kill me and have done with it!"

The words were in English. Some of them Ka-Zar understood; more of them he did not. But he gathered that the Om mistook him for one Sarput and that he feared death.

"Ka-Zar kneels beside you—not Sarput," he said slowly. "And Ka-Zar does not come to kill."

A violent tremor of agitation coursed through the white man's body at the words. He propped himself up on one hand, pawed wildly towards Ka-Zar with the other.

"Ka-Zar!" he whispered in a hoarse voice. Then he laughed mirthlessly in a cracked tone, slumped back to the ground. "Another of your devil's tricks, Sarput. Ka-Zar is a myth—a superstition of the blacks. But you won't be able to torture me for long. I'm finished—done." His voice became suddenly strong with hate and bitterness. "I wish to God there was such a person as Ka-Zar to drive you back to the hell you came from."

Ka-Zar had listened attentively and with a puzzled frown to the jumble of words. For the greater part they were meaningless to him. To him, there was no such thing as God or superstition, the devil or hell. He only knew that the man at his feet had suffered indescribable pain at the hands of one he called Sarput.

"Ka-Zar speaks," he said again. And then by way of explanation: "Ka-Zar, brother of Zar the lion."

Again the tremor of agitation swept over the dying white man. For a moment more he lay on the ground, panting heavily. Then summoning up the last of his fast-ebbing strength he struggled up to a sitting position. Blindly his hands sought for and found Ka-Zar's magnificent body. Eagerly his fingers swept over the bare muscles, hard and supple as drawn steel.

And as his fingers felt and read what his eyes could not see, a slow transformation came over his face. The lines of agony faded. A fierce glow of joy animated the wan features. His dying spirit rallied, sustained by the hate in his heart, by the urgency of what he had to say.

"Ka-Zar!" he muttered. "Brother of the lion! I used to laugh at the tales I heard about you. But you do exist—you're real." He clutched fiercely at Ka-Zar's arm, continued in a desperate whisper. "God or man, Ka-Zar, your jungle needs you."

"Your words are heavy with trouble," said Ka-Zar. "Speak on."

"A devil has come to your jungle," whispered the Om.

"Devil?" questioned Ka-Zar. "I know not of devils."

"A man," said the dying white. "A man like myself—but a

fiend. I was his guide. He kills for the joy of killing. And because I tried to interfere—" he clawed at his empty sockets and his voice rose to a shrill crescendo—"he did this to me!"

KA-ZAR KNEW THE inexplorable fate that awaited the sightless in the jungle. The best they could hope for was a swift and merciful death. The realization that a two-legged creature like himself had willfully blinded another, made his heart heavy. His few associations with man in the past had always been ones of trouble and death.

Now, with the sightless Om lying at his feet, panting out his last breath with his tale of the devil Om, a dark foreboding gripped Ka-Zar's heart.

"And this devil-man you speak of," he said slowly. "Where can Ka-Zar find him?"

"South—two day's march to the south," answered the other. "And if you find him, Ka-Zar, show him no mercy. Kill him for what he did to me—for the hell he intends to make of your jungle." He clutched frantically at Ka-Zar's arms, half-raised himself from the ground in a frenzy. "You'll kill him, Ka-Zar?" he pleaded. "Tell me you'll kill him!"

"If he is evil, if he harms one beast of the jungle," answered Ka-Zar slowly, "he will die. It is the word of Ka-Zar."

The strained muscles of the white man's face relaxed. A thin smile twitched at his lips. "So help me, I believe you," he whispered. "I can go easy, now."

And with the last faint echo of his words, he died in Ka-Zar's arms.

CHAPTER II

ZAR ANSWERS THE CALL

KA-ZAR ROSE TO his full height, turned slowly to face the south and stared unseeingly at the solid, emerald green wall of the jungle. His piercing amber eyes, keen as those of Pindar the eagle, clouded over and a frown settled heavily on his brow.

A thousand conflicting emotions stirred within him. For a long time now he had ruled over his jungle domain in peace. Now trouble had come again to the wilderness. Two days' march away an evil man, by his very presence, challenged him. He did not know this—Sarput did not know even that such a being as Ka-Zar, brother of Zar the lion, existed. And so he could not know that deep in the heart of the jungle a bronzed giant took up the challenge, flung back his majestic head and sent the mighty roar of the lion trembling through the forest glades.

For miles around, smaller animals fled squeaking to cover. And when the echoes of the cry died on the still, steaming air, a lone answer came to Ka-Zar. It was a thin, chattering voice that drifted down to Ka-Zar from the treetops.

He looked up and a moment later a little monkey scampered down from the leafy branches, bounded across the clearing and leaped up onto his shoulder. Spidery arms wrapped about his neck and from bright little eyes Nono the monkey stared down at the lifeless body on the ground. Agog with fear and curiosity, he jabbered excited questions in his master's ear.

Ka-Zar's smouldering eyes still stared into the south. He growled without turning his head. "Cease your chatter, silly one.

Go—find the mighty Zar, my brother. I go south—tell him to join me."

Nono squeaked once to show that he understood, eyed the body fearfully for a moment and then bounded off. When he had disappeared, swallowed up in the depths of the still forest, Ka-Zar looked down again at the thing that had once been a man. Except for the vestige of a frown that still lingered on his brow, his face was impassive.

The pity that had moved him a moment before died swiftly, for after all, Ka-Zar was of the jungle. In the jungle one slays—for food, or sometimes for vengeance or rivalry over the favor of a female. But the cruelty that had caused this Om to be maimed and left to die—that was beyond understanding. He puzzled over it, as he had often puzzled in the past.

A dim speck appeared in the cloudless blue dome of the heavens. It circled slowly, growing ever larger. It was Kru the vulture, the inevitable end of any jungle tragedy. Ka-Zar turned abruptly on his heel and with long, easy strides headed directly into the south.

As he plunged into the gloomy depths of the forest, his mind went groping back over the years.

HE DID NOT know that many years before, John Rand, a prosperous mine owner from Johannesburg, had started out from that city in an airplane, taking his beautiful wife and his infant son, David, to Cairo. They had crashed, to land in the heart of the Congo. A benevolent Providence had wiped out the memory of those first nightmare days and nights from Ka-Zar's mind.

With an effort that knitted his brows he now managed to recall vague glimpses of his beautiful and adored mother. Her tragic death, caused by a lingering jungle fever, was mercifully blotted out by time.

Ka-Zar's first clear recollections of his boyhood were those of happy days spent roaming the wilderness with his father. He did not know—and he would never know—that on the day before he and his father were to start on the long trek back to civilization, John Rand had been struck by a falling tree; that as a result of this accident, his father's mind had become unbalanced.

From that point on, the course of young David's life was changed.

To Rand's warped mind, the lonely grave of his wife in that God-forsaken stretch of wilderness, became a sanctuary. And all the miles of dense forest, of clearing and river and lake surrounding it, became his and David's—to hold sacred and inviolate against any trespasser.

The trespasser had come—in the shape of an evil and greedy white man and his native helpers. Keeping his fanatical trust, attempting to drive the newcomer from his wilderness home, John Rand had been slain. And young David, left alone, had come into his kingdom.

A true child of the wilderness, David had early made friends with the beasts. On one occasion he had saved Zar the lion, mighty lord of the jungle, from a treacherous bed of quicksand. And in his own hour of need, when his father died in his arms from a murderer's bullet, Zar did not forsake him. The watchful lord of the jungle had stood guard by the grief stricken boy and had led him at last to his own jungle lair.

There a pact of brotherhood had been sworn. There the boy ceased to be David Rand and became instead Ka-Zar, brother of Zar the lion. There he learned to speak the language of his brothers, the beasts. And there, aided by his superior intellect and the few weapons he had learned to fashion and to use, he had earned the right to rule over his vast heritage.

Years later the evil white man—the slayer of his father—had returned and Ka-Zar, fulfilling a vow made over the graves of his parents, had avenged the death of his father. He had learned many things in that encounter. He had learned to respect the white man's weapons; to mistrust the white man for his greed, his cruelty, his treachery. He had learned, above all else, that the coming of man to his wilderness spelled trouble. And that was why, as he strode swiftly along through the forest, his heart was heavy and dark forbodings stirred in his brain.

HE PAUSED SEVERAL times in his journey to drink from a meandering stream and to look back in the direction from whence he had come. But it was near sunset when at last his keen ear caught the sound for which he had been waiting. From somewhere far behind him came the distant rumble of a lion's roar.

Tossing back his head, Ka-Zar answered.

A hush fell over the forest. Ka-Zar swung up into the lowest branch of a nearby tree and squatted there on his haunches, like a great ape. A troop of brilliantly colored birds flitted across the open patch of sky that showed between the trees. The setting sun gilded the leaves of the topmost branches, slowly turned the square of sky to molten copper. From the northeast a vagrant breeze, cooled by its passage over a vast lake that lay in that direction, drifted like a sigh through the forest. It stirred the long locks of hair that tumbled down from Ka-Zar's shoulders. He raised his head and his nostrils flared as he sniffed. The scent of distant rushes and exotic flowers was mingled with other, more intriguing odors.

Again came the sound of Zar's call—nearer this time. And again Ka-Zar answered, while the denizens of the jungle listened in hushed silence to the interchange between the two great beasts.

The sun dropped swiftly to meet the waiting earth and mauve shadows crept out from behind the trees to gather on the jungle floor. The breeze shifted a trifle and Ka-Zar's frown was erased as a familiar, pungent scent came downwind to his nostrils.

With a low, glad rumble in his throat he dropped down from his perch. Twenty paces away the undergrowth parted soundlessly and a great, tawny shape materialized before him. Massive, formidable, regal, the lord of the jungle padded forward on great paws to meet him.

Never, under the sun, had there existed such a strange or such a true bond of brotherhood as bound these two. Their greeting was brief—an exchange of low, whining noises. Then Zar spoke in the guttural language of the beasts: "Trouble has come to my brother."

Ka-Zar fingered the string of his deadly bow. His eyes clouded again and he stared moodily into the gathering gloom. "Trouble has come to me and to the jungle," he growled in answer. "Again an evil Om has come to the forest."

Tawny gleams danced in the amber depths of Zar's eyes. The long hairs on the back of his neck rose to a stiff ruff. The tuft at the tip of his tail twitched slightly.

"Ka-Zar goes to find this Om," continued Ka-Zar.

With a majestic dignity Zar answered: "Where Ka-Zar goes, Zar goes also."

There was no need for more. Side by side they laid down together on the forest floor to refresh themselves with a brief sleep.

CHAPTER III

FEATHERED WARNING

THE MOON WAS already climbing over the tree-tops—a huge orange globe—when they rose. Zar melted soundlessly into the shadows of the jungle and a short time after, the night was shattered by a shrill cry. It was echoed by the deep roar of the lion's kill.

Zar returned soon, carrying in his massive jaws a young buck antelope. Ka-Zar drew his knife and together they squatted beside the kill, to eat their fill of the fresh meat. Then, after going to the stream to drink, they resumed their journey southward.

The dying guide could not have guessed at the speed with which Zar and Ka-Zar traveled through the forest. And so, instead of the two day's journey which he had predicted, it was a matter, of less than half that time when they reached their destination.

A flaming dawn blazed its riotous colors from the East when Ka-Zar pulled up short. Zar stopped at his side and together they listened for a moment. All about them and in the surrounding treetops, the jungle was awakening to a new day. While the animals who prowled at night were slinking silently off to their lairs, others awoke to noisy life. Parakeets took off in screeching flight, flashing iridescent sapphire and emerald across the path of the rising sun. Nono's cousins, the monkeys, came trooping down from the trees, to search for berries and nuts on the ground. One spied the graven figures of the two-legged giant and the enormous tawny lion beside him. His shrill alarm was instantly taken up by the others and they all fled, chattering with fear, up into the higher, branches. A plump, beady-eyed gnu wandered out from the underbrush, saw his peril and dove squeaking for cover.

Above all these sounds, Zar and Ka-Zar heard others. Their keen ears sifted the alien from the commonplace, recognized the distant crashing made by larger animals passing through the brush and voices that were not those of any jungle beast.

The dying guide had unintentionally conveyed a wrong impression. It was not a lone man, but a large party that traveled now through the forest.

Silently Ka-Zar turned to the left and resumed his journey in a wide, swinging circle that would bring him well in advance of the moving party.

Still guided by the sounds of the Oman's progress, he came out at last on a high ledge of outcropping rock. There he and Zar flattened themselves on their bellies and peered over the edge. They were directly above a faint, but discernible trail.

They could have stayed in that position, immovable and unblinking, all day if need be. But now they had not long to wait. The alien noises grew rapidly louder and soon, around a bend in the trail, appeared a great gray shape.

It was an elephant and, Ka-Zar studied it with interest. He had seen elephants before. In fact, Trajah, the mighty leader of the herd that made regular, pilgrimages through this jungle domain, was Ka-Zar's ally and true friend. This animal now approaching, however, was different from Trajah and his kind. He was not as large as any of Trajah's herd. His ears and his tusks, too, were small—even for his lesser stature. A brown-skinned man sat crosslegged upon his broad head and his back was heaped high with bulky burdens.

OTHERS CAME IN their wake. There were the familiar black men, whom Ka-Zar had seen before. These walked in single file, all bearing bundles greater than themselves, balanced miraculously on fuzzy heads and gleaming ebony shoulders. Ka-Zar was more intrigued by the brown men. They were dressed in fantastic garments and even their heads were swathed in strange, colored stuffs.

Several carried the dangerous, gleaming rifles that both Zar and Ka-Zar had learned to respect. When Zar first saw the sunlight glint upon the barrel of a fire-stick, a low growl rumbled deep in his throat. Ka-Zar stilled him with a single guttural sound.

"Quiet!" he warned in a low voice. "The Oman go from the jungle. Let there be no trouble—let them depart in peace."

Zar subsided reluctantly. The hated Oman were truly headed toward the southeast, toward the great grassy plains that lay beyond the edge of the forest. Ka-Zar was only too glad to see them go.

Yet it was not often that he had the opportunity to see and observe twolegged creatures like himself. And though they were the hated Oman, whose kinship he had renounced, his natural curiosity made him linger. Instead of returning at once to the heart of his kingdom, he edged back on his belly along the rock until he was well out of sight of the slow-moving column.

Then swinging up into the nearest tree, he took to the lower branches while Zar glided along like a great shadow below him. They paralleled the marchers, but in the direction from which the Oman were coming.

Swinging agilely and silently from bough to bough, Ka-Zar missed no detail of the long procession. His face grew grave when he saw the size of the party on the march. He was doubly thankful, now, that they were going.

He came at last to the end of the column. The stragglers at the rear kept glancing back over their shoulders. To Ka-Zar's ears came sounds that told him there were yet more of the Oman who had not passed him.

With a low call to Zar, below, he progressed swiftly forward. And soon, from the vantage point of a tall, leafy bao-bab, he was looking down on a strange scene.

An elephant, with a strange, tent-like contrivance upon its back, was kneeling on the ground. One of the fastenings that held the encumbrance had broken and several brown men were working frantically to repair it. Many Oman, both brown and black, clustered about them. But Ka-Zar's gaze went automatically to the central figure of the little drama.

The man was tall and thin. His skin was dark, but not shiny like that of the natives. Instead it was dull, ashen. A jet-black beard straggled from his chin. His eyes were gleaming slits, set close on either side of a hooked, predatory nose. His teeth gleamed white between thin, cruel lips.

It was not his gorgeous raiment, glittering in the brilliant sunlight, that told Ka-Zar that here was the devil Sarput. Evil radiated from that gaunt but gaudy figure. And right now, he was in the grip of a mounting rage.

From his perch, Ka-Zar watched with fascinated eyes. He was puzzled by an object that Sarput held in his hand. It looked like a stick, with something that Ka-Zar could only liken to a length of jungle vine dangling from it. He remembered suddenly. It was a whip—a favorite weapon of the Om he had killed many moons ago. He knew its purpose.

THE OM CALLED Sarput was shouting orders in a strange tongue. His voice was harsh and ugly to the ear. Each time he spoke, black men and brown alike trembled. Ka-Zar could see the expression of fear on their faces. Below him, Zar stood motionless and silent. Only now the hairs along the back of his neck stood up straight and stiff and his lips were pulled back a trifle from his bared fangs.

The noise of the advance party died off in the distance. Sarput fell to a restless pacing, stalking back and forth. A little brown man, whose twisted back began with a huge hump between his shoulders and ended in spindly legs, one shorter than the other, hobbled anxiously in his wake.

The men beside the kneeling elephant sweated copiously at

their labors. Suddenly the beast lurched, started to climb to his feet. The Oman shouted as the tent-like contraption slid down his broad side and collapsed as it struck the ground.

All Sarput's pent-up wrath exploded. With a shrill cry of rage he whirled. The hand that clutched the whip snapped up. Screaming with fear, his followers scattered.

The unfortunate hunchback was too slow. The whip hissed through the air, lashed out with all the speed and deadliness of Sinassa the snake, and slashed across his malformed back. He cried out—a high-pitched scream of mortal pain and terror. Then he stumbled and pitched headlong to the ground.

Sarput was upon him like a fury. Here was a ready victim for his blind rage.

With hoarse, inarticulate sounds issuing from his lips, he brought the hissing whip down again and again on the quivering form of the prone cripple.

At the first blow of the whip, Ka-Zar had been merely an impassive spectator to the scene. Now his gorge rose at the needless cruelty. Dimly he sensed that according to the jungle code, he was showing weakness. He could not know that his pity was a heritage of the white man's blood that ran in his veins.

Beneath the scourge of the whip, the hunchback's clothing ripped into tatters. His screams shrilled higher, more hideous, in the still morning air. And suddenly Ka-Zar, without knowing why he did it, straightened up to his full height on the leafy bough. Flinging back his head, clenching his fists against his mighty ribs, he sent the roar of Zar, the lord of the jungle, reverberating through the forest.

Instant silence fell upon the Oman. They stood as though turned to stone, only their eyes moving swiftly and fearfully in the direction from which the sound had come. Sarput, too, was momentarily paralyzed. He stood like a statue created by some fiendish genius, the murderous whip poised for another blow.

Then the hunchback stirred, tried feebly to crawl away. The

movement broke the spell that held Sarput. The whip started another vicious slash downward.

With a motion as swift as light itself, Ka-Zar snatched an arrow from his quiver, fitted it to his long bow, drew the string far back-and let fly.

SOMETHING STREAKED THROUGH the air, struck at a point exactly midway between Sarput and the terrified hunchback. And the devil, as the dying man had called him, stared at the long shaft of the arrow that stuck quivering in the ground before him.

With a concerted wail of terror, the native blacks flung themselves to the ground and covered their eyes. They had heard weird tales of a jealous god who ruled over this dark heart of the Congo. Now all the rumors that they had heard were verified. The god had spoken with the voice of a lion and from out of nowhere, he had sent a warning arrow. They had violated his sanctuary by their presence and each was fully convinced that within the next second, he would be slain by the wrathful spirit. Their plaintive wails for mercy filled the air.

In their turn, the brown men dropped to their knees, raised their eyes and hands to heaven and appealed loudly to their own alien, all-merciful protector.

Sarput, too, had heard of this strange jungle god who inhabited the depths of the forest. But he was loath to believe. He stood rigid, his beady eyes scanning the dense, emerald foliage from whence the mysterious arrow had come. More worldly than his followers, he was sure that a human hand—and not a godly one—had dispatched the deadly missile.

He was right in his surmise. But he would have known a touch of the fear that gripped his followers had his eye been able to penetrate those leafy depths For watching him in turn was a bronze giant, poised on a tree limb. And peering through the undergrowth, in the grip of a rage as terrible as Sarput's own, was an enormous, regal lion.

For a long moment, only the hunchback stirred. His eyes sought the trees from which his respite had come and they were soft with a gratitude that would not soon be forgotten. Feebly he crawled off and reached the shelter of a thorny thicket beside the trail.

Now that the cruel scene was ended, Ka-Zar knew a momentary regret that he had interfered. With a low call to Zar to follow, he retreated soundlessly from his vantage point, retiring well back into the shady depths of the jungle.

Sarput shook himself, as though to break a spell that had fallen upon him. Suddenly gone mad with frustrated rage, he whirled on his terrified followers.

"Fools!" he screamed, plying his whip freely among them. "It is no god—but a mere man who dares to mock Sarput! Into the forest! Find him and bring him to me! We shall soon see how vulnerable he is."

Crying out at the blows, the men stumbled and staggered to their feet. Torn between fear of their cruel master and fear of the strange jungle god, they moved reluctantly into the fringe of the forest. Half-hearted, driven on by Sarput's raging commands, they peered fearfully into the undergrowth and into the dense foliage above them

Several seized advantage of the moment to hastily repair the *howdah* and fasten it once more upon the back of Sarput's elephant. When their task was finished and the others came straggling in from the forest after a vain search, Sarput reluctantly decided to mount and take off after the rest of his party.

But as his lurching beast set off down the trail, he glanced back again and again at the point from whence Ka-Zar's arrow had come. And in the murky depths of his eyes, little red devils danced—a sign that, boded no good for the jungle god if he should fall into the hands of this hell-fiend.

CHAPTER IV

PRINCE OF DARKNESS

IF PUT TO it, Jan VanGelder, Royal Commissioner for the Belgian Congo, would have declared that he loved three things above all else. First, his daughter Claudette, next his honor and lastly the vast, primeval jungle it was his duty to administer.

And now, as he sat slumped in the high backed chair before his desk, be had a vague, uneasy premonition that all three were threatened.

VanGelder was tall and blonde; a man of simple dignity. His brow was high, his eyes of a placid blue; and his mouth was large and full. A fine man, VanGelder—just and generous to a fault.

Now as he toyed with the official documents on his desk, the lines of worry about his lips hardened and a heavy frown made a deep V between his brows. His cheroot had long since gone out. He was not aware of it and sucked greedily at the unlit weed. Vacantly he stared at the papers in his hand but did not read them. No need for that. He knew every syllable of their amazing wordage by heart.

But startling as those words were, they were not the exact cause of the apprehension in his heart. The real cause was embodied in the man seated opposite him on the far side of the broad, polished desk.

Gaudy in barbaric silks, his bony skull swathed in a colored turban, in which a single, large diamond gleamed splendidly, the Rajah Sarput lolled insolently in his chair. A mocking, half smile curled at his thin lips and in the ashen pallor of his face his beady black eyes gleamed malevolently. In one hand he carried a short but heavy riding crop and now he beat an impatient tattoo with it against his leg.

The sound irritated VanGelder, set his nerves on edge. He rustled the papers before him, muttered, beneath his breath: "I can't understand it."

However, it was a purely rhetorical statement. Commissioner VanGelder understood only too well.

The Rajah had heard his muttered words and now said with a politeness edged with ice: "I beg your pardon?"

VanGelder cleared his throat, played for time by lighting his cigar with elaborate care.

With precise strokes of his riding crop the Rajah demolished a large moth that had fluttered to the floor. With his beady black eyes still on his work of destruction he continued with studied insolence. "The papers are in order, of course?"

"Yes," answered VanGelder heavily. "They are in order. I have never seen before such perfect order in official documents." A tide of color coursed slowly up his cheeks and it was only with an effort that he kept the anger and resentment from his voice when he continued. "But my dear Rajah, I tell you I don't like the thing."

The Rajah Sarput raised his eyes slowly from the carnage that had once been a beautiful moth. He held the Commissioner's glance with his own and it seemed to VanGelder that an inner film dropped over his eyes, making them lifeless, soulless.

"Ah!" breathed the Rajah.

ONE WORD—ONE WORD only—but VanGelder had never heard a syllable contain such concentrated menace. He felt his anger rise within him as the color rose higher in his face. With one hand he gripped the arm of his chair, balanced his cigar carefully on the rim of an ash-tray with the other.

"Don't misunderstand me," he said carefully. "The entire

project is unprecedented. It is laden with danger—danger from a hundred sources. I was thinking of your Highness."

The Rajah Sarput showed his even white teeth in an amused and cynical smile. Placing one jewel-bestudded hand to his breast he inclined his head in an ironic bow. "I am touched—deeply touched, Your Excellency, that amongst your other worries you should have time to think of me. But let me put your mind at rest. I assure you that I am more than capable of taking care of myself." He cleared his throat with a little, coughing sound, added as an after thought: "In any situation."

VanGelder knew he was being laughed at, mocked. But there was nothing he could do about it. As he had mentioned before, the Rajah's papers were in order—perfect order. And those papers gave the Rajah title to and absolute sovereignty over a hundred square miles of the jungle that VanGelder had so long administered.

The thing would have been fantastic, unbelievable, if it had not been there before the Commissioner in black and white, sealed and authenticated by the royal seal of the King of Belgium.

Those papers on VanGelder's desk turned over to the Rajah a vast jungle kingdom to do with what he chose. To rule or ruin; to protect or plunder. And VanGelder thought he knew what the outcome would be.

The eyes of the two men, Belgian gentleman and Indian Prince—so utterly different in face and philosophy—met across the desk. They held, clashed like the steel of a pair of duelists engaging.

The Rajah smiled coldly. In VanGelder's heart the apprehension deepened. And with it his anger rose. The tension in the room built up charge upon charge. An explosion was imminent. And then, in that split second before it broke, the door opened and VanGelder's daughter entered.

She hesitated a moment on the threshold, on seeing that her father was occupied. VanGelder was about to dismiss her but the Rajah anticipated him and rose to his feet. There was no other alternative for the Commissioner but to present his daughter to the Indian prince. Rising, he nodded to his daughter.

Smiling, Claudette crossed the room to her father's side. She was lovely, fresh and piquant with youth. She had her father's wide blue eyes and her hair was the color of spun gold. A finely chiseled nose set off a sweet mouth and the determined line of her chin lent strength and character to her face.

"My dear," said VanGelder, taking his daughter's hand, "I want you to meet His Highness, the Rajah Sarput. Your Highness—my daughter, Claudette."

The girl acknowledged the introduction with a flashing smile. Then, as the veiled eyes of the Rajah took in her features one by one, swept slowly over the rounded lines of her body, the smile died from her lips and VanGelder felt her arm tremble beneath his hand.

THE RAJAH, LIKEWISE, was aware of the change that had come over her and of her shudder before his bold, desirous gaze. But for some perverted reason he was pleased that the girl should cringe before him. In his philosophy, it was fitting for a woman to fear her lord and master. Fearing, she was more pliable, a more willing slave.

Women were nothing new in the life of the Rajah Sarput; as a matter of fact, he was rather bored with them. In his native land he had but to clap his hand to have his choice of a resplendent harem. But now as his eyes continued to feast on Claudette's face and figure, he felt his sluggish pulses stir. Her blonde beauty would contrast well with his own dark features. She was as young and fresh as he was tired and jaded. The line of her chin bespoke spirit, despite her momentary fear, and he would therefor receive great joy in breaking her, bending her to his own superior will.

Of a sudden he coveted her with a passion full blown. And having thus far rode rough shod over life, he determined to have her—one way or another.

Claudette burned beneath his brazen stare. She sensed the sinister thoughts in his mind. Even more than her father she felt the cold, calculating cruelty that dominated his every thought and action.

The Rajah averted his gaze at last, fell to beating his leg again with the riding crop. Catching his lower lip between his teeth he bit it until one tiny drop of blood oozed forth. He addressed himself to VanGelder.

"Your daughter is a dream come to life. The dream of an opium eater."

The Commissioner was flustered and angered by such lavish praise. He muttered something to the effect that she was a good, Belgian girl and that she was returning home, soon.

The Rajah smiled but there was no humor in it. "That is unfortunate—for me. But perhaps we shall meet again before she leaves. It would be a pity, after meeting one so lovely, to lose sight of her forever."

"A damned pity," muttered VanGelder, forcefully, if not politely. Then feeling that the conversation was drifting into dangerous territory, he bluntly changed the subject. He turned to his daughter with a show of interest he far from felt. "The Rajah has acquired a tract of land up Uvalde way. A veritable kingdom. He intends to build himself a castle there and hunt." He turned to the prince. "That was your idea, wasn't it, Your Highness? To hunt?"

The Rajah inclined his head in a nod. "Exactly, Commissioner—to hunt," he answered with peculiar emphasis. "They tell me there are many strange and wonderful creatures in your African jungle."

VanGelder frowned. "Yes, many strange creatures. And many strange rumors have come out of the jungle."

THE RAJAH RAISED his brows in polite interest.

"There's tale the blacks tell of a jungle god," continued the Commissioner. "One who calls himself Ka-Zar, brother of Zar the lion. Of course it is pure superstition. But it's surprising how many things have transpired that can only be explained by the presence of such a jungle"—he hesitated, laughed—"jungle god or man." He shrugged, poked at the papers on his desk. "You might be interested to know that your domain lies in the westerly part of the forest this Ka-Zar is supposed to rule."

The Rajah tugged thoughtfully at the lobe of his left ear. In his mind's eye, he saw an arrow that still quivered in the ground between him and Ali the hunchback.

"Yes," he said slowly, "I have heard of the superstition. I am very interested in it. I shall look into the matter and when it is explained to my satisfaction, I shall send you a report."

Some sinister implication in his voice more than his words caught VanGelder's attention. He questioned the Rajah with a glance but the prince once more had his eyes on Claudette. With a tightening of his lips, VanGelder gathered up the papers on his desk.

Sarput turned to him slowly, bowed. "I think, Monsieur Commissioner," he said suavely, "that our business is concluded for the day. Let me congratulate you once more on your beautiful daughter."

VanGelder nodded his head in acknowledgment. Sarput cracked his whip against his leg once more, looked briefly from father to daughter, laughed for no reason at all, turned and strode from the room.

There was a long, uneasy silence in the office when the door had closed softly behind his retreating back. VanGelder broke it by slumping heavily into his chair.

"Damn that man!" he muttered savagely. "In his presence I have to fight down an overpowering impulse to choke him."

Claudette still smarted under Sarput's insolent stares. "I hate him, too," she said passionately. "He's evil! Beastly! He makes me think of things that crawl."

"He's all of that," agreed her father wearily.

"Who is he? What is he doing here?" demanded Claudette.

"And what is all this you were telling me about his kingdom?"

A scowl settled upon the Commissioner's usually placid face. He rose from his chair and paced the width of his office with impatient strides. "It's an outrage; it's a damnable shame!" he said bitterly.

"What?" asked Claudette.

Her father faced her squarely. "That man's coming here to the Congo. You are right, child, he is the personification of evil. He was driven from his own country by his native subjects who revolted against his inhuman treatment of them. Scandal after scandal followed his trail through all the capitals of Europe."

"Yes; but what is he doing here?" persisted the girl.

"That's the damnable part of it," answered VanGelder. "For political reasons Sarput is a figure of some importance to England. At some future time they might have need of him. It is their policy to humor him. When he was virtually driven from Europe by popular demand, England arranged with our Colonial Office to cede him a large tract of land here in the Congo.

"He intends to bring a thousand of his native subjects here, build a palace and set up a miniature kingdom in the heart of the Congo. He is to have complete sovereignty over it." The Commissioner paused, paced the width of his office a few times, then continued heavily. "From what little I know of the man, from my personal observation of him, I fear that his coming means trouble—trouble for all of us."

CHAPTER V

DARK TIDINGS

THREE DAYS AFTER Sarput and his entourage had vanished into the south, the rains commenced. The jungle and its inhabitants returned to their normal life. For many moons Ka-Zar was carefree and happy as he roamed the forest depths with Zar. Chaka and his tribe of great apes passed peacefully through on their way to new feeding grounds. Trajah, leading his herd of great gray beasts on one of their long, regular pilgrimages, lingered long enough for a delightful visit with his two legged friend.

And then, one day, Ka-Zar felt again a vague uneasiness. He tried in vain to shrug it off. He thought, at first that it might be the monotony of the rains that depressed him. Every day, once in the morning and once in the afternoon, with unfailing regularity, the deluge descended. Without warning the skies would open up and a veritable wall of water would pound down upon the forest. Any living creature, unfortunate enough to be caught without shelter, was instantly half drowned and reduced to sodden misery. Then, as though a gigantic spigot had been turned off, the downfall would cease as abruptly as it had started and the torrid sun would turn the jungle into a vast, steaming miasma.

At last the long rainy season was over and the blazing sun alone held full sway over the Congo. But Ka-Zar's uneasiness did not leave him and soon he discovered its cause. In ever increasing numbers, beasts were drifting in from the west, as though to seek refuge in his vicinity. They came at first singly and in pairs, then in groups and at last in vast herds.

Ka-Zar lost his interest in hunting and fishing, lay for long hours in front of Zar's lair and stared into the west. And sometimes at night he saw a dull, reddish glow in the heavens there, lighting up a distant volcanic peak.

He conceived and rejected many fantastic ideas as to it cause. It was a long time before he thought of Sarput and wondered whether that evil trespasser had returned. But once the possibility had occurred to him, the more he became convinced that that was the explanation for the vague unrest that had gripped the jungle.

Ka-Zar had never explored the full length and breadth of the vast heritage his father had left him. But he remembered the day when John Rand had led him to the top of a cliff overhanging the west shore of the lake and with outstretched arm, had described a huge circle around the points of the compass. He remembered that his father had included the high mountain peak in the western boundary of his dominions.

The boy David had never heard of the far-away king who, according to the white man's law, was the ruler of this vast wilderness. He accepted his father's word and trust and now as Ka-Zar, brother of the mighty lord of the jungle, he knew the grave responsibility of a rightful ruler.

He held a solemn conclave that night in the den, with Zar, his regal mate Sha, the lioness, and with their two cubs, Zoro and Sulandi, now rapidly approaching the full growth of their huge father. It was agreed that Zar and Ka-Zar should journey westward, seeking Trajah, whose herd moved slowly on the way.

Refreshed by a brief sleep, the pair set out shortly before dawn. Stopping only to make an occasional kill, or to drink deep from still pools and to sleep side by side in shady thickets by day and rocky caves at night, they traveled at a swift pace into the west. They skirted the mangrove swamp where Ka-Zar had once saved his tawny brother from the quicksands. And at sunset on the second day, they came upon the herd of elephants.

TRAJAH NEEDED NO urging to join them. Leaving Tupat, a big male, in charge of his tribe with orders to follow slowly in their wake, he took the trail with his two friends. Ka-Zar was soon ensconced upon his favorite perch, the broad back of the big gray beast.

Later that night the trio lay down in a grassy glade, twenty paces from a murmuring stream. The mountain peak loomed high and forbidding, now, against a sapphire sky studded with enormous low-hanging stars.

Ka-Zar slept lightly. It was in the first dim grayness, just before the dawn, that he awoke with a start. As his head snapped up, his companions likewise became instantly wide awake. All turned to listen.

Faint sounds drifted to them from the direction from which they had come. With a barely audible warning, Ka-Zar rose swiftly. He crossed the glade, in three long strides, then soundlessly he swung to the nearest tree. Like a darker shadow in the murky half light, he swung off towards the east, where a first faint tinge of color crept into the sky.

Trajah had left a plainly marked trail in his passing. Ka-Zar's keen ears told him that something, or someone, was cautiously following that spoor. He came to a place where a tall, dense-leaved oulangi overhung the narrow path and there, crouched on the lowest limb, he waited. His hand crept to the knife at his belt.

It was his keen sense of smell that told Ka-Zar first what to expect. So he knew no surprise when his eyes made out the ebony form of a native black, moving slowly toward him. Instead from his hidden point of vantage, he swiftly appraised this Om who came lurking on his trail.

The black was exceptionally big, exceptionally powerful. That was evident despite his stooping position as he studied the cold spoor. In one hand he clutched a long, gleaming spear.

Ka-Zar grasped the hilt of his crude dagger. Tensing his

muscles, he prepared for action.

The big black came closer, unaware of the hidden menace in the tree above him. Eyes on the ground, he stepped under the overhanging limb of the oulangi and like a plummet dropped from the skies, Ka-Zar swooped down upon him.

He landed full on the native's broad back. The black toppled forward under the sudden, crushing weight, the spear flying from his hand. Before he could recover himself, a sinewy arm slipped under his chin and jerked his head back. At the same moment, a razor-sharp blade pricked the skin above his throbbing jugular.

Despite his dire predicament, the huge black was no coward. Instantly he struggled to free himself from the death grip. His legs lashed out backwards and his spine arched. He flung himself to one side so violently that he suddenly found himself face to lace with his attacker.

He looked at the gleaming blade poised above him. Then his eyes traveled swiftly past the knife to the bronzed giant who held it. His eyeballs bulged.

"Ka-Zar!" he breathed in awe.

INSTEAD OF PLUNGING his dagger deep into the black's throat, Ka-Zar hesitated. It was the strange fact that instead of stark fear being mirrored upon the face of his helpless victim, there was instead a strange mixture of relief and worship—that caused him to stay his hand. Slowly he released his hold and stood up, still clutching the knife in readiness.

The big black climbed instantly to his knees and dropped his forehead to the ground in a gesture of reverence.

Ka-Zar drew himself up to the full of his majestic height. "Who are you?" he demanded. "And why do you follow my trail?"

Fortunately, the native had often had contact with the outposts of civilization and he could speak English.

"Ka-Zar," he breathed again. "I am your servant Wazi, chief of the Wurumba. I came seeking you, O mighty Ka-Zar."

Ka-Zar thoughtfully replaced the dagger in his loin cloth. "Rise, Wazi," he ordered. "What do you want with Ka-Zar?"

Wazi rose to his feet. With a proper mixture of pride and humility, as befitted a tribal chief before a powerful god, he picked up his spear and stood at rigid attention. "Wazi comes for aid for his people," he said simply.

Ka-Zar nodded. "Come with me. We shall join my brother and my friend and you shall tell your tale."

He started back towards the glade where he had left Zar and Trajah and silently Wazi followed. As they came into the clearing and the native saw the monstrous elephant and the huge lion waiting there, he stopped abruptly in his tracks.

"Come," said Ka-Zar impatiently. "They will not harm you."

He growled something in a low tone. Trajah waved his huge ears slowly from side to side and Zar sank down onto his haunches. As though in a daze, Wazi walked towards the waiting beasts. At Ka-Zar's command, he squatted down beside them.

"It is the evil Sarput who molests you?" asked Ka-Zar.

Wazi could not take his eyes from the two animals who, by some miracle, tolerated his presence among them. He answered without turning his head: "It is Sarput, O Ka-Zar. For years my people have lived peacefully in the shadow of M'Bele the big mountain. Now Sarput has come, bringing with him his strange brown-skinned tribe and many of the Bulangi who dwell to the south and west. Together they slay my people, torture them, hold them in slavery. Even the women and children are not spared. The very jungle beasts flee from that nest of evil, for they, too, die by the hundreds."

Ka-Zar's eyes darkened as he listened to Wazi's plaint. He stared into the west and the line of his jaw set at a hard, grim angle. Briefly he translated Wazi's words into the guttural language of the jungle so that Zar and Trajah might understand. A deep, menacing growl rumbled in Zar's throat. Trajah swayed restlessly from side to side.

Ka-Zar turned to Wazi again. "Who sends you to seek Ka-

Zar?" he asked.

"Ali," answered the chief of the Wurumba. "The brown one with the twisted back who attends the devil Sarput. He is our only friend in that place of evil."

Ka-Zar tossed back his long locks of dark hair. "We shall tarry only to drink at the stream," he answered. "Then together we shall go to see this devil." He repeated his words to Zar and Trajah.

Together they went down to the stream. The first slanting rays of the rising sun fell upon Ka-Zar's face as he knelt upon the mossy bank. He gazed down the path of golden light.

"Before many suns have come and gone," he said solemnly, "either Sarput or Ka-Zar alone will rule the wilderness."

CHAPTER VI

THE HUNT

WAZI'S HEART WAS a simple and credulous one. To him, Ka-Zar was a god. No mortal, not even Sarput and his many evil minions, could brave the wrath of a god and live. As far as Wazi was concerned, Ka-Zar had spoken—and the prayers of the harassed Wurumbas were answered.

As they resumed their journey, the black chieftain soon lost his fear of Zar and Trajah. And with the knowledge that it was the will of Ka-Zar that protected him from them, his reverence for the strange man-god grew.

As for Ka-Zar, he was burdened with a new problem. The Oman, white or black, were his sworn enemies. According to his code, Wazi's life blood should even now be spilled back there upon the trail.

But the chief had said that he and his tribe had always lived peacefully in the shadow of the mountain. Ka-Zar's brow knitted in perplexity. Perhaps, after all, these Wurumbas adhered to the jungle code and had a right to share the forest with the beasts.

There was no ready answer to the question, no precedent to help Ka-Zar make up his mind. So, for the moment he dismissed the matter and turned his attention once more to Sarput and his wrongdoings.

As they neared their destination the black chieftain took the lead. Familiar with his ground, he led his strange companions up onto a narrow, rocky plateau. They traversed this headland that jutted out into the forest and emerging from the thinning trees, came to a halt at its western edge, a sheer cliff.

The scene that greeted them widened their eyes with amazement. A clearing—the largest clearing that Ka-Zar had ever seen in the jungle land—stretched out below them. It extended from the base of the cliff on which they stood to the base of the majestic M'Bele. Ka-Zar saw with wonder that it had been created by the Oman, for the stumps of trees showed where the forest giants had fallen before the blows of their axes.

Many huts and tents, of all sizes and descriptions, dotted the encampment. And wonder of wonders, at the foot of the mountain stood such a shelter as Ka-Zar could not have visioned in a dream. Recalling the makeshift home he had occupied long years ago with his father, he could only stare and marvel. It was the Rajah Sarput's palace—a huge, rambling affair of tiered, sweeping roof; of gilded ornaments that gleamed in the sun; of broad, spacious verandahs. A high stockade enclosed the grounds about it.

There were many Oman about—Sarput's brown-skinned countrymen and the Bulangi blacks. Ka-Zar's face grew very grave as he realized the tremendous odds against him. Just how he was to drive this menace from his homeland, he did not know.

It was comforting to have his faithful allies beside him; to sense the implicit trust and faith that lived in the heart of the black chief. Wazi raised an arm and pointed off to his right.

"There, O Ka-Zar, you see the kraals of my people. Only the bravest remain in the village. The others have fled and live in hiding."

Ka-Zar followed the direction of his finger. In the distance he could make out the thatched roofs of the blacks' village.

SUDDENLY THEY ALL whirled, to stare off to the left. From that direction came a confused clamor. Men shouted; elephants trumpeted; there wag a loud, metallic clatter and the deep-throated clang of brazen gongs.

Ka-Zar scowled.

Wazi hastily, explained. "It is the hunt—I have seen it before."

"The hunt?" repeated Ka-Zar. "One stalks silently to hunt."

"Not the Rajah Sarput," answered Wazi. "His men make the noise, driving the game in mad flight through the jungle. They send the beasts across a chosen path. Then Sarput, mounted upon his largest elephant and armed with a high-powered rifle, goes to slay the animals as they flee in their panic. He does not kill for food but for the sheer lust of killing. He slays the beasts by scores—and laughs as they die, stricken down by his bullets, while he rides in safety upon his elephant. It is no hunt—it is slaughter."

He glanced towards the palace, then grasped Ka-Zar's arm. "See—there he comes now, eager for more of his cruel pleasure."

Ka-Zar saw the brown men lead an elephant, with a *howdah* mounted upon its back, up to the front of the palace. He saw the light glint from fire-sticks in the hands of others. Then the tall, resplendent figure of Sarput emerged from the building, received weapons from his followers. The elephant dropped heavily to his knees and the Rajah mounted, while his court stood in a respectful circle about him.

The clamor of the beaters sounded nearer. And now to Ka-Zar's ears came the cries of his jungle people—the shrill squealing of the wild pigs, the chattering of the monkeys, the yapping of jackals and the ear-splitting screech of a terrified leopard.

A strange, animal sound of rage rumbled in his own throat. "My brothers—the beasts," he said hoarsely. "I must save them." He whirled, growled at Zar and Trajah: "Come! We shall defy this devil-crazed Sarput!"

His face was dark with passion. He tilted his head to one side, listened for a moment to see in which direction the hapless animals were being driven. He could see the Rajah's elephant, with its master in the swaying *howdah*, leaving the enclosure that surrounded the palace. A turbaned Om sat cross-legged upon the beast's head, guiding it toward the appointed hunt.

Wazi shifted uneasily. "I was to tell my people if I found the mighty Ka-Zar," he said. "There was a signal agreed upon."

"Give it, then," snapped Ka-Zar. "Then find a place of safety and watch."

Wazi faced toward the kraals of his native village, off in the northwest. Throwing back his head, he sent the mournful, plaintive call of the gourali bird floating across the humid air. A moment later the cry came back to him, faint but clear, from one of his tribesmen.

With a single, gutteral command to his two allies, Ka-Zar sprinted back across the rocky plateau. Zar bounded after him, with Trajah lumbering along, at an awkward yet deceivingly fast pace, in their wake.

ONCE DOWN TO the level of the jungle floor, Ka-Zar swiftly took to the trees. Swinging from branch to branch, flying through the air in dizzying leaps, unerringly grasping trailing lianas and swaying branches at exactly the right moment, he traveled at break-neck pace, towards the approaching beaters.

Above a narrow, gorge-like ravine he dropped to the ground. A narrow canyon ran off from it at right angles. At this junction Ka-Zar took up his stand. Bitterly he smiled as he realized how cunningly Sarput had planned his drive. Once in the ravine the maddened beasts were unable to escape and when they emerged in mass formation at the far end, the slaughter would take place.

Unless the swirling tide of their blind rush was turned, diverted up the box canyon....

The first, fear-maddened van of fleeing beasts were upon him. They saw the bronzed giant standing before them, arms upraised commandingly. They slid along on their haunches in an effort to stop but like an irresistible avalanche the press behind them swept them forward.

"Turn!" bellowed Ka-Zar. "Into the west, my brothers. Go silently—make no cry. Turn into the canyon. Ka-Zar commands it."

Ten feet from the mouth of the spur, the line wavered. The walls of the ravine rumbled to the pounding of many hooves.

Beads of sweat popped out on Ka-Zar's brow. If he failed to divert that onrushing wave he would be ground to dust beneath a thousand grinding hooves.

"Turn!" he bellowed again. "It is I—Ka-Zar who speaks—Ka-Zar, brother of the lion."

His commanding figure more than his words penetrated into the fear lashed brains of the leaders of the pack. First one, then another turned up the canyon and the horde behind them followed blindly in their wake.

The avalanche was diverted and with a grateful sigh Ka-Zar expelled the air from his lungs. A moment later Zar and Trajah came up to stand beside him. He turned to them with shining eyes. "Now let us give this Sarput bigger game to follow!"

Flinging back his tossing mane of black hair, he unleashed the mighty roar of the lion. His loud defiance rang out over the jungle, setting the very leaves a-tremble on the great trees. And before the rumbling bass note had died away, it was echoed by the deeper roar of Zar and the booming trumpet of the huge Trajah.

The triple cry of defiance was followed by a sudden hush. Then a distant crashing told Ka-Zar that Sarput had turned his elephant in their direction and was heading for this new and more intriguing quarry.

Ka-Zar lingered only to make certain that the Rajah and his elephant were the nearest to him and that they would soon be far in advance of the slower-moving beaters. Then he turned and headed back towards the plateau, stopping only now and then to send the cry of the lion floating back to the following hunter.

Zar and Trajah did likewise. It was an old game in the jungle and they understood that Ka-Zar was leading Sarput in one direction, while the fleeing animals made good their escape in another.

CLEVERLY KA-ZAR LED his pursuer up the gradual slope of the plateau. The trio emerged from the thinner fringe of trees and took up their stand on the headland above the cliff. There they waited, listening to the sounds made by the approaching elephant.

Trajah tossed his massive head and his little eyes gleamed. Zar crouched, his tail twitching, his fangs baring every few moments for a low snarl. Ka-Zar stood erect, his nostrils flared a trifle, every nerve and muscle tense.

The branches of the nearest trees swayed and a gray form pushed out into the open. At the sight of the fantastic trio, silhouetted against the blazing sky, the *mahout* on the elephant's head squealed and jabbed frantically at the beast's ear with a hooked stick. Sarput shouted hoarsely, braced himself in the swaying *howdah* and swung up his high-powered rifle. His eyes glittered malevolently and his teeth showed beneath his beard.

But the Rajah's elephant was suddenly petrified with fear. He saw another animal like himself—only so enormous that it dwarfed him by comparison. He saw a great cat, bigger than the tiger that was his mortal enemy back in the far-off Indian jungle. When the *mahout's anke* ripped his ear, instead of turning to retreat, he reared high, throwing the man in the *howdah* off balance.

The rifle exploded in Sarput's hand as he grasped at the edge of the *howdah* to steady himself. A splatter of leaves flew from the nearest tree as the bullet tore through the foliage. And with the crash of the hated fire-stick ringing in his ears, Zar went berserk.

With a frenzied roar, he charged. With one mighty bound he landed high on the elephant's shoulder. His sharp talons dug deep into the tough gray hide and the elephant went mad with terror. He trumpeted shrilly as Trajah, with ears outspread and trunk high, joined the charge.

Sarput, shouting hoarsely at his unheeding *mahout*, whipped up his rifle again, aiming its muzzle full at the snarling lion.

But before he could fire, Trajah's trunk stretched out, wrapped about Sarput's middle and tore him from the *howdah*. Little red fires gleamed now in Trajah's eyes. His great tusks flashed in the sun and a lather of foam gathered at the corners of his pendulous mouth. Ka-Zar bounded forward as Trajah raised the Rajah high above his head.

It was Sarput's turn, now, to know a mortal fear. His legs and arms thrashed wildly. His dark face twisted into a mask of stark fear. For Trajah's intention was obvious—to fling him to the ground and crash out his brains against the rocks. Sarput screamed, begged wildly for mercy from the gods he had always defied.

"Stay!" Ka-Zar shouted to Trajah. "The evil one is mine to slay! Give him to me!"

Trajah hesitated, then reluctantly lowered his captive to the ground. Released from the elephant's trunk, Sarput was instantly seized by fingers of steel.

The rifle, which he had in continued to grip, was wrenched from his hand as though he were a child. Ka-Zar raised it, shattered it to matchwood and twisted metal across a rock.

Zar dropped from the flank of the Indian elephant and the beast, taking advantage of the moment, wheeled and lumbered off down the plateau. He crashed headlong into trees, blundered through thickets of thorn and nets of interlacing vines, while the *mahout* clung fearfully to his perch and proclaimed the rout with continuous shrieks and wails.

CHAPTER VII

THE KNIFE THAT FAILED

ZAR AND TRAJAH, holding their justifiable wrath in leash with an effort, watched Ka-Zar as he confronted their captive. The Rajah Sarput, who delighted in putting others to torture and to death, now experienced for the first time in his life, the torments that he had meted out to his helpless victims. Unarmed and alone, he was in the midst of a fantastic nightmare. A maddened elephant, an enormous lion with slavering jaws, a savage bronzed giant hemmed him in.

He stared at Ka-Zar dazedly and muttered hoarsely: "Who are you?"

Ka-Zar looked down at him from his majestic height and answered arrogantly: "I am Ka-Zar, brother of Zar the lion, lord of the jungle."

Sarput's bewildered brain reeled. He had heard of this legendary jungle God. Now he stood face to face with him. All the fanciful tales that he had heard were true. For with his own eyes and ears he had seen the lion and the elephant obey this strange man-god's command.

He searched Ka-Zar's stern face, tried to read the unfathomable depths of the amber eyes that steadily held his own. And with a sinking heart he realized that those eyes were like those of any other jungle beast. They were hard, implacable and there was no mercy in them.

Slowly Ka-Zar drew the knife from his belt. "Evil one," he said slowly, "you have molested my people. You have killed, not for food but for pleasure. And for that you shall die."

Zar heard the noise made by the Rajah's beaters as they came hurrying up the plateau. He growled a warning. But Ka-Zar, with the evil Om who had brought such misery to the jungle standing before him, did not heed.

Sarput, however, in his desperate need, heard his followers as they rapidly approached. His face which had turned ashen gray at the first sight of the unholy trio, gradually regained a little color. Frantically playing for time, he managed to twist his thin lips into a sneer.

"I have heard of you, Ka-Zar. And now I see what you are. A mad savage who prowls the jungle like any beast. Bah!"

A dull tide of crimson swept up Ka-Zar's bronzed cheeks. The tone of Sarput's voice more than the words was an unbearable insult.

"If Sarput is a man, Ka-Zar is glad that he may call the lion 'brother,'" he answered proudly. "The jungle knew peace before your coming—and soon the jungle shall know peace once more."

Slowly he raised the glittering blade.

But before he could strike, the Rajah's beaters burst through the fringe of trees. They halted a split second in amazement.

Without taking his eyes from the knife, Sarput shouted a volley of commands over his shoulder. And instantly the sun gleamed upon a score of leveled rifles.

Zar and Trajah turned to face the deadly fire-sticks. Ka-Zar acted instinctively, his motions swift as the lightning. With one hand he snatched the Rajah to him. The knife blade descended, quivered over the flesh at the back of Sarput's neck.

"If the fire-sticks speak—you die," he hissed in Sarput's ear. "Warn your people."

THE SHARP POINT of the knife pricked the skin and a single drop of blood oozed forth. A violent shudder wracked the Rajah's body from turban to toe. Hastily he translated Ka-Zar's words to the ring of beaters. They held their fire.

Ka-Zar knew a swift pang of regret that he had not allowed Trajah to put an end to the evil creature in his grasp. His desire to slay the transgressor with his own hand, had led to his undoing.

Now it was a stalemate. For he knew that the tableau could not hold long. Nerves were strained to the breaking point. Someone would make a false move—and disaster would follow. He must take advantage of the precious second allowed him.

His first thought was for his friends. They must not die, before the terrible fire-sticks of the Oman.

"Tell your people to throw their firesticks to the ground," he ordered, emphasizing the words with another warning prick of the dagger. "The lion and the elephant depart unharmed."

Reluctantly Sarput relayed his command. The beaters hesitated then one by one dropped their weapons. Ka-Zar growled to Zar and Trajah. "Go!"

They looked at him uncertainly. They were plainly unwilling to desert him then.

But Ka-Zar was insistent. "Go!" he repeated.

Obediently the two beasts moved off. And as they disappeared into the fringe of trees, high overhead a new spectator came to view the scene. Pindar the eagle, spiralling down on an enormous spread of wing, circled through the still air and with big keen eyes took in every detail of the tableau below him.

With the knowledge that his two allies were safe, a hundred conflicting thoughts came to claim Ka-Zar's brain. That he might escape with his own life was out of the question. With the first move that he made, the beaters would snatch up their rifles and he would be riddled by a score of bullets.

Grimly he made up his mind. If he must die, he would at least take this evil creature Sarput with him. The Om would no longer hold a reign of terror over the wilderness. Zar would rule the forest wisely and justly.

To come to a decision was to act. Ka-Zar jerked his dagger up a scant six inches, then drove it in a flashing arc toward a point midway between Sarput's shoulder blades.

It struck with terrific force—snapped!

Surprised, shocked, Ka-Zar stared with unbelieving eyes at the broken blade that remained clutched in his fist. The beaters, too, were stunned to immobility—unable to follow the swift turn of events. Sarput whirled and snatched out a short fire-stick that had been hidden in the folds of the cloth about his waist.

Now that the tables were turned, he was once more the satanic master. His bearded face was alight with an unholy joy. His beady eyes were mocking and his nostrils quivered with anticipatory pleasure.

"So you would defy the Rajah Sarput, eh, Ka-Zar?" he asked with an evil chuckle. "Well, we shall soon see whether you are a god—or just another mortal whose blood will run red from his veins."

HE RAISED HIS revolver, bringing its muzzle up to aim squarely at Ka-Zar's broad chest. And Ka-Zar, with the bitter knowledge that he would fail his jungle people even in death, prepared to die as arrogantly and proudly as he had lived. He drew himself up to his full height held his majestic head high and stared with level eyes at his executioner.

Sarput's finger tightened very slowly on the trigger. It was not every day that the fates sent him such lordly game and he was enjoying the moment to the full.

Then, suddenly, shouts rose from the ring of watching beaters. There was a mighty rush of air and a feathered fury dropped like a bolt from the blue. With wing-tips back, Pindar the eagle swooped down to the plateau.

Steel-hooked talons raked across Sarput's face. Blood spurted in their wake, dripping down into the Rajah's eyes and blinding him. He howled with pain as Ka-Zar quick to seize his reprieve, sprinted for the edge of the cliff.

Pandemonium broke out behind him. The beaters pounced upon their rifles and fired wildly. The air was shattered with hoarse shouts and the roar of many guns. Bullets whined through the air about Ka-Zar's head.

A vicious, leaden wasp stung him in the shoulder. He stumbled, regained his balance, sprinted forward a few more feet, then dropped over the sheer edge of the cliff. Sliding, falling, grasping at outcropping ledges he plunged down the face of the precipice. Rocks and gravel rasped the skin from his naked body in his rocketing descent. He reached the bottom at last on all fours. Breathless, panting, he sprang to his feet.

CHAPTER VIII

DAUGHTER OF THE JUNGLE

WITH THE TRIUMPHANT scream of Pindar ringing loud in his ears, high above the crack of the rifles, Ka-Zar plunged swiftly into the forest. For the first time in his life he was shamed that when he had meant to kill his blow had failed.

But more than shamed, he was puzzled, disturbed. Never before had his knife failed him; never before had anything stood up before the sweep of the hungry, steel blade.

The evil one called Sarput, had not only taken the thrust of the knife but the blade itself had snapped at the hilt. Ka-Zar had no remotest knowledge of mail or armor. It was entirely beyond his imagination that beneath his outer garments Sarput wore the finest shirt of link mail that money could buy.

And not knowing, Ka-Zar attributed strange powers of resistance to the dark-faced Om with the evil eyes. The adventure of the past few minutes served to increase his respect for the intruder and by the same token his determination to rid the jungle of him.

So busy was his mind with the new and difficult problems that confronted him that he was entirely unaware that a bullet had gouged a deep furrow across his left shoulder. Only when Zar paced up to him and with a growl, a sniff and a toss of his regal head indicated the wound, did he feel the pain in his shoulder.

He knelt swiftly and Zar tended the ugly gash with his tongue.

A moment later the jungle wall opened before the thrust of Trajah's broad shoulders. By his side strode Wazi, his ebon skin glistening in the sun, his eyes bright and intense in the black mask of his face. For a moment, mute with wonder, he watched Zar as the latter licked Ka-Zar's wound. To him, he was witnessing a miracle—a special sign of the kinship that existed between Ka-Zar and the beasts. Reverently he dropped to his knees and lowered his forehead to the ground three times.

It was the final, ultimate gesture of allegiance and forever after Wazi was to walk in the shadow of Ka-Zar.

Still kneeling, Ka-Zar turned to Trajah. A series of guttural noises rolled off his lips. "If it had not been for Pindar, Ka-Zar would have died before the fire-sticks of the Oman," he said. "How fared Pindar of the mighty spread of wing?"

Trajah flapped his ears, coiled and uncoiled his trunk. "Trajah saw from the edge of the clearing. Pindar flew high, leaving only a few feathers behind him."

Ka-Zar grunted his satisfaction. He acknowledged his debt to the eagle and promised himself that some day he would repay it. Then he turned to Wazi. "In truth," he said, "the two-legged white devil is evil. He has many followers, with many fire-sticks."

Wazi drew himself up to his full height. He was but an inch shorter than Ka-Zar and almost as superbly muscled. Now with a simple gesture of dignity he beat his massive fist against his ebon breast. "Wazi has many followers, also," he said. "They have no fire-sticks but they are brave. They will go where Wazi orders. If Ka-Zar will lead us we will drive the Oman from the jungle."

KA-ZAR LISTENED TO his words, pondered them for a long time in silence. Never before had he made an alliance with man, black or white. And now he hesitated to commit himself. All his past relations with the Oman had taught him to mistrust them. Yet with each passing moment it became increasingly clear to him that something had to be done. That he had to act and act swiftly before the evil one had plundered the domain he ruled.

He knew that with the exception of N'Jaga and the leopard tribe, he could count on the jungle beasts to aid him. But he dreaded to think of the frightful toll that would be exacted if he led his subjects boldly against the Oman.

Their fire-sticks killed from a distance. Therein lay their terrible advantage. For Zar or Trajah or Chaka to dispose of an enemy they must first come to grips with him. True, he, Ka-Zar, was deadly with bow or spear. But in the guerilla warfare he would be one against many.

All these things passed through his mind as he pondered the offer that Wazi had made. Unable to come to any decision himself, he propounded his problem to Zar and Trajah and asked them, from their store of wisdom, to decide for him.

Trajah was the first to reply. Swinging his massive head from side to side, he spoke. "Many times in my pilgrimages had Trajah observed the comings and goings of Wazi and his black brothers. They are indeed brave and their skill with the bow and spear is almost equal to yours, O Ka-Zar. If they will listen when Ka-Zar speaks, if they will do as Ka-Zar orders, if they will follow where Ka-Zar leads, the bargain is well made."

Ka-Zar nodded thoughtfully and turned to Zar for his opinion. With a short, peremptory growl the lion assured him that he agreed with what the elephant had said.

Ka-Zar tugged affectionately at the lion's mane; ran a hard palm down the length of Trajah's trunk. After all, the problem that confronted him was not his alone. The beasts of the jungle were concerned as much as he and he was pleased that two of the most mighty beasts had joined him in making the decision.

With a smile on his lips he turned to Wazi. "The animals have spoken and Ka-Zar heeds their words. Till the evil Om and his followers are slain or driven from the jungle, Ka-Zar will lead Wazi and his brothers against them."

Wazi beat his chest with both fists to express his joy, then dropping lowered his brow to the dust before the man he worshipped as jungle god.

"Rise, O Wazi," commanded Ka-Zar. "Lead us to where your followers await you so that we may see them."

Wazi leaped to his feet with alacrity and showing his filed teeth in a broad grin, started off on a long, easy stride into the northwest. Zar followed next, then Trajah and lastly came Ka-Zar bringing up the rear.

A burnished sun of molten metal was slowly sinking behind the rim of the forest when Wazi and the strange procession he led broke clear of the jungle wall into the open glade that sheltered the thatched roofed kraals of the Wurumba.

The low buildings of the village faced inward onto a rough quadrangle. Here the ground had been cleared of the rank undergrowth and had been tilled after a fashion. Even now a dozen native women, naked save for a scanty cloth around their loins, could be seen working in the open square with crude, blunt implements.

BEFORE EACH RUDE shelter a fire burned and thin spirals of smoke curled lazily upward on the still evening air. Over the fires bent old crones stirring the cook pots against the return of their warrior men.

Wild and primitive as the scene and setting were, this was the closest Ka-Zar had ever come to civilization. Never before had he seen so many Oman at one time. Eagerly, wide-eyed, he took in the strange sights, smells and sounds about him.

Before him on the trail, Zar growled his instinctive mistrust of the black Oman. Trajah, likewise, showed his primeval restlessness in the presence of man by the constant weaving of his trunk.

Ka-Zar spoke to them briefly, reassured them. And though he had implicit faith in Wazi, he nevertheless clutched his long spear a little tighter.

They had covered half the distance between the edge of the jungle and the nearest kraal before their coming was discovered. Then on a sudden a single, shrill cry went up from the village.

It was a girl's voice, eager, exultant, joyful. Immediately echoing it a hundred voices took up the cry in a wild paen of rejoicing.

As if by magic the village became a confused scene of movement and excitement. Men, women and children ran pell-mell from the kraals. The crones by the fires and the workers in the field threw down their implements and joined in the cry of welcome. At the first rising note of the tumult, Zar pulled up short in his tracks. A snarl rumbled in his throat.

Ka-Zar stepped forward and placing his hand on the lion's shaggy head, took his place at the head of the trail by Wazi's side. Zar's growl subsided and thus they proceeded, with the cries of the blacks growing louder in their ears.

"The Wurumba tribe cries its welcome," said Wazi, throwing out his chest with pride.

"It is good," answered Ka-Zar.

They had proceeded but a few feet further when suddenly from the milling throng of blacks, still within the quadrangle, a lithe figure darted forward. It was a girl and she ran with the grace and fleetness of the antelope, making straight for Ka-Zar and his allies. A few feet before them she flung herself to the ground, touching her forehead to Ka-Zar's feet.

Ka-Zar looked down at her lithe back and her well-formed head. Save for the vague, almost forgotten memories of his mother, he had no knowledge of women. This was the first one—black or white—that he had seen in twenty years. But with sure instinct he recognized in the girl at his feet, the female of the species Om—the two legged tribe of man.

He well understood her gesture of allegiance. He had accepted the same token as a matter of course from Wazi. But now, somehow, for some inexplicable reason, he felt uncomfortable that the girl should kneel before him. He looked to Wazi for help.

"My sister, Wamba," the black announced proudly.

"Rise, Wamba," said Ka-Zar. "Ka-Zar comes not in anger nor for gifts. He comes to help you and your people drive out the evil Om."

THE GIRL ROSE slowly to her feet. With a splendid unconcern she ignored the tawny Zar and the towering Trajah.

Unafraid, unashamed in the proud beauty of her nakedness she confronted Ka-Zar. For a long moment her soft black eyes bore deeply into the amber ones of the bronzed giant before her.

Ka-Zar stirred, restlessly before her ardent gaze. Strange, unaccustomed thoughts ran through his mind. The girl was beautiful, he told himself—beautiful like some wild, untamed gazelle. She moved him strangely.

And then, as if sensing his thoughts, Wamba flashed him a brilliant smile of ivory teeth, turned on her heel and fled back to the village.

Followed by his beasts, Ka-Zar was received in the village as the protecting god of the jungle. Food and drink were set before him and Wazi's proud warriors prostrated themselves before him, bringing as gifts their best and most trusted weapons.

Since the coming of Sarput some six months before the village had been sore pressed. One catastrophe after another had befallen it. Dozens of their bravest men had died before the fire-sticks of the intruders; dozens of their women had been carried off to slavery and worse.

Wazi had led his men bravely and wisely but against the combined forces of Sarput and the rival tribe of Bulangi he had been powerless. Now, with the coming of Ka-Zar new hope animated the breasts of the Wurumba; they were stirred by a new, fierce determination to drive the invading hordes from the jungle.

In their simple, superstitious minds, now that they had formed an alliance with the bronzed god Ka-Zar, they could not fail.

It was late before the feasting was over. And it was not until the moon had risen that Ka-Zar and his beasts held a council of war with Wazi and the wizard of the tribe.

And while the council was in session, a few miles distant in the Rajah's palace, another council was in progress.

CHAPTER IX

THE MAN WITH THE TWISTED BACK

THE RAJAH SARPUT was evil of temper by nature. He made a cult of cruelty. No devilish refinement of the torture and the wrack was beyond his cunning ingenuity.

On this particular night he out-did himself. To his perverted mind, his acts of depravity were an outlet for his rage over the ignominious outcome of his encounter with Ka-Zar.

At the expenditure of only God knows how much money, blood, sweat, life and limb his men—slaves is the better word— had hewn a large clearing in the virgin jungle. There they had erected for him a palace that rivaled in splendor any that had ever graced the shores of the Ganges in India.

It had turrets, it had minarettes. It had broad windows, lawns, sparkling streams cascading from pool to pool in exotic gardens. It had ceilinged rooms, broad stairways hewn from native stone. And it had dungeons deep and foul.

The palace of the Rajah was an expression of all the builders' arts. In its barbaric splendor it glittered like an evil jewel in the heart of the steaming Congo. And hanging over it, forbidding, threatening, was the jagged cone of M'Bele the volcano.

On the night of the coming of Ka-Zar, even as the lion-man and Wazi were laying down the plans of their campaign, the halls and the dungeons of Sarput's stronghold echoed and re-echoed to screams of anguish as the Rajah sated his frustrated lust on his helpless slaves.

He used the whip until his arm failed him. He used thumb-screw and wrack until even he sickened of the sport. And then, sated at last for the moment, he feasted and over his wine made plans for the morrow.

If truth were known, it was the incipient fear in his heart that fed his fires of lust. Gingerly he touched at the deep gashes in his face made by Pindar the eagle. Once more in his mind he felt the prick of the bronzed giant's knife at his jugular. If Ka-Zar had struck then, instead of later at his back, protected by the link mail, he would now be carrion for the vultures, his bones would already have been picked clean.

He shuddered at the thought and his lips curled back from his teeth. And as he lolled there at his table, planning how he might destroy this mad giant who contested his rule, there was a marked similarity between him and N'Jaga the leopard.

Never before had man so brazenly affronted him. Sarput determined that the measure of his punishment should be in keeping with the magnitude of his crime.

For a long time he considered all the myths and superstitions he had heard concerning the jungle giant. That Ka-Zar had strange powers; that he commanded the jungle beasts and that they obeyed him, was plain. But in his fear of a rifle or automatic, he showed that he was human.

Sarput smiled evilly. In his good time he would devise a far more interesting death for the jungle god than a bullet. More interesting for him—the Rajah.

But until that happy day dawned, he had to proclaim his sway over the jungle and all the living things in it, by some fitting spectacle. His day's sport had been ruined. He would have better sport on the morrow.

HE CLAPPED HIS hands and Ali the hunchback attended him. He spoke slowly, thoughtfully for a few minutes, considering each detail of the thing he planned. Then he dismissed the hunchback with a flick of his whip. "By the hump of your crooked back see that the arrangements are made," he said. "Let there be no slip, lest you, yourself, serve me for my sport."

Ali bowed and scraped his deformed body out of the room.

And if Sarput had seen the light in his eyes when the door closed behind him, he would have thought less of Ka-Zar and more of his own household.

Though the hour was late, in Wazi's kraal, no plan, either for good or evil, had been formulated. Ka-Zar still did not know how, even with the help of his new allies, he was to accomplish his purpose of driving Sarput and his minions from the jungle.

It was decided that now that Ka-Zar had come to aid them, the Wurumbas who had fled into the forest would surely return to the village by the morrow. In the meantime, Ka-Zar would refresh himself with sleep and then, after judging the numbers and strength of his black followers, try again to formulate some ingenious plan for action.

Wazi offered the use of his kraal to Ka-Zar and Zar. But they preferred the open jungle to either the village or the confining walls of the huts. Wazi walked out with them, under the gleaming stars. With Trajah, who had been waiting patiently outside the council kraal, they walked slowly through the sleeping village.

They had almost reached the encroaching fringe of the forest, when Ka-Zar and the beasts stopped abruptly in their tracks. They raised their heads and sniffed at the damp night air. A moment later, Wazi, too, heard faint sounds and scented an alien odor.

"Someone comes," he whispered....

Ka-Zar nodded. "From the direction of the Rajah Sarput's lair," he added darkly.

Grasping their weapons, with Zar stalking beside them and Trajah at their heels, they glided silently forward toward the trees.

The sounds came closer. They waited, tense. Ka-Zar strained his keen ears and knitted his brows as he listened. Then at last he growled something, low. Zar and Trajah instantly relaxed.

"It is but one who comes," Ka-Zar told Wazi. "One who is

crippled."

The black chief let his spear butt drop to the ground. "Ali of the twisted back," he answered. "He comes in friendship."

A few moments later the squat, misshapen form of the Rajah Sarput's attendant materialized from the forest. Several times he glanced back uneasily over his shoulder. Then he turned, limped forward a few paces and stopped abruptly.

It was his first sight of Ka-Zar and the two great beasts. In the silver rays of the moon his face was a study in awe and terror. He half turned around as though to flee.

WAZI STEPPED FORWARD. "Do not fear, Ali," he called out. "It is the all-powerful god Ka-Zar and his brothers. They will not harm you."

As the personal attendant of the Rajah, Ali had visited the capitols of the world with his master. He understood and could speak many languages, including the English in which Wazi addressed him.

At the familiar voice of the Wurumba chief and his reassuring words, he hesitated.

"Come forward, unhappy one," commanded Ka-Zar.

Slowly, still fearful, Ali came out several paces into the open. Then touching his breast and his forehead, he made a low obeisance before the strange, bronzed giant.

Again Ka-Zar felt the alien emotion of pity that he had first known when he had saved the life of this miserable wretch. "You have nothing to fear from Ka-Zar," he said quietly. "It was my arrow that stayed Sarput's whip, that day on the trail."

Ali had never forgotten that miraculous incident—the only time in his unhappy life that another hand had been raised in his behalf. His dark eyes melted into soft pools of gratitude and he flung his misshapen body to the ground before Ka-Zar.

Ka-Zar was annoyed with himself for the emotion that he felt in his heart. "Rise, foolish one," he said harshly. "Find the use of your tongue. What brings you here?"

Slowly, awkwardly, the hunchback rose to his feet. "I came to warn Wazi," he answered. "My master plans more deviltry."

Ka-Zar's face darkened; his eyes glowed. "What now?"

With another uneasy glance over his shoulder in the direction of the distant palace, Ali hastily explained. "The Rajah has just learned that his Bulangi black men are eaters of men. In the morning, five of his captured Wurumbas will be slain, to be eaten by their enemies the Bulangi. The Rajah will take keen delight in watching this terrible feast."

Ka-Zar was appalled. The taking of life and the eating of flesh were matters of course, of necessity. But that any creature would devour one of its own species was unthinkable—monstrous!

A low, stifled wail of anguish broke from the lips of the Wurumba chief. Tales had been passed on by his great-grandfather to his grandfather—by his grandfather to his father—of Wurumbas slain by cannibal tribes and eaten by their enemies. But to be slain in fair fight was one thing—to be slaughtered like pigs for a feast, was another. He bowed his head and beat upon his broad chest.

Ka-Zar drew himself stiffly erect and squared his mighty shoulders. "This must not happen—this *shall* not happen," he pronounced. "The five Wurumbas—where are they?"

Swiftly Ali explained. They were in a cell of the dungeon below Sarput's palace. Three Bulangi warriors guarded them. Others were posted about the building and at each gate in the high palisade that surrounded the grounds was yet another Bulangi, armed with a rifle.

KA-ZAR LOOKED UP at the deep blue dome of the heavens, at the rising moon which already bathed forest and clearing with a mellow light. Far off on the horizon hung a low bank of clouds.

"Return to the palace," he told Ali. "Soon I shall come. Once in the grounds, I shall give the low call of the gourali bird. Thus." He made a low, plaintive call. "When you hear this, be prepared to lead me down into the dungeon."

The twisted form of the hunchback trembled. He bowed his head. "I will do what I can," he murmured. "But if my master learns that I have betrayed him, I will die a hundred deaths, each more dreadful than the last."

Ka-Zar surveyed him gravely. "From what Ka-Zar saw on the trail, Ali has already endured many deaths. One more—a hundred more..." He shrugged.

Ali pulled himself together, made a last obeisance and turning, limped off into the forest. Ka-Zar turned to Wazi.

"The weapons which your people have given me are still in your kraal. Go swiftly and bring me back a knife."

Wazi hesitated. "For some reason which I do not understand, a knife is useless against the devil Sarput," he said. "I was watching from a place of safety and I saw the dagger break in Ka-Zar's hand."

"Bring the knife," repeated Ka-Zar sternly. "It is for another purpose."

Despite the fact that to him Ka-Zar was a god, Wazi instinctively objected. Then at Ka-Zar's insistence he went reluctantly back for the requested weapon.

While he was gone Ka-Zar explained the whole matter to Zar and Trajah. Though they wished to join him he refused their aid. If the rescue of the doomed Wurumbas was to be effected, it would have to be done silently and with great stealth. The approach of such a huge beast as Trajah would instantly arouse the encampment. And within the confines of walls, Zar would soon be hopelessly confused and trapped.

Only one detail of the task before him did Ka-Zar prepare for—the rest must be left to Ali and to chance. Throwing back his head, he sent a shrill cry echoing across the jungle.

Somewhere in the distance, the topmost branches of a huge oulangi stirred. A wizened little face with bright, beady eyes peeped out through the foliage.

A few minutes later, the same wrinkled visage looked out from a tree at the fringe of the clearing. Ka-Zar glanced up.

"Come down, silly one," he called. "It is Ka-Zar, brother of Zar the mighty, who has summoned you."

A series of squeaks came from the branches. Then the leaves rustled and a little monkey with an incredibly long tail dropped to the ground. Looking fearfully at the crouching lion and the elephant, he moved reluctantly forward.

Ka-Zar stretched forth a muscular arm. "Come," he repeated. "Ka-Zar will not harm you. Climb onto my shoulder, as your cousin Nono has done many times before."

Chattering, the monkey bounded forward, climbed Ka-Zar's arm and squatted on his shoulder. One tiny hand clutched at his long hair and a long, prehensile tail wrapped about the back of his neck.

When Wazi returned with a long, wide-blade dagger, Ka-Zar used it to slash a great length of tough jungle vine from where it hung in festoons from a broad-spreading baobab. Coiling it over one arm, he bade the Wurumba chief and his two friends to have faith and wait. Then with the monkey clinging tightly to his neck, he set off toward the distant palace.

CHAPTER X

ESCAPE

AS HE TRAVELED, the bank of clouds that had been on the horizon spread and crept up on the moon. By the time that Ka-Zar came to the edge of the clearing that the Rajah's men had hewn from the heart of the forest, the first gauzy titters of cloud drifted across the face of the silvery globe. Shadows flitted across the earth.

Warning the monkey to silence, Ka-Zar surveyed the strange city that had mushroomed in the wilderness. In the palace at the foot of the mountain, a light still glowed. The rest of the encampment was dark and still with the profound stillness of slumber.

Cautiously he made his way between the silent huts. Each time the moon was blotted out he sped forward on noiseless feet. Each time the moonlight flooded the clearing, he merged into the purple shadows cast by the nearest shelter.

It had been his intention to have the monkey scale the palace stockade, carrying one end of the tough liana with him. Once inside, the little beast would fasten his end of the vine securely to something so that Ka-Zar in turn might climb over the wall.

Now as he neared the palace, he saw that his plan was impossible. Beside the sentries at the gates, other Bulangi warriors stalked up and down outside the palisade. Swiftly Ka-Zar changed his plans. The gates themselves were much lower than the wall. If he could dispose of the guard at one, he could easily get over the obstacle without assistance.

He chose the center of the northern side for his attack. A black, with a rifle hung negligently in the crook of his arm, leaned against the portal there. Another, armed with a spear, was walking in the opposite direction on his beat.

The clouds gave Ka-Zar his opportunity. For a full two minutes they obscured the moon and he moved swiftly but sure-footedly through the blackness. He came up against the wooden stockade at a point between the two Bulangis and he knew that both their backs were turned to him at the time. With another faint, sibilant warning to the monkey on his shoulder, he clutched his knife and edged stealthily toward the gate.

The passing cloud thinned to vapor. In the ensuing half-light, the naked ebony back of the warrior loomed up suddenly before Ka-Zar's eyes. Ka-Zar crouched for a spring and a faint rustle of the grass betrayed him.

The black jerked erect. But before he could turn, a huge, powerful body struck him with terrific force from the rear. An arm of steel slid around under his chin and snapped his head back, shutting off his breath. A hand, clutching a gleaming blade, flashed over his shoulder and descended in a swift arc.

The razor sharp point of the dagger buried itself to the hilt at the base of the Bulangi's throat.

The monkey clung to his master's neck in terror but did not make a sound. Ka-Zar withdrew the blade and warm blood spurted in its wake. The body of the guard went limp in his arms as the life poured from it. He eased it to the ground and straightened up.

THE RIFLE THAT had fallen from the black's hand, Ka-Zar ignored. He would not have known how to use it. And besides, fire-sticks made a tremendous noise and for this night's work it would be folly to make a sound.

The kill had been accomplished in utter silence. Ka-Zar fought back the impulse to place a foot upon his slain victim and send the roaring challenge of the lion floating across the sleeping encampment. Instead, he swung up onto the gate, slid like a shadow over it and dropped noiselessly to the ground inside. Then crouching low, he voiced the low, plaintive call of the gourali.

A moment later the hunchback appeared to join him. He was trembling in a very ague of fear and only the whole-souled gratitude that he felt for this strange protector had made him keep his trust.

"The Rajah is wakeful—he does not retire to sleep," he whispered uneasily.

"Lead me to the dungeon then, quickly," said Ka-Zar.

Ali set off at once as fast as his spindly legs could carry him. In the dimness he looked like a huge, grotesque crab as he scuttled along. He made directly for the nearest side of the palace. Groping along the bottom of the wall, he stopped abruptly.

"Here," he whispered over his shoulder. "This window is near the ceiling of the cell you want. The door of it, leading to the dungeon proper inside, is solid and barred, with guards before it."

Ka-Zar stooped over. Overhead the moon showed its face briefly, illumined for a moment a square aperture cut into the base of the wall and blocked by two stout metal bars that divided the opening from top to bottom. A breath of hot, foetid air wafted from the window.

Ka-Zar's keen nostrils could tell him as much as his eyes. He had never seen a dungeon before, but the oppressive odor pictured it for him. He could fairly see the five miserable wretches in that stifling chamber below him. His eyes glowed in the darkness like those of a great cat.

"Call down to them in their own tongue," he whispered to Ali. "Tell them Ka-Zar comes to their rescue. Tell them to utter no sound."

The hunchback crouched by the aperture. He spoke rapidly

in a low, barely audible voice. Ka-Zar heard the sibilant intake of breath made by the imprisoned Wurumbas, startled by Ali's speech.

When the hunchback had finished, Ka-Zar thrust him aside. Kneeling before the window he grasped the two bars with fingers of steel. His powerful biceps bulged. His mighty chest expanded as he exerted all his magnificent strength against the rigid metal. The muscles rippled across his broad back.

The bars stirred in their settings. Slowly, very slowly, they gave, bent outward. Ka-Zar increased his pressure. The veins stood out like knotted cords at either side of his temples. His lips pulled back from his teeth.

THE BARS YIELDED further. Great beads of perspiration bedewed his brow. His eyeballs bulged. His breath whistled sibilantly through his clenched teeth. And while Ali crouched in wide-eyed amazement, watching, the bars curved still more outward—leaving a space large enough for a man's body to squeeze through.

Ka-Zar relaxed, climbed to his feet. Panting from his exertions, he tied one end of the jungle vine about the bottom of one of the twisted bars. Fastening it securely, he lowered the free end of the liana into the black, sweltering void below.

He leaned over and breathed in Ali's ear: "Tell the Wurumbas to be ready. Tell them to wait for the sound of confusion outside the dungeon door, then to climb swiftly, make their way to the gate in the north wall and flee with all haste to their village."

When the hunchback had relayed the message to the eager prisoners within the cell, he was ready for the next episode of the rescue.

"Lead me now to the dungeon within," he told Ali. "We must divert the guards so that the Wurumbas may make good their escape."

The unhappy cripple hesitated, then reading in the amber eyes that glowed down into his own a fierce determination that would not be stayed, he crept off along the wall.

Ka-Zar trod silently at his heels. They mounted two low steps, crossed a broad verandah and entered the dim halls of the Rajah Sarput's palace. The way to the dungeon was a devious one and though Ka-Zar marked each pace and turning upon his memory, he had small liking for this phase of his task. The confining walls and roof made him uneasy and he felt like a jungle animal that had blundered into a trap.

Ali was reduced to quivering misery. With every step he made, with every breath he drew, he trembled from head to foot. He was too near the presence of his evil master for comfort and he well knew what his fate would be if he should be discovered. He almost regretted his impulse to aid the Wurumba warriors and anxious to get his part in the drama over with, he made all the speed he dared.

Only when he began the descent of a steep, curving stair did he slow down. Again the hot, foul air of the cells wafted up to them as Ka-Zar drew up beside him. The steps were made of huge stone slabs. Fearfully Ali moved down them, then on the sixth he stopped and would go no farther.

"Around the bend of the wall below are the Bulangi guards," he whispered. "I dare go no farther."

Ka-Zar's eyes glittered. "You have done well, faithful Ali," he murmured. "Go."

With a vast relief the hunchback turned and fled. When he had vanished like a wraith, Ka-Zar proceeded cautiously down the curving stairs. Soon he saw the glow of light below. Another three steps and he peered cautiously around the wall.

A flickering torch set in the wall revealed the Bulangi guards. The trio apparently saw no need for vigilance here in the heart of the palace. One lay on the earthen floor, frankly asleep. Another squatted on his haunches, his head drooping drowsily upon his breast. The last, with his back turned in Ka-Zar's direction, was languidly searching the soles of his splay feet for burrowing jiggers. Their spears leaned negligently against the solid door of the Wurumbas' cell.

THERE WAS ONLY one thing that would serve Ka-Zar's purpose. Reluctantly he gave the knife, his only weapon, to the monkey on his shoulder. From his position he could see another flight of steps leading up from the dungeon. He pointed to it.

"Go," he whispered to the monkey. "Go silently so that the Oman will not hear you. When you are well up out of their sight, drop this shining-stick that I have given you. Then flee from this place."

The monkey squeaked once, softly, to show that he understood. Then gripping the haft of the knife in his skinny paw, he dropped lightly down from Ka-Zar's shoulder. Noiseless as a big spider, he crept like a shadow down the stairs, past the unseeing guards and vanished up the other steps.

Ka-Zar watched intently. A moment later there was a metallic clatter, loud in the utter silence, as the monkey dropped the dagger onto the stone steps.

Instantly the drowsy Bulangis were wide awake. They leaped to their feet and chattering excitedly, they seized their spears and rushed off to investigate. Ka-Zar listened with satisfaction. He heard the commotions that showed that the blacks had found the dagger, heard them noisily ascend further. His keen ears caught faint sound of scraping and a muffled grunt from beyond the barred door of the cell and he knew that the Wurumbas were making their escape.

CHAPTER XI

THE LION'S HEART

HIS WORK WAS done. Cautiously he began to climb back up the stairs on which he stood. He was half way up their curving length when suddenly he froze.

Directly above him a voice spoke—the harsh, unmistakable voice of the Rajah Sarput. The trembling tones of Ali answered.

Ka-Zar realized that he was alone, unarmed—trapped. His first vague dislike of the confining walls was confirmed.

Swiftly he reviewed his situation. Instinctively he sensed that Ali had not betrayed him, that the hapless hunchback had been unable to steer his master away from the approach to the dungeon. Escape that way was impossible. And if he went up the other stairs, he would run into the trio of Bulangi guards.

The Rajah's words had been muffled, unrecognizable. To get a better idea of what was afoot, Ka-Zar cautiously mounted five steps further. Flattened against the curving earthen wall, he listened.

For a moment there was a silence above him. Then he heard the rush of bare feet and a breathless voice addressed Sarput. Though Ka-Zar did not understand the Bulangi tongue, he realized that the guard from the north wall had just found the man that he had slain at the gate and had rushed to the palace to report to his master.

Then Sarput's voice drifted down as he addressed Ali in clear English. It was harsh with anger.

"You hear, ugly one? It was a widebladed Wurumba knife

that killed the black one at the gate. The prisoners—are they safe?"

In a quavering voice Ali replied that he had heard no sounds from below.

"We shall soon see," was the Rajah's grim answer.

Footsteps sounded on the stairs. Ka-Zar moved swiftly and silently. He reached the dungeon floor. From the other stairway came the clamor of the baffled guards, returning.

Between the flat, solid doors of the various cells, the earth walls were irregular and indented. The flickering torch had burned low and the light it threw did not penetrate far. A natural niche in the walls was beyond its pallid glow and Ka-Zar immediately made for it, flattened himself into the Stygian gloom of the recess.

From here, unseen, he had a clear view of both stairs and the pool of light before the cell door.

The Bulangi guards came first, panting from their running. They gathered in an excited huddle, chattering in hushed voices and gesticulating with their arms. Then they suddenly stiffened to rigid attention as the glittering figure of Sarput emerged on the other stairway.

Slowly, appearing a head taller in the aura of wrath that pulsed about him, he walked down among them. They fell back as he approached. Ali and the guard from the stockade followed at his heels.

Sarput addressed the trio of cell guards in their native tongue. Ka-Zar again had no need to understand the actual words.

THE BLACKS STARED foolishly at their master, shook their kinky heads. Then they turned and one raised the stout bars that stretched across the door of the cell they had been guarding.

It swung, creaking, inward. Beyond its threshold was only humid, impenetrable blackness. The Bulangi called into the darkness.

No one answered. Nothing stirred. From his hidden place

of vantage Ka-Zar studied the expressions of the men before him and the ghost of a mocking smile flitted across his lips.

Snatching the torch from its socket on the wall and clutching his spear, the Bulangi stepped into the cell. Sarput watched in stony silence, only his eyes glittering. The black returned, his face shining with perspiration and his eyes wide with unbelief. He mumbled something.

His two companions turned to stare into what was again empty blackness. Then, as they realized what had happened and how they had been tricked, a growing fear crept into their bulging eyes. They turned uneasily back to face their master.

What they read in his face made them cringe back against the wall.

Transfixing the unhappy trio with his wrathful gaze, Sarput spoke rapidly over his shoulder to the guard who had come from the wall.

As Ka-Zar guessed, he was ordering the man to rouse the entire encampment. But Ka-Zar was not disturbed. The fleeing Wurumbas be well into the jungle by now.

Then in the middle of his volleyed commands, Sarput suddenly ceased. A crafty gleam came into his eyes. Shaking his head, be countermanded the order he had just given and voiced another.

The warrior bowed, vanished up the stairs. This time Ka-Zar was mystified.

If he could have known what was passing through the sly, evil brain of the glittering figure there in the torchlight, he would have marveled more.

Sarput was shrewd. He knew his Bulangi followers had been vaguely disturbed by Ka-Zar's miraculous escape up there on the plateau. He knew that the blacks were a credulous and superstitious lot. He knew that subsequent mysterious happenings would be attributed to the strange jungle god and he had no desire to let them get out of hand.

Fortunately the guard who had discovered his slain companion had made no outcry and reported only to his master. The five Wurumbas who were to have furnished the morrow's feast were gone. Here were three Bulangis who had failed him. The slain man made another. And the guard who knew about the killing, the only other one who had any knowledge of the night's mysterious happenings, would be a fifth.

Sarput's wrath melted. A sardonic chuckle escaped his bearded lips. The Bulangis would have their feast; without knowing it, they would be eating not their enemies—but their brothers. The Rajah's sadistic nature relished the joke.

Calmly he drew the revolver from his belt. While, the three Bulangis watched him, petrified with terror, he slowly raised its muzzle.

THE HAPLESS TRIO could have slain him in a trice with their spears. But such was his evil domination over them, such was the awful fear that he had instilled in their black hearts, that they were powerless to move. From the shadows Ka-Zar impassively watched the scene. The lives of these three Oman, who were eaters of their own species, meant nothing to him.

Deliberately the Rajah squeezed the trigger. The first black plunged forward to the ground, dead before his body struck it. Low moans issued from the lips of the others. The revolver spoke again—and again.

Sarput looked down at the three huddled bodies at his feet. The bare earth, soaked up the crimson streams that poured from their death wounds. All huddled behind him.

The way of escape was not yet open to Ka-Zar. So he waited, as Sarput and his attendant did, in the foetid, steamy silence.

Soon the Bulangi warrior returned, bearing over his shoulder the body of the guard that Ka-Zar had slain. He stared at the three bodies on the ground, then at Sarput's command, added his burden to the grisly pile. As he straightened up, the revolver spoke again.

The strained nerves of the hunchback could stand no more. Ever since he had volunteered to help Ka-Zar, he had lived in mortal terror. Now, covering his eyes with his hands, he hobbled swiftly up the steps.

It was Ka-Zar's chance to make a break. But all thought of escape was wiped from his mind. Here, for the first time, was his opportunity. He was alone with his hated enemy. The urge to close his fingers about Sarput's skinny neck, to squeeze the life from his body, blotted all else from his mind.

Gathering his mighty muscles, he sprang like an avenging fury from the blackness.

Some instinct must have warned Sarput. He whirled, saw the figure of the bronzed giant appear in the torch light and whipped up his gun.

But before he could fire, fingers of steel closed like a vise about his wrist. They tightened in a grip so agonizing that a low cry of pain escaped his bearded lips. Needles of fire stabbed up his arm and the revolver trickled from his nerveless hand.

Ka-Zar kicked the fire-stick, sent it spinning off into the shadows. With an inexorable strength he drew the glittering figure of Sarput to him, his other hand reaching out towards the Rajah's skinny neck.

But even as his fingers closed over flesh, a babel of noise broke out somewhere above him. Ka-Zar's head snapped up. He snarled—a low, guttural snarl. For he knew that his chance had come too late.

Sarput clawed feebly at the bronze hand that choked off his wind. His eyes started from his head and his face turned slowly purple. Feet clattered down the stairs that the trio of Bulangis had searched a short time before.

Ka-Zar's whole being cried out in revolt. Bitterness gnawed like a canker in his heart. To have come so near to accomplishing his purpose and then to be forced to flee—it was the most cruel joke that the Fates had ever played upon him.

BUT SELF PRESERVATION was the first law of the jungle. In two more minutes, Sarput might have been an empty, glittering husk, the life squeezed from his body. But those two minutes' flow were as long as eternity.

Sarput's minions were clattering down the steps. Trembling with frustrated wrath, Ka-Zar flung the Rajah from him. As he struck the nearest wall and clung there, fighting for breath, Ka-Zar bounded towards the other stairs.

He ascended them three at a time and as he neared the top, he heard the mad confusion below as the Bulangis found their shaken master. When he emerged onto the main floor of the palace, he ran headlong into a group of blacks who came rushing into the building.

His sudden, startling appearance in the natives' midst was the signal for yet another bedlam.

Though they were armed with spears and rifles, Ka-Zar had the advantage of their surprise. Before they could recover he had leaped amongst them. His powerful arms lashed out. Men scattered before him like ten-pins. Like a devastating tornado Ka-Zar charged through the group, leaped through a doorway and landed on the broad verandah.

A dozen other blacks were just mounting the steps. Again the bedlam as he towered suddenly above them. His long arm flashed out, seized the nearest man and raised him kicking off the floor. With a mighty thrust he hurled the terrified Bulangi full at his companions.

The hapless warrior was impaled upon the spear of one of his comrades. His wail of agony shrilled through the air, died in a gurgling moan. The dead weight of his body crushed back the horde.

Before the Bulangis could recover Ka-Zar cleared the verandah with one bound and ran like a startled gazelle toward the gate in the north wall.

Behind him, howling men—black and brown—converged on the run from all directions. For the first time since he had darted from the dungeon, Ka-Zar was aware of cracking rifles. Bullets whistled about him. From the nearest of his pursuers came a flight of glistening spears.

As though the Fates were sorry for the trick they had played upon him, they drew a veil of clouds across the face of the moon. In the abrupt blackness that ensued, Ka-Zar gained the gate, leaped nimbly up it.

The clouds drifted on and the bright moonbeams revealed him silhouetted in stark relief atop the barrier—truly godlike in his superb nakedness.

A last hailstorm of arrows, spears and bullets sprayed the air about him. Then he dropped lithely down from the barricade and disappeared from view.

Once beyond the palace grounds his enemies could not find him. Among their huts, they milled about in noisy confusion. But Ka-Zar flitted swiftly and soundlessly from cover to cover, emerged from one pool of shadow only to melt into another. And with the bedlam of the pack in his ears, he gained the edge of the forest and leaped into the safety of the trees.

A moment later the tumult behind him was stilled. For from the dense cover of the jungle, the rumbling, defiant roar of the lion floated back over the encampment.

INSTEAD OF TEMPERING the Rajah's anger, the defeat he had suffered at Ka-Zar's hands served but to heighten it. Thenceforth he went forever armed, surrounded by a squad of picked retainers. By day and night his palace was guarded by detachments of crack riflemen.

Divided into two camps the jungle settled down for a long struggle. On the side of the invaders the men were armed with guns and revolvers. And against them Ka-Zar pitted the might of claw and fang, augmented by the bows and spears of Wazi's followers.

The odds against him were tremendous, yet he carried on the unequal struggle relentlessly with all the jungle wisdom at his command. Always his first consideration was for the safety of his beasts. It was he who invariably led the attack in the frequent skirmishes with Sarput's men. It was he who invariably retreated last in the face of threatened catastrophe.

But bitterly as he fought, wisely and bravely as he led his beasts and men, day by day saw him retreating further into the jungle before the fire-sticks of the Oman.

All his dark foreboding concerning Sarput had been fulfilled. Slowly he came to the bitter realization that here at last had come to his jungle a power to challenge his own—a power he could not cope with. And as each day's retreat left more and more animals behind, slaughtered by the fire-sticks of the enemy, his heart became heavy within him.

Sarput, on the other hand, gloried in the game. Here, indeed, was fitting sport for a Royal Prince. His native India had nothing to offer like this. However, he never lost sight of his chief objective—the capture of Ka-Zar, alive.

And in preparation for that day he whetted his appetite by practicing savage tortures on those of Wazi's men who fell into his hands. With each triumph in the field, his excesses increased, until even the Bulangi blacks, mortal enemy of the Wurumba, became restless.

It was Ali, wise in the ways of the black men, who started the rumor that they were engaged in the service of the evil one—embroiled in a war against the protecting god of the jungle. Further, that though success temporarily favored the Rajah, there could be only one outcome to the struggle. Ka-Zar, brother of Zar the lion, would triumph.

The rumor, spread and grew. The Bulangi became more restless, but Sarput was too blind, too arrogant to see.

CHAPTER XII

THE GIRL OF THE GOLDEN HAIR

COMMISSIONER VanGELDER, AS he sat at his desk, was a worried and troubled man. A frown sat heavily on his brow and his mouth was drawn with care. For the past six months ugly rumors had been drifting down to him from the interior. Each succeeding one had been more disquieting than the one preceding it.

Hardy traders, prospectors, explorers, all returned with tales of a seething unrest amongst the native tribes. An unrest that smouldered yet, but one that threatened to break out at any moment without warning, in a general uprising of the blacks. VanGelder well knew what that could mean. Once aroused and on the warpath, no white man would be safe in the entire region of the Congo.

And he knew, further, without being told, that the cause of the native rumblings was the Rajah Sarput. Tales, more ugly still, had come to the Commissioner concerning that dusky-skinned individual—tales that he found hard to believe.

Bitterly VanGelder cursed the diplomacy of far off European statesmen for burdening him and the territory he governed with a sadistic devil in the person of the Rajah Sarput. What did all the kings, diplomats and statesmen know of the vast dark region that lay south of the Equator? To them it was naught but primeval jungle, peopled by a handful of savage cannibals.

If a few of them should die for the pleasure of an Indian prince—what matter? But VanGelder knew better than that.

There was more than the lives of a few blacks at stake.

He came to a decision at last. He would make the long trek into the interior and investigate the rumors for himself. Only when he had the facts at first hand would he be competent to act.

Once the decision had been made, he felt better. The prospect of definite action appealed to him. But he had planned without his daughter, Claudette. When he told her of his intended expedition, she insisted on accompanying him. No recital of the hardships and dangers of the undertaking could deter her from her purpose.

"You know, Father," she said as her clinching argument, "you need some one to take care of *you*. And I have always wanted to penetrate into the interior."

"But, my child," protested VanGelder, "there are untold dangers of beast and man."

"*Poof*, for the dangers," answered Claudette impudently. "We will have guides, porters and what-not. And anyway, I want to make the acquaintance of this jungle god Ka-Zar I have heard so much about."

VanGelder frowned darkly. "You will more likely renew the unpleasant acquaintance of the Rajah Sarput," he said sombrely.

"You think he is back of all this trouble?" asked the girl.

"I know he is," answered VanGelder. "I wish to Heaven the devil was out of the country."

Even with the best of equipment, the most experienced guides and traveling light, it took VanGelder and his party two months to penetrate to the fringe of the jungle that had for so long been ruled by Zar and Ka-Zar. And during those two months, VanGelder's apprehensions had increased.

THE TRIBES WHO lived on the veldt, along the borders of the forest, had once been friendly but now they were suspicious. Some were openly hostile. To a man, the natives were sullen and surly and the antagonism they felt towards this latest party was a thing that could be seen in their eyes, heard in their muttered words.

And at night, the sullen unrest of the Congo was expressed in the wild, barbaric rhythm of the tomtom, rising from a thousand kraals.

VanGelder noted with increasing uneasiness that the blacks were surprisingly well armed and that they were never without their weapons. Taking a cue from the natives, he issued arms to every man in his company and a small automatic to his daughter. His orders were explicit and to the point. His men were not to shoot unless absolutely necessary—then they were to waste no bullets.

A hundred times during the past week VanGelder cursed himself for having permitted Claudette to accompany him. Under the most favorable conditions the Congo was no place for a woman. Now with each breath of air, each stirring leaf, each beat of the tomtom bringing a message of danger to him, he would have gladly sacrificed his chance of heaven if his daughter were safely back in his distant headquarters.

From a hundred sources he received ample proof of the rumors he had heard. They had not been exaggerated. If anything they had understated the real conditions. And as they neared the edge of the jungle, came whispers of the bronzed jungle god called Ka-Zar, brother of Zar the lion. Tales, myths, sagas of his deeds and daring as he struggled with the new menace that had come to his wilderness.

VanGelder was not superstitious and he scorned such tall tales as jungle gods. But he was convinced that there was some basis for the wild, fantastic tales whispered by the blacks. There was some power deep in the forest—a very real power—that was combating Sarput. What that power was, he would have given a great deal to know.

They left the great, grassy plain behind them and plunged abruptly into the depths of the jungle. VanGelder would have been amazed to learn: that before he had progressed a day's

march through the dense bush, slitted amber eyes had seen
them from the protection of the jungle screen. He would not
have believed his eyes if he could have seen fleeting glimpses
of a tall, naked, bronze giant who followed his progress, or of
the massive tawny lion that padded softly along at Ka-Zar's
side.

Ka-Zar's struggle with Sarput had been raging now through
two rainy seasons. And at the end of that time, the lionman's
base of operations was a two days' march from Sarput's stronghold.

Ka-Zar was no longer the carefree bronze leader of the jungle
beasts. He was care-worn and drawn and there was a new expression in his amber eyes. Anguish was there. Not that he
himself had suffered physical pain and hardship. No. He did
not consider himself. But during the past few weeks of fighting
he had seen many of his allies fall before the murderous fire-
sticks of the Rajah's henchmen.

He was sick at heart. For slowly but surely Sarput was driving
him and his beasts and his new allies, the Wurumbas, ever
further from the vicinity of the palace. He dreaded to think
what the end might be.

IT WAS WHILE he was prospecting, with Zar beside him, for
straight limbs of the dakka tree to be hardened in a slow-
burning fire into spears and arrows, that he first scented the
presence of Oman in the immediate vicinity. Head flung back,
his quivering nostrils told him that there were white men and
black.

His eyes hardened and his lips became a cruel straight line.
He growled a word of warning to Zar and clutching his spear
firmly in one hand, swung up into the nearest tree with the
other. Agilely he swung off through the trees, more swiftly,
more silently than Chaka, the great ape. Below, the tawny shape
of Zar kept pace with his rapid progress.

Ka-Zar had proceeded but a short distance when his ears
brought him verification of what his nose had already told him.

Off to his right he heard a confused hubbub of noise that could have been made only by a large party of men on the move. With a mighty leap he swung off in the direction from whence the sounds came. There was a steely glitter in his eye and his heart picked up a faster beat.

It was his fervent hope that Sarput had rashly invaded too deep into his domain. If such were indeed the case, Ka-Zar assured himself that his spear or knife would not fail him a second time. He would strike for the throat this time—and he would not miss.

A few minutes later he slackened his headlong pace. He steadied himself in the crotch of a tall tree that overlooked a narrow game trail, following the course of a winding stream. Below him, following that trail north and west, were Oman, indeed, both white and black.

Ka-Zar took in the party with one swift, all-inclusive glance. There were three white men, the rest were blacks. Then his heart sank. For of all that score of men, the one his spear ached for was not there. The Rajah Sarput was not one of the party. More, Ka-Zar knew that he had never seen any of them before.

The white Oman were strangers to his land and he was sure that the blacks belonged neither to the Wurumba nor Bulangi tribes.

A dozen questions assailed Ka-Zar at once. Whence came these Oman, so heavily armed; and where were they going? He realized that the trail they were following would take them to the stronghold of Sarput. Were these men new enemies of himself and his beasts, come to help Sarput in his work of destruction?

His fingers tightened around the haft of his spear as he loosed the bow swung over his back. Between his spear and his arrows he could account for a dozen men.

Once more his eyes swept over the moving column. Starting with the head he took in each figure one by one. A lean white led the way. Following him was a large, massive man with one of the strange mushroom hats upon his head. And by the side of this latter Om there strode another.... No. This was no man.

Ka-Zar's eyes narrowed and the fire faded from them. By some irresistible impulse he was impelled to get a closer view of this other creature who walked beside the towering Om. Calling down a sharp command to Zar to keep to cover, he swung swiftly off through the trees to the very edge of the trail.

There, moving noiselessly and unseen through the dense foliage of the lower branches he kept abreast of the party as it traveled north and west. From this point of vantage he was able to secure a good view of the face and figure of the two-legged creature that had intrigued him.

HE HAD NEVER seen a face so lovely before. He marvelled at the delicately chiseled features, the clear blue eyes and the golden hair, longer than his own, that was stirred by the vagrant breeze.

With something of a shock that both surprised and confused him, Ka-Zar realized that he was staring at a female of his own species, the first white girl he had ever seen. Something stirred within his breast. It was the primeval urge in man for a mate, though he did not realize it.

Hungrily he took in the radiant, beauty of Claudette Van-Gelder's face. And so ardent, so compelling was his gaze that the girl turned her head and stared questioningly at the jungle wall. She saw nothing—not even the trembling of a leaf to mark the passing of the bronzed giant. Yet she was troubled by the feeling that someone was watching her. She turned back to her father with a laugh.

No creature in the jungle has the power of laughter. Ka-Zar had never heard such a bewitching sound before. And with swift, sure intuition he knew that no matter what other Oman might be, this laughing, blue-eyed creature who set his pulses hammering was good. That she meant no harm to his beasts or his jungle, he was convinced.

CHAPTER XIV

SPEARS IN THE SUN

A DOZEN TIMES that morning Claudette was troubled by the uncanny feeling that she was being watched. She tried to shake off the annoying impression but it persisted despite herself. Half laughing, half in earnest she mentioned the matter to her father.

He looked at her closely for a moment, than smiled and patted her hand. "Don't let this jungle hell get under your skin, Claudette. Another day's march or so and we will be at Sarput's palace."

Claudette frowned and shook her head. "You think I'm silly, I know," she protested. "Or else you think the sun has touched me. It's neither of those things, I'm sure. I just have a feeling that someone has been watching me all morning."

"From where?" asked VanGelder.

Claudette waved her tiny hand, at the immutable jungle wall hemming them in. "From in there," she said vaguely. "First from one side of the trail, then from the other."

From wide, intent eyes she scanned the dense screen of foliage about her. A frown of worry about his eyes, her father did likewise. Both of them, for long moments, stared directly at the spot where Ka-Zar stood hidden in the brush. But neither of them saw aught but the unchanging face of the jungle.

VanGelder made an effort to rid himself of his uneasiness by a short laugh. "You're imagining things, my dear," he said. "Barry and Holt are the best guides in this part of the country.

If anything, man or beast, had been on our trail all morning, they would have known it long ago."

With the words he dismissed the matter but not so Claudette. When the party came to a halt for the midday meal, she explored a little way ahead on the trail. What she expected to find she did not know. But nevertheless, she was pleasantly exhilarated.

At times she passed so close to Ka-Zar that he could have reached out from behind a leafy screen and touched her. At other times Zar could have felled her with a stroke of his paw without moving. Her untrained eyes and senses, however, perceived nothing. The jungle appeared to her as always.

She halted after a short while and started to retrace her steps. Half way back to the encampment, her eye was attracted by a cluster of large, red berries that hung down invitingly from a slender vine. The bloom of freshness was upon them, doubly appealing beneath the hot midday sun.

With a little gurgle of surprise and pleasure she plucked the fruit. Eyes sparkling in anticipation of some strange, exotic flavor, she brought the first berry to her mouth. But before she could crush the fruit between her lips, there was an excited whir and chatter from the tangle of vines that lined the trail and a long-tailed, wise-faced monkey leaped from the brush straight for her.

The girl was startled for a moment into immobility. Nono, for it was he who had leaped from Ka-Zar's shoulder at a whispered command from his master, sprang agilely onto Claudette's shoulder. Scolding furiously, he dashed the berries from her hand, perched a moment on her shoulder, scolded some more, then grimaced owlishly into her startled eyes.

CLAUDETTE WAS NOT afraid. She was merely surprised at the boldness of the wild creature. The more so, as she thought she could almost understand the message he was trying to convey to her. It was obvious that the monkey did not want her to eat the berries. Undoubtedly they were poison. She stared at them a moment where they lay at her feet, faced Nono and nodded.

At this assurance the monkey sprang from his perch and was swallowed by the jungle screen.

Claudette tried to follow his erratic course, but lost him almost immediately. Slowly, in deep thought, she continued on her way back to the encampment. And so absorbed was she in the strange thoughts that assailed her, that a few steps further on she walked straight into danger again.

Her eyes were trained on inner things, strange and wonderful. She failed entirely to see the emerald green snake coiled on a hot rock in the center of the trail. It was a five foot mamba, the fastest to strike and the most deadly of all the snakes in Africa. At the girl's unheeding approach it reared up suddenly, prepared to strike. Its slender head swayed hypnotically from side to side and its unblinking eyes were pinpoints of venom.

A scant five feet from the reptile, Claudette saw her peril. She stopped dead in her tracks. Fear gripped her. She was unable to advance or retreat. Fascinated she stared at the mamba's swaying head and the darting fork of its tongue. Horrified she saw the slender coils of its body tense.

She wanted to scream, but no words came. Then, just as the snake reared up to strike, she heard a sibilant hiss, twice repeated, issue from the leafy screen.

As if it had received a verbal command, as if some will greater than its own dominated him, the mamba lowered its head. In utter bewilderment but fascinated still, Claudette watched. The forked tongue of the snake darted in and out for a few times. Then with a dry rustle of scales it slid from the rock and skirting the girl slithered across the jungle floor.

Not until it had vanished was Claudette able to move. Then, ashen of face and with some strange and inexplicable thing touching at her heart, she sped down the trail towards the camp.

She was still pale and shaken when she pulled up by her father's side. VanGelder was quick to see her agitation. "What's the matter, Claudette?" he asked anxiously.

The girl's eyes were sober and her voice steady when she

answered. "Tell me," she said slowly, choosing each word with care. "Are we anywhere near the domain that this mythical jungle god Ka-Zar is supposed to rule?"

"Why, yes," replied VanGelder. "We're in the very heart of that district. But of course you don't believe that superstitious rot?"

"I don't know," answered the girl without smiling.

Her father looked at her narrowly. "Are you sure you feel well? No head-ache—no buzzing in the ears?"

Claudette smiled for the first time, shook her head. "No, dad, I'm not getting one of your weird jungle fevers. But I tell you there's magic hereabouts. Black magic."

"You've seen something—you've heard something," said VanGelder. "What?"

IN MINUTE DETAIL Claudette told him what had happened when she had plucked the wild berries; how the monkey had dashed the fruit from her hand and scolded.

It was her father's turn to pale. "From your description you were about to eat the gangi berry. It is a deadly poison. The natives use it to poison their arrows."

"I guessed as much," said Claudette soberly. "I do believe that monkey was trying to tell me so."

"Nonsense," replied VanGelder, wiping the sweat from his brow. "A pure coincidence. Monkeys are impudent and curious."

"Yes?" challenged the girl. "And have green mambas suddenly become gentle and full of pity?"

"Green mambas!" echoed VanGelder in a startled voice. "What about green mambas?"

"I almost stepped on one," said Claudette. "I was paralyzed with fear and could not move. It was about to strike. And then, just as I steeled myself for the bite of its fangs, I heard a hizzing— sharp and commanding—from the side of the trail. I swear it. Something—some one was talking to that snake. Ordering him—commanding him. And the snake heard and understood, for it didn't strike after all. It lowered its head, slid off the rock and disappeared. Now what do you, think of that?"

VanGelder swallowed at his Adam's apple and mopped at his brow again. "My dear, if what you say is true, I don't know what to think. It's wonderful—it's miraculous—it's…."

"Exactly," put in Claudette. "Either it's magic of the blackest kind or this—this god Ka-Zar does exist."

CHAPTER XIII

BLACK MAGIC

VAn**GELDER WAS IMPRESSED,** more by the girl's conviction and earnestness, than by her words. He found no ready answer for her and tried to dismiss the matter with a laugh that did not quite come off. No further mention was made of the strange incidents throughout the remainder of the day. But when the party got under way again after the meal, VanGelder advanced to the head, of the trail with his two guides and his eyes were sharp and intent. The automatic was loosened in his holster and he gave Claudette strict orders not to stray from the party.

The day wore on. The sun swung through its zenith and began a slow, majestic descent in the west. No untoward incident occurred to break the monotonous spell the sun cast upon them all.

On one occasion, Barry, the chief guide, commented on the scarcity of game. He had never seen the jungle so depleted of the bigger, meat eating beasts.

VanGelder frowned. "That's a clear indication that we are nearing Sarput's stronghold. The animals that he hasn't slaughtered have fled."

Barry grunted. "Despite everything I've heard about Sarput, I'll be glad when we reach his encampment. We ought to make his place by tomorrow sunset. And tonight I'll want you to stand guard with Holt and me."

VanGelder looked at him questioningly.

"I don't trust our own blacks too much," explained Barry. "They're full of talk of this jungle god Ka-Zar. This is supposed to be near his stamping ground."

"Just what is back of the myth?" asked VanGelder.

The guide shrugged. "Anything can be back of it. But mark my words, it's something damn queer."

"Then we go on guard against this Ka-Zar? But I thought he was the benevolent, protecting god of the jungle?"

"Sure, he's all that, if you listen to the blacks," said Barry. "And they say he hates all white men. But it's not Ka-Zar I'm worried about."

"Then what?"

"We're entering the Bulangi hunting grounds. They're bad medicine. Cannibals—with a partiality for whites."

"Yes, I know," replied VanGelder. "But I understand the Bulangi have formed an alliance with Sarput."

"Maybe so," answered Barry skeptically. "But I wouldn't trust a Bulangi any further than I could see him. And that on a dark night, too."

Barry's fears and skepticism were well founded—too well founded. If he had only known, he should have put the men on guard then, instead of deferring until they made camp for the night. For it seemed no more than a minute after he had declared his intentions that the party was surrounded by a swirling horde of naked blacks.

The faces of the natives were painted into grinning masks. Their teeth were filed and hanging from their throats were necklaces made from the finger bones of their past victims. Each black carried a long spear and as the pack danced grotesquely about VanGelder's party, they brandished their weapons threateningly.

BARRY RECOGNIZED THEM immediately as the dread Bulangi. And from their painted faces and their grisly regalia of human bones, he knew that they were on the war path.

So swift and silent had been the surprise attack that Van-Gelder's men never had the opportunity to fire a shot before the party was surrounded. True, VanGelder half drew his automatic from his belt, but at a sharp word from Barry, let it fall back into its holster.

"We're hopelessly outnumbered," said Barry. "We could get a handful of the devils with our guns, but in the end we'd all be served up as long pig. Our only chance is to parley with them. Give them gifts for a safe passage to Sarput's palace. If they won't listen to reason we can always go to work with the guns."

VanGelder was not thinking of himself or of his own safety. He was thinking of his daughter, Claudette. For the hundredth time, more bitterly than ever before, he cursed himself for a fool for having permitted her to accompany him. He had only one consolation and that a mighty slim and bitter one. If worst came to worst, he knew that Claudette would not hesitate to turn her automatic on herself.

Gnashing their teeth and rolling their eyes, the Bulangi had closed in their circle until the little party of whites and terror stricken blacks were huddled close together in a compact group. By every suggestive gesture the dread intention of the Bulangi was obvious.

When the dance had somewhat subsided, Barry stepped out a few feet from the party and held up his hand, palm outward.

"Greetings to the mighty warriors of the Bulangi," he said in the native dialect. "The white men come in peace."

A derisive howl from the blacks greeted his words. Levelling theirs long spears they edged in closer. Once more VanGelder's hand crept furtively to his holster.

"The white men are the friends of the Rajah Sarput," continued Barry. "They travel through the jungle under his protection. And to the brave Bulangi, the Rajah's allies, even as we, we bring many gifts."

At the mention of gifts another howl arose from the blacks.

One who towered a foot above his fellows and who was apparently their leader, stepped forward.

"What gifts do the white men bring to the Bulangi?" he demanded of Barry.

Without hesitating Barry extracted a cheap dollar watch from his pocket, held it to his ear for a moment, then tossed it to the native.

The black caught it deftly, held it to his ear as Barry had done and showed his teeth in a wide grin. He held it to the ear of one of his followers. But instead of appreciating the ticking of the watch, this latter one jumped back in fear. He chattered excitedly for a moment and with a scowl the black chief threw the watch to the ground and ground it to bits beneath the butt of his spear.

"Damn," said Barry beneath his breath.

"What's the matter?" whispered VanGelder.

"They think the watch is magic—evil. We're in for it. They'll parley for another few minutes, then charge without warning. Pass along the word. Be ready for them and when they come— let the devils have all you got."

VanGELDER'S FACE WAS set into hard lines as the passed along Barry's word of warning and advice. Claudette came up to stand by his side and for a moment he pressed her hand. "Courage," he whispered.

She nodded and he looked into her face. It was pale, true, but her eyes were clear and bright and her head was held high in proud defiance. Even though death was near, Claudette showed no fear. VanGelder marveled at her cool courage—and wished her a thousand miles away.

Then as Barry had predicted, the black leader was continuing the parley. He spoke rapidly and though VanGelder could not understand the words, he knew that they were spoken in anger.

"What does he say?" he asked Barry.

"He wants fire-sticks—guns," replied the guide.

"And when they get the guns they'll slaughter us with their spears just the same," said VanGelder bitterly. "Tell him to go to the devil. As for me, Barry, I'd sooner die fighting. The sorry business will be over sooner, that way. I've heard what fiendish torture these devils put their prisoners to before finally killing them. And I want none of it."

"I feel the same way myself, sir," answered Barry grimly. "Too bad about the Missy. You might tell her it would be better to…."

"She understands that already," cut in VanGelder.

"She would, sir," said Barry. "She's got pluck."

Abruptly an ominous silence fell upon the blacks. In the brilliant sun their sweating hides gleamed like sable satin. Now each man of them crouched low, presenting an unbreakable circle of spear heads to the surrounded party.

VanGelder knew that he could look for no help from the native bearers of his party. Knees knocking together, his blacks were huddled in a pathetic group. Strange animal whimperings of terror came from their lips.

He laughed shortly and snapped up his automatic. Claudette followed suit. Barry and the other guide held their rifles in readiness.

"Steady!" whispered Barry. "Let them make the first move. But unless I miss my guess, they'll be on us in another minute."

For the space of ten, never-ending seconds, a terrible silence held them all. The very air was brittle and electric with tension. The two opposing parties, each with death in their hearts, confronted each other, stared at each other from hot eyes across a short ten feet of jungle clearing.

No one moved, no one spoke—not a breath was drawn, even. The myriad voices of the jungle suddenly stilled as if all creation awaited the explosion that hovered in the air. It was as if both groups had been miraculously turned to stone in that split second before they threw themselves at each other.

BUT THOUGH NO man visibly moved—black or white—each side knew that the other was steeling themselves for the first shock of the battle. The supple muscles of the blacks tensed for the spring. The fingers of the white men tightened slowly on the triggers of their guns.

The black chief moved forward an inch. A low, unearthly wail floated from his lips. But even before Barry could still it with the roar of his rifle and a crashing bullet to the black's throat, an unseen, powerful bronzed hand had moved.

An arrow sped more quickly, more truly than the bullet could have done. There was a sudden whirring sound, an abrupt fanning of hot air and a long, feathered shaft dug deep into the Bulangi's throat and quivered there.

The unearthly wail of the black rose to a high crescendo note, then broke on a bursting bubble of blood. Already crouched far forward on the verge of his spring, he swayed there an agonizing moment as if reluctant to die. Bulangi and whites alike stared at him with incredulous wonder.

No one had the power of movement. Not even the dying black, who could not follow his life's blood to the earth, which was already stained red.

Then the spell that held them all was shattered. From high in the topmost branches of a towering dakka tree came the stentorian bellow of a lion—a male lion who has made his kill.

The rumbling roar—proud, mighty, defiant—echoed and reverberated through the jungle. And there was that in it more potent than the arrow. For on the last booming note of the roar, the will that had kept the stricken Bulangi on his feet was snapped and he pitched headlong to the ground.

Claudette heard the loud howl of terror emitted by the blacks, but she did not see them leap back from the crumpled body of their chief and scatter pell-mell into the brush. She did not see, for her eyes were raised to the tree from whence the roar of the lion had come.

Was it her imagination? Was it a trick of the copper sun? Was it a vision conjured up by her strained and overwrought nerves? For a fleeting moment she saw something move in the treetop. Something that was tawny as a lion, yet was a lion for all that. Something that was bronzed and gigantic, with flowing hair. Something that moved erect through the branches with the sure swiftness of the great apes—yet was no ape for all that. Something that held her gaze for a long moment with eyes that were human.

That something was man or god.

"Look, Father!" she said breathlessly.

But when VanGelder turned his head to look, Ka-Zar had vanished.

"What?" he asked in a startled voice, jerking up his, automatic. "What did you see?"

CLAUDETTE BLINKED HER blue eyes, passed a hand across her brow. "It must be the heat, the excitement," she said wearily. "But for a moment I could have sworn that I saw a man, a bronzed giant, in the top of that tree."

VanGelder threw his hand comfortingly across her shoulder. "It's this trip—the danger and excitement," he said solicitously. "The Bulangi have fled. There is no danger now. Tomorrow we will be at the palace of the Rajah."

"Yes, Father," she said in an awed whisper. "But someone *did* shoot that arrow and the roar of the lion came from the treetop!"

VanGelder's jaw sagged. "By Jove," he said in a hushed voice. "You're right. In the excitement I forgot that. From the tree-top an arrow—then a lion's roar. And you say you saw—what?"

Claudette's head came up and she smiled into her father's eyes. "I saw Ka-Zar, Father," she said simply. "Ka-Zar, brother of Zar the lion: Ka-Zar, the benevolent god of the jungle."

VanGelder made a series of choking sounds, swallowed three times before he was able to speak.

"But that's nonsensical superstition, child," he protested at last.

"As you will," she said, still smiling. "But I saw him." Then, so softly that her father could not catch the words, she added: "A god you may be, Ka-Zar—but you looked at me with the eyes of a man. I'm glad," she whispered.

"What did you say?" asked VanGelder sharply.

Claudette smiled at him enigmatically. "I said I was glad, Father—glad."

CHAPTER XV

POMP AND CIRCUMSTANCE

THE **RAJAH SARPUT** had just finished his evening meal and
reclining upon a cushioned divan, he gave himself up to his
latest favorite diversion. His mind never tired of devising new
and more terrible fates for Ka-Zar, against the day when the
jungle god should fall into his hands.

Sarput's keen mental pleasures were abruptly interrupted
when Ali came hurrying into his presence. Swiftly the hunchback made the customary obeisance and then poured forth a
flood of words.

"Master, the Bulangi at the south wall reports that a party
approaches. It is a large party, of both white men and black."

With an oath, Sarput jumped to his feet. Crossing to the
nearest window, he looked out over the city of huts toward the
forest beyond. The news had spread swiftly and every shelter
spilled forth its inhabitants. All clutched weapons and looked
into the south.

Even as a runner came speeding up to the palace to report
further details, the party came out of the forest and into the
Rajah's view.

He saw the slanting rays of the setting sun reflected on chalky
helmets and swore again. Then among the approaching expedition he saw a slim little figure, topped with a cloud of hair that
gleamed like gold. The oaths died stillborn and his lips curled
up at the corners in a smile.

For he recognized the daughter of VanGelder, who had

aroused a flaming desire within him on the day when they had first met. And he realized now, as he saw her headed for his wilderness palace, that that desire had smouldered within his breast ever since that time. It needed but the distant sight of her fair face to awaken the old desire once more within him.

He whirled on his heel, clapped his hands sharply. "Why do you stand there, misbegotten son of a swine?" he thundered at Ali. "It is Monsieur VanGelder who comes. Quick—tell the warriors to meet him at the gate—to form a rank of escort to the palace. Have the servants here marshalled to receive him with all due honor. It is a visit of state."

As Ali hurried off to issue a hundred hasty orders, Sarput turned once more to the window. A thin hand caressed his straggly beard. His eyes gleamed. His thoughts were pleasant ones.

He watched the blacks hurriedly form a column and march toward the edge of the village. Somewhere a bugle shrilled and then a chorus of drums began a chant of welcome. The entire palace was a-stir with preparation.

The Rajah's eyes followed the slim form of Claudette Van-Gelder. Already his scheming brain grew busy with the possibilities of this unexpected visit. The jungle god Ka-Zar was being bested. Soon he would either fall into Sarput's hands or flee back into the eastern jungle from whence he had come. VanGelder was a confounded nuisance. But the old fool's hands were tied with much official red tape. And anyway, for being the father of such a charming bit of feminine loveliness, the Rajah could afford to overlook a few unpleasantries.

THE HUNCHBACK CAME once more into the room. His arms were heaped high with things that he had hastily gathered up—the necessary paraphernalia for a formal visit of state. And while in the grounds below, the Rajah's elephants were swiftly attired in gorgeous trappings and lined up in a double row from the main gate to the steps of the verandah, Sarput donned his official splendor.

From a turban of the richest brocade an enormous solitaire diamond gleamed. His tight-fitting coat was encrusted with embroidery of gold threads. The sash about his middle would have put a rainbow to shame. The jeweled emblems of a score of Eastern orders were hung upon his flat chest.

While Ali held up a mirror he strutted for a moment like a vain peacock before it. Then leaving the room, he went at once to the main hall of the palace.

It was a large and imposing place. Its doors were intricately carved and gilded by the artisans he had brought with him. Costly brocades and tapestries hung upon the walls. Deep-piled Oriental rugs covered the floor. At the far end was an imposing dais, on which a canopy of crimson velvet, upheld by gilded spears, hung over the magnificent throne of his forefathers.

Nasib, the keeper of the elephants, led forth the Rajah's hunting leopard. A jeweled collar encircled Dhar the cheetah's neck. The bracelet at the other end of the chain attached to it, Sarput snapped around his wrist. Dhar glided silently beside him as he mounted the steps of the dais. Then as he seated himself upon the throne, the cheetah stretched out at his feet. The entire household of the palace lined up in formal ranks around the walls and from somewhere a muffled drum began to beat.

VanGelder and his party had been astonished beyond measure by the fantastic city that had mushroomed here in the heart of the Congo. Now, as they were ushered into the palace, they were struck dumb by the splendor about them. They crossed the threshold, stepped into the great hall and drew up to a concerted halt.

The scene before them was unreal in its magnificence. Van-Gelder had been prepared for strange things that might be going on in his province—but hardly for such a parade of Eastern pomp as this. Recovering himself and his official dignity with an effort, he found the use of his legs and moved slowly forward.

Sarput graciously rose from his throne and came down from the dais to meet him. Dhar snarled, flattened his ears against his head. The Rajah stilled him with a single harsh command, then affectionately stroked the animal's sleek head.

VanGelder stopped, removed his helmet, clicked his heels together with military precision and executed a stiff, formal bow. Sarput inclined his turbaned head forward a few inches, touched his breast, lips and brow in a gesture that was at the same time humble and yet arrogant.

"I'm delighted," he said, showing his teeth in a thin smile, "to welcome Monsieur VanGelder, His Belgian Majesty's respected Commissioner."

The sight of Sarput's face, grave except for a mocking light in his eyes, took VanGelder's mind swiftly back to their first meeting. He frowned heavily, then rising to the pomp of the present occasion, he erased the frown from his face and bowed again.

"His Majesty's servant greets the Rajah Sarput," he answered stiffly.

SARPUT RELAXED A trifle. The chain that hung from his wrist clinked softly. "My welcome," he added significantly, "extends also to Monsieur VanGelder's party—and to his gracious and beautiful daughter."

Reluctantly VanGelder turned. The two guides still stood near the entrance of the hall, negligently at their ease but taking in every detail of their strange surroundings with alert eyes. At her father's signal, Claudette stepped forth from between them.

Holding her head high, she walked gracefully up the length of the hall, the cynosure of all eyes. She drew up beside her father, bowed her head in what was the minimum show of respect that the occasion demanded.

"Your highness," she said coolly, "has outdone himself and I am tremendously impressed by such an imposing reception."

Her tone implied that she was not impressed in the slightest. Perversely, Sarput was delighted. It was her spirit, equally as much as her fair beauty, that had first attracted him. He surveyed her now—a picture that would quicken the pulse of any man. He noted her slim, shapely legs were attired in khaki riding breeches. Her shirt, open at the neck, was torn and soiled by the journey. Her hair was touseled into unruly golden curls. Yet her visible pride more than matched his own.

Under the bold scrutiny of his burning gaze, a flush crept up from her throat and tinged her smooth cheeks a faint rose color. She shifted uneasily from one foot to the other.

At the movement, the crouching cheetah at Sarput's side suddenly glared at her, lashed his tail and snarled. At the sound, at the sight of the glowing greenish eyes and the bared fangs, Claudette unconsciously shrank back a pace. A faint shudder raced through her body.

Sarput swiftly gathered up the glittering length of chain, drawing Dhar up against him. He placed a restraining hand on the growling beast's head, spoke soothingly to him in his native Indian tongue. As Dhar subsided, he turned apologetically to Claudette.

"A thousand pardons if Dhar has frightened you," he murmured. "It is because of his very ferocity that he has become my favorite companion." Seeing the faint shadow of fear on Claudette's face as she still stared into the cheetah's glowing orbs, he continued: "Dhar has the soul of a devil—in his black heart he knows only the urge to kill. No one but Nasib, the keeper of my elephants, and I can manage him. You needn't be afraid now—you see he obeys me implicitly."

Claudette did not reply. Some deep-rooted instinct told her that she had made a bad mistake in letting Sarput see her fear of the beast.

The Rajah turned, called to Nasib and removing the bracelet, ordered the keeper to take the cheetah away. Then, satisfied with the success of his imposing welcome, he said to VanGelder and Claudette: "Come. I think we could enjoy an informal chat in a little more privacy."

CLAUDETTE, HOWEVER, A little shaken in her confidence, preferred to be alone for a few moments. An attendant was dispatched to lead her to her room. Barry and Holt, because they were white men, were also put up in the palace. Sarput ordered that the rest of the party be comfortably quartered and after arranging that a bountiful feast be hastily prepared, led VanGelder to his own suite.

There, over whiskey and sodas brought by Ali, they talked. Sarput reclined at ease upon his cushioned divan and regarded his visitor with mocking eyes.

"To what, my dear Commissioner," he inquired, "do I owe this heaven-sent visit?"

VanGelder put down his glass, rose and strode several paces across the door. Then he turned and regarded the glittering figure of the man sprawled negligently before him.

He sensed the mockery and with sudden determination, threw diplomacy to the winds and answered bluntly.

"I've heard things—ugly things. I decided to come up here myself and find out if they were true."

The Rajah waved a jeweled hand. "If all this," he made an expansive gesture, "is what you've been hearing about...."

"Not exactly," cut in VanGelder. "I've heard other things. The wholesale slaughter of game, for instance. And the slaughter of—men."

Sarput shrugged his thin shoulders. "Oh, that," he said. "Of course, there's been a bit of trouble. That jungle god you warned me about—or rather, some crazy white man who roams the forest—seems to dislike the idea of progress. He managed to stir up a fuss, but I have him well in hand now."

VanGelder straddled his legs, frowned. "Perhaps. I never believed in that yarn, exactly. But if there is such a god or man, the blacks in this region believe in him. You've stirred up a devil's mess of trouble in the Congo."

The Rajah raised an insolent eyebrow. "So? Well, after all, my dear Monsieur VanGelder, you are just a servant of your government. And that government ought to be well pleased with the magnificent civilization I have built up in the heart of this rank jungle."

The words were insulting. VanGelder realized that he was being made the butt of insolent mockery and his face flushed a dull crimson.

"It was a sad day," he retorted, "when officials back home got you off their hands and thrust you onto mine. They surely knew what deviltry you'd soon be up to and they expect me to tolerate it. But you're going too far." He stabbed the air with a warning forefinger. "It doesn't take much to wind up the blacks of the Congo. Rebellion spreads with the speed of a forest fire. And my government would not stand for the wholesale slaughter of every white man, woman and child in East Africa, just to satisfy your infernal pleasure."

It was the Rajah's turn to flush. An unhealthy, purplish color stained his swarthy cheeks. The little red devils danced in his murky eyes. Then he remembered Claudette.

He laughed softly, his teeth showing through his straggly beard. "Come, come, my dear Commissioner," he murmured. "After all, you are my guest. Your dinner will soon be ready and after you have eaten, we shall find some pleasant diversion to make you forget your official troubles."

CHAPTER XVI

MERCY—AT A PRICE

DESPITE THE RAJAH'S last words, VanGelder did not find his stay in the palace a pleasurable one. Each day, each hour brought some new evidence that the ugly rumors he had heard were not only true, but far short of the truth.

He saw the fate of Wurumba slaves, laboring under the blazing sun until they dropped exhausted in their chains. He saw the hunchback Ali struck because he moved slowly on his crippled legs. He saw jungle creatures that were both harmless and beautiful die needlessly, merely because they crossed the path of the Rajah, whose ruling passion was to slay.

But most of all he was disturbed by a vague unrest that disturbed the blacks. He was present when a party of Bulangi warriors, who had been sent out to harass Ka-Zar and his Wurumbas, returned in ragged, confused disorder. The terrible punishment that the angry Sarput immediately meted out to them for their defeat, disturbed VanGelder far less than the mutterings of their watching brother. The Bulangi were a bold and war-like race and though at first they had been happy to serve a master far more cruel and domineering than themselves, the first rumblings of revolt were stirring among them.

Claudette, too, saw all these things. To her father these acts were mainly warnings of a possible mass uprising and his responsibility included the life of every white man in the Congo. To her, they were subtle, far more personal threats. She knew that by her coming here, she and her father had put themselves in Sarput's power. She knew that Sarput desired her and wondered how long it would be before his passion burst all bounds of restraint. And every new act of wanton cruelty that she witnessed was a foretaste of what she might expect at his hands.

Bravely she maintained a show of pride and courage. But in her heart she knew many misgivings. Though she did not mention the name of Ka-Zar again, her thoughts turned often to the surrounding jungle. She visioned again the bronzed giant as she had glimpsed him in a tree. With sure, feminine instinct she knew that he was good, that he was just and kind. His image formed in her mind as that of a god-like saviour and she found herself longing to meet him, to pour out her troubles to him and place herself under his protection.

Despite her growing fear of Sarput, she was woman to the core of her being and her soul revolted at each new act of cruelty.

It was in the afternoon, exactly three days after her arrival, that her stout heart could stand no more of it. Early that morning, Nasib had come to the palace and fearfully reported that during the preceding night, Dhar had broken from his cage and vanished into the jungle.

The loss of his hunting leopard, his most prized possession, enraged Sarput as nothing else had done. All through the morning, exhorted by the trembling Nasib, parties had searched through the forest. Now the hapless keeper came to report their failure.

Sarput was alone with Claudette, paying her his bold, hateful compliments. The intrusion as well as the reason for it made him tremble with rage.

Because of the girl's presence, he suppressed his flaming temper. It smouldered beneath an icy exterior, doubly dangerous because it was pent up within him.

In stony silence, only his eyes glittering, he listened to Nasib's halting words. Then still without speaking to the keeper, he summoned two of the brown men, who also tended the elephants. Not until they stood on either side of the unhappy keeper, did he address them in their native Indian tongue.

CLAUDETTE DID NOT understand. But she saw Nasib's face grow suddenly ashen-gray, saw his knees turn to water and his eyes became pools of stark horror.

Never had she seen a man show such mortal terror. It struck through her like a knife, set her own pulses hammering. Her own fear of Sarput was nothing compared to what she saw mirrored on Nasib's face. She whirled on the Rajah.

"What are you saying?" she asked hoarsely. "What have you told him?"

Sarput looked down at her, his face still stony. In a cold, unemotionless voice, he told her.

"The fool has let Dhar, my cheetah, escape. He'll pay for his carelessness. I have just ordered him to be chained between a pair of my elephants, to be drawn and quartered."

A low cry burst from Claudette's lips. She stifled it with the back of her hand, recoiled a step and stared at Sarput. In her mind she saw the hideous spectacle and the vision made her brain reel.

"No—no!" she breathed, shuddering. "You can't do that!"

Sarput shrugged. "Why not?"

He made a signal and the two elephant herders seized Nasib's arms and started the stumbling wretch toward the door.

All Claudette's pride, all her courage and her fear, were blotted from her mind. She could think of nothing but the horrible fate that waited for the keeper. Words came to her lips now, in a tumbling rush.

"Don't," she begged wildly, holding out her hands in a piteous gesture. "Spare him—for my sake."

The Rajah looked down at her. Her last words stirred in his brain. Slowly the little red flames died down in his eyes and a strange glow came into them instead. He let his lids droop to hide it.

With another gesture, he stayed the men at the threshold.

Then to Claudette he said slowly: "Dhar meant a great deal to me. I must be compensated for my loss—one way or another."

Claudette heard and understood. She turned pale. All her old fear of Sarput rushed back in a tide that overwhelmed her. She stared from his hateful face to the pitiful figure of Nasib, near collapse at the door.

It was a horrible choice. Either she sent that poor wretch to a ghastly doom, or she chose a fate equally as terrible—or far worse—for herself.

FOR A LONG moment, various emotions clashed and warred within her. Blind hatred of the man before her, pity for his victim, the instinctive urge for her own self-preservation. Her father's daughter, truth and honor were deep-rooted in her soul. Then suddenly she reached a decision. Her head came up and she faced Sarput squarely.

"For my sake," she repeated, "let him go."

Sarput made no further effort to hide the exultant gleam in his eyes. A wolfish smile parted his beard as he turned immediately toward the trio at the door.

"The ill-born, thrice-accursed rascal is forgiven," he said rapidly. "Lead him instead to the edge of the forest, but let him remember that if he is seen again, he will die as I promised!"

FOR A MOMENT Nasib stared in unbelief. Then a vast relief swept over him. To be set, alone and unarmed, in the wilderness, was nothing compared to the fate that had threatened him. Somehow, he would survive. In a flood of gratitude, he broke from the grip of the others and flung himself at Claudette's feet.

The Rajah scowled blackly, gave a sharp order. The two men dragged Nasib to his feet and hustled him out of the room.

Sarput turned back to Claudette. "There—your wish has been granted. But I am satisfied that the reward will be well worth it."

Claudette stepped back. With a noncommittal, meaningless remark, she walked to the opposite side of the room. Sarput's close-set eyes followed her as she toyed with various objects in turn, set them down again wandered aimlessly on. Each step, however, carried her nearer to the door.

At first the Rajah was content to watch her obvious dilly-dallying, her transparent subterfuges to delay issue between them. It prolonged his delightful anticipation.

But at last he grew impatient. He strolled towards her, a sensual smile curling the corners of his lips.

"Enough of that game, my dear," he said softly. "Come—it isn't every day that I let myself be twisted about a woman's fingers."

Claudette stood with her back to the open door, confronted him with chin held high and eyes level. She knew that by now Nasib was well out of reach of Sarput's vengeance. "You are laboring under a mistake, Your Highness," she answered calmly. "For once, you see, I was forced to overlook my principles."

The smile died on Sarput's lips. For a moment he stared at her, then suddenly he realized what she meant. His face turned a mottled purple and he took another step toward her. "You lied to me?" he demanded hoarsely. "You tricked me?"

Though her pulses fluttered, she held her ground. "Yes," she answered evenly. "I lied—for the sake of that miserable man."

The Rajah's nostrils flared. The flames danced again in his eyes.

"No—you wouldn't dare…" began Claudette.

He stepped forward, grasped her wrist and drew her roughly to him.

At the touch of his moist, hateful fingers, at the feel of his panting breath on her face, Claudette's whole being rose up in revolt. Fear again claimed her. She acted instinctively. Her free hand flashed up, her open palm struck with all her force against the Rajah's cheek. It came away, leaving the livid outline of five fingers against the swarthy flesh.

Then, terrified at the consequences of her rash act, before Sarput could recover from his startled surprise, she wrenched herself free from his grasp and fled.

CHAPTER XVII

BATTLE ROYAL

HER EVERY INSTINCT and sensibility outraged by the scene she had just witnessed and by her interview with the Rajah, Claudette fled blindly from the palace. Her whole soul was in revolt against the evil genius whose mere presence seemed to cast a blight upon the virgin wilderness.

And though she had faced a cruel death before the spears of the Bulangi unflinching, fear now stirred in her heart. A terrible, nameless fear of the thing she had seen in Sarput's eyes. Her cheeks flamed a dull crimson with shame. She knew only one thing. She had to get away from that palace of evil, lest she suffocate.

At a word from her, the black on guard at the gate threw back the portal. Without a backward glance, unarmed, alone, she stumbled blindly for the encroaching fringe of the jungle wall.

Vaguely in her mind, though the thought was never definitely formed, was the hope that she might once again see the bronzed giant who had looked down at her from the top of the dakka tree, to meet Ka-Zar, talk to him and tell him of her fears.

Without analyzing her thoughts or emotions, she knew that she could put her trust in Ka-Zar; knew that her safety as well as that of her father was dependent upon the bronzed giant of the jungle.

Ever before her, as she fled, was the leering face of Sarput—

his cruel, sensual lips, his possessive black eyes—and his hands, whose touch on her bare arm had made her flesh crawl and her soul revolt.

To rid herself of the dark image that still pursued her, she stumbled ever deeper into the jungle wilds. She took no heed of her direction; she followed one blind game trail after another, only to move off down a third at a tangent.

And when at last Sarput's eyes pursued her no longer, she came to the sudden realization that she was lost. There was no trail; so thick were the inter-twining limbs of the trees overhead that there was no sky. There was naught but impenetrable jungle growth about her, so dense that her inexperienced eyes could not even tell her where she had last broken through the brush.

Claudette was more impatient with herself than afraid. She assured herself that she could not be very far from the palace and the doubtful safety it afforded. She would return to it after a while. First she had to think, had to plan, had to build up her reserves against further advances of the Rajah

She sank down onto the fallen trunk of a tree and cupped her chin in the palms of her hands. From what Sarput had told her, from all the whispered words that she had heard in the palace and from the scenes she had witnessed, she knew that Ka-Zar was engaged in a death struggle with Sarput. But with a sinking heart she realized that from all indications, her jungle god was being bested in the unequal struggle—that each day he was being driven further and further away from the territory surrounding the palace.

Claudette could have wept from sheer anger—from the sheer hopelessness of the situation. What could one man—bronzed giant though Ka-Zar might be—do against a thousand men with rifles?

THE DISTANT ROAR of a prowling lion penetrated her sombre thoughts. She looked up and was startled by the ever-deepening gloom of the forest. She had tarried longer than she knew under the protection of the tall trees. Dusk was falling. Unhappy as the thought was, she knew that she had to return to the palace.

Wearily she rose to her feet, glanced once coolly about at the trees that hemmed her in, then started boldly off to the right. If she had only known, the palace lay directly to her left.

She found it hard going. A thousand thorns pulled at her rough clothing, a thousand unseen prickly fingers held her back with malicious hands. Vines tripped her and she stumbled over the holes of burrowing mammals. Strange, she thought, how on entering the jungle she had not noticed how difficult the going was.

She became hot, tired. The turgid air that had been coming from the north died for a breathless minute, to mark the transition between day and night. Then it came again, but this time from the south.

A myriad of swarming insects assailed her, with vicious bite and sting. The noises of the jungle by day ebbed and died away, yielding place to the more sinister noises of night as the larger beasts began their nightly prowl.

Claudette changed her course a dozen times in as many minutes. Once with a cry of joy she stumbled on what she thought was a trail, only to be bitterly disappointed a moment later when she found that it led her to the edge of a deep ravine.

The light was fast ebbing now. In the center of a small clearing she stood still and considered her position. Fear stirred at her heart. With a grim realization of all that it implied, she admitted to herself that she was hopelessly lost. With a sheer effort of will she tried to be calm. She must not lose her head, yield to panic. Once her father discovered her absence from the palace, he would start out in search of her. Of that she was sure. Then her lips curled bitterly. Sarput, even, would join in the hunt.

She was startled by a furtive lashing in the underbrush at her right. Whirling, she faced in that direction. A pair of large, malevolent green eyes glared at her from the tangle of growth.

Then there came a sibilant, snarling hiss. Once more Claudette heard the lashing of the tail of the unseen beast. Then, where the baleful green eyes had been boring holes into the night, was naught but blackness.

With an icy hand clutching at her heart, the girl realized that the beast was stalking her. What it was—large or small— deadly or harmless—she did not know. The soul-searing fear of the unknown held her in thrall.

But not for long. A moment later the unknown danger that threatened took shape and form, materialized into the dread, slinking form of Dhar, the hunting cheetah of the Rajah.

Through generations and generations of his kind, Dhar's lust for the kill had been bred and in-bred within him. It was instinct with him, once the chain had been loosed from the collar around his throat, to stalk his prey, strike like lightning and slay with his ripping claws.

BELLY TO THE ground, his small, wedged-shaped head jutted forward, the cheetah crept from the fringe of the jungle into the small clearing. With malevolent green eyes he held the girl transfixed. He edged forward another few feet, then slowly, arched his hind quarters and his slavering jaws gaped.

Now that she realized the shape and form of her peril, Claudette's fear did not lessen. It only changed in kind. With stark vividness, the tales the Rajah had told her of the cheetah's ferocity, came to her mind. He would leap for her throat and as his long, saber teeth sank into her jugular, his ripping claws would slash.

She tried, to move but could not. She tried to call for help but no words came. She saw the tensing of the cheetah's limbs, saw the raw, red cavern of his mouth, saw the beginning of his leap.

Then three things happened simultaneously, with such startling swiftness that she was dumb with sheer shock and surprise. There came a challenging roar from nearby; the jungle screen parted. And from the opening a regal lion leaped into the clearing.

It was Zar aroused, terrible in all his might.

Even in mid-air, Dhar, with a spitting snarl, changed the direction of his spring, from the girl to this new threatening beast.

Lion and cheetah met in mid-air and the crushing shock of their impact sent them both back on their haunches. Then with a silent ferocity, a singleness of purpose that was appalling, they closed once more.

Wide of eye, the nails of her hands digging deep into her palms and her heart beating a trip-hammer tattoo in her throat, Claudette watched them as they fought. She could not have fled even if she had had the strength. Some irresistible force, greater than her own, held her there, rooted to the spot.

Zar the mighty was bigger, heavier than the cheetah. But by this very token Dhar was faster and his ripping claws more sharp. It was an abysmal, primeval struggle between the two jungle beasts for supremacy, with a lone white girl for witness. The law of fang and claw was being put to the supreme test.

Instinctively Zar hated this alien beast; hated him doubly for the smell of the devil Om that was strong about him. For his part Dhar knew that he was fighting for his life and the knowledge lent a new swiftness," a new cunning, a new ferocity to his attack.

They slashed with claw, ripped with fang. There was no sound save the hissing pant of their hot breaths. And the girl watched them spellbound.

After the second shock of their coming together, Dhar was quick to roll upon his back—his favorite fighting position. Like steel-tipped pistons the claws of his four feet ripped at the lion's belly.

Zar felt the flames of pain rip at his entrails. This strange beast he was engaged with fought like N'Jaga and his tribe. And like N'Jaga he must be dealt with.

WISE FROM LONG years of jungle survival, bold with the dignity of his sovereignty, cunning from a thousand battles won—for to lose once meant death—Zar swiftly changed his attack from one of claw to one of fang. With a sudden movement he threw his tawny body off that of the cheetah and to one side away from the ripping claws. At the same moment his massive jaw clamped on Dhar's throat in an unbreakable grip.

The skin and fur protecting the cheetah's jugular were thick and tough. Zar hung on, nevertheless. In a frenzy the cheetah pivoted around on the back of his skull to bring his claws into play once more. Savagely they ripped at the lion's quarter. Zar ignored the burning wounds, concentrated on his own grip. Slowly, inch by inch he worked his teeth deeper and deeper into the flesh of the cheetah's throat. Slowly, inch by inch, he gathered more and more of the loose flesh covering the jugular into the vise of his gaping jaws.

Dhar's breath was coming now in tortured gasps as Zar's jaws shut off his air. Blinding lights flashed before his bulging eyes and a rushing, roaring sound started in his brain, to end with an explosion like that of a bomb. The slashing blows of his claws became weaker. And at this sign of approaching victory, Zar's grip became still more inexorable. He worked his jaws forward, his teeth still deeper. Making a lever of his hind legs he crushed the cheetah's head to the ground and exerted his last ounce of magnificent strength.

Suddenly he felt a spurt of hot blood in his mouth and he knew that the battle was won. He had reached the jugular at last. Dhar's body lashed once in a wild, convulsive movement, then collapsed with a weak striking of paws.

His jaws still clamped tight about the cheetah's throat, Zar raised his head, lifting the body of his victim clear of the ground. For a moment he shook the limp body from side to side as if it were a miserable bush rat. Then sure at last that the battle was over, he let the body of Dhar slump to the ground.

He turned slowly to confront Claudette, who still stood transfixed. Then his regal head came up and the stentorian challenge of the lion who has made his kill, rumbled brazenly across the jungle.

Claudette's brain whirled dizzily. She was assailed by a cruel thought. Was she after all to fall prey to the ravening beasts? Had she been saved from the cheetah, only to die before the fangs of the lion? Her cool courage could stand no more. Her eyes swam, her knees turned to water beneath her and would not support her weight.

She knew that she was fainting; she knew that she was falling. The earth rose up dizzily to meet her. But in that second before she crashed she felt strong arms about her, felt herself swept off her feet, to be held close against a hard and mighty chest.

Warm breath fanned her cheek. Then she had the sensation of being carried swiftly off through the jungle.

With a sheer effort of will she held onto her consciousness long enough to breathe one prayer to Heaven. She thanked the all-knowing God, who in his infinite wisdom had made man and beast alike, for having sent Ka-Zar to save her. For that it was Ka-Zar who carried her so securely in his arms, she was sure.

With a little sigh of weariness and contentment, consciousness slipped from her.

CHAPTER XVIII

FOREST IDYLL

SARPUT'S BOAST TO VanGelder that he had driven Ka-Zar deep into the jungle was not quite exact. For ever since the arrival of VanGelder and his daughter at the palace, Ka-Zar had been within bowshot of the Rajah's stockade. He admitted to himself that it was the presence of the beautiful female Om who had brought him there, where every tree and every shadow concealed a lurking menace against his life. Yet so innocent was he of the workings of his own nature that he could not analyze or understand the power that impelled him.

Zar understood and might have told him, but in the language of the lions there is no word for love.

So for three days, with Zar ever at his side, Ka-Zar lurked outside the stockade walls, seeing all that transpired within, but never being seen himself. On several occasions he caught fleeting glimpses of the golden-haired creature and each time he marveled at the rapid beating of his heart.

He was not far off that third afternoon when Claudette fled so precipitantly from the palace. Sensing that something was amiss he swung to the trees and followed after her. A frown darkened his brow when he saw her plunge deeper and deeper into the jungle, all unheeding.

He and Zar were standing but a few feet behind her when she sat down on the tree trunk to rest and think. And when a few minutes later she started to retrace her steps and became hopelessly lost, he could have reached out his hand and guided her to safety.

On more than one occasion he was tempted to do just that. But his wild and untamed instinct, his natural mistrust of man, deeply rooted in him almost since birth, held him back. And in addition to this he felt a strange shyness, an alien uneasiness, whenever he was near the girl.

Ka-Zar was reveling in the subtle perfume that drifted downwind to him from Claudette, when Zar brought him out of his abstraction with a low growl of warning. His head snapped back and his nostrils twitched as he sniffed at the air.

Then a moment later both he and Zar saw the slinking form of the cheetah. Dhar had been creeping upon them and the girl with the wind and they had not been aware of his presence until that moment when he was about to strike.

Ka-Zar was swift to realize the danger that threatened the strange female Om who so intrigued him, but he was not so swift to act. For one of the few occasions of their long companionship, Zar was the first one to strike. With a challenging roar he broke through the jungle wall and met the diverted charge of the cheetah with his broad shoulder.

And once the battle was on, sure of the outcome, Ka-Zar did not interfere.

An hour had passed since Claudette had experienced the sensation of being carried, when her eyelids fluttered open. She was aware of a pale, unearthly light. It came from the silver orb of the rising moon. And silhouetted in the soft glow, bending directly over her where her head lay pillowed on a low hummock of moss, was the leonine face and piercing eyes of the bronzed giant she had first seen in the top of the dakka.

UNAFRAID, SHE SMILED up into the amber eyes and immediately the face relaxed. The fierce lines softened, the eyes became mellow.

"Ka-Zar!" whispered Claudette.

With one hand Ka-Zar brushed back the raven hair from his forehead. Surprise took possession of his face. "You know my name?" he said in wonder. "Who are you who calls Ka-Zar by name and walks alone in the jungle?"

"I am Claudette VanGelder," answered the girl. "My father is Commissioner of this territory. He came here to investigate the rumors he had heard concerning the Rajah Sarput and I came with him."

A frown puckered Ka-Zar's broad brow. "Ka-Zar knows little of the white man's tongue. I hear your words but know not their meaning. The Rajah Sarput is evil. He wages war on Ka-Zar and his jungle beasts. In time, he shall die. But first Ka-Zar must know whether you come as a friend of the evil one."

Claudette shook her head violently from side to side in a decided negative. "No, no," she said hurriedly. "I and my father would fight the Rajah, even as you, if we had the power."

At her words Ka-Zar's mobile lips broke into a smile. "I knew as much," he said simply, "since I first saw you. Your face is like that of the golden lobali flower in a sunny clearing. Evil could not live in a face so beautiful."

Many polished courtiers had flattered Claudette before, but never had words thrilled her so much as these issuing from the lips of the bronzed and naked savage bending over her. She knew that this was no pretty, practised speech; not the cheap flattery of the effete drawing room, where compliments are cheap and bandied about from one woman to another until they lose all meaning.

So simply had they been stated that she knew they were sincere. They came unguarded from the heart. Without guile, without any ulterior motive, they were the honest expression of an honest man.

Savage though this Ka-Zar might be, Claudette sensed instinctively that there was a splendid nobility about him. He was not so much savage as decivilized, she mused. No, it was that civilization had never touched him. He was that unspoiled, rare and impossible thing—nature's nobleman.

She sighed and wondered whether he could hear the furious

beating of her heart. Then she flushed, beneath his steady gaze and struggled up to a sitting position. She found herself in a small clearing on the bank of a gurgling stream. The rim of the moon was just clearing the tops of the surrounding trees. Off to her right she saw a faint, reddish glow in the sky.

Ka-Zar interpreted her questioning look. "The lair of the evil Sarput," he explained.

Claudette shuddered at the name, then for the first time made out the massive form of Zar, by the stream. The lion was busily engaged in bathing his wounds in the clear water. Instinctively her hand went out to Ka-Zar. "It was he—the lion who saved me?" she asked.

KA-ZAR'S FLESH BURNED at the cool touch of her hand. He looked straight ahead, unseeing, before him. "Yes," he answered. "It was Zar who saved you. It was Zar who killed the beast of the evil one."

"Zar the lion?" she asked. "Zar—your brother?"

Ka-Zar nodded. "Yes, Zar the mighty. Zar, brother of Ka-Zar."

Claudette knew that she was speaking foolishment, but she could not keep back the words. "Are—are you a god?" she asked in a small voice.

Looking deep into her eyes he answered slowly, significantly: "Ka-Zar is a man—even as you are a woman."

Claudette hid her face before the burning look in his eyes.

"You fear Ka-Zar?" he continued softly.

"No," she answered.

A great exultation filled Ka-Zar's heart. "Ever since your coming, Ka-Zar has been disturbed," he said. "Now he knows what has bothered him. Ka-Zar needs a mate."

The words were uttered with a simple dignity and they filled Claudette's heart with a strange glow. Never had a girl received such a proposal before, she knew. She was thrilled to the core of her being. From any other man those few blunt words would have been insult. She would have resented them. But from Ka-Zar's lips, their very elemental quality made them beautiful. Her emotions mastered her for a moment. She could not speak.

"I shall drive out the evil Oman," continued Ka-Zar swiftly. "Then together with Zar we shall roam the jungle." He paused a moment, but still Claudette did not answer. "You do not speak," said Ka-Zar with a troubled frown. "Has Ka-Zar offended you?"

Claudette had not answered for the simple reason that she could find no words for the emotions that surged in her heart.

"No, no," she answered swiftly to his last question. "You have not offended me. But I am bewildered by so much that has happened. Everything is so strange, so impossible. It is almost like a dream. I—I..." she stumbled over her words, hesitated and fell silent.

"Ka-Zar is mighty but just," he continued, pleading his cause.

"I know," said Claudette. She talked on hurriedly at random, trying to cover her confusion. "And I haven't thanked you yet for saving my life. Tonight and three times back on the trail before we reached the palace of the Rajah."

"Ka-Zar saw that you were good but blind to the signs of the jungle. By my side you shall learn what is to be eaten and what is to be cast aside; where to step and where not to step. The beasts of the jungle shall befriend you and no harm shall come to you."

He continued on and in simple words depicted the life she might expect if she honored him by becoming his mate. Her head spun. For a mad moment she was tempted to accede to his wish. Then all her background, all her traditions, all her training fought down the impulse.

"I cannot answer now," she said at last. "Later."

Ka-Zar bowed his head. "Ka-Zar hears and understands," he answered. "Ka-Zar's patience is as long as that of Trajah the elephant."

CLAUDETTE WAS DEEPLY touched by his humbleness. Her fingers strayed across his clenched fist for a fleeting moment. There is no telling what the outcome might have been had not a distant commotion broken the stillness of the jungle at that moment.

Claudette raised her head and looked at Ka-Zar questioningly.

"It is the Oman," he explained. "Sarput and the white man who is your father search the jungle for you with many men."

At the mention of her father, the spell that had held Claudette on the verge of making a mad plunge into the unknown future with this equally unknown man at her side, was broken.

"I must go," she said.

"Ka-Zar will take you. But you will come again?"

"Yes."

"With the setting sun, tomorrow?"

"Yes," said Claudette breathlessly.

"Here," said Ka-Zar. "The way is simple and the trail plainly marked. You will not lose your way and it would not matter if you did. For Ka-Zar will be watching for you."

Once more Claudette thrilled to his voice and words. Then, as if she were but a leaf floating on the breeze, he picked her up in his arms and indicating the trail as he walked, started off towards the red glow in the sky that marked the palace of the Rajah.

CHAPTER XIX

"HELL HATH NO FURY—"

K A-ZAR TARRIED LONG enough by the edge of the jungle that surrounded Sarput's lair to see Claudette safely within the gate, to hear the beating of drums, the noise of many fire-sticks and the loud shouts of rejoicing that greeted her return. Then he turned once more and moved off down the trail he had just traveled.

He had gone but a few feet, however, when his path was blocked by a slender, shadowy figure. It was Wamba, the sister of Wazi, the Wurumba chief. And in Wamba's black eyes there was a light that Ka-Zar had never seen before, a light he could not fathom. But being filled with the glory of Claudette he smiled upon her.

Wamba answered his smile with flashing eyes. She spoke rapidly, angrily in her native tongue. Ka-Zar by now understood some of the Wurumba dialect and could speak a few words.

"Why is Wamba angry with Ka-Zar?" he asked.

"The white girl," she answered. "She belongs to the evil men."

Ka-Zar frowned. "The white girl is good," he said bluntly.

Wamba's lips curled in scorn. "Ka-Zar is god of the jungle. There can be nothing between him and the white-faced girl."

If Ka-Zar had been more experienced in the ways of women he would have realized that Wamba was jealous and he would have known further that hell hath no fury greater than a woman scorned. But, his mind was occupied with other things. He laid his hand gently on Wamba's shoulder.

"Ka-Zar is no god, O Wamba. He is man."

With an angry movement she shook off his hand. "Your beasts and my people are in great danger before the deviltry of the evil one and his friends. Has Ka-Zar become soft that he makes love to a foolish girl when danger threatens?"

"Enough!" said Ka-Zar sternly, stung by her bitter words and by the realization that perchance they might be true. Then more softly: "Go now, Wamba. Ka-Zar would be alone. Ka-Zar has not failed you or your people."

For a long moment Wamba stared from bold eyes into his amber ones. And what she read there filled her heart with bitter jealousy. With a single, sibilant word that Ka-Zar did not catch, she turned on her heel and melted into the dark shadows.

His heart still uplifted by his meeting with Claudette, Ka-Zar continued on his way to where Zar waited for him and from thence to the Wurumba village.

But not so the black maiden, Wamba. Her savage heart was filled with anger. The tender passion she had felt towards the bronzed jungle giant who had come to save her people was changed to black resentment. She had desired him for her own, but from the look she had seen in his eyes, she knew that that would never be.

Equally the wrath was directed at the white-faced girl who in Wamba's unschooled mind had stolen Ka-Zar from her. But Claudette was beyond her powers of good or evil.

Not so Ka-Zar. Through him she could hurt them both.

All the cunning of her savage mind began to work. If she could not have Ka-Zar, she would see to it that the white-faced one did not have him either. Her eyes glinted as each new cunning thought prompted another. And finally she evolved a scheme that was Machiavellian in conception.

IT WAS LONG past midnight when the Rajah Sarput finally retired to his quarters that night. Though he had lost Dhar, his favorite hunting cheetah—the mangled body of the beast had been discovered in the search for Claudette—he was well pleased with the events of the day.

Slowly he sipped a final whiskey and soda while his mind's eye explored anew the many charms of the lovely girl who had fallen into his power. For though Claudette and her father were not aware of it, they were his virtual prisoners.

Sarput's thin lips curled and he stroked his straggly beard. VanGelder was a fat, pompous ass, he told himself—a nuisance. He would be disposed of later, at some opportune time. Or better still, if need be, he could be used as a lever to bring the girl to her senses and final surrender.

Sarput flattered himself smugly for conceiving that bright idea. The girl was a spitfire, he mused. She had spirit, pride and courage. She would not be easily broken. But he liked her the better for it. Had he not tamed the ferocious Dhar? In a few months under his patient tutelage she would be as docile and submissive as any slave.

Sarput scowled. And when that time came he would tire of her as he had done of a hundred women before her. He would cast her out, her pride humbled; her spirit broken. Or maybe he would give her as a gift to the black Babi, chief of his Bulangi braves.

The Rajah's pleasant thoughts were interrupted at this point by the shuffling entrance of Ali.

"What now, misbegotten one?" he asked.

Ali bowed low as he made obeisance to his master. "There is one at the gate, sire. The black girl Wamba, of the Wurumba tribe. She seeks an audience with you."

Sarput's eyes narrowed craftily. From past experience he knew that where women were concerned there was apt to be treachery.

"Speak, witless fool," he said harshly. "What would this Wamba have of me?"

"Master," replied Ali, concealing the reluctance with which he reported the news, "through an interpreter I have learned that she brings news of Ka-Zar. But she will unburden herself only to you."

Sarput half rose from his chair. "Misshapen cripple," he stormed, "why do you tarry? Run—fly! Bring her to me with the interpreter. At once!"

Ali scraped his twisted leg in a bow and as fast as his affliction permitted him, fled from the chamber.

He returned a few minutes later, trailing behind him Wamba and the black who was to act as interpreter. His duty performed, Sarput ordered him to leave. When the door had closed behind the hunchback, Sarput eyed the black girl shrewdly from worldly, experienced eyes. He guessed at the tumult surging in her heathen breast, guessed at the reason that brought her there. To add to her temptation he let a string of sparkling jewels trickle slowly through his fingers.

BOLDLY UNABASHED, WAMBA confronted him, her dark eyes darker still with passion.

Sarput turned to the interpreter. "Ask her what brings her here?"

The black spoke a few guttural words to Wamba. She answered and her reply was in turn translated for Sarput's ears. "She brings news of Ka-Zar."

The Rajah's eyes narrowed. "What news?" he asked.

Again the black spoke and again Wamba answered. The black interpreted once more. "She comes to betray Ka-Zar. She says not to let Ka-Zar know who betrays him."

"It shall be as she says," replied Sarput eagerly. "And this string of jewels shall be her reward for her information."

The Bulangi spoke rapidly to Wamba, whose eyes glittered at the mention of the jewels. Then she answered him with a hurried flow of words.

The interpreter turned to Sarput at last and translated. On the morrow at sunset, Ka-Zar would be at a certain place in the jungle, a half-mile removed from the palace. The girl Wamba described the place in detail. He, Buku, knew the spot well and could lead his master there.

A swift surge of elation filled Sarput's heart at the possibility of at last getting Ka-Zar into his power. The day he had looked forward to for so long was about to dawn. For a sunset on the morrow, if the girl had not lied to him, Ka-Zar the jungle god would be enchained like any slave.

The Rajah fondled the string of jewels for another moment, then with a gesture of contempt tossed them to Wamba. Just as she was in the act of catching the glittering baubles a low, ominous rumble filled the air, shaking the palace to its very foundations.

Startled, Sarput looked up. Wamba and the black froze in stark terror.

A moment later the Rajah, from his worldly wisdom, guessed the answer. The towering volcano at the foot of which he had built his splendid palace, was not extinct as he had supposed. Now, after centuries of slumber, it was awakening to activity.

"It was the voice of the mountain M'Bele," he told the Bulangi.

Instead of being reassured, the black was more mystified and more fearful than before.

Eyes wide with a nameless terror, Wamba listened until the last rumble died away. Then forgetting the jewels that had slipped from her fingers, she fled to the door.

CHAPTER XX

CHAINS

WITH THE IMPATIENCE of any man awaiting the appointed time of a rendezvous with his beloved, Ka-Zar arrived at the trysting place a full hour before sunset. Ever since he had returned Claudette to the keeping of the palace the preceding night, his heart had been filled with her. A thousand times he had pictured her face, her voice, her smile; again and again he had re-lived the brief moment when she had touched his hard fist with the tips of her cool fingers.

A new song was in Ka-Zar's heart, a new strength in his mighty limbs. All his old reckless confidence returned to him. He laughed at the threat that the Rajah Sarput represented, confident that in the next encounter between them he would triumph.

His brief, incomprehensible scene with Wamba had been forgotten a second after it had transpired. His mind was filled with too many other things to consider treachery. And so it was that when he came to the glade where Claudette was to meet him, he threw himself on the ground and from the sheer joy of living, dug his hands deep into the moist earth.

If the subtle perfume that emanated from Claudette had not been so strong in his nostrils, he might have scented the danger that crept up on him, nearer, ever nearer. If the sound of his beloved's voice had not been in his ears, he surely would have heard the warning whisper of the jungle as Sarput's blacks surrounded him.

As it was, he was still lying on the ground, his spear and his long bow cast carelessly to one side, when he first scented danger. He made a long, lithe dive for his spear, came up with it in his hand. But too late. The points of a dozen other spears pricked the skin of his throat and another score hemmed him in with a ring of steel.

For a fleeting instant all of Ka-Zar's fighting instinct was aroused. He knew that he was trapped, but nevertheless he intended to die with the challenging roar of the lion on his lips.

Then with sudden, blinding force came the realization that he had been betrayed. For a moment he was stunned, incapable of thought, action or emotion. That the flower-faced girl he had wooed as his mate had been capable of such infamy, shook his inner-most being as nothing had ever done before—as nothing would ever do in the future. It was she who had betrayed him! Under the pretense of listening to his words of courtship and mating, she had tricked him, led him into this trap.

Ka-Zar's soul sickened within him. The fire died from his eyes. He had no desire to live or fight. Let the Bulangi do with him what they might; let the evil Om enjoy his revenge to the full.

And it was thus, broken in spirit, head bowed on chest, that the once proud Ka-Zar, king of the beasts, was led captive in chains to the Rajah's palace.

And as he was thrust through the stockade gate on the point of a dozen spears, M'Bele stirred once more in its sleep and settled down again with an eruptive shower of sparks and ash.

SARPUT WAS THERE to witness Ka-Zar's arrival. For the occasion he had turned out his entire household, made a gala celebration of the affair. Standing high on a balcony, his gaunt form silhouetted darkly against the setting sun, he watched with gloating eyes as the bronzed giant who had defied him for months was dragged across the courtyard.

By his side stood Claudette, her face drawn and haggard, her eyes wide. With frantic hands she gripped the rail of the balcony before her lest she fall.

Sarput saw her extreme agitation and the lids of his eyes drooped while his lips curled back from his teeth in a wolfish smile.

When Ka-Zar and the procession surrounding him had reached a point directly beneath the balcony on which the Rajah stood, Sarput raised his hand in a commanding gesture and ordered a halt.

In a loud, mocking voice he addressed the naked giant in its midst. "Welcome, Ka-Zar, brother of the lion. I have long wished to extend the hospitality of my dungeon to you. There you can roar your inhuman roar and gnash your teeth against bars and chains like any savage beast."

Ka-Zar barely heard the words and surely did not understand them. But at the sound of the hated voice he raised his chin from his breast and stared upward at the balcony.

He favored Sarput with but a brief, contemptuous glance. Then his burning eyes focused on Claudette, who stood swaying by the Rajah's side.

And what she saw in them of hate, contempt and bitterness struck her like a physical blow. She staggered back, would have fallen had not Sarput's ready hand steadied her.

"You see?" whispered Sarput in her ear. "Your jungle god is only a savage beast after all. He hates you. His eyes were like those of Dhar, my poor cheetah."

"Please," said Claudette. "Let me go. I can stand no more."

But standing in chains in the courtyard below, how was Ka-Zar to hear? How was he to know that it had been Wamba and not Claudette who had betrayed him; that even at the moment Claudette, her father and the two white guides of their party were all prisoners behind locked and bolted doors?

Knowing naught but bitterness, at a sign from Sarput he permitted himself to be dragged away.

In a cell of the foul and noisome dungeon deep beneath the palace, Ka-Zar was chained to the wall. Here he rotted for two weeks, his sole companions a horde of vicious bush rats. Once daily a black would enter his cell, leaving a jug of water and a bucket of swill beside him, and then vanish again.

There was no other sign from the outer world that he had not been forgotten, that his fate was not to be this—that he was to be literally buried alive in his cell. Ka-Zar did not mind. He had lost the most priceless thing the jungle had bestowed on him—the will to live.

He did not eat; he did not sleep. The face of the golden-haired girl whom he thought had betrayed him haunted him eternally. He remembered her vividly as he had last seen her, standing on the balcony at Sarput's side. In his mind's eye he saw the evil one lean over and whisper something in her ear. Despite her flower face she, too, was evil. With all the will at his command he tried to put her from his mind. But to no avail.

TO RID HIMSELF of her hated presence he pondered at times on the fate that awaited him. He knew Sarput's lust for cruelty too well to believe that he would be permitted to die by slow starvation. No; his death would be made the occasion of some fantastic spectacle.

At other times to drive the mocking thoughts of Claudette from his mind, he strained at his chains until his magnificent body was exhausted.

He grew thin, emaciated. It was not that he lacked food. Many times in the forest he had gone for days without meat. It was that his soul was sick.

And as if Nature had adapted itself to his mood—as if the very heart of the jungle protested at his captivity—the rumbling from M'Bele became more frequent and more threatening. Sulphurous fumes hung heavy in the already foetid atmosphere of the cell; a fine ash sifted down from the narrow, iron-barred window high up against the ceiling. And at night an intermittent red glow pulsed fantastically on the far wall of the dungeon.

Ka-Zar would have smiled bitterly if he had known the reason why his ultimate fate had been so long deferred. The

Rajah was preparing for him his ultimate achievement in barbaric sport.

It had been the Bulangi chief who had first told Sarput of the enmity that existed, between Ka-Zar and N'Jaga, the leopard that limped. It was more than enmity—it was a death feud. On hearing the tale, an idea was born full grown in Sarput's mind. Immediately he dispatched a score of his retainers to hunt for the leopard that limped. N'Jaga was to be captured alive at any cost, no matter how long the chase took or how far afield it led. And woe betide the men if they failed.

It was the eleventh day after Ka-Zar's captivity that the hunters returned from their long trek westward, with their prize. N'Jaga was mad with fear and hate. Tail lashing, teeth gnashing, he endlessly paced the width of his narrow cage, while his baleful orbs gleamed like twin opals of venom.

Sarput examined his latest prize with the keenest delight. With relish he studied N'Jaga point by point, noted the flat skull, the saber-like teeth. He gloated over the breadth of chest, the powerful haunches and the claws of steel, each one capable of disemboweling a man at one stroke.

In comparison to this raging jungle beast, Dhar the cheetah had been but a purring kitten. And to heighten N'Jaga's rage, Sarput issued orders that for the ensuing three days the leopard was to be starved and perpetually tormented by the points of spears.

CHAPTER XXI

AN OLD SCORE IS SETTLED

IT WAS ON the fifteenth day of his captivity that Ka-Zar first saw a face from the outside world. Early in the afternoon he heard the muffled tread of naked feet in the corridor outside his cell, accompanied by the characteristic shuffle that marked the coming of Ali. Apathetically he raised his gaunt and haggard head and stared at the door. A key grated in the lock, a bar raised and slowly the portal swung inward.

The hunchback Ali, followed by four Bulangi warriors, stepped into the cell. Each of the blacks was armed with a spear, while from Ali's hand a key swung at the end of a stout chain. The four natives showed their filed teeth in grins, but the hunchback's face was pale.

"Courage," he muttered, as he fitted the key to the lock, of the chains that held Ka-Zar to the wall. "Your hour of judgment is at hand."

"Ka-Zar asks no more than to die," replied Ka-Zar. He took a deep breath as the last chain fell away from his wrists. "His heart is already dead."

Ali muttered something beneath his breath, then issued a sharp command to the blacks. Swiftly they surrounded Ka-Zar and with their spears pricking at his ribs, marched him out of the dungeon.

As they mounted upwards toward the light and fresh air Ka-Zar felt his strength revive. Calmly, without fear, he wondered what fate the evil one had in store for him. Then one last spark of his spirit asserted itself. If the devil Om thought that he—Ka-Zar—would beg for mercy, he was doomed to disappointment. For, Ka-Zar told himself, he was beyond all pain, all hurt. Death in any form would be a sweet release from the traitorous fair face that haunted him.

The party reached the ground floor of the palace at last and after negotiating many intricate passages and turnings, emerged at last into the courtyard, into the full blaze of the sun. Ka-Zar was momentarily blinded by the strong light. He blinked his eyes a few moments, then when they became accustomed to the relentless brilliance of the sun, he looked about him.

He was puzzled for a moment by what he saw. Directly beneath the window of the Rajah's suite a large arena had been erected. It was enclosed by a fine-meshed wire netting, which extended upward for some twenty feet. At one end was a small, cage-like contraption; opposite it was a small door.

On the far side of the arena, drawn up in all the regalia of a state function, was the entire household of the Rajah. And next to them in massed formation, their long spears shining brightly in the light, stood the Bulangi warriors.

Ka-Zar's appearance was greeted by a rising howl of derision from the blacks. They showed their teeth in hungry smiles, pranced about and shook their spears above their heads. Now that the mythical Ka-Zar was laid low and captive in their hands, they could afford to forget their superstitious fears. The retainers of the prince, likewise, expressed their feelings in a strange jargon of words.

KA-ZAR DID NOT know what was expected of him but it was plain to see that of all that surging mob, there was no one to call him friend. They had congregated there, he realized, to see him die, and the more terrible and prolonged his death—the more they would relish the spectacle.

A low growl of disgust rumbled in his throat but that was the only sign he made. Verily, of all the creatures that roamed the jungle, the two-legged ones were the most evil. If his death was what they awaited, they would be satisfied. He would not fight for his life; would not make a spectacle of himself to satisfy the blood lust of a horde of yelling blacks.

Then of a sudden the hoarse cries that had greeted his appearance were stilled. All eyes were raised to the Rajah's balcony. Slowly Ka-Zar raised his head from his chest and glanced upward.

Sarput had just emerged onto the balcony. Standing at his side, the Rajah's arm hooked familiarly under hers, was Claudette. Behind these two stood VanGelder and the two white guides. And bringing up the rear stood a squad of the prince's native retainers, each armed with a rifle.

There was no way for Ka-Zar to know that Sarput's arm was hooked under Claudette's to prevent her from swooning. There was no way for him to know that VanGelder and the guides had walked onto the balcony under compulsion; that they were in reality prisoners of the guards behind them.

Ali he saw was the devil Om who had brought such misery to his jungle. And by his side stood the girl who had betrayed him. They had come to witness his humiliation, to mock him in his hour of death.

Some deep, atavistic spirit was aroused in Ka-Zar's heart. What the jeers and gibes of the throng of blacks had been unable to do, the sight of Claudette's face accomplished. His head snapped up—proud, arrogant, defiant. His chest expanded to the full and his muscles bulged. For a long moment his burning eyes gazed deep into Claudette's blue ones. He saw her blanch, pale, shrink back. Then he transfixed Sarput with compelling eyes.

"O evil one," he called out in a loud, commanding tone that all might hear. "More craven than Dikki the jackal, more foul than Janko the hyena, lower than Sinassa the snake who crawls upon his belly—I, Ka-Zar, brother of Zar the lion, spit upon you that all may see."

And then to suit his words, he spat volubly towards the

balcony.

It was Sarput's turn to pale—not with fear but with hate. His features convulsed, twisted into a mask of consummate rage. It was a moment before he could speak and when at last he finally found his voice, it trembled with passion.

"To the arena!" he commanded in a hoarse voice. "Let his flesh be pierced by spears that his blood may run red."

Ka-Zar's four guards jumped at their master's commands. In a trice the points, of their spears had cut long ribbons of flesh from Ka-Zar's body. Then with the blood streaming from a dozen wounds, he was roughly propelled forward to the wire cage. The trap door was raised, he was thrust violently inside and the door rattled shut behind him with an ominous bang.

KA-ZAR STOOD STOCK-STILL for a moment on straddled legs, his leonine head swaying slightly from side to side. That some unknown, unseen danger threatened he knew, but from which direction it would strike—he did not know.

Once more the blood pounded strongly through his veins. He felt his muscles bulge and swell and he was reassured. For some unaccountable reason he felt supremely confident that he would conquer whatever thing—man or beast—who attacked him.

An awed hush had fallen over the thronged assembly. No one spoke; no one moved; even M'Bele had ceased its warning rumblings. Only the sun blazed down relentlessly, infusing Ka-Zar with new strength.

Then, as Ka-Zar still stood poised by the trap door on the balls of his feet, the silence was shattered by the blood-curdling scream of a leopard. His head snapped round to face the cage at the far side of the arena. He recognized a familiar accent of hate in that scream and a moment later his suspicions were verified as the door of the cage swung up and N'Jaga bounded into the arena.

Ka-Zar threw back his head and laughed—a short and bitter laugh.

At the sound, N'Jaga checked his charge in full stride and flattened down, belly to the ground, ears back against his flat skull. His recognition of his ancient enemy had been almost as swift as Ka-Zar's recognition of him.

But for once the sight of the jungle god aroused no fear in N'Jaga's heart. It merely increased the insane rage that had consumed him since first the net of the Rajah's hunters had fallen over his head.

And as his rage increased, so did his cunning. With malevolent eyes he examined Ka-Zar swiftly. One glance was sufficient to tell him that the bronzed two-legged creature was unarmed. No knife glittered at his belt or in his hand. For once the advantage was N'Jaga's and he determined to press it to the full.

With the savage snarl of the lion rumbling in his throat, naked and empty-handed, Ka-Zar advanced slowly on the leopard. N'Jaga, however, did not yield ground as was his ancient wont. Instead his muscles coiled, rippled along his flanks like bands of steel. The talon-like claws of his forepaws arched.

Ka-Zar saw. He knew that N'Jaga realized that he was unarmed. He knew that the feud that had existed between him and the leopard was to be settled for all time. Only one of them would leave that arena alive.

To retreat meant a swift and terrible death. At the first sign of weakness or fear N'Jaga would be upon him. Half crouched, his powerful hands with fingers spread reaching before him, he advanced slowly. If N'Jaga in all his feline beauty was a savage beast of the jungle, no less was Ka-Zar. The same impulse animated them both—to strike first, swiftly, surely and without mercy.

With but a short ten feet separating the two, the reeking scent of blood dripping from Ka-Zar's bare body went to N'Jaga's head. He could restrain his hate no longer. Throwing caution and cunning to the winds—an ear-splitting scream curdling in his throat—he leaped for Ka-Zar's throat.

KA-ZAR NEVER HEARD the frenzied shout that arose from the spectators. His eyes, his ears, his every sense and perception were concentrated on the three hundred pounds of spotted fury plunging for him.

He felt the foetid breath of the leopard hot on his face; saw the huge jaws gaping wide. And in that second before N'Jaga struck, he lowered his head and caught the full weight of the great cat on his shoulder, hurling him to one side.

N'Jaga's ripping forepaws, instead of disemboweling him, tore long gashes in his upper arm. In mid-air N'Jaga pivoted. He landed on four springy paws but for a moment he was off balance. He never regained it.

For even as his mentor, Zar the lion, charges in to kill— Ka-Zar was upon him, fast as light. His powerful left forearm flashed for the briefest of seconds in the sun, then clamped from behind in a strangle hold around N'Jaga's throat. With his right fist he gripped the fold of loose flesh beneath the leopard's jaw and bracing his feet against the floor of the arena, heaved mightily upward.

N'Jaga plunged and lashed; he heaved and twisted his supple body until a lather covered his spotted hide. But the arm about his throat did not relax—the powerful fist under his jaw continued to push his sleek head backward. The claws of his forefeet were impotent. He brought the terrible talons of his rear into play. Again and again they slashed at Ka-Zar's thigh, cutting deep to the bone. Then he dug them in deep and using the sturdy column of Ka-Zar's body as a lever, he arched his back in a supreme effort to break the strangle hold on his throat.

The muscles of Ka-Zar's arms stood out like knots of oak. His very sinews threatened to snap beneath the strain. A pulse beat violently at his temple and an immense gong beat brazenly inside his skull. Slowly, inexorably, inch by inch he forced back N'Jaga's head.

Now the baleful green orbs of the leopard were glaring up into his own; now they were blinded by the dazzling sun that seemed to stand still in the heavens above them.

Fear came to N'Jaga's heart at last. And so subtle was the bond between Ka-Zar and the jungle beasts he ruled that he sensed it immediately. It was the added stimulus his flagging muscles needed. Exerting his last ounce of strength he heaved up still further on N'Jaga's jaw. Back—back went the sleek head. For a moment the fires of hell were concentrated in the green eyes. Then there was a sudden sharp snap as N'Jaga's neck was broken and the fire died from the glazing eyes.

N'Jaga lashed convulsively once, then his body went limp in death. Slowly Ka-Zar loosed his terrible hold, permitted the body of his ancient enemy to slump to the ground. N'Jaga, the leopard who limped, was dead. Never again would he dispute the trail with Zar. The blood feud he had nursed for so many years had come to an end at last.

Slowly Ka-Zar straightened his aching body to its full height. Placing one naked foot on N'Jaga's throat he turned to confront Sarput. His head whipped up. A hot breath of air stirred the raven locks that fell down to his shoulders. And even as the lion, his brother, with a thundering roar he proclaimed his might—not to the jungle this time, but to the dusky-faced man and the girl who stood at the balcony's edge above him.

Claudette was on the verge of fainting. Sarput knew a wrath greater than he had ever known before. He choked, he sputtered, he fumed. His dark face turned an apoplectic purple. Trembling from head to foot, a thin stream of saliva drooling from the corners of his mouth, he shouted commands to his retainers below him. Then, before waiting to see them executed, he dragged Claudette from the balcony.

CHAPTER XXII

ALI PAYS A DEBT

O **NCE AGAIN, KA-ZAR** was confined in chains in the stifling, foetid dungeon. But the respite gave him little comfort. He knew that somewhere up above, the baffled Sarput was busily scheming some new and more terrible punishment for him. When he thought of Claudette, such a bitterness rose up in his heart that he thrust the vision of her from him. Again and again he exerted all his strength upon the chains that held him, until panting and exhausted, he ceased his futile struggles. And as if the Fates were determined to add the last, final straw to his burden of trouble, M'Bele continued to rumble.

The intervals between the growls of the volcano grew shorter. More and more frequently the earthen walls of the subterranean cell trembled, as a violent disturbance heaved the bowels of the earth. The air became more oppressive and strange, noxious gases crept in to mingle with its other odorous scents.

For long hours Ka-Zar stared hopelessly at the small square of sky that he could see from the floor of his dungeon. He thought longingly of the green depths of the jungle, of murmuring streams and the immense sweep of a cloudless blue sky that touched the horizon. Then the hopelessness of his predicament swept over him and left him trembling. In vain he cudgelled his brain for some hope, for some idea that might save him, for something that would at least give him the anodyne of action.

But the square of blue sky far above him turned slowly to the flaming reds, golds and purples of an African sunset. The vivid colors blended and merged, changed to deeper hues. And at last, after the brief gray twilight of the tropics, night fell.

He was looking toward the east, and he could not see the volcano that towered up behind the palace. But like a bit of dark mirror up there on the wall, the patch of sky reflected the flames of M'Bele. A reddish glow pulsed continuously and with each deep-throated rumble, it flared to brighter incandescence. A fine sediment of ash sifted down from the aperture.

Sleep, of course, was out of the question. Though his body felt on the verge of physical exhaustion, neither the wounds made by N'Jaga nor his uncomfortable position in the chains and the dark forebodings that claimed his mind, would let him find surcease in slumber. His head hung low on his breast in hopeless despair, when at last he heard a sound beyond his cell door.

His head came slowly up and his eyes turned blankly to stare at the closed portal. The reflection of the glowing heavens il-lumined the cell with a dull, reddish half-light.

Had Sarput devised some torture fiendish enough to satisfy his mad soul? Was Ka-Zar going to be led at last to his final end? For a moment he remained apathetic, thinking that it might be just as well to see the end of such mental and physi-cal tortures as he had suffered.

Then he realized that whoever was beyond the door was working stealthily and cautiously. Some deep-rooted instinct gave him new hope, brought him up to rigid attention.

The bars squeaked faintly as they were raised. A key grated in the massive lock. Then slowly the heavy door swung inward and the turbaned head of Ali peered into the cell.

Motioning Ka-Zar to make no sound, the hunchback listened for a moment. Then slipping across the threshold, he limped up to Ka-Zar and fitted a small key into the lock that fastened his fetters to the wall. Holding the chain carefully so that it would not clank, he whispered urgently into Ka-Zar's ear as he released him.

"M'Bele growls louder," he said hoarsely. "The entire encampment is terrified and everyone wishes to flee. But my master thinks of you and of the golden haired girl and tarries."

A GRUNT OF thanks rumbled in, Ka-Zar's throat as the last chain fell away.

Ali looked at him from limpid eyes—the man or god—he did not know which, who had earned his undying gratitude. "Flee now, it is your only chance."

Free from his chains, with a chance at freedom, the dark jungle called once more to Ka-Zar. He drew himself up stiffly, squared his broad shoulders and turned with glowing amber eyes to Ali.

"You have done well, faithful friend," he said. "I go into the forest but I shall return. When the moon rises, meet me inside the north gate. Ka-Zar is still bewildered when he is within walls and he will need you to lead him through the palace."

Ali nodded slowly. "If my master learns what I have just done," he said soberly, "Ali will not see the moon rise. But if Ali still lives, he will be at the appointed place."

Ka-Zar dropped a hand lightly on a misshapen shoulder. His heart was stirred, as always, by the loyal soul that dwelled within that grotesque body. "Courage," he whispered. And there was such an intensity of conviction and courage in his own tone, that Ali's troubled mind instantly knew a strange peace.

Ka-Zar waited until the hunchback had gone. Then speedily and with all caution, he made his own way out of the dungeon.

The halls of the palace were deserted. The entire household was huddled outside on the grounds, fearfully watching the flames of M'Bele. Ka-Zar had no trouble in reaching the stockade unmolested.

He soon found that the entire population of the encampment were likewise absorbed by the threatening volcano. Moving silently as a wraith, he made his way among the outlying huts and reached the jungle wall without having been missed or detected.

Once in the forest, he was at home. After the vile, close air of the cell, despite the new sulphurous fumes, the atmosphere of the jungle was perfume in his nostrils. He breathed deeply of it, expanded his mighty lungs and then took to the trees.

Travelling swiftly, with sure instinct, it did not take him long to find the camp of the Wurumbas. They had built their evening fires in a small clearing and like the Bulangis and the brown men back at the palace, they were fearfully watching the volcano.

Wazi was sorely troubled. For the first time, an unthinkable heresy persistently knocked at his brain. A god was a god. A god was invincible. Ka-Zar was a god. Ka-Zar had promised to protect the Wurumba. Why, then, did Wazi dare to doubt?

YET WAZI KNEW that Ka-Zar had been taken prisoner by the evil one. And again and again the impious thought came to him—was Ka-Zar, at that very moment, alive or dead? Would he soon triumph, wreak his vengeance on those who had not only incurred his wrath but had dared to lay hands upon his person? Or was Ka-Zar already only lifeless clay....

A tall, bronzed familiar form materialized suddenly in the firelight. It was as though Ka-Zar had read Wazi's mind and appeared magically before him to shame him for his doubt. Apparently the rest of the Wurumbas had been likewise disturbed. For as one they cried out and with their chief, they dropped to their hands and knees and prostrated themselves on the ground.

Ka-Zar halted, looked down at the prone forms of his allies.

"Rise, Wazi," he commanded. "Rise, warriors of the Wurumba."

They got to their feet. Eagerly the chief came forward to meet him.

"Ka-Zar is truly a god," he said reverently. "He has come back to us."

"More than that," replied Ka-Zar. "He has come back to lead you to victory against your enemies and his."

Hastily Wazi translated to his eager followers. Their faces lit up and their teeth gleamed in the firelight as they showed their pleasure.

Ka-Zar looked about the camp. "Where," he asked Wazi, "are my brother the lion and my friend the elephant?"

"They stay nearby in the forest," answered Wazi. "They do us no harm and they wait for your return."

Flinging back his head, Ka-Zar sent forth the rumbling roar of the lion. A moment later it was answered from the jungle depths by Zar.

While he waited for Zar and Trajah to come, the Wurumbas brought him a gourd of water and a kettle of the stew that had been their evening meal. The cooked food tasted flat and unpleasant to Ka-Zar, used to fresh-killed meat. But hunger gnawed his belly and he was weary. Squatting on his haunches, he dipped his fingers into the kettle and ate.

He had just finished his meal with a long drink of water when the underbrush beyond the camp parted and Zar and Trajah moved toward him. While the Wurumbas stared at this ever-marvelous miracle, he went to greet his friends. With low growls and guttural sounds, they talked.

Trajah told him that Tupat and the rest of the herd had come up to join their leader. They were back in the jungle now, in the direction from whence he and Zar had just come.

"It is well," answered Ka-Zar. "For tonight we shall drive the Oman at last from the wilderness. Trajah and his people can do much to help."

Turning to face the Wurumba, he addressed Wazi. "The hour has come. In the camp of Sarput, the Bulangi and the brown men are possessed by great fear because M'Bele growls and spits forth flame. They are not on their guard and we shall surprise them."

GUTTURAL SOUNDS OF approbation followed Wazi's translation of his speech. The warriors raised their spears in salute, then stood at rigid attention.

Swiftly Ka-Zar gave his orders, laid out his plan of attack. The Wurumba were to be divided into three parties, to attack from the south, east and the north. Since all eyes in the Rajah's camp would be toward the west, upon the flaming mountain peak, they would be able to approach without being discovered. Wazi would go with the central party; Zar with another; Trajah with the last. The rest of the elephants would be distributed equally among them.

Ka-Zar would give the signal for a concerted attack. Then he would be busy with his own particular business. The elephants would smash great gaps in the stockade, enabling the warriors to push through into the palace grounds.

The orders were swiftly explained to the Wurumbas and to the two beasts. With a long, shrill trumpet, Trajah summoned his herd from the forest. The three separate parties were quickly formed, the women bringing every available weapon to arm the warrior. Then losing no time, Ka-Zar led his strange army toward the distant palace.

CHAPTER XXIII

M'BELE GROWLS

IN AN UPPER room of the palace, Claudette VanGelder paced the floor. Several times she stepped out onto a little balcony that overlooked the palace grounds and stared down dully at the milling men below. Each time the volcano rumbled and the building trembled to its foundations, they huddled into wailing groups. Each time she shuddered.

The door of her room was locked. There was no escape, except....

She fought with a mad impulse to fling herself from the balcony, to end this series of horrors that was making her weak, sapping her courage. With an effort she turned, walked over to another locked door, set in the south wall of her room. Pressing her lips to the panel she called softly: "Courage, Father. I am still here and safe."

No voice answered her. She did not expect an answer. For she knew that in the room beyond her father and the two guides, Barry and Holt, were helplessly bound and gagged. She had called in at frequent intervals, trying to reassure them a little.

She hoped that her tone conveyed more hope than she felt. She moved wearily away from the door, sank into a rattan chair. Her thoughts shifted to Ka-Zar.

A faint sigh escaped her lips as she recalled the emotion that the magnificent bronze giant had aroused within her. Then bitterly she reflected that something had come between them. What it was, she did not know. His last glance toward her, as he stood in the arena, had been inscrutable, unreadable. But in it she had sensed not hate, exactly, but a cold aloofness which she did not understand.

With all her heart she longed to see him again, to find out what barrier had grown between them, to tear it down and know once more the ineffable peace and contentment that she had felt in his arms.

A violent rumble from M'Bele shook the palace. The heavens glowed with a pulsing crimson light. Then as the echoes of the thunder died away for a moment into silence, she heard a key turn in the lock of the outer door. Thinking that it was Ali come again to bring her food or water, she merely turned her head in that direction.

The portal swung inward—and she stiffened in her chair. For it was not the grotesque form of the hunchback, but the tall, glittering figure of Sarput who entered the room. Unable to move, she gripped the arms of the chair until her knuckles stood out white beneath the skin and watched him.

To her relief, he crossed over to the window, stepped out onto the balcony and looked down. Then he laughed harshly and said over his shoulder: "The poor fools! They've never seen a volcano before. They haven't the faintest idea what might happen. That's what makes their antics so very funny."

Claudette found her voice. "I fail to appreciate your humor. A volcano, after all, is no respecter of persons. Or of palaces, or princes."

Sarput turned around, came slowly toward her. "Don't worry about M'Bele, beautiful lady," he murmured. "In my native land, the sacred peak Khalli towers over the Great Temple of Niva. I've observed it often."

HE STOPPED BEFORE her, looked down at her with burning eyes and slowly shook his head. "So you'd have me start trekking through the jungle, eh?" he asked mockingly. "No—I'm sorry, but it would be most inconvenient, just now. There's another little matter that demands my attention immediately."

Again Claudette froze. Though his words were lightly spoken, she knew instinctively to what he referred. Her face blanched. An icy finger of fear raced down her spine.

"You—you mean…" she began haltingly.

Sarput bowed. His eyes gleamed. He stroked his straggly beard with a jeweled hand. "You, my dear," he answered suavely.

That was all. That was all he needed to say. Claudette's heart sank within her. Gathering the last remnants of her flagging courage, she rose to her feet, raised her chin and confronted him.

"Never," she cried proudly. "Never—I'd rather die!"

Sarput's face flushed dark with passion; his bushy eyebrows met in a ferocious scowl. Then abruptly, on the surface at least, he became his usual sardonic self.

"You are too gorgeous to die, my dear," he answered. "Even I could not find the heart to send you to your death. I could far sooner condemn a man—say, an elderly one."

Claudette recoiled a step. One hand flew to her lips. "You mean—my father?" she gasped. "You would threaten my poor father?"

Sarput's only answer was a laugh—a mocking, mirthless laugh.

A flood of words, a torrent of pleas for mercy rose to Claudette's lips—only to die still-born before they were uttered. All this fiend's inhuman cruelties paraded before her eyes. She closed them for an instant to blot out the picture. A numbness possessed her. For she realized that she must face the horrible choice—that any pleas for pity would be only music in Sarput's ears.

To add to her distress, she realized that in the adjoining room her father must have heard the Rajah's words. Unable to stir hand or foot, unable to utter a sound, his mental torture surely must be greater than hers.

She knew, as surely as if he had cried out to her, what he would have said. Spare herself from this outrage, even at the cost of his life!

She did not have to consider the matter—she did not have to ponder long over her choice. She drooped her head for a moment, breathed a silent prayer and then slowly raised dull, lacklustre eyes to Sarput's glowing ones.

"There is only one possible answer," she said simply. "I love my father."

The Rajah received the words with a sibilant, indrawn breath. Then, his suave manner dropped from him like a discarded cloak. His lips showed in a wolfish smile. His eyes narrowed to gleaming slits. His hand came up and with thin lingers outstretched, reached out toward her.

It was at that moment, a moment as long as eternity to Claudette, that pandemonium broke loose outside.

SARPUT STOPPED IN midstride. His head jerked around. Baffled and angry by the intrusion, he hesitated.

The bedlam came from all sides. There were the hoarse shouts of men, the shrill trumpeting of elephants, the rumbling roar of a lion.

With a low snarl Sarput leaped for the balcony. Moving almost like an automaton, without her own volition, Claudette followed and peered past him.

The gigantic torch of M'Bele illumined the entire panorama before them with a flickering crimson light. It gleamed on the spears of the Wurumba warriors who had burst *en masse* from the jungle. It revealed the great gray shapes of Trajah's elephant herd, charging down on the startled encampment

With shrieks and cries, the Bulangis and the brown men rushed frantically for their own weapons. So sudden was the attack that they were badly confused. They ran aimlessly about, bumping headlong into one another and incipient panic seized them. Before they could rally to repulse the invaders, the Wurumba were upon them.

Ordinarily a peaceable people, Wazi's blacks had suffered too long at the hands of these traitors to their own kind. Now they were aroused to frenzy and they were driven with the old, atavistic urge to slay their enemies. They gave no quarter and swooped down upon the milling Bulangi in wave after wave of gleaming black death.

It was a weird, unholy scene. The reddish glow from M'Bele bathed them all with the sinister tint of blood. Spears glistened for a moment, then plunged deep into naked bodies. Rifles cracked in spasmodic chorus. Above the terrifying war cry of the Wurumba, shrieks of mortal agony floated through the air.

A madness fell upon them all. In their wild panic, the Bulangis could scarcely distinguish friend from foe. Trumpeting, with the reek of blood strong in their nostrils, the elephants charged the stockade.

Most terrifying of all was Zar. The Bulangis, like all other natives, feared the lion above all beasts of the jungle. Now he was devastation let loose among them. A bounding, massive tawny fury, he charged headlong at group after group. His jaws slavered. His huge claws raked quivering flesh. A single blow of his mighty forepaw snapped an enemy's spine.

From his window high in the palace, on his face the most horrible expression that Claudette had ever seen. Sarput watched the rout. As though he were rooted to the spot, as though his vocal cords were paralyzed, he stood in stony silence.

His own elephants, lashed to insane fear by the trumpeting of Trajah and his herd, suddenly broke from their confines. With shrill squeals, ears flapping, they burst from the enclosure and headed in mad flight for the forest.

That was the signal for the Bulangis and the others. A screeching group raced for the jungle. Following their example, the rest did likewise. Warriors, women and children fled from the encampment as though the devil were at their heels.

Some of the Wurumba raced after them, harassing the retreat. The rest swarmed through the gaps that Trajah's elephants had made in the stockade and poured into the grounds of the palace.

IT WAS NOT till then that Sarput seemed to realize that he was in deadly peril. His face a hideous mask of baffled rage and stark fear, he whirled about and shouted hoarsely for Ali.

The door of the room burst inward. But it was not the hunchback who entered. Claudette cried out sharply as the tall, bronzed figure of Ka-Zar loomed on the threshold.

Sarput blanched, his cheeks turning a dirty ashen-gray color. Then his right hand flashed for his sash and whipped out his revolver. The barrel jerked up and its muzzle gaped hungrily at Ka-Zar's broad naked chest.

The sound of its explosion was drowned by a reverberating thunder roll from M'Bele. The bullet sprayed splinters from the edge of the door, for Ka-Zar had leaped at the instant the gun was fired.

His rush carried Sarput crashing back against the wall. The gun flew from the Rajah's fingers, struck the floor and slithered off into a far corner of the room. Then while Claudette watched in breathless fascination, the death duel between these two sworn enemies began.

It was mercifully brief. To the now continuous growls of the volcano, they swayed in silent, desperate struggle. Ka-Zar's lightning movements were too swift for her eyes to follow. She saw Sarput suddenly whirled around, clasped hard against the massive chest of Ka-Zar. Bronzed hands slid around the Rajah's thin body, came up and closed behind his head.

Even as Sarput realized the deadliness of the hold, there came a snap. The turbaned head jerked suddenly forward, then the Rajah's chin lolled loosely on his breast.

For a moment Claudette stared dumbly, wondering vaguely why Sarput had ceased to struggle. Then she realized that his neck had been broken and a low cry escaped her lips. She swayed dizzily, grasped the back of a chair for support.

But Ka-Zar ignored her. Dragging the limp form of his slain enemy, he stepped out onto the balcony. Holding aloft the glittering empty husk that had once been the Rajah Sarput, he flung back his head and sent the mighty roar of the lion's kill floating out above the din below.

The cry rang like a paean of triumph in the ears of the Wurumbas, like a death knell in the ears of the Rajah's minions. For a moment the hubbub ceased and all eyes turned up to the balcony. At the sight of the lifeless form in Ka-Zar's arms, the Wurumbas echoed the kill with a blood-curdling war cry. Then the clamorous rout began again as the victorious blacks pursued their enemies toward the forest.

Ka-Zar turned back from the balcony, let the body of Sarput drop to the floor. Thrusting it disdainfully aside with his foot, he approached the girl.

A cataclysmic roar split the night. The heavens flared in a burst of flame and the floor heaved up beneath their feet, throwing them off balance. Claudette stumbled forward, grasped Ka-Zar's arms.

"The volcano!" she gasped. "Hurry...."

He bent down and swept her up into his arms. Ali crept into the room, approached the prone form on the floor and crouched over to survey the still thing that had once been his cruel master.

CLAUDETTE STIFFENED IN Ka-Zar's arms, struggled up and pointed toward the door in the south wall of the room. "My father..." she said breathlessly. "Locked in there... with the two guides...."

Ka-Zar instantly set her on her feet. Hunching one massive shoulder, he sent his body hurtling like a battering ram at the panel. It shattered with a splintering crash. Ali limped after him as he plunged into the room beyond.

Swiftly they released the prisoners. Then with a terse command for them to follow, Ka-Zar went back into the other room and again picked up the girl.

As they made their way down through the palace, they could see the towering cone of M'Bele. A mile-high column of lurid flame rose toward the heavens. With each echoing roar, a shower of rocks was belched from the bowels of the mountain. Blazing cinders and powdery ash rained down over the palace.

Ka-Zar gained the courtyard, set off at a swift pace. Glancing back over his shoulder, he saw the crater vomit forth a mass of molten lava. It spilled out, began to creep sluggishly yet inexorably down the eastern slope of the mountain. It swallowed up great jungle trees as it moved down toward them.

The encampment was now utterly deserted. As they reached the edge of the jungle, Wazi came forward to meet them.

"The enemy have fled and they will not stop until they have reached their distant land," he told Ka-Zar. "My people go away from the burning mountain, back to the camp and their women to celebrate the victory."

"It is well," answered Ka-Zar. Slowly he set Claudette down to the ground. "Take these Oman to your camp, also. Let no harm come to them tonight. In the morning, I shall come to decide what will be done with them."

Wazi saluted gravely. Claudette had turned to her father and clung to him in a tight embrace.

With a curt order to them to follow Wazi, Ka-Zar left them and headed in the direction of the plateau. Barely had the jungle swallowed him up when a massive, tawny shape materialized from the undergrowth beside him. Silently Zar padded forth on great paws and fell into step beside him.

There was no need for words between them. Ka-Zar let his hand drop onto the lion's shaggy head. Together they climbed swiftly up onto the plateau, walked out and halted at the top of the cliff.

From there they watched M'Bele complete its awesome destruction. Again and again rocks spewed from the crater and lava spilled out over its lip. The sluggish stream of hissing, molten rock made its winding way down the slopes, licked out at the edge of the encampment. The flimsy huts were crushed by tons of liquid rock, the remnants of the stockade bent inward before the irresistible force of the stream.

The Rajah's courtyard, his fabulous gardens and fountains, and lastly the great palace itself, were obliterated from their view. The lava flow moved slower, stopped at last at the fringe of the jungle. And where the fantastic city what Sarput had reared in the heart of the wilderness had stood, was now only a gray sea that bubbled like a witch's cauldron.

CHAPTER XXIV

HAIL AND FAREWELL

WITH THE DAWN the last rumbling of M'Bele died away and a heavy downpour came to cool and refresh the jungle. After a short while the rain ceased and the sun came out to bathe the world in golden splendor.

Ka-Zar rose from where he had lain through the night unsleeping by Zar's side. Silently he stalked through the camp of the Wurumba which still slept, exhausted after the victory and celebration of the night before. He glanced once briefly at the hut that sheltered VanGelder's party, then proceeded on to where Ali the hunchback slept by the smouldering embers of a fire.

With a gentle hand he roused the cripple. "Rise, O Ali," he commanded.

Ali scrambled awkwardly to his feet, touched his hand in turn to his breast, lips and brow and bowed low before him.

Ka-Zar smiled down upon him, let his hand fall affectionately on his misshapen back. "There is one more task for the faithful Ali to perform."

"Ali hears and obeys," said the cripple.

"In the hut, there," said Ka-Zar, pointing to a rude shelter in the center of the clearing, "are many fire-sticks and provisions. Take them to the Om VanGelder. Tell him that a new day has dawned. Tell him that peace has come again to the jungle. Tell him to go in peace—but to go at once." He paused, gripped Ali's hand in his own. "As for you, Ali, I and the jungle owe you

302

a debt we can never repay. Know that you have earned the gratitude of Ka-Zar."

The hunchback looked at him from swimming eyes. "Ali obeys if Ka-Zar so orders. But it has been in Ali's heart that he might stay here in your jungle to serve as your slave. In all my miserable life you are the first man who has spoken to me with the voice of kindness."

Ka-Zar was deeply moved by the simple words. For a moment he was tempted to consent to Ali's plea. Then with clear vividness he realized the insurmountable difficulties that would forever confront Ali in the forest, due to his deformity.

He shook his head in a kindly negative. "Ka-Zar has no need for slaves. He would rather remember you as friend. It is better, Ali, that you return with the Om VanGelder."

The faithful hunchback bowed his head in submission. "As Ka-Zar wills," he said simply.

He turned and had started for the supply hut when Ka-Zar spoke to him again. "Your eyes are bright, Ali. On the long trail back, keep them on the golden haired girl Claudette, that no harm might befall her."

"It shall be as Ka-Zar says," replied Ali.

An hour later, VanGelder's party was ready to take the trail. From the top of the high plateau, Ka-Zar watched them trek slowly across the encampment. The rising sun sent golden shafts of light to him from the crown of Claudette's hair. They pierced his heart and all his old anguish returned to him.

Like a bronzed god he stood on the high bluff, silhouetted against the sun. It was thus that Claudette saw him for the last time.

Her hand went out to him appealingly. "Ka-Zar!" she called in an anguished voice.

KA-ZAR HEARD AND for a mad moment he was tempted to leap down from the bluff, sweep her into his arms and flee with her into the jungle depths. Then he mastered the impulse. It was she who had betrayed him into the hands of the evil Om.

As if sensing the inner turmoil in his breast Claudette called again.

Then deliberately, so there was no mistaking the import or significance of the gesture, Ka-Zar turned his back upon her.

Thus it was that the beautiful creature who had come into Ka-Zar's life went out again. But her flower-like face was to haunt him forever. The girl he had loved—the girl he had desired for a mate—had betrayed him. Aye, verily, the ways of the Oman were dark and inscrutible.

His heart was heavy. With a sigh he frowned at the ground. Then Zar stalked up to take up a position beside him and the darkness that veiled his soul lifted. Together, Zar and Ka-Zar—lion and man—they surveyed their domain. Where Sarput's palace had stood was now naught but a leveled heap of smouldering ash and lava. Ka-Zar knew that in an incredibly short time the jungle would once more reclaim the clearing, blotting out the last vestige of the Prince of Darkness, who had appeared amongst them and who was now gone.

His heart lifted within him. Unlike the white girl his jungle and his beasts were unchangeable, immutable. Zar would be his faithful friend and ally to his dying day and together they would rule, wisely, justly—and in peace.

BOOK III

THE LOST EMPIRE

KA-ZAR THE GREAT, powerful lord of the jungle, battles against the cunning and cruelty of the warriors of the Lost Empire and the heathen gods of that mysterious world.

CHAPTER I

THE ABYSS

RICH, ABUNDANT, OVERFLOWING with life, yes. Yet, that dark and impenetrable corner of the globe known as the Belgian Congo, is cruel. It is the land where the inexorable Law of Claw and Fang still reigns supreme. In fact, it is the only Law. Let the strong survive; let the weak beware lest they perish from the face of the earth. For the jungle knows no pity and mercy is dealt out only in swift death. There in the heart of a primeval wilderness, the price of life is eternal watchfulness.

Cruel, yes, is this steaming, miasmic jungle world. But there, hard on the equator, even more cruel is the brassy face of the sun as it shines from the vast dome of heaven at high noon.

So intense are its rays that they can fell an ordinary mortal in a matter of minutes. When the sun crosses its zenith, the heart of Darkest Africa stops beating. The lizard buries himself in the mud, the hyena slinks in his noisome den and no bird sings.

High noon. The earth lay panting. Yet from behind the matted screen of the jungle wall came unmistakable sounds of movement; the scarlet leaves of the shubah bush trembled, yet no breeze had stirred.

Who was this—man or beast—that came down the jungle trail in open defiance of the molten sun overhead? What dire necessity, what restless soul urged him on beneath the leaden weight of the sun?

Before the thrust of a massive gray head, the tangled wall of the jungle parted. Trajah the elephant, wise and venerable leader of his herd, moved slowly into the clearing. But Trajah was not leading his pack of cows and young bulls on one of their far-flung pilgrimages. Behind him came a far more strange and awe-inspiring procession.

Stepping where Trajah had stepped, came Zar the lion—Zar the Mighty, with regal head and saber-tipped talons. Clinging precariously to his ruffled mane, was a grimacing, ring-tail monkey.

But that was not all. Stranger still, more startling yet was the figure that brought up the rear of the procession—the figure of a man. He was naked save for a scant loin cloth around his middle. Tall like a God, proportioned like a Viking, his muscles rippled and flowed like tempered steel beneath his bronzed skin as he moved.

More arresting than his superb body, however, was his head. It was massive, leonine, topped by a thick shock of black hair that fell down to his shoulders. And out of his face stared two eyes, cold, alert—all-seeing, tawny eyes—that gave him a strange kinship to the lion who stalked before him.

Thus came Ka-Zar, Brother of Zar the Mighty, at high noon.

Whence did he come? From his jungle domain many moons' journey behind him. Where was he going? Ka-Zar could not have said. He only knew that a strange restlessness was upon him—a restlessness so compelling that it even urged him on during the heat of mid-day.

As he moved forward across the clearing, his mind went groping back over the years.

He did not know, of course, that many years before, John Rand, a prosperous mine owner from Johannesburg, had started out from that city in an airplane, taking his young wife and infant son, David, to Cairo. He did not know that the ship had crashed, to land in the heart of the Congo. A benevolent Providence had wiped out the memory of those first nightmare days and nights in the jungle.

Now, twenty years later, vague and disturbing memories of his beautiful and adored mother rose up to haunt him. Her tragic death, before the onslaught of a mysterious jungle fever, had been mercifully obliterated by time.

Ka-Zar's first clear recollections of his boyhood were those of happy days roaming the wilderness with his father. He did not know—and he would never know—that on the day before he and his father were to start on the long trek back to civilization, John Rand had been struck by a falling tree; that as a result of that accident, his father's mind had become unbalanced.

From that time on, the course of young David's life was changed.

TO RAND'S WARPED mind, the lonely grave of his wife in that God-forsaken stretch of wilderness, became a sanctuary. And all the miles of dense forest, of clearing and river and lake surrounding it, became his and David's—to hold sacred and inviolate against any trespasser.

The trespasser had come—in the shape of an evil and greedy white man and his native helpers. Keeping his fanatical trust, attempting to drive the newcomer from his wilderness domain, John Rand had been slain. And young David, left alone, had come into his kingdom.

A true child of the wilderness, David had early made friends with the beasts. On one occasion he had saved Zar the lion, mighty lord of the jungle, from a treacherous bed of quicksand. And in his own hour of need, when his father died in his arms from a murderer's bullet, Zar did not forsake him. The watchful lord of the jungle had stood guard by the grief stricken boy and had led him at last to his own jungle lair.

There a pact of brotherhood had been sworn. There the boy ceased to be David Rand and became instead Ka-Zar, brother of Zar the lion. There he learned to speak the language of his brothers, the beasts. And there, aided by his superior intellect and the few weapons he had learned to fashion and to use, he had earned the right to rule over his vast heritage.

Years later the evil white man—the slayer of his father—had returned and Ka-Zar, fulfilling a vow made over the graves of his parents, had avenged the death of his father. He had learned many things in that encounter. He had learned to respect the white man's weapons; to mistrust the white man for his greed, his cruelty, his treachery.

And later, he had learned to his sorrow, to distrust the white man's mate-woman. Especially one, the laughing, blue-eyed, golden haired girl, Claudette. Since that day, two long rainy seasons ago, when he had said his last farewell to her, he had known no peace.

Claudette had betrayed him; or so he thought. He had sent her away forever, without a backward glance. He well knew that leagues without measure separated him from her, yet the bitterness of it was, that she was forever in his heart. In every pool of water he saw her laughing face and blue eyes. No gazelle bounded across his path but he saw her tantalizing figure dancing before his eyes.

And it was to flee from her—though in his heart he knew there was no escape—it was to flee from himself and the memories that haunted him, that Ka-Zar roamed farther and ever farther away from his domain at high noon.

Half way across the clearing, Nono the monkey squirmed around on the lion's back and with one long, agile leap sprang to Ka-Zar's shoulder. Wrapping one spidery arm around his master's neck, he pointed the other towards the end of the glade where a growth of luscious green grass marked a water hole. He showed his teeth in a simian grimace and chattered vivaciously.

Ka-Zar pulled at the monkey's left ear with a rough affection. "Enough, silly one," he said with mock severity. "If you find the trail too hard, return to your long-tailed brothers and gossip all day in the tree tops."

Nono suddenly became absorbed in a burr that had caught in a tangle of Ka-Zar's hair and forgot what he had originally pointed out.

After one brief glance behind, Trajah, still in the lead, continued on across the glade. He, too, would have liked to have wallowed in a pool of cool water but his two-legged friend was driven on by a force greater than himself.

Trajah was old and very wise. He had battled through a hundred mating seasons and in his shrewd animal brain he understood the thing that gnawed at Ka-Zar's heart. He was in search of....

Abruptly, without warning, the earth beneath Trajah's massive feet began to tremble. A second later there came a sinister, ominous growl from deep down in the bowels of the earth. Instinctively, with a squeal of warning, the huge, gray beast spurted forward.

AND AS HE charged, the earth that appeared so stable a moment before crumbled and melted away behind him. There was a sustained, cataclysmic roar, an enveloping cloud of dust as a thousand tons of earth sank from view.

By one short step, Trajah had managed to reach solid land. It was fifty yards, however, before he could check his charge and turn. Slowly, cautiously, his huge ears flapping and his trunk upraised he made his way back, testing the ground carefully at each step.

He approached the abyss far closer than was wise, considering his weight. The cloud of dust still hung over it and from far below came the last rumble of the falling earth. Slowly, as he waited with puzzled, worried eyes, the cloud of dust thinned out. And there, where Ka-Zar, Zar and the monkey had been but a minute before, was naught but a yawning hole in the ground.

In his long life Trajah had had experience with an occasional land-slide in the season of heavy rains but this was something beyond understanding.

A vague uneasiness possessed him. It was clear that his friends had disappeared down that yawning chasm. How deep was it?

He edged forward cautiously but as the earth began to slip again beneath his tremendous weight, he lunged swiftly back again.

For once Trajah's greatest asset, his bulk, became a distinct handicap. It prevented him from edging close to the lip of the chasm. Helpless, confronted for once with a situation he did not know how to meet, he flung back his wrinkled trunk and gave vent to the trumpeting call of the bull elephant. The shrill note echoed and re-echoed throughout the jungle but from the bottom of the pit came no answering call.

Again and again Trajah split the silence with his clarion call until the very leaves trembled on the trees. No answer. After each challenge it seemed that a pall of silence fell over the world, more brooding than the one before.

All through that long, hot afternoon, the faithful Trajah hovered near the rim of the chasm, sending forth his call at regular intervals. He felt sure that if Zar or Ka-Zar were still alive, they would have answered him at once. The heavy silence that greeted his straining ears could mean but one thing.

The two-legged lion-man who had brought peace and justice to the jungle was dead—dead along with his brother the lion and the chattering monk.

Trajah knew that sooner or later, death comes to all things that live in the jungle. Yet a great sadness filled his heart. He would miss the two-legged one, whose delight it had been to ride upon his broad back. At sunset he trumpeted his call for the last time, then looked up and searched the heavens.

On a spread of pinioned wings, Kru the buzzard—the in-evitable end of every jungle tragedy—was wheeling down to investigate.

Slowly Trajah went to spread the dire tidings throughout Ka-Zar's domain.

CHAPTER II

SIGNS OF THE OMAN

BUT KRU WAS not to feast that day!

When the rumbling cave-in precipitated Ka-Zar and his friends deep into the bowels of the earth, Zar was the only one of the trio who did not lose consciousness. A spitting, whirling fury, he was enveloped by the deluge, tumbled over and over by the rush of sand, earth and stone. Buried completely, instinctively he fought for his life. Choking, gasping, he clawed desperately to escape his tomb.

His paws were raw and his lungs were filled with suffocating dust when at last his muzzle broke through the debris. Pausing only long enough to inhale deeply of damp air, he wormed his tawny body free.

Far overhead was a distant patch of blue sky—the gaping hole in the earth's crust through which they had fallen. It seemed to Zar that he stood in some strange kind of a cave, but the light was too dim to see far in any direction. Near him he could make out the tiny form of Nono, piteous and motionless huddle of fur. But the monkey was not Zar's chief concern. The great lion swung his shaggy head about and peered into the Stygian gloom for his brother.

But Ka-Zar was not to be seen. He was buried—somewhere under that pile of earth and sand. With a low whine of anguish issuing from his throat, Zar sniffed the staggering mound. Whether he detected the faintest of faint scents or whether by sheer instinct, he paused before a certain spot of loose sand.

Then, with his worn and bleeding claws he began frantically to dig.

Never had the jungle trio been closer to death—if death had not already struck. Never had they been in such strange and repelling surroundings. They were creatures of the open, of shady forest paths and of sun-bathed clearings; of emerald trees and sparkling streams. Here was a place of perpetual gloom; of dank, foul air; of silence broken only by the hushed drip of water.

The nearest that Zar's stout heart could know of fear, was the uneasiness which now possessed him. It was more than faith and loyalty that spurred him on. Nono was a silly, helpless creature—Zar needed his courageous and wise two-legged brother to stand by his side in the emergency.

If he was not already dead—Ka-Zar must not die!

It was in reality a matter of moments. But in that place of eternal twilight and eerie silence it seemed eons before Zar's torn paws flung back a last shower of earth and exposed a patch of bronzed skin. And it seemed centuries more before at last the unconscious giant had been dragged from his tomb—unconscious but still breathing faintly.

Dazed, whimpering, Nono crawled over and squatted at his master's feet.

Ka-Zar's return to consciousness was a slow and painful process. His head throbbed; his mouth was hot and dry; his lungs were a torture. With an effort he struggled up to a sitting position and looked around him. Every inch of his body had been battered by the heavy earth and the rocks that had swept him downward. He was a welter of livid bruises, of torn and bleeding flesh.

Slowly his brain cleared. He heard Zar's low growl of relief, saw the huge lion tenderly licking his torn paws and guessed what had happened.

"My brother has saved me," he acknowledged simply, in the guttural language of the beasts.

Zar looked significantly about him. "Zar has need of his brother," he answered.

Nono crept forward, climbed up on Ka-Zar's shoulder, wrapped both arms about his neck and whimpered. Twinges of pain wracked Ka-Zar's body as he rose to his feet but a hasty examination soon told him that by some miracle, no bones had been broken in his perilous fall. Wistfully be looked up at the patch of sky so hopelessly remote above him.

If he but had Pindar's wings....

IN VAIN HIS eyes searched the sides of the shaft that led up to the light and life. They were sheer walls of rock—not even Nono could have attempted to scale them. By some evil mischance the trio had traveled over a treacherously thin crust of earth that had waited like a trap to snare them.

Trajah had been in the lead. It had been his tremendous weight that had started the cave in, and they in the rear had had no chance to escape.

Reluctantly he lowered his eyes and gazed about his prison instead. And as he became accustomed to the semi-darkness, he saw that it was not the small pit he had first imagined it to be. On three sides were rocky walls, down which water dripped steadily and monotonously. He walked over to the nearest, put one hand against the damp surface. Then his eyes flicked upward.

Just above the level of his head, strange marks had been scratched in the smooth face of the stone. Ka-Zar drew in his breath with a sibilant hiss. His eyes narrowed and he leaned forward to study the mysterious signs more closely. He made out a crude but unmistakable representation of the sun; several others were surely meant to be beasts; others still held no meaning for him. With a puzzled frown he turned to Zar.

"Others have been in this place before us," he explained in a series of low growls and grunts. "Oman—two-legged creatures like Ka-Zar."

At the mention of men, Nono squeaked and tightened his grip around the jungle giant's neck. The long hairs on back of the lion's neck rose and bristled, his slitted eyes gleamed and the tip of his tail twitched, Oman—in the language of the jungle, the name that meant men. A name to be conjured with, and dreaded. At first, instinct alone had warned the beasts to mistrust those strange two-legged creatures. Later, experience had proven the dire import of the warning.

Men had brought swift death and cruel suffering in their wake. The creatures of the forest had learned to hate and fear them—to hate their blood lust and their greed, to fear their sly and treacherous cunning.

Ka-Zar alone, ruler of the jungle, was the exception. And he, himself, though he had met good men and bad, had renounced them. He had learned to be wary of strangers, be they black men or white. And now as he stood irresolute in the subterranean chasm, he reminded himself that even though he walked upon two legs, in heart and soul he was a beast—the sworn brother of the mighty Zar and the ruler of the jungle creatures. Man, then, was his natural enemy, also.

It was with a strange mixture of emotions that he studied the curious hieroglyphics upon the dank wall. A thousand wild speculations crowded through his brain. The Oman who had scratched those marks—did they still exist? Or were they long dead and forgotten? Neither beast nor jungle native had mentioned this mysterious underground cavern. Where had these Oman come from? Who were they? Where had they gone?

Grimly Ka-Zar told himself that he would soon find out. To stay where he was meant a slow and agonizing death by starvation. With Zar at his side he must set out into the unknown and together they would face whatever might befall them.

Turning his back on the walls, he faced the vista of gray dimness that stretched out before him. His jaw was set at a hard angle as he called to Zar. "Come!"

The little monkey chattered with fright as he strode with long, purposeful steps into the dank twilight.

"Hush, silly one," warned Ka-Zar. "You may betray us with

your chatter."

Zar fell into place beside him, suspiciously sniffing the air, feeling the earthen floor with every padded step. Ka-Zar fingered the keen knife that still dangled in its sheath at his belt, and thought longingly of the stout bow and the quiver of arrows that were buried deep somewhere in the landslide. It was futile to look for them he knew, for even if he could find them, they were undoubtedly shattered and useless.

NOW FROM AHEAD there came to their ears the subdued roar of rushing water. Their progress became slow and cautious for as they moved further away from the hole high up on the earth's surface, the light below grew dimmer.

A draft of air came up the tunnel through which they moved, touched Ka-Zar's cheeks with chill, damp fingers. And then around a sharp turn in the tunnel, they came at last to the source of the roaring—a swift-flowing, dark, subterranean river. Here they paused to bathe their bleeding wounds and to clear their dust-choked throats with drafts of the icy waters.

Somewhat refreshed, they resumed their cautious advance. The bank of the river was slippery footing. In places the stream was wide and its dark surface gleamed unbroken like a black mirror. In others it narrowed sharply and tumbled frothing over rocks and boulders in its bed. Once Ka-Zar stumbled over something and paused to examine what had tripped him. In the gloom, his sensitive fingers told him as much as his eyes. He picked up the object and turned it over and over in his hands. It was a vase of clay—he had seen similar objects in the kraals of the jungle black men.

Again his mind was haunted by wild speculations as to what danger lay before him and his friends. Small wonder that he found this underground passage a place of deepest mystery. He did not know it, but the most courageous explorer in the world would have known a touch of fear in the place; the most erudite scientist would have been baffled there. For Africa is the Dark Continent and the Congo is the Heart of Darkness. And here in the depths of the Congo lay things more fantastic than any civilized man had ever dreamed.

Several times Zar growled deep in his majestic throat, telling that this subterranean world of gloom was not to his liking. Each time Ka-Zar stilled him with a guttural warning. Nono had long since subsided into shivering misery.

Twice something swooped down over their heads, brushed noiselessly by with only a sudden rush of air to tell of its passage. Then far ahead they saw that the dimness of the tunnel was lightened by a flickering, reddish glow.

They turned the corner of an abrupt bend in the passage and saw, set in the wall ahead of them, a burning torch. Now their vigilance was redoubled. Their eyes peered ahead, past the spluttering beacon. Ka-Zar saw that the stream they had been following grew wider. Several times his fingers crept to the haft of the knife at his belt. But still the silence was unbroken. Nothing moved; nothing stirred. Shrewdly he guessed that long hours had passed since he and his friends had been swept down by the treacherous cave-in. It was now night and if by any chance there were Oman in the vicinity, they would probably be sleeping.

With a last warning for silence, he moved forward. His stomach muscles were drawn in, his belly was empty and he was hungry. Somewhere, somehow, they must find food.

CHAPTER III

THE TEMPLE OF PTHOS

A **SHORT FEW** minutes later they rounded a last bend and halted in amazement. The river widened out abruptly before them into a vast lake. From its shores the walls of the tunnel leaped upward in vaulted arches, tier upon receding tier, until they were lost in utter blackness. Here and there on the high parapets, like evil eyes in the blackness, other torches had been set into the rocky walls. And at their feet the tongues of flame were reflected eerily in the dark, still waters of the lake.

Straight ahead, far distant across the water, gleamed a steady pillar of flame. It was different in several respects from the sputtering tongues of the torches. For one thing it rose from an elevation higher than any. And its light was a pure, pale glow. Its very distance and the surrounding gloom made it seem detached, as though it floated in space.

Suddenly Zar's ruff rose. A quiver ran down the length of his huge, tawny form. His lips pulled back from his bared fangs and he snarled.

"Still!" warned Ka-Zar in a low voice.

He, too, had caught it—the faint but unmistakable scent of man! From slitted, tawny eyes he surveyed the black and silent lake and the towering cliffs hanging over it. Along the rocky walls his keen eyes made out many oblong patches of black shadow and his jungle instinct told him that they were the entrances to caves. As far as he could see, the cliffs were honeycombed with them.

His jaw tightened. Then he shrugged his massive, naked shoulders. Where there were Oman, there also was food. The thought whetted his already keen appetite. He turned and started off at a swift but silent stride, following the shore of the lake.

The hated scent of man grew stronger in his nostrils. And soon he came to the first shadowy opening in the bare face of the cliff. Peering into it, he saw a long, narrow tunnel leading into the rock. Another torch illumined its length.

Zar fell in behind him as he entered the passage. Soundlessly they traversed its length and at the far end, found that it branched off into two opposite directions. There was nothing to indicate what might lay at the end of either.

Ka-Zar detached the clinging monkey, dropped him lightly to the ground and then stooping over, laid his lips close to Zar's ear. "Go with Nono," he ordered in a low, hoarse whisper. "Ka-Zar goes the other way. Go silently—seek food, not trouble. Ka-Zar will meet his brother here at this spot later."

With a subdued growl to show that he understood, Zar turned into the left hand passage and glided off like a monstrous tawny shadow. The fearful Nono scampered nervously in his wake. Ka-Zar watched them a moment, then turned off to his right and with equal stealth moved off in the opposite direction.

He soon found that he had entered a veritable labyrinth. Here in the cliff, the narrow tunnels crossed and recrossed each other in a tangled maze. He halted in dismay and wondered if Zar, too, had been lost in a similar tangle. But there was nothing for it now. Of one thing he was certain. Men—many men—his traditional enemy, were here. And he did not relish the prospect of meeting them with a hungry, gnawing stomach.

One lead was as good as another. He turned off down the nearest shaft. In many places he had to stoop to clear the low rocky ceiling. It terminated in an elaborate, bronze door.

Ka-Zar halted before it, surprised. He studied the closed portal for a moment. Two straight pillars flanked it on either side. They were decorated with vividly colored paintings that made no sense to him. Some were of two-legged creatures whose heads were those of Nono the monkey or Nyassa the fish. Others had bodies of Sinassa the snake and the wings of Kru the vulture.

WITH EVERY SENSE alert, with every nerve on trigger edge, he tried the door. To his surprise, it opened easily, swung noiselessly inward under the steady pressure of his shoulder. With one hand near his belt, he glided across the threshold, let the door swing back into place behind him.

After the low ceiling of the narrow tunnel, he was not prepared for the vastness of the chamber he had entered. Nor had the bare rocky passage prepared him for the dazzling splendor that now greeted his eyes.

Around him the walls rose high and sheer, decorated by pillars far more resplendent than those that flanked the doorway outside. Here were more vivid paintings, but these were augmented by embellishments of gleaming metals and twinkling gems. Before him a flight of steps, polished until they shone, led up to a broad dais. On either side of the platform were slender columns topped by glowing braziers. Blue smoke curled up from these, drifted down to him heavy with the pungent scent of incense. And between the two columns, in the center of the dais, stood the most repelling, the most amazing, object that he had ever seen.

Around its massive base many lamps burned with a strange, bluish light. It rose sheer, towering, threatening—an enormous figure that was far more grotesque than any of the painted representations on the walls.

Ka-Zar had seen the pot-bellied figures of clay that the jungle blacks worshipped as gods. But it took him a few moments to realize that this enormous figure before him was also a god. He walked slowly forward, studied it curiously. He saw a squat, misshapen body that was grotesquely human. Claw-like hands were folded across the swollen belly. The head of a hideous monster, with empty sockets for eyes and curved horns jutting from its low forehead, leered down at him.

Ka-Zar had no knowledge of history nor of religions. His clear eyes saw in that repulsive face all the greed and lust and cruelty of the Oman. And he sensed that men who would worship such a god must have hearts as black as the darkness in which they lived.

He forgot what he had come seeking. He was obsessed suddenly by a yearning for the brilliant sunshine of the world above, for the luxuriant green growth of the forest, for the familiar sounds of insects and birds and beasts.

But it was no sound that roused him suddenly from his nostalgic reverie. It was but a feeling—a vague warning that was born in his own brain—that made him suddenly tense and wary. He knew, without knowing why, that he was not alone. The flesh at the nape of his neck crawled where the gaze of invisible eyes rested upon him.

His nostrils flared a trifle and from slitted tawny eyes he searched the vaulted chamber. Slowly, very slowly he turned to face the door through which he had come. Then his gaze was irresistibly drawn upward. He stiffened as his own eyes met a pair of greenish orbs that glared malevolently back at him.

On a narrow ledge above the doorway crouched a sinister ebony form. Ka-Zar stiffened to rigid immobility as he recognized N'Jagi, black cousin of N'Jaga the leopard. Around N'Jagi's sleek throat was a slender collar of gold, studded with gems. His long tail switched. He lay flat on his belly, his ears back—the hideous guardian of this unholy temple. And Ka-Zar knew that if he took one step toward the portal, a spitting, clawing black death would descend upon him.

Only one beast had ever dared to challenge Ka-Zar's supremacy in the jungle. N'Jaga, the magnificent spotted terror of the forest, had dared to defy the might of Ka-Zar and his mighty brother Zar the lion. The feud had been a long and bitter one; a feud that would never die as long as the leopard tribe roamed the earth. In the final test, when N'Jaga and Ka-Zar had met in fair battle, N'Jaga had died by the jungle giant's hand.

NOW HERE WAS N'Jagi, far more treacherous, far more powerful, far more cruel than his spotted cousin. The black hate mirrored in his gleaming eyes was a challenge, a reminder to Ka-Zar that he was the ruler of the jungle and all its people. He rose to it. Flinging back his mane of long dark hair, he straddled his legs and faced his hereditary enemy—a magnificent figure, arrogant and commanding. Then with a reckless disdain for whatever men or beasts dwelled in that place, he expanded his mighty chest and sent the stentorian roar of the lion echoing and re-echoing through the temple.

The crouching N'Jagi heard and understood. Never before had the black leopard known fear. The two-legged creatures who dwelled deep in the earth had always trembled in terror before his baleful glare. Only one of them dared to approach him—and between him and this Om was a bond of black deviltry, a strange brotherhood of evil. Now this strange two-legged creature dared to defy him! He spat, but in his heart of hearts he knew a strange apprehension.

It angered him. He lashed his tail. A whining snarl issued from his throat. And then the two legged one spoke to him in the language of the beasts.

"Spring, N'Jagi!" came the defiant taunt. "Spring at Ka-Zar— brother of the mighty Zar—and die!"

The glow from the braziers was reflected in the shining steel that leaped with lightning swiftness into Ka-Zar's hand. Still N'Jagi hesitated, glaring in impotent hate from his slitted emerald eyes. A blind lust to slay possessed him. He gathered his powerful muscles and his lips curled back from gleaming fangs.

"N'Jagi waits," called up Ka-Zar scornfully. "He is wiser than his cousin N'Jaga. For N'Jaga died by Ka-Zar's bare hands."

At the words, the smouldering fury in N'Jagi's heart burst

into searing flame. His arrogant soul would admit of no master. His crafty brain urged him to back down, to bide his time and wait for vengeance. But the challenge of the jungle is not lightly ignored. There is no word for mercy in the language of the beasts. The weak are killed and the strong survive. And an enemy is forever an enemy until he is slain. Torn between the urge to destroy this bold two-legged creature and this strange apprehension that had come for the first time to trouble him, N'Jagi wriggled uneasily on the ledge.

Ka-Zar waited no longer. Grasping his knife, with another guttural taunt he stepped deliberately forward. One step. Two steps. Three steps....

Two more strides would carry him to the door. N'Jagi's fury overmastered his caution. With a hideous scream, his terrible claws spreading out into glistening steel hooks, he sprang.

Ka-Zar leaped nimbly aside as the shrieking black fury descended upon him. The foetid breath of the leopard was rank in his nostrils as the beast hurtled down beside him. The malevolent hate in the green orbs—a hate heightened by the knowledge that his first lunge had missed—was a living thing.

Then, before he could recover—before he could rip Ka-Zar from throat to loin with a slash of his saber claws—the jungle man leaped into action. And the jungle man was quicker, more sure and deadly than the leopard had been. With his shoulder he smote N'Jagi's shoulder, throwing the leopard back on his haunches. Then his left hand flashed out, knotted in an iron fist around the collar of gold that encircled the black cat's throat.

In his right hand the blade of his knife glinted brightly for a moment, then descended in a swift arc.

N'Jagi saw the blow even as it fell. Using his two hind legs as levers, he lunged violently to avoid it, at the same time lashing out with his fore-paws. Five streaks of liquid fire seared their way across Ka-Zar's chest as the leopard's claws drew blood. But his grip on the collar never loosened.

The blade descended, driving home through the satiny skin

of N'Jagi's throat. Hot blood spurted up to Ka-Zar's hand. The leopard's eyes were glowing coals of pain and hate. He lunged again, slashed futilely with his claws at the empty air—then slumped in Ka-Zar's grip.

WITH A LONG, drawn-out breath the pent-up air escaped from Ka-Zar's lungs. Still holding up the limp body of the leopard by the golden collar around his throat, he disdainfully wiped his knife against the satiny hide, jammed it home into its sheath again. Then with a guttural snarl he cast the body from him.

As if the arrogant gesture had been a signal the massive bronze door swung open. The temple became a bedlam of shrieking shouts and cries and the rush of many naked feet. Ka-Zar whirled, his chin fell on his chest and his shoulders hunched. His knife flashed up again—but ere it could descend a horde of naked black men had thrown themselves upon him.

The dagger was clawed from his fist. Thumbs gouged his eyes; teeth sank into his flesh. By sheer weight of numbers the blacks overwhelmed him, sent him crashing to the floor of the temple beneath a pile of sweating, stinking bodies.

Even the mighty giant of the jungle was no match for such a horde. And after the brief but furious melee, when Ka-Zar was jerked roughly to his feet, he was truly a prisoner. Around his neck the blacks had slipped a collar of copper, to which was attached a heavy chain.

Dazed, sick at heart, trembling with impotent fury he straddled his legs and glared at his captors. As the reddish film dissolved gradually from his eyes, he saw them clearly for the first time. They were black, true, but strangely different from the jungle creatures he had known. These men were puny, their arms and legs spindly and misshapen. Instead of glistening ebony, generations of living deep under the ground had turned their skins to a dull, unhealthy-looking gray. Their eyes were sunken deep in the sockets of their skulls and they wore only ragged and filthy loin-cloths. They jabbered excitedly to one another in a tongue that he could not understand.

Like a lion at bay surrounded by a pack of mangy dogs, Ka-Zar stood in their midst. Though he could not understand their talk or the gibes they spat at him, their expressions were easily readable. Their lacklustre eyes mirrored at the same time a cold fury against the violator of the temple and a superstitious awe as they saw the lifeless body of the black leopard.

Ka-Zar faced them without fear. That the fate which awaited him was probably a dire one, he did not care. It was the feel of the collar about his neck that revolted his very soul. The symbol of bondage—about the neck of the mighty Ka-Zar—King of the Jungle—brother of Zar the lion! It was unthinkable!

The chain clinked as he flung back his magnificent head, squared his massive shoulders and once more set the temple throbbing to the challenging roar of the lion.

CHAPTER IV

THE QUEEN CONDEMNS

THE FIRST WAN light of dawn was breaking over the Congo when in another temple, not far distant, a radically different scene was transpiring. Here the walls and the vaulted ceiling were of purest white. In the center of the tiled floor was a sunken pool. Papyrus plants fringed its edges and enormous lotus buds floated upon the still water.

Set in a vast niche in one wall was the towering statue of a goddess. Her countenance was at the same time benevolent and yet stern; implacable and yet merciful. Her blank eyes looked down at the figure of a young girl who lay prostrate on the tiled floor at her feet.

The girl raised her head, lifted her arms in supplication. She was hauntingly beautiful. Beneath straight brows her eyes were deep pools of darkness. Her nose was finely chiseled and her mouth was a splash of vivid scarlet. Her slender body was exquisitely formed and of the rare tint of old ivory. A slender gold circlet in the form of a twisted snake bound her forehead and beneath it her hair fell to her shoulders, sleek, blue-black.

From a jeweled girdle that encircled her hips hung a sheath of some gossamer stuff. Above the girdle her ivory tinted body was nude save for cupshaped discs of gold, that upheld her firm young breasts.

Her scarlet lips parted and aloud she communed with her deity in the strange language that had puzzled Ka-Zar.

"O all-seeing and all-powerful Isis," she began in a low, husky chant, "deign to aid thy troubled daughter. Remember in thy wisdom that when my forefathers fled their beloved Egypt the most precious burden of their blacks was thy image."

There was deep sorrow in her whisper as she continued: "Now my father the king lies buried beneath the temple. Times are troublesome in Khalli and my people are restless. O Isis, aid the proud Queen Tamiris who kneels so humbly before thee. Counsel me—guide me!"

The last faint whispers of her voice died away into silence as she prostrated herself once more on the tiles. For a long time no sound broke the stillness. If the goddess spoke words of wisdom, they were voiced only in the heart of the kneeling girl.

She rose at last. Her head came up and with a regal gesture of command, she clapped her palms sharply together.

Instantly the door to an ante-chamber opened and eight girls garbed in filmy white draperies—the vestal virgins of the goddess—glided into the temple. Some bore urns of incense, others huge fans of peacock feathers. One carried tame doves upon her arms and shoulders. As they approached, the humility Tamiris had displayed before the goddess dropped from her like a discarded mantle. She held her head imperiously high, her eyes flashed brightly and her lips were set in a straight, uncompromising line.

The priestesses fell into place about her and to the accompaniment of a melancholy, minor keyed chant, Queen Tamiris walked slowly from the temple.

Already the first hot rays of the sun were slanting over the Congo. The high circular wall of unscaleable cliffs was shaded from deep purple at the base to a pale turquoise at the summit.

Jungle, lush and vividly green as Ka-Zar knew and loved it, covered the floor of the lost valley. On the far side of it, visible over the tree-tops, rising tier upon tier of sun-baked clay and stone stood the fabulous lost city of Khalli.

From its summit, pale now in the light of day, rose a steady pillar of flame. It was this eternal light that Ka-Zar had seen through a break in the cliffs the night before, when he had stood in the tunnel and looked out across the underground lake.

TAMIRIS' ROYAL VISIT to the Temple of Isis was an occasion of state. It was a sumptuous procession that awaited her as she emerged from the building. Stepping into her gilded palanquin she sank back against its silken cushions and the conveyance was raised to the shoulders of four black slaves. The sun gleamed on fluttering banners and brazen trumpets as she was carried in regal style towards the distant city.

As the column traversed a broad path along the shaded floor of the jungle, the beauty of the Queen's face was marred by a dark frown. True daughter of the Ptolemies, she was quick to anger—slow to forgive; and she was more proud than Lucifer, himself.

She mourned her father now that he was dead, yet living, she had secretly despised him for his weakness. A keen child she had long guessed that the wise and crafty Zut was the real ruler of Khalli. And now, though she was still hardly more than a child, she vowed that Zut's reign was ended. For long years she had brooded in secret upon the matter and now that the time had come, she was determined to assert her own dominance.

The fringe of jungle thinned and from narrowed eyes Tamiris surveyed her fantastic kingdom. It was a strange city indeed that had grown up here in the depths of the Congo—an imposing pile that pyramided upward in flights of hewn stone steps, of terraces and hanging gardens, of palaces and hovels, of obelisks and market-places and tombs.

The procession began the long climb up the steps. The palanquin lurched as the leading slave stumbled, throwing Tamiris back against the cushions. Instantly her face flamed a dull crimson with rage. Thrusting her head from the side of the conveyance she addressed the trembling culprit.

"For that you shall have twenty lashes, clumsy one!"

The unhappy slave bowed his head and plodded on. Somewhat mollified, Tamiris allowed her mind to brood once more upon the tangled affairs of state.

When at last she dismounted before the vast portal of her magnificent palace, a breathless black emerged from the building, prostrated himself panting at her feet.

"Speak," ordered Tamiris coldly. "What do you wish with your Queen?"

"Daughter of the Sun," murmured the slave, "Zut desires your presence in the courtyard of the palace. There are those who wish audience with you."

Tamiris drew herself to the full of her diminutive height. Twin spots of color flamed in her smooth ivory cheeks. So Zut dared to summon her thus? The time had come to throw down the gauntlet and defy him. Let this slave tell him....

She bit her under lip, changed her mind. No. Better to wait until she was in the audience hall. Let the multitude hear her challenge this usurping schemer. She made a gesture to the slave.

"Go. Tell Zut that the Queen comes."

Dismissing her cortege, Tamiris entered the building. At every step of the way guards saluted her with upraised spears, men and women of the household made obeisance as she passed. She walked past them, unseeing, unhearing, oblivious to their presence. Crossing a long hall, she found Zut waiting for her near a door that gave out onto the main courtyard of the palace.

She surveyed him with ill-concealed hostility as he bowed gravely. A yellow robe was wrapped about his tall, cadaverous figure, his bare feet were shod with sandals made of thongs of leather. His sole adornment was a ring that held a monstrous moonstone, that looked out of place on his thin, clawlike hand. An unprepossessing figure, until one looked at his face.

ZUT WAS AGELESS. As long as Tamiris could remember his skin had always looked like wrinkled, yellow parchment. His loose and pendulous lips were hidden by a straggly beard. It was his eyes that were noteworthy, that held the gaze with an hypnotic fascination. Beneath jutting brows, set close on either side of a hooked and predatory nose, they were small but piercing. There was something of the power, the cunning and the cruelty of a bird of prey about this crafty statesman.

It was the Queen who spoke first. "You have requested my presence," she said coldly. "See to it that your reason for doing so is sufficient to warrant such presumption."

Zut allowed his lashless lids to droop over his eyes, veiling whatever expression her arrogant words might have brought to their depths. "It is a matter of the greatest import," he replied. "The Daughter of the Sun knows that trouble is brewing in Khalli. Through the long centuries the black slaves who dwell in the catacombs have multiplied, while the descendants of their masters, here in Khalli, steadily decline. The blacks realize the power of their numbers. They grow avaricious and resentful. Revolt simmers below the surface even now."

Tamiris squared her slim shoulders. "Let them revolt, if they dare. Every traitor shall die."

Zut shook his head, combed his beard with skinny fingers. "Spoken like a Ptolemy, Queen Tamiris. But such words must be backed with swords and with warriors. Thus far, only my persuasion with Seti, the High Priest of Pthos, has kept the embers of rebellion from bursting into flame."

Though she would not admit it, Tamiris knew only too well that what Zut said of the blacks was true. When her forefathers had fled down from Egypt with a handful of slaves, they had stumbled by accident into one of the natural tunnels that ran through these cliffs. A cataclysmic earthquake had sealed the passage behind them and doomed forever to live in this place, they had builded the city of Khalli in the little valley of jungle. Here the nobles had maintained, as well as they could, the culture and the arts of their native land.

But time and again slaves had fled and taken refuge in the caves that honeycombed the cliffs surrounding the underground lake. There in eternal twilight they had multiplied in number and degenerated in body and soul. Forswearing the goddess

Isis they had set up a temple to the evil Pthos and rumors of obscene orgies and sacrifices drifted out to the city.

Now these worshipers of darkness had become a decided menace to Khalli and its inhabitants. The devil could rule them but not Tamiris the Queen.

All this passed through Tamiris' mind, but to Zut she said only: "Your reason for summoning me—what is it?"

Zut opened the door that led to the courtyard and as they stepped through onto a broad terrace, he explained: "The dwellers in the catacombs have captured an outlandish prisoner. Whence he came from, no one knows. They claim he has desecrated the temple of Pthos and they clamor for his blood. You can see for yourself what manner of man is this creature."

Tamiris walked to the edge of the terrace, looked out over the courtyard. It was filled from one end to the other with a milling throng of blacks, who sullenly and reluctantly prostrated themselves as she appeared before them.

Standing in their midst, bruised, battered but still magnificently defiant, Ka-Zar towered above them. Despite the hateful fetters about his neck he was still untamed, still the monarch of the jungle.

The daughter of the Ptolemies surveyed him with interest. No sculptor in Khalli could have modeled such a superb head, such a massive, muscular body in bronze. An instinct as old as Eve, but something which she did not as yet understand, stirred in the breast of the youthful Queen.

ONE OF THE blacks jerked at the chain fastened to the collar about Ka-Zar's neck. Ka-Zar glared at him and a low growl rumbled deep in his mighty throat.

"You see?" said Zut in Tamiris' ear. "He speaks no language, but growls and snarls like a beast. He is naked, save for the skin of an animal about his loins."

"Yet," retorted Tamiris, "he is worth ten of Khalli's best warriors—and worth a hundred of these puny slaves."

Zut rubbed the side of his hooked nose with a bony knuckle.

"Perhaps. But the blacks demand his death. And the daughter of the Sun would be wise to placate them."

Without reply, Tamiris turned her back to him and walked majestically down the steps of the terrace. Placate these grotesque, malformed creatures who dared to question her sovereignty? Never! She would defy them, here and now. Defy Zut, also. How this jungle giant had managed to appear mysteriously in her domain did not matter, at the moment. Had it suited her purpose to toss his life away, she would have done it without a second's hesitation. But as a pawn in the game, he would be spared.

She walked up to Ka-Zar, came to a halt before him. All eyes in the courtyard were upon her, all ears waited for her to speak. Her scarlet lips parted—the multitude would soon hear her momentous challenge!

But she had reckoned without Ka-Zar. With powerful arms folded across his bronzed chest, he stared at the slight figure confronting him. For long months he had been tormented by the vision of a girl who be believed had betrayed him. To his simple soul, then, woman meant treachery and his hate had grown to include them all. That in itself was reason enough for him to feel instant antagonism for the exotic creature who now stood before him.

But that was not all. Despite his hatred, Ka-Zar had never been able to rid himself of a yearning for the golden-haired vision of his dreams. Claudette of the laughing face and eyes as blue as the skies after rain. Now he looked upon the face of Tamiris and her flaming beauty was an affront. It was a mockery—the fact that she should remind him of Claudette. For her eyes were hard and as brilliant as jet; her scarlet lips were set in a thin, straight line. And her lithe body was that of a jungle cat ready to spring.

Ka-Zar did not stop to analyze such complex emotions. In his simple heart he knew only that the sight of this exotic Queen was hateful to him. And he expressed that hostility in the natural way for him to do so. He distended his nostrils. A guttural, animal snarl rumbled in his throat. Then with a contemptuous gesture he tossed back his regal head and clenching his huge fists, he loosed from his lips the rumbling bass challenge before which the very jungle had always trembled.

A wail of terror rose from the blacks as they fell back. Their hands brandished the varied assortment of weapons they bore. Only Tamiris held her ground. She did not flinch; she did not stir. But there was no mistaking the defiance, the disdain, that this jungle giant was directing at her.

A pulse beat dully in the ivory column of the Queen's throat. Twin spots of angry color flamed in her cheeks. A violent rage, the heritage of her arrogant ancestors, possessed her. This naked savage—this—this jungle animal—dared to mock her!

With the roar of the lion, Ka-Zar had swept the carefully planned chessboard of diplomacy into a heap. Tamiris forgot that this creature was but a pawn in her royal game, forgot that a moment before she had been about to speak the word that would set him free.

In a torrent of the staccato, corrupted Egyptian that was her language, she showered the dire curses of the gods upon his untamed head. Ka-Zar listened and watched in scornful silence as she denounced him. His judgment of her was vindicated— in her flashing eyes, in her twisted lips, in the tiny hands that clenched and unclenched at her sides—she was every inch feline, cruel, savage.

Suddenly she straightened, raised one hand in an imperious gesture and spoke a swift sentence to the surrounding blacks. A concerted yell of triumph welled from their throats as they closed in about their prisoner. Then without a backward glance Tamiris turned, majestically ascended the terrace and disappeared inside the palace.

CHAPTER V

THE QUEEN RETREATS

WILLING HANDS PULLED savagely at the chain attached to the collar encircling Ka-Zar's throat. Leaping and howling the blacks dragged him swiftly across the flag-paved courtyard toward the base of a massive monolith. It was fantastically carved in bas relief with more of the strange creatures that were neither bird nor man nor beast, but fantastic combinations of the three. Ka-Zar could see that encircling the monolith, head high, were a series of massive bronze rings.

He soon learned what they were for. A last painful jerk of the chain and one end of the linked halter that held him was slipped through one of the rings and cunningly secured.

He was chained—truly chained.

All his old hatred of the Oman swept through his heart. He had experienced nothing but sorrow and trouble at the hands of man. The first had slain his father—and in time he had died. The second had brought untold woe to his jungle domain—and he, too, had died. The third—the golden-haired girl....

Bah! It was a raven-haired she-devil who held him enslaved now. Not with a laugh and a caress of soft hands—but with chains.

With a bitter snarl of resentment, Ka-Zar relaxed. Head on his chest, he brooded on his fate. The black-eyed she-devil had condemned him and if he could have understood her last words, he would doubtless know also the manner in which he was to die.

With pleased grins now, the blacks hovered about him. All through that day, with the broiling sun of the Congo beating down upon his head, he stood immovable, unblinking, chained to the monolith. The black men came to taunt him, to spit upon him, to lash him with gibes in their outlandish tongue. To Ka-Zar, brother of the mighty lion, they were but a pack of mangy hyenas—he ignored them all.

Their vile words he could not understand and they hurt him not. The occasional spear with which they prodded him, or the stones they flung, were but indignities and irritations beneath his notice. His contempt was magnificent.

Only once did his amber eyes flash fire, only once did the lion's growl rumble in his throat. One of the blacks approached him, a broad grin showing the sharp points of filed teeth. In his two hands he held a small urn out of which the water spilled as he walked.

He held out the vessel invitingly but as Ka-Zar reached eagerly for it, he let it slip from his hands to crash to the flags of the courtyard. It shattered into a thousand bits and the precious fluid trickled away across the sunbaked stones.

A fiendish howl of derision went up from the encircling blacks at the incident. Ka-Zar understood then that he had been tricked. His eyes smouldered. He lunged forward suddenly to the full length of his chain. Like a piston his long right leg flashed out and the toes of his bare foot, hard as granite, caught the culprit under the chin.

The black hurtled backward, crashed into three of his fellows and brought them down with him in his fall.

The jeers of the others gave way to a gnashing of teeth. Once more Ka-Zar fell back into his stoic calm. He regretted his wrathful outburst. Never again would these jackals arouse him from his superior indifference.

Thirst! He knew its tortures. First it made man or beast mad—then it destroyed them. Was that the fate that awaited him? Again he reflected on the wanton cruelty of man. The beasts of the jungle slay—slay for food. But the refinements of torture, of prolonged agony before the release of death—that was the product of the cruel, twisted brain of man alone.

He must conserve his strength. His belly was empty. The day wore slowly on. The sun wheeled through its zenith, descended at last into the west. Ka-Zar's mouth was hot and dry as the dust on the flags at his feet but not by one sign did he show the anguish of his body. The night would bring surcease and he had yet to test the full of his strength against the chains which bound him.

AS THE LONG shadows fell at last across the courtyard, the blacks melted reluctantly away. Then, a moment before the sun sank below the rim of the encircling cliff, the Queen stepped silently out onto the terrace.

From long, narrowed eyes she looked down at her captive, studied him. The level shafts of the dying light glinted brightly off the jeweled ornaments that spangled her bare body, stabbed at Ka-Zar's eyes and betrayed her presence to him.

Slowly his head came up, swung toward the terrace. Coolly he surveyed the girl, a barbaric picture bathed in the warm light of the dying sun. Then his lips curled with hatred. For a long moment piercing amber eyes met glowing black ones as their gaze met and held—Tamiris, Queen of a lost civilization—Ka-Zar, jungle King of a domain to which civilization had never come.

Tamiris' cheeks flushed and her breasts arched against the jeweled discs that covered them. A growing curiosity had brought her out to the terrace to study this strange jungle giant. Who was he, this magnificent creature who spoke with the voice of the lion? Whence came he? What did he seek in Khalli?

At the sight of his superb figure, still proudly defiant in spite of the fetters, the alien emotion that had disturbed her before came again to her heart. In a sudden confusion that she could not explain, she turned abruptly and hastily retreated from the terrace.

CHAPTER VI

ZAR'S KILL

THE TWILIGHT OF the tropics is brief. Purple shadows gathered at the base of the cliffs, crept silently forth and stole toward the city.

Alone at last in the courtyard, Ka-Zar watched the coming of the night. Far above him the strange, steady flame glowed brighter against the deepening sky. The hubbub of noise that had arisen steadily from the lower reaches of the city died gradually away. For the first time he could hear the distant sounds of the surrounding jungle.

The chattering of monkeys, the squawk of a sleepy bird disturbed by some prowling snake, the shrill yapping of a jackal came faintly to his ears. To Ka-Zar this was far more torture than the pangs of hunger or the torment of thirst. His soul yearned for the dark stretches of the jungle, for the wide expanse of forest and lake and star-studded heavens that were home and freedom.

His head sunk dejectedly on his breast. Now that there was no one to watch him he let his wide shoulders slump. The long strain of prolonged hunger and thirst, of the fierce rays of sun that had burned down upon him all that day, began to tell on him. A weariness of spirit as well as body descended upon him.

Then suddenly his head snapped up. From the distant jungle came a familiar cry—the rumbling bass notes of the lion's kill. The sound was distorted by the encircling cliffs, which flung it back and forth in diminishing echoes. Ka-Zar's eyes glowed.

Zar—could that have been Zar?

Hardly. But if the cry was not that of his kingly brother, at least it was that of a friend. Straining his ears, he listened.

It came again—like distant thunder—challenging, triumphant. And this time Ka-Zar thrilled to every fibre of his being. For he could not be mistaken.

Too often he had exulted to that same majestic voice. Too often he had set the wilderness ringing with his own answering call. He knew that it was none other than Zar the mighty who now made the night tremble.

Ka-Zar's body stiffened to the full of his imposing height. His head tilted back, his lips opened. The first rumbling notes of the cry started in his throat—then died still-born. His jaws snapped shut.

Often during that long and terrible day he had thought of Zar and Nono and wondered at their fate. He knew now that Zar was free, that somehow he had eluded the cave-dwellers and had reached the expanse of jungle in the sunken valley. But to answer his call would have been a fatal mistake.

To the inhabitants of Khalli, the roar of a lion in the wilderness would have no significance. But let that same cry ring from the heart of the city in the darkness of the night—and instantly the courtyard would be swarming with alarmed men. If he responded to the cry—and Ka-Zar knew that his loyal brother would—Zar would only fall into a trap.

So with the consolation that at least the lion had escaped his fate, Ka-Zar let his head droop once more upon his breast. Zar could do nothing for him anyway. Despite all the strength of his massive tawny body he could not free the jungle giant of his chains.

The chains....

Seizing the glittering links in his hands, Ka-Zar pulled at the hateful fetters. His powerful biceps bulged; his forearms stood out in hard knots of muscle; his broad back rippled. Beads of sweat popped out on his forehead. His brain swam giddily.

In a sudden outburst of fury and desperation he gathered the last ounce of power in his flagging body, tugged and heaved.

But all his efforts availed him nought. With a bitter sigh of resignation he let the clinking chain drop from his hands. Weariness overcame him at last. His eyes dulled and his lids drooped over them. His tortured, aching body relaxed, crumpled slowly, joint by joint. He sank to the flags, crumpled at the base of the monolith. There was no need to fight against the merciful sleep that came to bathe him in oblivion.

It was a light touch that roused Ka-Zar to instant wakefulness. The stillness was absolute. The moon had risen over the Congo, but her face was wreathed in tattered wisps of cloud and only a dim, half-light pervaded the courtyard of the palace. Ka-Zar was aware, at first, only of tiny fingers on his bare arm as his eyes accustomed themselves to the darkness.

A moment later he made out his nocturnal visitor. Nono the monkey bent over him. Ka-Zar's throat was aflame with thirst. He could not even voice his gladness. Then Nono's beady-eyed face came closer; the mouth of the monkey came to meet his own.

PRECIOUS DROPS OF water moistened Ka-Zar's dry lips. He opened them greedily and a thin stream of the fluid entered his mouth and trickled down his throat. It was tepid, but to Ka-Zar it was the elixir of life itself. Hungrily his parched body absorbed it and those few priceless drops revived him.

He struggled up to a sitting position as Nono dragged forward a chunk of raw, fresh-killed meat. Ka-Zar fell upon it and devoured it in ravenous gulps. With each mouthful new strength flowed into his weary body and the languor that had descended upon him evaporated.

"My brother's kill?" he asked the squatting monkey as he feasted.

Nono kept glancing fearfully about him. "Zar's kill," he squeaked. "Zar sent me."

Already the mouthful of water and the taste of raw meat had

routed the blank despair from Ka-Zar's heart. The knowledge that he still had his two faithful allies to help him gave him new courage, new hope. The old instinct to survive, to cling to life, was strong within him.

"The silly, long-tailed one has proved a true friend to Ka-Zar," he whispered to the monkey. "If he would do more—let him bring more of the water. Nono is agile, Nono is swift. Nono can move like a silent shadow. Go—steal one of the gourds which the Oman use to carry water. Bring drink to Ka-Zar."

With a single clucking sound to show that he understood, the little creature scampered like a huge spider across the courtyard. For a brief instant his slender form was outlined against the full glow of the moon, then he vanished.

He reappeared a short time later, hugging a clay vessel in his skinny arms. Ka-Zar took it from him, drank first sparingly and then with long draughts of the cool liquid.

When the last drop had been drained, he handed the pot back to the monkey. "Take the gourd—keep it," he ordered. "Bring water to Ka-Zar when it is needed. And tell my brother the mighty Zar to lie low in the jungle."

He stood erect, a sculptured figure with one bronze arm raised in farewell, as the monkey left him.

CHAPTER VII

JUNGLE MIRACLE

IN **THE PALACE,** another had found no restful sleep that night. Queen Tamiris, after tossing fitfully on her resplendent couch, had risen at last to pace the length of her magnificent chamber. Lanterns of pierced bronze that glittered with multi-colored lights, hung pendent from the high ceiling. Columns of glittering bits of mirror, cunningly set into clay, shimmered against the walls. The fragrance of burning sandalwood rose in a cloud from a huge urn and permeated the room. Luxurious rugs covered the floor and silken cushions covered the royal couch and several divans. But tonight all this evidence of queenly splendor gave Tamiris no comfort.

A frown made a deep V between her straight, dark brows. Before her eyes was always the vision of the strange jungle giant, chained to the monolith. With growing fury she thought how this man, who had come unbidden and unwanted to Khalli, had upset her carefully laid plans.

Her first test—her rights as supreme ruler against the insidious dictatorship of Zut—had come and she had failed. It was all the fault of this naked jungle savage. He had dared to insult her and in her fury, she had blindly acceded to the wishes of the usurping Zut.

Her tiny feet in their gilded sandals made no sound on the deep-piled rugs as she paced back and forth across the room.

In vain she tried to forget her fatal blunder, tried to formulate some new plan to break Zut's power and quell the incipient rebellion of the degenerate slaves. Always her mind came back to the naked bronze savage she had doomed to a lingering death.

With clenched fists she confronted the tawny-eyed vision before her. "The fault is your own that you must die thus," she whispered passionately. "Tamiris is not needlessly cruel. But in this game of empire you have made yourself a pawn. You have interfered with the plans of a Ptolemy—and so you must die."

Angry with herself, she tried to turn that anger into a mounting hate for this man whose image had come to disturb her. Wildly she prayed that he had already succumbed, so that she need no longer think of him.

And so it was that the first slanting sunbeams of the new day found her, garbed in sheer black draperies and bedecked with gold and silver, making her way toward the courtyard. Her heart was beating strangely faster in her breast as she stepped out onto the terrace.

Already a group of blacks had come to gloat upon the fate of their captive. But Tamiris found these slaves in a hushed, whispering group, gazing openmouthed at the monolith.

Her gaze shifted to one corner of her long, slitted eyes, expecting to see the jungle giant in a limp huddle at its base. She stifled the gasp that came to her lips. For there, standing more arrogantly than ever, was Ka-Zar.

There was no visible sign of the ordeal to which he had been subjected. His level eyes were just as inscrutable, his lips just as scornful, his head just as high as it had been when he had first been chained to the shaft.

One of the blacks, braver than his fellows, went closer and essayed feebly to repeat the taunts and gibes with which they had showered him the day before. But the others turned to face the Queen and in their dull, ashy faces she could read baffled wonder, baffled rage and a growing uneasiness towards this stranger.

Had they dared to approach her, they would have sought an

answer to this miracle. And biting her scarlet underlip, Tamiris realized that she would have been unable to answer their question.

Other blacks came—came to stare and wonder. Swiftly Tamiris turned and in a growing perplexity that she did not dare to show, vanished once more into the palace.

ANOTHER DAY PASSED. And another. And another. And another. And still the strange bronze giant faced each flaming sunrise in the full of his glorious strength.

All Khalli buzzed with a growing excitement. The uneasiness of the superstitious blacks who dwelled in the catacombs mounted. Each night they wended their way to the dim temple in the bowels of the earth and weird rites were performed at the feet of their ugly god. Seti, the crafty High Priest of Pthos, seized his opportunity. He pointed out that the mysterious captive was in the outer city, where Isis was the ruling deity. It was a sign that the power of Isis and of Ra, the sun-god, was weakening. And a sign also that the long dominance of the Ptolemies was diminishing in the frail hands of a woman.

These rumors spread and came at last to the tiered city. They came to the keen ears of Zut and the Machiavellian brain of that ageless schemer mulled them carefully over.

Were the Queen's prestige alone damaged by this strange happening in Khalli, Zut would have bided his time and allowed events to take their course. But he, too, lived in Khalli and in this instance, his own power was questioned. Better than Tamiris he realized that once the blacks threw off their serfdom and ran amuck, it would take an iron hand to control them. Unless he also was to be swept into oblivion by the threatening torrent, he must act.

He found Tamiris in her own apartments, sitting upon a divan with her determined chin resting in her palm. Her cheeks were flushed darkly and her ivory brow was wrinkled in a frown. She had just come from a brief visit to the courtyard.

Zut made a deep obeisance. "Daughter of the Sun," he said

gravely, "I come as a friend and as a loyal counsellor. As the trusted servant of your father before you, I dare to speak the truth; as one whose years are so many more than your own, I dare to advise you."

Tamiris moved her head in a barely perceptible nod. "Speak, then," she said coldly.

Zut bowed again. "This naked animal man fails to die. By some miracle he survives without food or water. Even Zut in his wisdom is puzzled and the blacks who dwell in the caves are greatly affected. It is as though this jungle-man defies the will of the Queen in refusing to die when she has condemned him."

Tamiris leaped to her feet, stiffened her slight body and clenched her hands at her sides. Her eyes flashed. "For once, Zut speaks the truth. Tamiris will have no more of such brazen defiance. Come. I shall speak the word and the blacks will fall upon him with their spears and swords. We shall see whether he is invulnerable to the bite of pointed steel."

The pale moonstone on Zut's finger glinted as he raised a claw-like hand. "Well-spoken, Favored of the Goddess. But for days the people have been in a state of growing tension. Such a hasty execution would not still the emotions that have been aroused. Such a swift death would be too merciful for one who has dared to bring the wrath of the Queen upon his head. No. I have a better plan."

He leaned forward and there was a glint in his close-set eyes as he spoke rapidly and earnestly to the listening girl.

A slow tide of color crept up from her heaving breast and mounted up the ivory column of her throat. Twin fringes of jet lashes dropped over her eyes to veil their depths. Then as Zut finished, she answered huskily: "It shall be as you say. Choose a hundred picked men, equip them with what they ask and send them into the forest. And let there be no delay."

With an humble attitude that did not betray his elation at this second triumph, Zut bowed and hurried off to carry out her orders.

When he had gone, Tamiris walked unsteadily over to the nearest window and stared, unseeing, out over the expanse of her isolated, buried kingdom.

BLOOD BROTHERS

A **T FIRST KA-ZAR** exulted over the consternation of his captors. His own simple animal soul had never known the hold of superstition. Had he understood their strange language, he would have been as baffled as they. Miracles, gods and goddesses had no meaning for him.

Often he marveled at their stupidity in not setting a guard over him in the night time, wondered why they did not suspect that somehow he was obtaining food and drink. True, the courtyard was surrounded on three sides by a high wall and on the fourth, by the towering facade of the palace. Occasionally men did make surreptitious visits to his open prison during the night. But Nono was swift and noiseless and cunning and he left no tell-tale tracks on the bare flags.

But though Ka-Zar did not die, the hateful fetters were still about his neck. With each passing day he became more conscious of the symbol of his bondage. They weighed more heavily on his spirit than on his body. Despite the instinctive urge to survive, he could not restrain a vague wish that even death should come to end his monotonous and hateful captivity.

Each night he had heard the familiar roar of his tawny brother, trembling faintly across the still air. Each night the sound had whipped his flagging spirits, given him new courage to face the coming of another dawn. Then one night, as he waited with a faint smile on his lips for the cry of his brother, he heard a new note in the lion's voice.

Ka-Zar's heart froze to an icy lump within him as the lion's roar rang out again and again from the distant jungle. This was not the triumphant pronouncement of another kill. There was a note of fury, of desperation, in the sound. Tense, drawn, his face set in lines of anguish, Ka-Zar stood rigid at the base of the monolith and listened. With a sinking feeling at the pit of his stomach he knew that now the sounds coming from Zar's mighty throat were compounded of baffled rage and pain. They were echoed by a concerted howl, fiendish shrieks of triumph from the lips of many Oman.

A short time later, Nono scampered over the wall. In the stress of his excitement he had brought neither meat nor water. Ka-Zar seized him as be approached.

"Zar?" he asked in a guttural growl. "What has happened to Zar?"

His teeth chattering with fright, Nono confirmed his worst fears. Oman—many Oman—had crept quietly into the forest. The mighty Zar had been captured by a trick and now he lashed helplessly in a great cage.

Ka-Zar took the blow in stoic silence. Already the first wan tinge of dawn was lightening the east. Enveloped by a poignant grief such as he had never known, he bowed his head as Nono disappeared from the courtyard.

Sunk in silent apathy, Ka-Zar had not yet moved when the first blacks came as usual to look upon him. Dully he raised his head and from lack-lustre eyes he surveyed them.

Now their manner towards him was radically changed. Triumph was in their harsh voices. An unholy anticipation gleamed in their sunken eyes. They forgot their recent fears and gathered in a milling throng to torment him.

That some new plan for deviltry was afoot, Ka-Zar could readily see. He longed to understand the outlandish chatter of these jackals so that he might learn the fate of his brother. He was indifferent to his own. After all, though he had forsworn them, he was actually one of the despised two-legged species.

He had some understanding of the dark impulses that motivated them, that had led them to fetter him with chains. But
the animal brain of Zar was yet simpler than his own. Ka-Zar's
heart bled for the sufferings of the king of the jungle, finding
himself penned up by hateful bars.

Occasionally, above the chatter of these yapping jackals, he
heard the angry voice of Zar, each time nearer to the city. And
as the sun climbed higher in the heavens more people than ever
before appeared to congregate in the courtyard.

This time, apprehension came to Ka-Zar's troubled brain. It
was soon evident that some momentous event was due to
happen. Zut appeared on a balcony high above the terrace, a
striking figure despite the simplicity of his garb. The white
dwellers of Khalli, dressed in brilliant, outlandish costume,
joined the throng. Like Zut, they were tall, swarthy of skin and
hawk-eyed, hooknosed and bearded.

A MAN KA-ZAR had never seen before, but obviously a personage
of importance, appeared beside Zut on the balcony. Seti, the
High Priest of Pthos, was a glittering but repellent figure. He
was fat to the point of obscenity. His features were all but invisible in his doughy, putty-colored face. His priestly vestments
swathed an enormous paunch and he waddled as he walked.
Soon he and Zut had their heads together in low but earnest
conclave.

The noise and confusion mounted. Still Ka-Zar neither
moved nor spoke. Only his watchful eyes observed them all
and his busy brain tried to guess what was to come.

A sudden hush fell over the multitude. All eyes in the courtyard turned upward toward the balcony. There was a concerted
intake of breath and then as one man they prostrated themselves
face downward upon the flags.

Ka-Zar's eyes flicked upward. On the balcony, flanked by the
deferential figures of Zut and Seti, ringed about by female
attendants and tall Egyptian soldiers, stood Tamiris. A huge
peacock feather fan shaded her from the brilliant rays of the

sun. An elaborate headdress of gems and feathers covered her
sleek hair and a fabric woven of shimmering metal threads was
wrapped about her slender hips. Her face was pale and her eyes
were darkly-burning coals in a wan mask.

Just for one fleeting moment did her glance rest on the
captive. A swift intuition told Ka-Zar that it was in the last
futile hope that he showed signs of weakness. But he did not
know why she wished this. And so with the ghost of a smile
he mocked her and was pleased to see that her bosom rose and
fell as she tore her eyes away. Instead, she looked out over the
west wall.

What she saw there made her eyes widen. She leaned forward
with sinuous grace, grasped the edge of the balcony. Ka-Zar
was reminded of N'Jagi the black leopard. There was the same
savage beauty, the same lithe grace, the same feline cruelty in
every line of them both. Both aroused the same instinctive
antagonism in his heart.

Tamiris raised her hand and a brilliant sunlight was reflected from a score of tinkling bracelets that encircled her bare
arm. Her husky tones floated out over the prone multitude in
unmistakeable command.

The gathering came hastily to its feet. Like a receding tide
blacks and Egyptians swept back from the monolith, helped
one another scale the walls and perched safely atop them. Every
balcony of the palace was crowded, other spectators peered
down from the roof and from the topmost tiers of the city.

Alone in the deserted courtyard, Ka-Zar knew that the ordeal
had come. His anxious eyes sought the faces of the people who
had come to witness. All were looking out beyond the west wall
and he alone could not see what waited there.

Then startlingly near, like a throbbing reverberation of a
mighty thunder, came the roar of Zar the lion. The spectators
gasped, cried out, then cheered.

At the sound of his brother's voice, Ka-Zar jerked as though
he had been struck. It was Zar—Zar in his cage—who was on

the other side of that high blank wall. The knowledge that he was so near his friend brought a sudden surge of relief.

And then that relief died in Ka-Zar's heart. A ghastly thought came to his brain. These crafty Oman—these wicked creatures with their twisted souls and twisted brains—had found the supreme torture for their captive. By some cunning trick they had captured Zar and now they intended to slay his blood brother before his own horrified eyes!

For the first time Ka-Zar's stoic calm was completely shattered. In a frenzy born of desperation, his brain filled only with the dire need of his friend, he went berserk. As though the chain that bound him was a living thing he seized it, grappled with it, tore at it. He clawed at the bronze collar around his throat. But the glittering links held and mocked him with their slender strength.

THE ASSEMBLED MULTITUDE saw his sudden outburst and mis-interpreting it, shrieked with delight. Ka-Zar stared up at the Queen, his lips pulled back from his teeth in a snarl, his tawny eyes glinting through a shock of touseled hair, his handsome features distorted into a scowl of hate. He longed to climb up onto the balcony and spring upon her slender figure. He breathed a silent prayer that he would live long enough to get his chance and vowed that when he did, his huge hands would encircle that ivory column of throat and squeeze the breath of life from it.

But again all eyes had shifted away from his figure. He followed their direction and saw a small section of the west wall—a cunningly-concealed door whose existence he had not suspected—open slowly inward.

Again there was a clamor of the multitude and to a blood-curdling chorus of howls and shrieks, echoed by another rumbling roar, an enormous tawny shape bounded through the portal.

Zar, roused to a frenzy by the jabs of many spearheads, charged into the courtyard. A red film of hate dimmed his eyes. A smouldering fury burned in his breast. Like a yellow hurricane of death he sprang at the only creature he saw before him. His great fangs were bared and his talon-like claws were arched to rip the hated Om to ribbons.

The mad chorus of the onlookers rose to a shrill pitch. Tamiris leaned forward again, gripping the rail of the balcony until her knuckles stood out white beneath the skin. All the color had gone from her face. A thousand emotions in turn crawled over her features and her dark eyes were haunted.

Oblivious to the din, Ka-Zar stared at the tawny fury that catapulted toward him. A strange half-whine, half-growl tore from his lips. It was the same sound, though no other knew it, that Zar's cubs would make when Sha their mother cuffed them too roughly.

The massive body of Zar jerked in mid-air. He landed on stiffened forelegs, slid to a sudden halt that brought him up short at the feet of the man chained to the monolith.

The shrieks of the crowd rose to fever-pitch. Then they were stilled as though a sudden stroke had paralyzed every throat. This lion was the most enormous beast they had ever seen. They were prepared for the sight of a terrible, bloody slaughter. But they were not prepared to see the bronze giant stoop to the limit of his chain, throw his arms about the neck of the lion and bury his face in the beast's shaggy mane!

For the space of long seconds no one stirred; no one spoke. It was as though the walls and the balconies and the ramparts of Khalli were lined with images of stone. And in that moment Ka-Zar knew at last the fate that the Queen had planned for him. She did not know he was the king of the jungle, lord of the jungle beasts.

For a last precious second he clung to his mighty brother. Then he rose, turned to face the balcony where Tamiris, Zut, Seti and the rest still stood petrified with astonishment, and flung back his head and laughed.

Zar rose from his crouch, strode to Ka-Zar's side and turned to face the silent audience. A regal pair—magnificent specimen of man and beast—they confronted their enemies with kingly dignity.

The silence was shattered as abruptly as it had fallen. With a piercing shriek a black flung his arms to the unseeing heavens, wailed in terror and then buried his face in his hands. The spell once shattered, the others broke out in a confused clamor. Some, trying to flee, fought in blind panic against the packed throng that hemmed them in. From the balcony Tamiris shouted an order, but her voice was drowned by the tumult and none heard.

Ka-Zar was quick to sense the brief advantage. He leaned over and growled something low to Zar. For a moment the lion hesitated. Then the caution that along with his might had made him ruler of the wilderness, made him see the wisdom of Ka-Zar's command.

Without warning he loosed another earth-shaking bellow. His captors had underestimated his prowess. Two tremendous leaps took him to the nearest wall, he gathered his great haunches and another bound catapulted him to the top. Screaming men spilled in every direction. One stroke of Zar's death-dealing paw sent another hurtling far out through the air, his last mortal cry quivering from his lips. Then before the startled assemblage could recover either their courage or their wits, the great lion was gone.

CHAPTER IX

TEST OF THE GODS

UP ON THE royal balcony the Queen, the High Priest and Zut were as dumfounded as the ignorant slaves below. Zut, by far the keenest of the three, was the first to realize the full possibilities of the situation. Whether he had indeed witnessed another miracle, or whether the strange jungle man had worked some mysterious black art on the charging lion, he was not sure.

But he was the first to note the change in the attitude of the Egyptians and the blacks below.

The cave dwellers in particular had forgotten that a short few moments before, they had cried for the blood of the victim. Now as they recovered from their first shock, they gazed upon him with open-mouthed awe. There was both respect and fear in their faces.

Zut's cunning brain interpreted his knowledge swiftly. The blacks had seen a miracle—this creature, to them, was a god! At least, it would need but a single voicing of that thought to bring them all to their knees. Zut suddenly changed his mind about the fate of this prisoner. In his supreme ego and ambition he decided that he could make use of such a god.

Tamiris' reaction was entirely different. As Zut had said, this lion-man's refusal to die was a personal affront. And each day that he continued to live, increased her agitation about him. She grew furious at him—mainly because she sensed that she—a daughter of the Ptolemies—was weakening.

Seti saw only that she was quivering with rage. He waddled

356

forward, made an awkward bow.

"Daughter of Isis," he pleaded, "this man desecrated the Temple of Pthos by his unbelieving presence. The followers of Pthos demand his death. Let Pthos himself decide his fate."

In spite of her fury, the Queen blanched. "Seti means…?"

The High Priest bobbed his bald head. "Yes, Daughter of the Pharoahs. Let him drain the Cup of Pthos. If the god wills that he be spared, he will live. If he has angered the god, he will surely die."

Tamiris' face grew sombre. The Cup of Pthos was a draught of the bitter waters of a poisoned spring, that bubbled in a cavern far under the cliffs. Three times in her life she had seen suspected traitors drain the chalice. In each instance the ordeal had proven them guilty, for each man had died writhing in excrutiating agony. She hesitated.

Zut stepped forward, bowed. "Would it be wise, O Queen?" he demurred. "Look. See your subjects down below—see…."

For once in his life, Zut had made a bad tactical error. Tamiris whirled on him, her eyes flashing fire. "So! Zut dares to dictate to his sovereign? Skulking schemer! Base usurper of the right of Kings! In a woman you have met your master! I hear you and I defy you!"

All the carefully thought out words with which she had planned to deliver her challenge were forgotten in her passion. In an uncontrolled outburst she cursed Zut with all the unspeakable curses of the ancient gods. Then in a last paroxysm of rage her hand lashed out quick as a snake and her open palm struck the side of Zut's gaunt cheek. It fell away leaving the livid imprint of five fingers that all could see. And leaving, what they could not see—a wound in his warped soul that would never heal.

Whirling to face Seti, Tamiris commanded: "Send one of your men, swiftly, for the Cup."

Then conscious that she had thrown down the fateful gauntlet, she turned and grasped the railing of the balcony once more.

Seti called down to one of the awestruck slaves. Zut stepped back a pace. The imprint of the Queen's hand paled slowly on his cheeks as he combed his straggly beard with one hand, twirled the moonstone ring on his finger with the other. But there was a glint in his close-set eyes that no one had ever seen before and the other people on the balcony shrank imperceptibly away from him.

STILL STANDING ALONE in the courtyard, Ka-Zar, too, had noticed the change that had fallen over the multitude. Though he was still in chains, no longer were gibes and insults hurled at him. Instead he noted with secret amusement the awe and respect in the faces now turned toward him. It appeared, though he did not experience as vast a relief as an ordinary man would have known, that he was to be spared further torment.

And so it was that when at last a black entered the courtyard, bearing a small chalice, that he suspected no treachery. The slave's respectful attitude, was in fact, genuine. As he came up to the monolith and proffered the cup with a reverent bow, Ka-Zar remembered that in the excitement of Zar's capture the night before, Nono had forgotten to bring him water. He was thirsty and unsuspecting, he reached eagerly for the chalice.

Had he glanced up at the royal balcony as he touched his lips to the brimming cup, had he seen the deep anguish in the eyes of the Queen, he would have dashed it from him. But instead he drank.

The water was bitter, unpleasant to the taste. But thirstily he drained the vessel to the last drop.

Even as the slave retreated with the empty chalice, he felt the first pangs. Then for the first time he realized his mistake. A single, sweeping glance at the tense faces above him confirmed his suspicions.

A slow fire burned at his vitals. The pain of it mounted swiftly to an agony of torment. Ka-Zar was sure, then, that his last hour had come. He only prayed that the torment would end swiftly, before even his iron will would break and he would betray his suffering to the human fiends who watched him.

Stabbing darts of flame shot through his body. The insidious poison spread swiftly, numbing his limbs. He knew that he was powerless to move, even if he tried. He bit his tongue to keep from crying out as liquid fire coursed through his veins.

But such was his iron self-control that the watchers could see no visible evidence that the poison was taking effect. Only Zut was keen-eyed enough to discern the beads of sweat that bedewed the suffering giant's forehead and guess the truth.

Without seeming to move fast he sidled off the balcony.

"Another drink—of mere water—to hasten the work of the poison," he muttered and disappeared before the startled Queen might stop him.

A moment later he reappeared on the terrace and stepped down into the courtyard. In response to his command a slave hurried off, came back bearing a clay pot of water. Zut took it from him and walked up to the agonized Ka-Zar.

The film that had descended over the latter's eyes cleared just long enough for him to recognize Zut and to see what happened as the Queen's counsellor proffered him the drink. For a moment Ka-Zar believed that his brain was already poisoned and that it was all part of a ghastly nightmare when Zut performed a swift bit of legerdemain over the cup.

But the rays of the sun glinted on the huge moonstone and Ka-Zar could plainly see Zut's clawlike fingers loosen the stone with a single twist; could plainly see the stone hinge back and a fine white powder sift into the clay pot.

More poison? There was no need for that. He was already doomed. But even if by chance it were, it would perhaps end his agony more swiftly. When Zut raised the vessel to his lips, he drank avidly.

Zut waited until he had drained all the potion. Then as though through awkwardness he let the pot slip through his fingers and shatter into shards on the flags. Then stepping back he watched Ka-Zar through half-closed eyes.

FOR A MOMENT of crucial agony Ka-Zar dug his nails deep into the palms of his hands and prayed that his next breath would be his last. Then gradually, to his growing wonder, the fires of torture began to die down. The leaden feeling left his limbs. His body was still racked with pain but it was definitely lessening.

Zut saw the first tinge of healthy color come back to the stricken giant's face. He saw the man's tense limbs gradually relax. He saw the tawny eyes clear, saw them turn to him in dumb gratitude.

He fingered the moonstone ring. In all Khalli, only he possessed the secret of the white powder, which was an antidote for the lethal waters of the poison spring. Against the day when he himself might have to undergo the ordeal, the ring in which the powder was cunningly concealed had never left his finger. Now, smarting under the outrage the Queen had committed against him, he had found ready use for it.

Zut could not read the lion-man's thoughts, but that did not matter, for what ensued was sufficient for his own purpose.

As the pain left him and his brain cleared, Ka-Zar's first thought was that Zar was free and he himself had still survived. The warm surge of life swept through his veins, exhilarated him. He turned his face toward the sun that he had thought he would never see again, raised his fists to his brawny chest and with a thunderous bellow, sent the roar of the lion echoing over the heads of the silent multitude.

As though this were a signal, blacks and Egyptians alike set up a mournful wail. And Zut seized the chance for which he had been waiting.

Stepping forward, he raised both arms dramatically to the watching throng.

"Men of Khalli!" he cried. "The god has spoken! Henceforth whosoever harms this man's sacred person—let him beware—for he shall incur the wrath of Pthos!"

Shouting, yelling, pushing, his listeners poured over the walls and jammed the courtyard. They dropped on their knees before Ka-Zar, touched their foreheads humbly to the flags to beg his forgiveness.

Zut turned his eyes toward the royal balcony. "Even the Pharoahs," he cried out, "bow before the will of the gods. Daughter of the Sphinx—give the order to liberate this man who is favored of Pthos!"

All through the ordeal Tamiris had remained clutching the rail of the balcony. Now she looked down into the sea of expectant faces upturned to her own. Again Zut dared to command her!

Dimly she sensed that somehow he had tricked her. In helpless fury she saw that the black descendants of the the slaves were with him to a man. It was their god who had spoken. If she dared to refuse—the submerged fires of rebellion would break out into instant flame. A single glance showed her that the blacks outnumbered the residents of Khalli in hopeless measure. The cavedwellers would fall upon them and wipe out her people in a swift and terrible massacre. Ankhamen, the stalwart leader of her army, and her soldiers surrounded the courtyard. But they were too few—too few....

Somehow she found her voice. Somehow she managed to speak the command.

Instantly the horde leaped to their feet and surrounded Ka-Zar. The key to his bonds was produced amid cheers. Willing hands loosed the chain from the ring in the monolith, then jerked the bronze collar from his throat. Seti lumbered across the balcony, entered the palace and a moment later joined the crowd in the courtyard.

It was only Tamiris' hold on the balcony that kept her steady on her feet. Her pride had suffered many blows, she had made a powerful enemy in Zut, her high-handed ambitions were dangerously threatened. Yet though her world trembled beneath her feet, she watched Ka-Zar being freed with relief instead of displeasure.

Her face, however, was inscrutable. And when the collar dropped from his neck and he glanced up at her, he could not guess that in her heart of hearts she exulted with him. Without a word, without a gesture, she watched him as flanked by Zut and Seti and with a mob of howling, grinning blacks at his heels, he was escorted in triumph from the palace.

CHAPTER X

SACRIFICE TO PTHOS

WITH ZUT AS his mentor, Ka-Zar began a new life in Khalli. The freedom of the tiered city, of the jungle, of the caverns, was his. He roamed where he willed and everywhere he was greeted with the respect which was now his due.

Under Zut's tutelage he made rapid progress learning the language of this lost people. He owed a debt to this ageless, enigmatic man who had saved his life. Ka-Zar had his own code of honor—a strange compound of the teachings of his dead father and the jungle code of the beasts. Some day he would repay that debt.

The first thing that he did, as soon as he could escape the homage of the worshiping blacks, was to set out alone toward the forest that lay between the city and the opening in the cliffs that led to the underground lake and the caverns. His call of the lion immediately brought an answer from Zar and soon his brother and the little monkey joined him on the shady jungle floor.

In the limited vocabulary of growls and grunts that was the language of the beasts, he told them of his new freedom. It was possible that Zar might once more take his place by his brother's side, but the wise old lion preferred the familiar haunts of the wilderness. It was Nono, on his favorite perch atop the bronze giant's shoulder, who accompanied Ka-Zar back to the city.

That was the first of many surreptitious visits during which the trio decided that they would undertake the seemingly hopeless task of finding a way out of this sunken valley. In the heart of each was a longing for their distant jungle home that grew with each passing day until it became a driving obsession.

The people of Khalli marveled when Ka-Zar appeared with the little monkey clinging to him, marveled still more when it was seen that man and beast spoke to one another. The only one who really understood was Zut. To his newfound friend, in his newly-acquired tongue, Ka-Zar explained his life in the wilderness, his dominance over the beasts and the manner in which he had arrived in Khalli. And that was why Zut alone knew that this bronze giant was but a man, however a strange one. He knew why the massive lion had failed to slay him and he shrewdly guessed that this little monkey was the reason that Ka-Zar had not died of hunger and of thirst in the courtyard. And so, though he was careful to pay due homage to his protege before the eyes of others, he was merely friendly when they were alone.

Ka-Zar avoided the palace. On several occasions he glimpsed the Queen, once when she was on her way to the Temple of Isis, once when she appeared at a festival. But each time he kept well out of sight, grateful that he no longer had to suffer her hateful presence.

His mind was filled day and night with the desire to escape. Having an instinctive dislike for the underground catacombs and the creatures of darkness who dwelled in them, he began his explorations in the open bowl of the sunken valley. Sometimes Zar accompanied them, sometimes he and Nono were alone. The high wall of cliffs was many miles in circumference. Starting first from a point north of the city, Ka-Zar prowled about their base. Time and again he found openings in the rock, entered only to find that they were shallow caves that had no other outlet. Time and again he found a precipitate path leading up the face of the walls, scaled it at perilous risk only to reach a point beyond which neither man nor beast could ascend higher.

Every home, every cave in Khalli was open to him. He would return weary in body and limb, sleep in mansion or in jungle, and with the next sunrise be off again on his ceaseless quest.

And so it was that he failed to notice the ever-growing tension in the isolated kingdom. Many times be found Zut and Seti with their heads together in solemn conclave, but he did not guess that they were surreptitiously stirring up the simmering brew of rebellion.

ONE EVENING, AS he was just about to set forth for the jungle to find Zar and report another day of fruitless search, a slave came running to him, flung himself on the ground at his feet and panted a message.

"All day, O Favored of Pthos," said the black breathlessly, "Zut has sought you. He desires your presence at once in the Temple of Pthos."

With distaste, Ka-Zar remembered the dim underground chamber where he had first been made captive. It was on his tongue to refuse, then he remembered also the debt he owed to Zut. Reluctantly he made a gesture to the black to rise. "Very well. Come."

Together they made the journey down the long road that had been hewn through the heart of the jungle. Not many ventured to traverse it after nightfall. Now the black strode hurriedly along the dim forest floor, his eyes fearfully searching the shadows on either side. A faint smile flitted across Ka-Zar's lips each time the man's face turned ashen at the howl of a hyena, the scurrying of a rodent across the trail or the mysterious rustling of branches overhead.

They came at last to the break in the cliffs, turned into the tunnels lighted with flaring torches. This was the first time since his capture that Ka-Zar had returned to the place of caves and catacombs. But he had not forgotten the dank, foul air that rushed to assail his nostrils now, the vast, dark reach of the underground lake, the constant drip, drip of water.

This time, though, free and with no need for caution, he saw things that he had not noticed before. There were boats drawn up along the shores of the lake—high-prowed vessels painted in red and black and yellow, with figureheads of carven monsters. He saw bats, enormous creatures, who flitted through the tunnels on phantom wings and hung in great pendent clusters from the rocky roof. He saw wrinkled bags, incredibly ragged and dirty, steal from the catacombs, fill clay pots with water from the lake and scurry back into their holes again.

"Where are the men?" Ka-Zar asked his companion.

"They are already in the temple," answered the slave. "There is to be a ceremony."

The answer meant little to Ka-Zar. He asked no more. He found Zut waiting for him in the corridor, at the exact place where he had left Zar that first fateful night.

Zut dismissed the slave, then bowed to Ka-Zar. "Tonight there is a sacred rite in the temple," he explained. "A sacrifice is to be offered to Pthos and Seti, the High Priest, has given you the great honor of performing the task that is reserved only for his own holy hands."

Ka-Zar shook his head. "I know not what you mean. This matter of gods and ceremony and such is beyond my comprehension. I want none of it."

"It is to honor Pthos," reminded Zut gravely. "Remember, it was Pthos who spared you."

Ka-Zar did not believe that. But his own eyes had seen this man save him. With the reminder of his debt, reluctantly he agreed to accompany Zut into the temple.

They opened the heavy bronze door and stepped into the great chamber beyond. The temple was jammed with a dense throng of blacks, squatting on the floor before the towering image of their god. On the dais, at the feet of the hideous statue, stood Seti. His obese form swathed in multicolored raiment, he stood with arms upraised and a weird chant issued from his lips.

Ka-Zar stepped a little to one side, then suddenly he stiffened as a low snarl sounded directly behind him. He whirled about and the hairs crawled at the back of his neck. Twin orbs of emerald glared balefully back at him. For a moment of stark unbelief, Ka-Zar stared at the ebony form of N'Jagi, the black leopard.

Instinctively Ka-Zar fell into a crouch and a low growl rumbled in his throat as he waited for N'Jagi to spring. Then he saw that the leopard was chained. Glittering links fastened his collar to a ring set in the wall. That explained why the blacks were able to worship here in the temple without fear of the beast.

IN HATE AND fear, N'Jagi laid his ears flat back against his narrow skull, curled his lips back from his sharp fangs and spat. Zut came over hurriedly, walked up to the leopard, laid a hand upon the animal's flat head, spoke low, soothing words. N'Jagi subsided, only his eyes glaring malevolently at his enemy.

"So the leopard did not die?" said Ka-Zar.

"No," answered Zut. "He was sorely wounded, unconscious. But I have nursed him back to health and he is once more guardian of the temple."

"You do not fear him, like the rest," said Ka-Zar.

Zut shook his head. "No. It was I who raised him from a cub. It is I who feed him. The leopard knows me and loves me and would lay down his life to defend me."

Again Ka-Zar had occasion to be puzzled by the ways of these Oman. N'Jagi was Zut's brother, even as he himself was the brother of Zar. If man or beast harmed either one, the other would hunt the culprit down and slay him. Yet Ka-Zar had almost killed N'Jagi and Zut, the leopard's master, held no resentment against him.

He shook his head, dismissing such a matter that he would never understand.

Leaving the leopard, Zut beckoned him to follow. Together they wended their way through the dense throng, gained the dais at last and mounted it. The High Priest ended his chant on a shrill, high note.

"Do as Seti tells you," Zut whispered to Ka-Zar, then drew back to a shadowy corner.

Slaves replenished the burning braziers and the flames mounted higher. As Seti came toward Ka-Zar, the assemblage touched their heads twice to the floor before them, then fell to a slow, rhythmic swaying.

Ill at ease, wishing that the cursed rites were over, Ka-Zar submitted to his role. He allowed Seti to drape a resplendent cloak over his naked body, allowed him to set a headdress in the form of a golden, winged lion upon his brow, allowed him to thrust a golden wand that ended in a serpent's head into his hand.

"Do as I do," hissed the High Priest in his ear.

And because of his debt to Zut, Ka-Zar obeyed.

The strange ceremony that followed was ever after a blur in Ka-Zar's mind. The air was close and oppressive with the scent of many unwashed bodies. The light was dimmed by the clouds of smoke that issued from the braziers. Sometimes the crowd was hushed as Seti harangued them; sometimes there was a hubbub as all tongues broke out into a babble. Twice a black shrieked, writhed about on the floor frothing at the mouth, and was carried out by his fellows. Once N'Jagi, aroused by the sight of his old enemy, made the vaulted chamber ring with his hideous screech.

Ka-Zar was not yet proficient enough in the language to understand it when it was sung in minor chants or spoken in a swift torrent of passionate words. But he did see that the assembled cave dwellers were working themselves up to a higher and higher pitch. Strange music added to the bedlam. From off to one side came the clash of brazen cymbals, the thin, reedy wail of a flute, the muffled beating of a drum.

Again Seti raised his arms to the leering face of the god looking down upon them. Then he turned and looked off to the left. There was a stir in that direction. A small door opened. The assembled worshippers craned their necks, then raised their voices in a concerted shout of anticipation.

Ka-Zar looked, also. He saw a slave, bound with heavy ropes, shoved forward toward the dais by the eager hands of his fellows. The man was in the grip of abject terror. His knees trembled so that he could hardly move. His eyes were wide open in blank despair. His loose lips quivered, but no sound issued from them.

ONCE ON THE dais, he dropped to a kneeling position as the High Priest turned once more to address the god. Ka-Zar saw the blood lust on the faces of the worshippers. When Seti had finished, he walked to the edge of the platform, received something from another slave.

Ka-Zar saw the dim light reflected on a huge, naked sword. Its curved blade, he could see even at that distance, was keen and razor-sharp. In blank amazement he watched Seti waddle toward him and before he could recover his wits, the monstrous weapon was in his own hands.

The High Priest gestured toward the kneeling man. The words he spoke were lost in the deafening clamor that rang out from the crowd.

Dumbly Ka-Zar stepped forward—one step, two, three....

Then at last he realized what was expected of him. He was expected to use that sword—he was expected to slay the terrified victim. A swift vision crossed before his eyes. He could see the hapless creature already dead—see the warm blood trickling down over the steps of the dais while the bloodthirsty mob shrieked their delight.

He raised the sword. Then with all his might he flung the glittering weapon at the foot of the idol!

The shriek froze in every throat. A hush as profound as the stillness of death fell upon the temple, as all faces stared in shocked amazement. Such a thing had never happened before.

And in that utter silence Ka-Zar denounced them.

"Despised Oman!" he cried, his amber eyes blazing and his huge hands clenched. "To think that Ka-Zar—brother of Zar the mighty—king of the beasts and the jungle—would do this shameful thing! To slay in fair battle is one thing—to slay a helpless victim is another. Crawl back into your holes—rats that you are!"

Fortunately, for him, he was still not proficient enough in his new tongue to speak it with such passionate speed. His flow of words was unintelligible.

Zut, as always, was more quickwitted than the rest. He leaped forward, took his place by Ka-Zar's side and with consummate artistry, raised both arms in a dramatic gesture.

"Again the god has spoken!" he cried. "Again Pthos commands you through his new disciple! He needs no sacrifice to appease him—he smiles upon you! His intended victim shall live to worship, in humble gratitude, the mercy of Pthos!"

Seti still had not found either his wits or his tongue. Cheated of the bloody spectacle, the mass of slaves looked sullen and disappointed. But too ignorant to question the words of such a wise man as Zut, they heard and believed. There was only a subdued mutter as Zut and Ka-Zar swiftly unbound the dazed victim and he scurried off.

Ka-Zar had had enough. With a nauseous feeling at the pit of his stomach, he stalked off the dais, strode through the crowd and left the temple.

Zut followed him, caught up to him in the passage outside. Ka-Zar surveyed his friend and mentor from cold eyes.

The latter combed his straggly beard. "Such things are the custom," he explained. "For long years the slaves have made human sacrifice to Pthos."

"Such customs are evil," retorted Ka-Zar. "If the slaves do such monstrous things, they should be punished."

Zut moved his finger, rubbed the side of his beaked nose. "I am not the ruler of this kingdom," he said slowly.

Then, having cleverly implied that she was responsible for the unholy practise, leaving Ka-Zar with a vision of the youthful Queen as he had last seen her standing on the balcony, Zut moved off.

CHAPTER XI

THE CATACOMBS

ZUT DID NOT make the mistake of again inviting Ka-Zar to join in the worship of the evil Pthos. Free once more to renew his search for a way of escape, Ka-Zar continued his round of the valley.

But he failed to find what he sought. Though he did not relish the prospect, he decided that the underground tunnels and caverns were next.

He started out one morning just as the dawn brought a faint, pinkish tinge to the East, though in the bowels of the earth he knew it made small difference whether it was night or day. The night before he had sent Nono to Zar with a message and so he went alone on his quest.

He knew what a hopeless maze of tunnels and passages opened off the banks of the underground river and lake. Once before he had blundered headlong into trouble. It was not trouble but a way of escape that he was now seeking. Sooner or later, perhaps, he would have to try every passage. But first he would go in the direction he remembered—southward towards the spot where he and Zar and Nono had first blundered into the lost kingdom.

The cavedwellers were just beginning to stir in their lairs when he skirted the shore of the lake. The flares were sputtering low in their brackets. But Ka-Zar's eyes were like those of a great cat and his pupils widened to accustom them to the dimness. He reached the place where the river emptied its swift-flowing waters into the silent lake, turned the sharp bend and followed its slippery bank.

Again the bats wheeled on ghostly wings about his head. In the dying light of the last flare he saw great, bloated spiders crawling on the walls of the passage. The darkness deepened as he went on. Before him, reptiles he could not see slithered off the mud bank and splashed into the stream.

With sure instinct he turned at last into the tunnel through which he and his friends had first come. But as he progressed deeper, he began to wonder why the darkness did not lighten. The landslide that had brought him tumbling downward had left a gaping hole in the earth above. The daylight it admitted should have filtered to the spot where he now stood.

He found the answer fifty yards farther on. The way before him was blocked—blocked by a solid mass of earth and rock.

Ka-Zar scowled in the darkness. He remembered that the week before, a violent tropical storm had wreaked its fury upon Khalli. Perhaps the torrential rain that fell then had battered down more of the earth above, packed it in a mounting heap that blocked off the tunnel.

Morosely he turned back and returned to the river. Standing again on its bank, he hesitated for a moment. Then abruptly he turned and went further along its muddy shore. He had not gone far when he discovered another tunnel opening in the rocks. With the same dim hope that had sustained him in his quest, he turned into it.

This time, he had not gone far when he pulled up short in his tracks. A low, ominous rumbling came to his ears. It grew louder with alarming rapidity. The very earth trembled beneath his feet.

For an instant Ka-Zar was paralyzed. For an instant numb horror froze his heart. Then the spell was broken and turning, he fled blindly back through the passage.

He had not acted a moment too soon. With a reverberating roar that thundered in his ears, an avalanche of earth and stones poured after him. A shower of mud, a spatter of pebbles sprayed upon his retreating back. With a last burst of speed that threatened to burst his lungs, he reached the opening of the tunnel, sprinted a few more yards up the river bank.

Panting, he mopped the perspiration from his brow as the landslide rushed through the tunnel, came to a slithering halt upon the bank and sent a last shower of debris splashing into the water.

Once before he had been buried alive by such a treacherous torrent. Now again he had barely escaped being entombed. This was a dangerous vicinity, here in the bowels of the earth. Apparently these landslides were frequent and they came without warning.

SHAKEN BY THE narrowness of his escape, and yet reluctant to give up the search that by now had become a symbol of life itself to him, he did not re-trace his way at once toward Khalli. The last rumbles of the falling earth died away, leaving the silence broken only by the monotonous drip of water and the murmuring rush of the stream.

The river. Ka-Zar's brows knitted. Why had he not thought of it before? It came from somewhere—it had some source. Did it merely bubble out of the rocks from some hidden spring? He determined to find out.

Despite his better judgment, a growing hope mounted in his breast as he set off along the bank. And therefore when he had penetrated as far as he could go, he knew the keenest disappointment. He had come to a place where the stream boiled out of a hole in the rocks barely big enough to permit its passage. Whether that hole led to its very source—a spring—or whether it was but another tunnel that made a natural length of pipe, with the river widening once more beyond it, he could not guess. But no living creature could attempt to go through that aperture, through those seething waters, and live.

Bitterly Ka-Zar turned and wearily he headed back in the direction from whence he had come.

Late that same afternoon, the Queen Tamiris was on one of her frequent pilgrimages to the Temple of Isis. Surrounded by all the pomp and glitter of her court, she reclined on the soft cushions of her palanquin as slaves carried it down through the city.

Contrary to the impression she had so unfortunately made on Ka-Zar, Tamiris was honorable and just. She had a stern sense of duty and toward that duty, she would willingly sacrifice any life in Khalli if need be. But needless cruelty, the taking of life without any justification whatsoever, she could not tolerate.

At the head of her procession were several black slaves whose duty it was to clear the way. People drew respectfully back to either side of the road to make obeisance as their sovereign passed.

A mangy, homeless cur, intent only upon a morsel of refuse on the opposite side, scurried across the roadway. Though he was well in advance of the slow-moving cavalcade, one of the foremost slaves shouted angrily, stooped and picked up a great rock. He hurled it at the cowering dog with deadly accuracy.

There was a sickening thud, a single yelp of terror. Then with piteous whines the dying beast dragged itself a few more yards, collapsed, kicked once convulsively and then lay still.

Tamiris had viewed the whole incident. It had transpired too swiftly for her to intervene and spare the life of the brute. Now in a sudden flare of outraged passion, she leaped from her litter. Snatching the jeweled girdle from her hips she strode angrily toward the slave.

Ka-Zar, turning a corner, was just in time to see her confront the black—a barbaric picture of slim legs disclosed by whipping draperies, of raven hair tossed by the wind and eyes like great pools of jet.

He saw the culprit fling himself face downward in the dust, saw the Queen's right arm flash up. The glittering girdle described a short arc through the air, then descended with all her might across the back of the slave. The sharp-cut gems bit deep into the bare flesh, leaving a long welt that turned slowly scarlet. Once more the lash rose and fell and a second raw stripe crisscrossed the first.

Then with a gesture of revulsion Tamiris flung the glittering girdle into the dust, turned on her heel and returned to her palanquin.

At the first stroke of the lash Ka-Zar knew a momentary impulse to leap out and interfere. Then he downed it. Queen or slave—these Oman were nothing to him. Let them torture or slay each other, if it pleased them to do so he did not care.

He had, so he thought, witnessed just one more display of cruelty on the part of this bloodthirsty female. Soundlessly he stepped back into a nearby doorway and waited, silent and unseen, while the procession went past.

When it had gone he emerged and slowly headed for the palace in search of Zut.

CHAPTER XII

INTRIGUE

THE ATTENDANTS AND soldiers at the gates admitted Ka-Zar without hesitation to the palace. He needed no escort to find his way to Zut's quarters, the only ascetic chamber in that massive pile of decadent splendor.

His bare feet made no sound on the tiled floors of the long corridors and unannounced, he finally thrust aside the coarse draperies that curtained the door of the counselor's room.

A single glance showed him Zut and Seti, seated close together and engaged in earnest conversation. Letting the curtain drop silently back into place, Ka-Zar stepped back. Ever since the fiasco that he had made of the sacrifice to Pthos, he had avoided meeting the High Priest. And he had no desire to meet that repellent, obese creature now.

He lingered outside the portal, thinking that he would wait until Seti had finished his visit. Inside, the two men were speaking in low, hushed tones that carried to the curtain only in an indistinguishable murmur.

Indistinguishable, that is, to ordinary mortal ears. But Ka-Zar's ears were of the jungle—keen—delicately attuned to catch the faint murmur of a dying breeze, the thin hum of a mosquito, the barely audible hiss of a hidden snake. Standing outside in the dimming hall, he heard Seti's voice and he could distinctly make out the words.

"…and I can no longer wait; I can no longer hold them."

"The time has come then," he heard Zut answer. "You have

only to await my signal." He paused a moment as if considering. Then: "When the eternal flame burns crimson—strike!"

"Tomorrow." That was Seti, more urgent this time.

And after another brief pause, Zut echoed: "Very well. To-morrow."

Though the conversation was at once recorded indelibly on Ka-Zar's brain, it held no meaning for him. Hearing the scrape of feet and knowing that the visit of the High Priest had ended, he moved a few yards further on down the hall, stepped back into a shadowy recess in the wall.

He waited until the figure of Seti appeared, waddled out of sight in the opposite direction. After the High Priest had gone but before he stepped out of his hiding place, Ka-Zar heard the harsh but muffled sound of a brazen gong in Zut's chamber.

For some inexplicable reason he stayed where he was, watching. His instinct was rewarded when a moment later a black shadow materialized soundlessly from nowhere. The lamps set in the brackets upon the walls had not yet been lit. A gray, obscure twilight filled the halls but Ka-Zar's slitted eyes recognized the moving shadow as one of the black slaves, taller and more powerfully built than his stunted fellows. Silently he watched the man dart a quick glance to right and to left, then vanish through the curtains into Zut's chamber.

That something was afoot was now evident. This time Ka-Zar approached the portal very deliberately and very cautiously, laid one ear against the curtain and listened.

It was well that he did, for the words that drifted out to him were very startling, indeed.

"Zoab," Zut addressed his surreptitious caller, "I have a task for you—a very, very dangerous task."

"My master has but to speak," answered the slave.

"Very well, then. Ask me no question and if you value your life, breathe no word of what I tell you. Find your brother Mu and bind him to the same secrecy. Tonight, at midnight I shall admit you both to the palace by the north gate. Make your way swiftly and silently to the Queen's bedchamber. A single thrust of a dagger as she sleeps—that is all."

KA-ZAR HEARD THE slave's sharp intake of breath, realized that for an instant his own heart had stopped breathing.

"It shall be done," came Zoab's low voice.

"Yours shall be the hand of destiny," murmured Zut.

Again Ka-Zar glided noiselessly away from the door, melted into the shadows as Zoab appeared and swiftly vanished again. His own brain reeled. Now for the first time he remembered the growing tension of the people of Khalli. Something dark and dire was brewing. But the murder of the Queen....

His face was thoughtful when at last he pushed aside the curtains and entered Zut's meagrely furnished quarters. His enigmatical mentor greeted him in friendly but absent-minded fashion. Ka-Zar returned the greeting as briefly, squatted as always in jungle fashion on his haunches.

For long moments each was busy with his own thoughts. Both were dwelling on the scenes that had just transpired, but each from a different angle.

To Zut, the message that Seti had brought him had been dark tidings. Zut realized that he and the High Priest had done their work too well—they had stirred the blacks up to revolt, stirred them up too far. In his wisdom Zut knew that he was no longer safe, that when the deluge broke, he could not stem it. And so though he had given his word to give the fateful signal the following day, he had no intention of signing what would prove to be his own death warrant. No. He would strike tonight. With Tamiris slain, he would seize the reins of power. With the Queen they had been taught to hate removed—with this favorite of the gods, of his own creating, who now sat before him—he would be able to control them.

Ka-Zar, too, was thinking deeply. Though he could find only hate in his heart for the she-leopard who ruled these Oman, he was strangely disturbed. For the first time he felt the beginnings of a vague distrust for this man who had been his friend and mentor. To strike in the dark—to slay without warning one who was unarmed and defenseless—that was not Ka-Zar's way.

Forgetting what had originally brought him there, and not caring to voice his troubled thought, he rose at last, spoke a few idle words and took his leave.

Once more out in the hall, he hesitated. Then on the spur of a sudden impulse, instead of leaving the palace, he turned and sought a hiding place instead.

A few moments later attendants came with tapers and soon the palace was a blaze of light. But none dreamed that within its walls, unseen, unheard, the jungle giant waited for the coming of midnight.

CHAPTER XIII

DEATH COMES CREEPING

THE WINDOWS OF Queen Tamiris' bedchamber were opened wide to the warm night air. An enormous, swollen globe of a moon hung low over the Congo, sent its effulgent light streaming in broad bands through the aperture. The mellow moonlight picked out the pattern of the rugs, glistened from the steps of a low dais, bathed a silken-covered couch and the still form that lay upon it.

A tall screen of paper made from papyrus threw a dense black shadow in one corner of the room. And in that patch of blackness, only a pair of glowing, amber eyes betrayed the fact that Ka-Zar kept his vigil. He had stolen into the chamber as silently as the moonbeams themselves and now not even the sound of his hushed breathing disturbed the youthful Queen in her slumbers.

In profound meditation he stared at her. The night was sultry and she had flung aside the covers of the couch. All her tinkling ornaments had been discarded. A sheer robe of cobwebs and delicate in color as the first blush of dawn, swathed her slender figure. Her raven hair spread across her pillow and her eyes were closed.

In repose, all the harshness, all the arrogance was gone from her features. In the magic alchemy of the moonlight she appeared but the child that she really was—frail, helpless, innocent, virginal. And Ka-Zar, watching, was strangely perturbed. All the hate melted from his heart and a protecting tenderness crept into it instead.

It was no sound that roused him from his reverie. It was, rather, some sixth jungle sense that stirred the hairs at the nape of his neck. His head jerked around and he stared off to his right.

In the dimness beyond the brilliant bars of moonlight, a solid black shadow took form. Then another.

Ka-Zar tensed as the twin dark blotches stole soundlessly forward toward the royal couch. The course of the assassins would bring them past his own hiding place.

He crouched; his huge hands opened. Nerves on edge, he waited.

Zoab was in the lead. There was the subdued glint of bared steel in his hand. He moved forward slowly—one step—another—then another. Gathering his muscles, Ka-Zar sprang.

A bronzed arm wrapped itself about Zoab's body, tightened like a vise. A sinewy forearm slid under his chin, jerked it violently back. There was a faint but ominous *snap*. The blade slipped from Zoab's hand and dropped noiselessly onto the deep-piled rug underfoot.

With only a tiny, sibilant sigh whistling from his lips, his neck broken, Zoab collapsed in the arms of the jungle giant.

Ka-Zar let the lifeless body slump to the rug as he whirled to confront his victim's brother. Mu's eyes glittered in the darkness as he bounded forward, a wicked-looking dagger in his upraised hand. With a strangled snarl, the second black aimed full at Ka-Zar's bare chest.

The gleaming point descended in a swift downward arc. Then it was arrested in mid-air as Ka-Zar's hand flashed out, clamped about the wrist of the black. A single deft, powerful twist and the course of the hungry blade was deflected. Still carried by the momentum of the original stroke, it swooped down, bit avidly into the soft flesh at the base of Mu's throat.

Warm crimson spurted in its wake. The knees of the traitorous slave buckled. The life poured from his body as he stood swaying on his feet. Then, a sodden corpse that would never move again, he collapsed over the body of his brother.

The whole incident had transpired swiftly and with hardly a sound. Like a great shadow, Ka-Zar melted into the blackness once more and vanished, leaving the Queen's bedchamber in possession of the mellow moonlight and two dark, sinister objects that had not been there a few short moments before.

KA-ZAR DID NOT know that Tamiris had been sleeping lightly. He did not know that her fringe of dark lashes had lifted just in time for her to witness the silent struggle. There was no mistaking the terrible purpose of these two armed slaves. But before she could stir or cry out, she had seen them meet their fate. And she had recognized, in the dimness of the room, the brawny form of the bronzed giant who had outwitted them.

As he disappeared, with mingled emotions she rose from her couch, crossed the room and stared down at the lifeless bodies on the floor, at the spreading blotch of crimson that stained the rug. She was shaken by the narrowness of her escape; grave, as she realized the far-reaching significance of this treacherous attempt to slay her. The fact that Ka-Zar—who had openly defied and scorned her—had saved her life, was something to marvel and puzzle over.

He had not lingered to receive her thanks, apparently he had not even wished to be recognized. What then, was his motive in thus risking his life for one he scorned?

Tamiris could not guess. To her, the only thing that was obvious was that the strange jungle giant, for some reasons of his own, did not wish his midnight exploit to be known. And therefore, summoning her most trusted slaves and binding them to secrecy, she bade them remove the bodies and dispose of them with the utmost caution.

There was no more sleep for the Queen that night. Morning found her still pondering the fact that her throne was trembling upon its foundations, that a dire crisis was approaching in the affairs of Khalli. Digging the painted nails of her hands into her palms, she reminded herself that she was the daughter of the Ptolemies.

She lashed herself to a rage against these degenerate blacks who dared to threaten her, worked herself up into a fury against the scheming Zut. Somehow she sensed that he was behind the attack of the night before. The crafty counsellor was avaricious for power. He would go to any lengths to attain it.

Once, in a moment of weakness, unwanted and unaccustomed tears welled suddenly to the eyes of the youthful Queen. She flung herself on a divan and buried her burning face in her ivory hands. All the attributes of her sovereignty, all the hard shell that she had imposed upon herself, slipped away. She became her natural self—a young girl alone and lonesome and apprehensive for the future.

If only—she mused bitterly—she but had a real man to fight by her side. A man she could trust. And with the thought the inscrutable amber eyes of Ka-Zar blazed once more before her.

The breath caught in her throat. The tears ceased miraculously and with intent and burning eyes she straightened slowly on the divan.

Those eyes had surveyed her with scorn, with mockery, with contempt—true. But they were honest eyes, fearless ones—innocent of the faintest breath of treachery or deceit. Daughter of kings for ten thousand years, Tamiris was the end product of a super-civilization. And now she sensed that the same heritage of royal blood flowed through the veins of this jungle god.

God indeed! He had dominance over the savage beasts of the wilderness; he had dominance over men, both black and white. Tamiris' pulse beat faster and twin spots of color blazed in her cheeks. Swiftly jumping from the divan she crossed the room to an ebony chest, inlaid with mother-of-pearl. Lifting up the lid she picked up a gem-encrusted mirror and holding it before her flushed face, she gazed at her reflection for a long time.

Then with a sudden, impetuous movement, she flung the mirror from her.

"Yes," she whispered dramatically. "And he has dominance over you, Tamiris! I read it in your eyes!"

Her turbulent young heart became a welter of seething and conflicting emotions. For a long time she struggled with herself, fought with her pride—and lost. She told herself that it was a matter of state business that made her clap her hands and bring her slaves and maids running to serve her.

"Go," she said imperiously to one, "find this Ka-Zar. Tell him that the Queen desires him to attend her at once."

Then as the black scurried off, she turned to her maids. "My finest jewels—my most resplendent garments. Hurry—a scented bath—my hair...."

KA-ZAR RECEIVED HER summons with a grunt that did not betray his emotions. A scowl made a deep V between his brows and his eyes darkened. What did this disturbing Queen want of him now? He longed only to be free of the encroaching confines of this outlandish city, longed to be many moons journey away in the distant forest that was his home. His jungle called him. What of Trajah the elephant and Sha the lioness? How fared Zar's cubs and Nono's brothers? What was transpiring in his wilderness domain? A shadow crossed his mind and his tawny eyes became hard. During his long absence, had any intruder come to violate the sanctity of the jungle?

Very well. He would see this barbaric queen. Then he would not rest until he had found a means of escape from this lost kingdom.

He met Zut as he walked through the halls of the palace. Zut stroked his greasy beard with a skinny hand. "The Queen has sent for you, Son of Pthos?" he asked.

Ka-Zar answered with a growl of assent.

Zut did not know that the bronze man before him had foiled his dastardly attempt on the life of the Queen. He was still sorely mystified and much upset by the fact that the plot had somehow miscarried and his trusted emissaries had failed to return. Matters were coming fast to a climax. He might need this jungle god and he did not like this summons of the Queen.

"Beware the wiles and snares of a woman," he whined. "Honey can drip from the tongue of Tamiris even as she weaves plots like a crafty spider weaves its web."

Ka-Zar's nostrils flared. His new mistrust of this old schemer grew in his heart. The whining voice sickened him.

"You speak with the voice of the jackal," he retorted. "Or in the manner of Sinassa the snake who crawls upon his belly. This Queen is but a woman—the female of her species—to be mastered like any other."

Zut shrugged. "Rash words, my son, spoken bravely but in ignorance. The enmity of Tamiris, once aroused, is not to be scorned. Her craving for power holds nothing sacred. Did you know that the old king, her father, died of a mysterious gnawing of his vitals? Yet during the days of his illness, all his food and drink were prepared only by the hands of his daughter."

With the terrible insinuation ringing in his ears, Ka-Zar turned on his heel and with his mind in a turmoil, he headed for the Queen's apartments.

CHAPTER XIV

THE QUEEN COMMANDS

AT HIS ENTRANCE, Tamiris dismissed her maids. They had done their work swiftly and well. Her body was oiled and perfumed. An elaborate headdress of sapphires and emeralds, formed in the shape of the Sphinx, crowned her sleek hair. The precious stuff that sheathed her slim hips was of iridescent blues and greens. Every inch of her semi-nude body was covered with glinting jewels.

She was proud, striking, as a peacock in her dazzling finery—and beautiful beyond mortal dreams. Ka-Zar stopped short, confronted her squarely and unabashed, boldly appraised her.

A delicate flush mantled Tamiris' ivory cheeks and her heart beat with a dull pounding against the jeweled discs that covered her breasts. But equally unabashed, unashamed, she let his eyes drink their fill. Royalty was meeting royalty on an equal footing. And if Tamiris was feminine loveliness incarnate, Ka-Zar was the most magnificent specimen of manhood shehad ever seen.

She raised her hand at last and as Ka-Zar strode forward, she rose to greet him.

"The Queen welcomes you, Son of Pthos," she said in her low, husky voice.

At the mention of the god of darkness, a scowl descended on Ka-Zar's face. "Your Pthos means nothing to me," he said evenly. "I am of the jungle where only the sun is god."

Tamiris drew herself up to her full height. "I, too, am a Daughter of the Sun. And on that common ground, we shall talk."

"Ka-Zar listens," he answered noncommittally.

"Very well. Hear then. Troublous times have come to Khalli. At any moment my kingdom will be torn by uprising and revolt. The degenerate slaves, under the evil banner of Pthos and under the leadership of the scheming Zut, will attempt to wrest Khalli from the true followers of Isis. It will be a combat between the forces of evil and the forces of justice and right.

"By some miracle the gods have sent you, king of the jungle, to my country. Was it really Pthos—were you destined to aid the powers of darkness? I cannot believe it. You cannot escape—you must make your choice. Your eyes are fearless and honest. I can only believe that you belong to the side of right."

For a long moment Ka-Zar did not answer. Tamiris sounded sincere, the passion with which she spoke was genuine. Was this what Zut meant? Was this more of her artful deceit? Was she daring to make a fool of him?

With keen feminine intuition, Tamiris guessed his thoughts.

"Zut has told you evil of me. Is it not so?"

Ka-Zar did not speak.

"Answer!" she commanded.

"It is so," he challenged, his eyes level.

The Queen's face paled. "And you believed?" she asked huskily.

"Ka-Zar has eyes to see."

"Yet Ka-Zar is blind."

"Ka-Zar knows that it was you who had him chained by the neck to the pillar of stone."

Tamiris bit her scarlet underlip, then confronted him un-flinchingly. "In your jungle, O Ka-Zar, there is but one law—the law of survival. It is the same here in Khalliland. I, too, must obey it. That law is greater than you or me. You are a man grown but your heart is simple and your mind is that of a child." She stepped closer to him and a passionate earnestness and plead-ing came into her voice. "Believe not the tales concerning me with which Zut has poisoned your mind. Zut is evil."

"Yet he of all in Khalli befriended me," answered Ka-Zar stubbornly.

Tamiris stamped her regal, sandaled foot. "Fool!" she burst out impetuously. "For his own evil ends. He sees that you have power over the blacks. They fear you—worship you. Zut would use you like bait in a trap. And then when he has accomplished his dark ends, he would discard you. Cast you to the prowling jackals."

AT HER WORDS, anger swelled the veins in Ka-Zar's throat. But be did not know whether that anger was directed at the girl or at Zut.

Tamiris was quick to see his confusion and pressed her advantage. "Zut is a traitor. His tongue drips with lies. He is black of heart. My father died of some slow, insidious poison. Yet the only poison known in Khalli is the bitter waters of the underground spring, that kills swiftly and surely.

"Tamiris has no proof. Zut is the direct descendant of Egyptian magicians. Somehow the black arts have been passed down secretly through the generations and he possesses strange, dark knowledge of which we others know not. My father's death was a lingering one. Zut did not believe that in my youth, I would dare to challenge him. He thought to usurp my throne and now his thwarted ambition will not let him rest."

Her words only confused Ka-Zar the more. His simple mind was not fitted to cope with such intrigues, with such plot and counter-plot. Zut had just insinuated that Tamiris had murdered her own father. Now she claimed that the counsellor was the true murderer.

If she was telling the truth, Ka-Zar could understand much, forgive all she had done to him. For his own father had been murdered by a covetous white man.

Now Tamiris laid bare her heart. With the humility of a woman and the pride of a Queen, with her chin held high and in her eyes a melting appeal, she spoke in low but steady tones.

"You have scorned Tamiris and mocked her. You have confounded all her plans and been the cause of her undoing. Yet she has searched her soul and found not hate, but love for you. Even the Daughter of the Sun is but a woman, with all a woman's weakness.

"Smile upon me, Lord of the jungle. Take your place by my side. Together we shall rule Khalli. Together we shall quell our enemies and reign, a royal and truly-mated pair, upon my now lonely throne."

Ka-Zar could scarce believe his ears. With wide eyes he gazed at the girl who stood proud and unashamed before him, laying her heart and her throne at his feet. Suddenly he realized that since the night before, the vision that had tormented him both day and night had been banished forever. The laughing blue eyes and sunny hair of Claudette had been blotted out by eyes of midnight blackness, by hair as sleek and blue-black as the raven's wing.

It was the sight of her, as he had watched her the night before, that had worked some subtle magic. He had seen her then unadorned, slim and virginal. Now she faced him in all the glory of her love, perfumed, glittering, alluring, utterly desirable.

A fever possessed him. His blood pounded through his veins, set a pulse throbbing at his temples. The exquisite face of this barbaric Queen swam before his eyes. His brain reeled. The thought of taking her for his mate set every fibre of his being aquiver.

A rare confusion assailed him. In sheer panic, without speaking a word, he turned and fled from her presence.

Dazed, rooted to the spot, the Queen stood and watched him vanish. Her bosom rose and fell once convulsively. Her tiny hands clenched at her sides. It was beyond belief. She—a daughter of the Ptolemies—had offered her heart to this naked, jungle savage. And instead of prostrating himself at her feet—he had gone without a word!

For a moment she trembled under the lash of outraged pride.

Then suddenly she flung herself upon the divan, buried her hot face in her arms. A single bitter tear squeezed through her lids and made a darker blotch upon a silken cushion.

BLINDLY KA-ZAR FLED the palace. His soul was in a turmoil. Without aim or purpose he wandered through the narrow streets of the city. Vaguely he was aware that the people he passed seemed equally perturbed. Each looked askance at the other. Fear and mistrust was written on every face. Little groups gathered in doorways to talk in hushed whispers, fell silent as he stalked past.

Twilight fell at last, bringing with it no relief. The oppressive heat of the day became a sultry night. Still Ka-Zar prowled restlessly through crooked alleys, wandered like a lost soul up and down endless flights of hewn stone steps.

The Egyptian inhabitants retired into their houses at an early hour that night, barring their doors behind them. By the time the huge golden moon came up over the rim of the cliffs, the streets of the city were deserted.

Not till then did Ka-Zar's brain clear a trifle. Not till then did his mind hark back to the day before, not till then did he recall Zut's promise to Seti.

"When the flame burns crimson—strike!"

The words could only refer to one thing. Unconsciously Ka-Zar's glance traveled upward, came to rest on the pillar of flame that rose in a steady shaft from the topmost tier of the city, far above him.

Now he realized the full, terrible import of that signal. And with sudden dismay he realized that at any moment he might see the eternal light suddenly change to a glowing crimson.

There was no time to question why he should be so appalled at the thought. With one stroke he wiped from his mind all the thousand and one conflicting thoughts that had harassed him. Then with but a single, clear-cut purpose, he made all speed toward the top of the city.

In the same manner that Chaka the great ape swung through

the trees of the jungle, Ka-Zar scaled the ramparts of Khalli. With the sure-footedness of the antelope he ran lightly across the rim of the walls, hardly conscious of the perilous depths below. With leaps a leopard might have envied, he went ever upward.

At last, panting, he gained the topmost terrace of the city. He found it to be a luxuriant hanging garden, a rectangular plot of swaying palms, dripping orchids, splashing fountains. From its center rose a sheer-sided pylon built of clay bricks. It was from the top of this pylon that the eternal flame flung its steady banner skyward.

The moonlight and the pillar of fire overhead checkered the gardens with patches of brilliant light and alternate patches of Stygian shadow under the spreading palms.

Ka-Zar had arrived with not a moment to spare. Even as he flung himself over the wall and dropped nimbly to the ground, he saw a black figure dart across the garden, scale nimbly up the side of the pylon. With a low growl rumbling in his throat, he sprinted off in hot pursuit.

With all the agility of Nono the monkey, despite his massive body, he climbed up the slanting pile of clay bricks. Each was recessed a half inch from the one below it and that was all the purchase that his fingers and bare toes needed.

He emerged on a narrow, bare platform. Apparently the pylon was hollow, for the mysterious flame issued from a hole in its center. The black stood balanced on straddled legs a scant few feet away. The light gleamed on the ebony skin of his upraised arms. Both his fists were clenched—he was about to throw something into the heart of the flame.

He never completed the movement. With a low snarl Ka-Zar flung himself upon him and an instant later they were locked in a death-grip.

It was a silent, atavistic struggle that transpired there up on the topmost peak of the city. In vain the black struggled to free himself of the giant's grip. They swayed back and forth, perilously close to the edge of the pylon. But the black was no match for the mighty man of bronze. Suddenly he was plucked from his foothold, raised high on powerful arms.

KICKING AND STRUGGLING in a frenzy of fear, the helpless black guessed Ka-Zar's intention. But he could do nothing. Even as a shrill wail of terror tore from his lips, he was hurled through the air as though he had been shot from a catapult. His body turned over and over as he flew far out over the walls, then plunged precipitately downward.

He vanished from his victor's sight. Then his last frenzied shriek, cut off abruptly, floated back to tell that he had been smashed on the rocks far below.

Atop the pylon, the glowing flame shimmering on his naked bronze body, Ka-Zar looked out over the valley toward the distant caverns. Over there, many eyes were watching, awaiting the crimson signal that would unleash bloody war in Khalli. Flinging back his head, squaring his brawny shoulders, he sent the thundering roar of the lion floating across the sultry air.

As the cliffs picked up his cry of defiance and sent it echoing back and forth across the valley, with the back of his hand Ka-Zar mopped the great beads of sweat that bedewed his brow. A fine black powder had spilled from the hands of the black. It strewed the top of the pylon; it made daubs on his sweat-streaked body. Carefully he blew it off the clay bricks, away from the steady burning flame; rubbed it off his flesh. Then he lowered himself over the edge of the platform and climbed down the side of the pylon.

As he retraced his way through the dappled stretches of the gardens, he realized that once again he had impulsively foiled Zut's plans. He determined to seek out the counsellor, speak out openly, try to get at the real truth hidden in the network of lies, suspicions and intrigues in which he was caught like an insect in a spider's web. That he must take a hand in the coming clash, on one side or the other, was now inescapable. Perhaps a talk with Zut would help him to make up his mind, help him to decide once and for all which way he should choose.

CHAPTER XV

DELIVERED UNTO PTHOS

KA-ZAR WASTED MUCH time in Khalli trying to find Zut, only to learn at last that directly after the cry of the lion had floated down from the top of the pylon, Zut had betaken himself hurriedly toward the underground habitations on the other side of the valley.

Ka-Zar started off in the same direction.

He was halfway down the long, dim jungle road when a great black shadow materialized from the brush at one side of the road and Zar padded silently into place beside him. Nono dropped down from a branch, climbed swiftly up onto his master's shoulder.

Ka-Zar dropped a hand onto the tawny head of his brother. "Like Sinassa the snake, trouble rears its ugly head in the valley," he told Zar in the guttural language of the jungle. "Soon there will be much fighting and bloodshed. Lie low here in the jungle. If Ka-Zar needs you, he will call."

Zar did not understand why his two legged brother must share the doings of these hated Oman. Yet if he must, he would fain go by his side.

But Ka-Zar was adamant. And at last Zar, bowing to a wisdom greater than his own but with his heart filled with gloomy forebodings, faded once more into the underbrush. Ka-Zar tried to loosen Nono's grip about his neck, told the silly creature to scamper off into the safety of the forest. But Nono clung tighter and chattered his protest. The little monkey's eyes were filled with such pleading that Ka-Zar finally shrugged and permitted him to remain.

Once he had left the forest and plunged into the dark caverns under the cliffs, a slave told him that he would find Zut at the Temple of Pthos. Again Ka-Zar had to overcome his old aversion to the dim chamber with its monstrous, leering god.

He found his way surely and swiftly around the edge of the lake. All along the route he passed groups of muttering blacks. Each time they prostrated themselves before him, gazed in the same awe and wonder at this bronze giant with the little monkey atop his shoulder. As Ka-Zar turned into the passageway, there was barely room for him to pass. The tunnel was jammed with a throng of blacks, keeping a respectful distance away from Zut and Seti who were speaking earnestly together before the bronze door of the temple.

The animated conversation of the counsellor and the High Priest died abruptly as the tall form of Ka-Zar approached them. Zut's face, with its skin of wrinkled old parchment, betrayed no sign of emotion. Yet at the sight of his naked bronze disciple a slow fury smouldered in his breast. The wily counsellor's schemes had availed him nought. The plot on the life of the Queen had failed and he had been obliged to keep his promise to Seti, taking the chance that he might somehow survive the holocaust. Yet the signal had not been given—and the roar of the lion echoing out from the top of the city had told him why. It explained, also, why Zoab and Mu had never returned.

Zut turned to confront Ka-Zar. His fingers clawed at his beard. "So—you did not heed my warning," he accused. "You listened to the lying words of the Queen—listened and like an utter fool, believed. You call yourself a man. Bah! You are a weakling—a lump of clay in the hands of a woman!"

Had he weighed his words carefully for days, Zut could have found no taunt more sure to rouse Ka-Zar's wrath. This insult stabbed him to the quick and a swift retort came to his lips.

"Zut is angry only because he wishes me to be clay in his own hands," he answered hotly. "Zut speaks of being a man. Is he a man who plots in the dark, who sends others with knives to slay a defenseless woman?"

ZUT DID NOT know that Ka-Zar was still undecided, that he had come seeking him in a last desperate effort to make up his own mind about the justice and right in this matter which had split up the kingdom. Zut did see, though, the swift suspicion that glinted in Seti's eyes as he heard Ka-Zar's last words. This wild man of the jungle was causing much trouble and something would have to be done immediately, lest he menace Zut's very life.

The last tattered remnants of the cloak of friendship dropped from the counsellor. He drew his skinny form erect and his hawkeyes glittered beneath his craggy brows.

"Very well, then," he said. "It matters not what an ignorant savage thinks of Zut. It was I who made a fool of you. I lied to you for my own ends, but I do not need you after all. It was I who poisoned the old king. I was the real ruler of Khalli, and though now this chit of a girl dares to defy me, I shall yet be the ruler in name as well as fact."

He whirled on the mob of blacks who crowded in the passage. Stretching forth a scrawny arm, he pointed a bony finger at Ka-Zar. "This man is a traitor!" he denounced. "It was he who blocked the giving of the signal. And now he dares to defy us in our own stronghold!"

The blacks gasped, stared back openmouthed. In the long centuries of primitive cave-life, their brains had degenerated along with their bodies. They were too dull-witted to understand Zut's sudden change of heart. They had been taught to venerate Ka-Zar as god and now Zut called him a traitor.

Ka-Zar saw the blank, stupid faces of the blacks. He realized that though his fate hung once more in their hands, that without a leader to point the way, they were incapable of making any decision. And with that realization, he found the answer to the question that had been so long troubling him. For centuries these blacks had grubbed meekly away in their caves. The spark of rebellion had been planted in their dull wits by some unscrupulous, keener brain than their own. It was Zut, with the aid of Seti, who had stirred up this devil's brew in Khalli.

Zut saw the hesitation of the slaves, remembered with growing fury that he himself was responsible for the false miracle that had spared Ka-Zar. Such an idea once implanted in those thick skulls was not quickly dispelled. One false move and they might turn upon Zut and rend him. He had a sudden inspiration.

"This man is a traitor!" he cried again. "Zut denounces him— but Zut does not ask you to believe the word of a mortal man. If this Ka-Zar has dared to commit treason against the god who has protected and befriended him—that god alone will sit in judgment on him. Throw him into the Temple of Pthos—leave him alone to face his god. At sunrise you will find whether Zut has spoken the truth."

Seti's doughy face quivered. Echoing Zut's thundering accusation with a torrent of high, shrill words, he waddled to the door, flung the portal open.

His movement broke the spell that held the blacks. Like automatons, with harsh cries, they surged down the passage. At the sight of the horde rushing at him, Ka-Zar held his ground. But the little monkey squeaked in terror, dropped from his perch and with fearful glances over his shoulder at the oncoming blacks, scampered blindly in the opposite direction.

In vain Ka-Zar braced himself—in vain he lashed out as the first slaves charged at him. There was no stemming that leaping, shouting, black tide. Ka-Zar was almost lifted from his feet, rushed through the open doorway and hurled with terrific force into the Temple of Pthos. The bronze door slammed behind him with a crash like the knell of doom.

CHAPTER XVI

THE IDOL IS SMASHED

KA-ZAR SMASHED HEAVILY into the far wall, spun around with the spitting scream of N'Jagi ringing in his ears. Instinctively his hand whipped to his belt for the blade of steel that had always hung there. Then with a bitter laugh he realized that it was a long time since the blacks had taken his knife from him, on that first fateful night here in this very temple. Head crouched low between his shoulders, his body weaving slowly from side to side, bare-handed he set himself for the leopard's spring.

But almost to his disappointment, N'Jagi's black body did not plunge down upon him. Again the shrill scream of the beast echoed through the vaulted temple, followed by the clink of a metal chain.

His narrowed eyes orbing the semidarkness, Ka-Zar looked up to the narrow ledge that extended over the door. Gleaming opals of hate glared down at him. And there, straining against the chains that held him fast to the wall was N'Jagi.

His fangs were bared; his gaping jaws slavered. A strange, unearthly cry issued from his throat as with frustrated rage he threw his weight against his chain.

Arms akimbo, Ka-Zar rocked back on his heels and laughed up at the leopard. "So, N'Jagi," he taunted in the guttural language of the beasts. "Your master the evil Zut fears for your life, so he chains you in safety."

At his mocking voice the devil was aroused again in the

leopard. Once more his scream split the silence; once more he crouched back, then flung himself forward.

"Fool!" said Ka-Zar. "Break the chain, O N'Jagi—and you surely die."

Then with a show of utter disdain and contempt he turned his back on the snarling beast and swiftly surveyed the temple. He had been put into the Temple of Pthos to die, he knew. But if not before the sabre claws of N'Jagi—then by what dark agency? More trickery, this? More evil cunning of the bloodthirsty Oman?

Then slowly, as if impelled by some irresistible fascination his eyes were drawn to the hideous idol of the god that stood upon the dais. Again all its malignant evil assailed him like a living thing. The flesh crawled on his back; he bared his teeth. Then he flung back his head and sent the challenging roar of the lion crashing through the dim chamber.

The hated cry lashed N'Jagi to a new outburst of demoniacal fury.

Ka-Zar ignored the leopard, concentrated his suddenly narrowed eyes on the idol. Some sixth psychic sense told him that whatever the danger that threatened him, it was represented by that hideous image of stone.

All the dark tales he had heard concerning it came crowding back to him. It was evil. It demanded human sacrifice. Its appetite was insatiable. Once a victim had been delivered up to Pthos, he was never seen again.

Ka-Zar knew that he was intended as such a victim. But though the idol held him with a dread fascination, he feared it not. Pthos to him was but a name. He knew naught about gods, good or evil—and he cared less. He trusted in the might of his own right arm and in his friends, the jungle creatures.

Spells, magic, terrible curses—Bah! He took a long challenging step forward towards the idol. A thing of stone could not hurt him!

True.

But the thing behind that thing of stone could slay him! The hideous and grinning face of the idol concealed a second face equally as repulsive. The only difference between them was that this second one, instead of being carved from stone, was compounded of living flesh and blood and bone.

IT WAS THE face of Zut—evil, passion—distorted. To his pursed thin lips he held a short reed pipe that jutted an inch through one of the holes that made the idol's sightless eyes. And quivering at the end of that pipe was a tiny, poisoned dart. No man in all Khalli save Zut knew the secret of that poison—knew that it struck swifter than the poison of the burning well and left no tell-tale trace behind.

That was the dread secret of the idol of Pthos. It was hollow. And now crouched behind it, squinting through its gaping eye-socket, Zut expanded his lungs and waited for his victim to approach closer.

The blood pounded swiftly through Ka-Zar's veins and though beads of sweat popped out on his brow, he felt cold and numb and strangely apprehensive. His nostrils flared to the scent of danger; every nerve and sense flashed a shrill warning to his brain.

Instinct told him that danger lay before him. And he met it in the only way he knew how—by advancing. The stony face of the idol held him fascinated. It was a form of hypnotism.

And so intent was he on the leering face of the image—so intent was Zut on his steady approach—that neither saw the rapidly moving blur of shadow that scurried across a narrow ledge on the rear wall, then dropped agilely to the dais.

Zut's lips were pursued around the mouth of the blowpipe; his lungs were expanded to the full. Squinting through the narrow aperture in the idol he drew a deadly bead on the base of the bronzed column of Ka-Zar's throat, that loomed ever larger below him. He could not miss. He had done the selfsame thing a score of times before and never once had he had such a splendid target.

Already in his mind's eye he saw the sudden recoil of the jungle giant as the poisoned barb sank home; saw him shudder convulsively, claw at his throat, then sink to the ground. So the jungle god had fallen for a woman's wiles. Fool! He could have ruled in Khalli along with Zut.

Now, instead, he would fall victim to the very hungry Pthos!

He tongued the mouth of the reed—expanded his lungs—he....

There was a sudden hiss behind him—a patter of running feet—then needlelike claws dug deep into his spine and a pair of long and spidery arms wrapped themselves around his neck.

The impact of the unexpected weight on his back deflated the air in Zut's lungs—and spoiled his aim. The poisoned dart whizzed from the blowpipe, whined angrily past Ka-Zar's ear.

From behind the grinning idol and muffled by it came a guttural curse, followed by a furious, scolding chatter. Ka-Zar recognized both sounds. The first was human and he would have sworn that that familiar chatter came from no other than Nono the silly one.

He leaped forward. With one mighty spring he bounded up onto the platform. Three long strides took him to the rear of the idol. And there, gray of face, stark fear in his eyes, Zut vainly essayed to choke the life from the monkey with one hand, while he wrenched at the dagger at his belt with the other. He never succeeded in either attempt.

With a guttural snarl Ka-Zar leaped in. The steel fingers of his right hand closed around Zut's scrawny neck, as the momentum of his charge flung the Egyptian back against the cold body of the idol.

ZUT DROPPED THE whimpering monkey as his dagger cleared his belt. But long before he could whip it up Ka-Zar had caught his wrist in a grip of steel. As if it were but a green twig, Zut's arm bent back beneath the jungle giant's pressure. He winced, he cried out in agony—he screamed and the dagger fell to the floor with a metallic clang.

His cries of agony, however, were drowned in the hideous screams of N'Jagi as the black leopard, fangs gnashing, wracked his sleek body against the chain that held him.

For once Zut had been too sure of himself. He had overplayed his hand.

Powerful arms swept him from his feet, held him high aloft above the idol's head. Looking down into the implacable tawny eyes of Ka-Zar, Zut read the fate that was in store for him. Instead of being the executioner, he was to be the victim that was to satisfy the blood lust of the unholy Pthos. In another moment his skull would be crushed like a rotten gourd against the stony face of the idol.

In that moment the Machiavellian Zut begged for his life. "Hold, O Ka-Zar," be pleaded. "Forget not that it was Zut who gave you the antidote to the poison cup of the Queen."

Ka-Zar's mighty limbs trembled with the hate that was upon him. Yet what the crawling thing in his hands had said was true. His eyes smouldered. "You tricked me," he said. "You have fed me with lies."

"Yet forget not that it was I who saved you," quavered Zut.

"Ka-Zar does not forget," said the jungle giant. "A life for a life. I give you back yours, now."

He suddenly lowered the trembling figure to his hip. Then implanting the sole of his bare foot high up on the base of the idol, he heaved mightily. The stone image trembled, groaned, loosed on its moorings. Then, with a final thrust, Ka-Zar sent it crashing down from the dais to the hard floor of the temple, where it broke into a dozen pieces.

Directly behind where the idol had stood, a small section of the masonry jutted out from the wall. It had been cunningly fashioned and hinged, this secret aperture and it explained how Zut had so mysteriously gained his devilish place of concealment.

The crash of the toppled idol was still rumbling in the vaulted temple, when Ka-Zar threw back the bronze door and stood silhouetted for a moment in the doorway. High above his head at arms' length he held the trembling Zut. Below him, their startled and terror-stricken faces lit up by the weird lights from a score of torches, Seti and his followers fell back.

A howl of consternation rose from their wolfish lips. They would have been less startled if the stone image of Pthos, itself, had appeared in the doorway. And before they could recover, Ka-Zar sent the screaming Zut hurtling down onto their heads.

The packed ranks of the slaves wavered, broke. Even the flaming torches were knocked from their brackets as the mob fled. And when Seti managed at last to recover one and to hold it aloft the temple door was empty.

Ka-Zar had vanished.

CHAPTER XVII

FIRST BLOOD

THREE MINUTES LATER his towering form leaped through the main gate to the City of Khalli. The sleepy sentrys on duty there, looked up with wide eyes at his precipitate entrance, grasped their spears more firmly.

Pulling to an abrupt halt, Ka-Zar spoke to them swiftly. "The gate! Close it at once!" he commanded.

The guards looked at him stupidly and impatient at the delay, Ka-Zar presented his broad shoulders to the massive gate and slowly swung it to. Not until the heavy bronze bar had been set securely in its place did he turn again to the guards.

"There will be dark trouble in Khalli, tonight," he said prophetically. "Dark trouble and much bloodshed. Spurred on by the treacherous Zut and Seti, the blacks are rising."

The faces of the sentries showed swift alarm.

"The gate to the city is to be opened to no one," continued Ka-Zar hurriedly. "Least of all to Zut. Mark my words well and if you fail you shall have Ka-Zar to reckon with. Blow thy horn, trumpeter! Arouse your men! Man the walls!"

He broke off abruptly as from somewhere far towards the south came a deep, ominous rumble, the distant clamor of angry voices.

"The slaves are already on the march," continued Ka-Zar. "Blow, trumpeter, blow! And if need be, let each man of you die tonight for your city and your Queen!"

The savage clamor of the approaching blacks rose louder in

their ears. The trumpeter was paralyzed for a moment. Then he clapped his horn to his lips and blew three shrill blasts of alarm.

With the brazen notes still echoing back from the cliffs that hemmed in the city, Ka-Zar sped from the gate and made straight for Tamiris' palace.

He found the place in a confused turmoil as he brushed by the guard at the outer door. Men, rudely awakened from sleep, milled about in confusion as they buckled on their short swords. Others stared questioningly at one another and muttered a last prayer to the gods.

His bronzed figure towering above them, Ka-Zar commanded their attention with an upraised arm. "Men of Khalli," he called. "Hear me, hear me all. Led by the traitorous Zut and Seti, the black slaves have revolted. Even now they march on the inner city to slay and plunder—to slay your queen and to put the tyrant Zut upon the throne.

"To the walls, men of Khalli. Let your hearts be stout, your spears well aimed; and may the gods of Khalli lend strength to your sword arms."

His ringing words of challenge and defiance worked a miracle on the demoralized soldiers. They felt that they had in Ka-Zar an invincible ally—one favored by the gods. Their backs stiffened, their eyes glittered and shouting hoarse cries of alarm to the still sleeping city, they rushed from the palace and made for strategic positions on the walls.

When the last man had vanished, Ka-Zar sped across the now deserted entrance hall, leaped up the broad flight of marble steps at the far end, and without the formality of knocking entered Tamiris' apartment.

He found her dressed and waiting for him, surrounded by a handful of trembling maids. True, her face was slightly pale but her lips were resolute and there was no mark of fear upon her. Her eyes glowed with a steady, intense light and all the while she fondly fingered the jeweled haft of the short dagger that hung from her girdle....

Without waiting for an exchange of greetings she spoke. "Ka-Zar brings tidings?" she said.

"Dark tidings, O Tamiris," he answered. "The blacks have risen."

"I heard your words in the hall below," said the Queen. "And Ka-Zar—Lord of the jungle—does he fight or flee?"

KA-ZAR DREW HIMSELF up to his full height and looked down for a long moment into her glowing eyes. Anger surged within him at her insinuating words. Then with a rush of sudden relief, he understood. Well might Tamiris be the daughter of an ancient civilization, but nevertheless, she was a true daughter of the jungle. In her own peculiar way she was spurring her mate onto battle, even as Sha might have done to Zar in defense of their cubs.

"Ka-Zar—brother of the lion never flees from danger," he said. "Ka-Zar has come to fight—not for your city, not for your civilization, not for the men who call you Queen—but for you."

He laughed suddenly, swept her into his mighty arms, crushed her against his bronzed chest and kissed her fiercely.

Tamiris was breathless and bruised when he deposited her gently on her feet a moment later but in her heart was a great exultation. But before she could stay him, Ka-Zar was gone. And as the door clanged to behind his retreating back, a mighty shout went up from the walls and surrounded the city.

On his way out of the palace, Ka-Zar commandeered a long spear and a heavy, two-bladed sword. He balanced the first in his hand for a moment, then tested the blade of the other with his thumb. He found both to his satisfaction. His soul exulted and his heart beat swifter as once more he felt the weight and heft of weapons in his hands. For many moons now, he had been unarmed. True, his bare fists were weapons enough against any dozen men in Khalli, be they white or black.

But now be was confronted by overwhelming hordes. Death would be swift. He determined to deal it more swiftly still.

When he reached the outer wall, he found the men of Khalli

grim and alert at their posts. The dying moon glinted dully off spear head and broad sword. A mighty shout of welcome went up from the hosts that manned the wall.

Ka-Zar brandished his spear aloft in greeting, then swiftly surveyed the hurried scene of activity about him. A dozen paces back from the wall men sweated as they piled up huge mounds of stones beside strange looking devices. They looked to Ka-Zar like young trees of a dozen seasons' growth. One end of each was firmly implanted into the ground and attached to the other was a small platform of wood some two feet square.

Other groups of men bestirred themselves with bellows around a dozen fires. Over them, on iron bars, hung suspended as many steaming cauldrons of boiling water and oil. Ka-Zar had never seen such preparations before but shrewdly he guessed for what purpose the steaming liquid was to be used.

Outside, from beyond the wall, came a throaty, ominous rumble—the swelling guttural cries of a vast multitude.

Twenty paces from where he stood, Ka-Zar noted a group of men with their heads together in consultation. From their jeweled weapons and the purple of their robes he knew them to be chiefs—leaders of the white men of Khalli in time of emergency.

He hurried up to them and at his coming their teeth glinted brightly as they gave him welcome.

"I am Ankhamen," said a tall, patrician Egyptian. "It is my honor to command the Queen's men. In her name I welcome you to our ranks."

Ka-Zar smiled. "My spear is thirsty. My sword cries out for blood."

"Well spoken, O Ka-Zar, God of the jungle," said Ankhamen.

BUT THE JUNGLE giant shook his head. "Ka-Zar is no god. He is a man, even as you. He is here to fight. Once tonight he gave back to Zut his miserable life. He shall not spare him a second time. Why do not the blacks attack?"

"Zut has asked that we yield the city. He promises mercy. If not his hordes will storm the gate."

"And your answer?" asked Ka-Zar.

"We have been debating the issue."

Ka-Zar shook his head violently from side to side. "O foolish men of Khalli. Trust not the word of Zut or Seti. If you would answer, let your swords speak and your spears."

Ankhamen nodded in agreement. "Ka-Zar speaks with the tongue of wisdom. It shall be done as he says. I, myself, from the wall shall denounce the infamous Zut and Seti."

With the words he started for one of the flights of narrow stone steps that led to the top of the parapet.

Ka-Zar laid a heavy but gentle hand upon his arm and stayed him.

"You are old, Ankhamen," he said, his eyes shining with admiration. "Up there on the wall, a hurled javelin would be hard to dodge. And more, you are trusted of the Queen. She needs you. Let Ka-Zar speak to Zut and his followers. If they listen, all may be well. But if not, it shall be war."

So saying he turned abruptly, snatched a blazing torch from a soldier and crossed to the stone steps. He mounted them swiftly. Inside the wall all eyes followed his progress with breathless attention. Outside, the angry clamor rose to a frenzied din.

Awaiting the moment when the cries of the blacks had reached their peak, Ka-Zar suddenly leaped to the top of the parapet. High above his head he held the burning brand and the leaping tongues of flame bathed his bronzed body in rippling sheets of fire.

At the sudden appearance of the jungle god—the man who but a few short hours before had been considered by the slaves as the favored son of Pthos—the eternal symbol of light in one hand, a glinting spear in the other—a sudden hush fell over the packed ranks of the revolting legions.

For a long moment Ka-Zar stood there, straddle-legged on the parapet, motionless, immobile as if he had been carved from bronze. Only his slitted eyes were alive as they eagerly searched for the wizened face of Zut in the sea of faces below him.

He spotted the arch-traitor at last in the front line, flanked on one side by the obese Seti. Keeping one eye on the unholy pair he threw back his head, expanded his lungs and addressed himself to the multitude.

"Sons of Pthos," he began, "you have listened to evil words of counsel and have risen against your Queen. Know you that those who lead you, the evil Zut and the fat Seti, are willing to betray you unto death to achieve their own ends....

"Queen Tamiris knows all. But the queen is merciful. Throw down your arms. Return you to your caves now and peace and justice shall reign again in Khalli."

He paused dramatically and a strained silence answered him. His commanding presence, his heavy, weighted words had made a deep impression on the blacks.

BEFORE THE VERY walls of the City, with the power for which he had lusted so long almost within his grasp, Zut saw that an overwhelming defeat confronted him. Worse yet, a defeat without having struck a blow.

A passionate hate for the jungle savage he had befriended welled up in his breast. But there was no time to consider that now. He had to act at once before the aroused slaves turned upon him and rent him limb from limb.

With a loud cry he leaped out from the rank and facing his followers raised his arms aloft. "Sons of Pthos!" he screamed. "Listen not to the words of the jungle savage. He has desecrated your temple and mocked your gods. The blood of the sacred leopard is upon his hands. Believe not that he is favored of Pthos. It was only by black magic that he shattered the idol of your protecting god."

His voice rose to a wild crescendo of passionate appeal. "Pthos cries out for vengeance! Kill the unbeliever, the profaner of your temple—kill those who harbor and shelter him...."

A loud wail of approval and approbation went up from the

slaves at the frenzied appeal. Spears were brandished, swords were thrust towards the walled city in a symbolic gesture.

And alone, immovable on top of the wall, looking down into a sea of hideous, lusting faces, Ka-Zar knew that he had lost. He flung up his arm again, holding the spear aloft. At the gesture the clamor subsided.

"So be it, sons of evil!" he bellowed. "You have asked for war and by war so shall ye die!"

His mighty torso arched suddenly backward. Balanced on one foot he poised for a moment. Then with a mighty thrust he hurled his spear from him. With an angry drone it sped true to its mark and the reckless black, who, in his eagerness for the taste of blood had leaped for the wall, was impaled in mid-stride.

The slave screamed once, dropped his weapons and with two clawing hands strove to tear the hardened bronze from his vitals. Then, with a final agonized wail he collapsed on his face.

Ka-Zar had drawn first blood. And in that second in which the dead slave had hit the hard packed earth, a hundred javelins were launched at his breast and a thousand men surged forward.

The siege of Khalli had begun.

CHAPTER XVIII

THE SEIGE

AND THROUGH SEVEN long days and seven long nights the siege continued. Time and time again, like a black wave the slaves surged forward to the wall, only to be repulsed with frightful slaughter.

The ancient Egyptian builders of the lost city had done their work well. The wall surrounding it was high, was thick. And so long as those defending it were faithful to their trust, almost impregnable.

Lashed on alike by fanatical zeal and blood lust the black slaves launched charge after charge against the frowning walls. While atop the parapet, the defenders hurled them back.

Full well they knew what fate awaited them if once the slaves succeeded in scaling the wall or breaching it. Outnumbered a hundred to one the white rulers of the city would be engulfed in a surging tide of black humanity. And the blood thirst of the ever insatiable Pthos would be slaked at last.

Of all those stout-hearted defenders, none showed more bravery, more daring, more reckless abandon than Ka-Zar. Wherever the fighting was hardest—wherever the walls were most sorely pressed, there would be found his herculean figure— there would be heard his defiant challenge of the lion.

Long since the attacking hordes had learned to fear it, to tremble before its might. And as the walls still held, in more than one heathen heart a doubt was born.

Ka-Zar fought with the strength and valor of ten men. He

was untiring, ever vigilant—ever the first to jump into action when a new danger threatened.

Single-handed, alone, his companions swept to oblivion from about him, he fought off a score of raiding blacks until re-enforcements swept up beside him.

A dozen wounds scarred his mighty body. His eyes were red-rimmed and heavy from lack of sleep. Yet the arm that swung his mighty broad sword never failed him and his aim in hurling his long spears was never better.

Many times he longed for his stout bow and a full quiver of arrows. Bitterly he cursed himself for a fool for not having made one during his long idle days in Khalli. But moments of such futile contemplation were few and far between. It was hack with the broad sword! thrust with javelin!—and in close quarters fight for one's life with blood-stained dagger.

The first night of the siege he learned the purpose of the strange contraptions that had puzzled him. He saw men with straining backs, bend the stout saplings back like a bow; saw others load the small platform at their ends with heavy boulders.

Then, with a screaming rush of wind the saplings would be suddenly released and the heavy stones would hurtle over the wall to crash into the milling throng before the walls.

The contrivances were crude catapults but they were efficient and Ka-Zar marveled at them. A clean death and far to be preferred to the agony of boiling oil poured from the top of the parapet onto the heads of the blacks attempting to scale the wall.

Towards the close of the eighth day there came a temporary lull in the fighting. The decimated ranks of Zut's followers drew back from the wall out of spear range, leaving only a thin circle of warriors before the parapet to harry the defenders.

Grateful for the momentary respite Ka-Zar squatted on top of the wall and gave his attention to the knicked and dulled edge of his great sword. He was testing it with his thumb a few moments later, when Ankhamen limped hurriedly towards him.

The old man's face was drawn and pale but there was an indomitable light in his eyes. For a week he had been fighting gallantly at Ka-Zar's side, despite the fact that during the first night of the siege a spear had pierced his thigh.

Ka-Zar placed a bracing arm around the old man's shoulders. "The blacks retreat," he said cheerily. "They have tasted death and like it not."

Ankhamen smiled up at him and shook his head. "Would that it were so. It is but a respite. Zut has some new cunning afoot. His blacks but rest to gather strength for a new assault."

KA-ZAR FROWNED DARKLY and tested the blade of his sword again. "And how fares Tamiris, Queen of Khalli?"

For a fleeting second Ankbamen looked at him keenly, then turned away with a little sigh. "She is true daughter of the Pharaohs. Even in the face of ultimate defeat, her courage never falters."

At the words, Ka-Zar's head snapped up. "I understand you not, Ankhamen? Why speak of defeat when the blacks have fallen before us like flies? For seven days and seven nights they have stormed the walls and failed."

Ankhamen nodded. "If it were but a matter of defending the walls…. But go. The Queen would talk with you."

"Tamiris?"

"Even so—Tamiris. She would look upon your face again, and she has words for your ear alone." He held out his hand in a simple gesture and instinctively Ka-Zar grasped it in his own. "Go," said Ankhamen again, "and may the gods that brought you here, preserve you. For the gods know that Khalli has need of you."

CHAPTER XIX

HUNGER

THE DARK EYES of the Queen grew soft as she saw the lines of weariness etched in Ka-Zar's face, his care-worn brow, the still defiant angle of his lean jaw. She raised her hand in greeting as he approached and there was both anxiety and a melting tenderness in her voice as she asked: "How goes the siege, O brave Protector of Khalli?"

Ka-Zar shrugged his tired shoulders. "Your Egyptians are loyal and brave. All the legions of the devil cannot pass them."

Tamiris sighed. "No," she murmured huskily. "With such a leader, no one could admit defeat." Then lowering her eyes, she frowned, traced the pattern of the rug with the toe of a tiny gilded sandal. "But there is one enemy more powerful than even the mighty Ka-Zar. And now that enemy rears his ugly head here in the heart of Khalli."

Ka-Zar's eyes narrowed. "You mean…?"

"Hunger," answered Tamiris simply. "The supply of food is almost gone. Even the stoutest heart grows faint when the belly is empty."

Ka-Zar scowled. "There is food in the caverns of the blacks. There is game aplenty yet nearer at hand, in the forest." His hands clenched at his sides. "Yet your Egyptians are outnumbered, a hundred to one. To sally forth from the safety of the walls—means death."

Tamiris' eyes were haunted. She turned, walked unsteadily to the window and looked out over her beleaguered city. She raised a hand, brushed it across her ivory brow. "Must I, then," she asked faintly, "surrender? Turn my kingdom and my faithful subjects over to the mercies of these blood-crazed rebels?"

A hushed silence followed her words. Ka-Zar saw a swift vision of the slaughter, of the terrible fate of this unhappy girl, once the black horde poured in through the gates of the city. The prospect of a lingering death by starvation was equally unbearable.

He inhaled a sharp breath. His massive chest expanded; his nails dug into the palms of his clenched fists.

"No!" The word tore from his lips.

Tamiris whirled. Startled, she stared at him. And there was that determination written upon his face, that reckless glint in his eyes, that brought a faint ray of hope to her own.

She ran to him in a sudden burst of passion, placed her tiny hands upon his broad chest and turned her face up to his own.

"Speak!" she begged hoarsely. "There is yet hope?"

Ka-Zar seized her wrists, his fingers tightened about them until she winced with the pain.

"Ka-Zar will never surrender to the evil Zut!" he said, his face distorted, his amber eyes glinting fire. "Somehow— someway—he shall yet outwit him."

He thrust her roughly from him, turned and stalked across the room. With the lithe stride of Zar the lion he paced the width of the chamber, while Tamiris watched him, hardly daring to breathe. Suddenly he flung back his head, whirled to confront her.

"To send out an expedition for food would be fatal. This war must be ended swiftly—it is our only hope. Heed my words. These blacks who have dared to rise against you are but a pack of slinking jackals, brainless, without courage, helpless without a leader. Zut and Seti may be slain. Without those masters of evil to spur them on those jackals will flee yelping for their black holes."

Breathlessly Tamiris nodded. "True! You are keen as well as

mighty, O Ka-Zar. But to slay Zut and Seti—how could that be done? I know those skulking schemers well. Surely they keep well away from the dangers of the battle. Doubtless they save their precious hides somewhere in the safety of the distant caverns."

Ka-Zar's lips curled with scorn. "So, too, thinks Ka-Zar. There he will go, there he will find them—and there his knife shall seek out and find their black hearts!"

THE FERVOR OF his words brought a flush to Tamiris' cheeks. For a moment she exulted with him. Then suddenly she paled. One hand flew up to the ivory column of her throat.

"But—but Ka-Zar has said that not all the Egyptians together dare to venture from the walls. Who, then, goes with him to seek Zut and Seti?"

Slowly Ka-Zar drew himself up to the full of his majestic height. "Ka-Zar needs no companions," he said arrogantly. "They would but hinder him. He goes alone."

The last vestige of color drained from Tamiris' face. All her newborn hope turned to ashes in her mouth. She was torn between her last desperate chance for salvation and the love for this bronzed giant that filled her heart. Her slender body quivered from head to foot.

And while she stood as one turned to stone, unable to utter a sound, Ka-Zar turned abruptly and strode out of the room.

CHAPTER XX

THE POISON SPRING

WHEN HE EMERGED from the palace, night had fallen over the lost kingdom and a misty glow on the horizon foretold the rising of the moon. Great stars studded the sky, remote, coldly indifferent to the woes of men on the insignificant earth so far beneath them. Like reflections of the stars on a dark lake, the campfires of the besiegers made a twinkling ring about the city.

Ka-Zar sent a messenger to Ankhamen, warning him only that he would be absent for a while and bidding him to stay on guard until he returned. Then anxious to run the gauntlet before the moon rose, he made his way swiftly down from terrace to terrace.

As always he was naked except for the skin of an animal about his loins, and save for the keen blade tucked into that belt, he was unarmed. He moved lithely as N'Jagi, as silently as Sinassa the snake. Even his own vigilant sentries did not see him as he slid like a shadow over the lowest rampart, dropped cat-like to the ground outside the walls.

His enemies, too, were weary of the prolonged warfare. They had retired to huddled groups about their fires, where they squatted and partook of their evening meal. But though the defenders of Khalli were silent in this brief respite, these slaves were already drunk with victory. Long before he reached their circle Ka-Zar could hear their voices raised in animated conversation, in discordant song, in quarrel among themselves.

He headed for a point where the blacks were encamped at the fringe of the encroaching jungle. From beyond the chatter about the camp fires there drifted the squeals of Quog the wild pig, the chattering of Nono's long-tailed brothers, the fiendish laugh of Janko the hyena. And as he listened to these familiar sounds, all the thin veneer of civilization that Ka-Zar had acquired from his contact with men, dropped from him. He became a beast once more—the two-legged, super-animal who was the lord of the jungle.

His massive shoulders dropped into a crouch. His eyes closed until they were but gleaming amber slits. His nostrils flared and he sniffed at the damp night air. As he glided forward his bronze body closely resembled the tawny form of his mighty brother.

It was amazing the way his huge form shrank to cover behind a stunted bush, disappeared behind the narrow bole of a tree. Gliding soundlessly from one patch of shadow to another he approached the nearest group of jabbering blacks.

They were ensconced beneath the spreading branches of a huge oulangi tree. Whether the firelight in their eyes blinded them, or whether their full bellies had lulled their caution, they lolled at their ease even as the black shadow of the jungle man rose from behind nearby shrubbery, flitted across an open stretch and melted into the huge bole of the tree. Ironically, one walked over, squatted down at its base and leaned his back against the rough bark.

Ka-Zar's lips pulled back from his teeth in a soundless snarl. His nostrils wrinkled from the strong, foetid odor of the unwashed black. It seemed incredible that the senses of these creatures could be so dulled that they had no warning of his presence.

One of his enemies yawned. Another scratched listlessly at the sole of his foot. One poked at the fire, sending a shower of sparks hissing up toward the branches. And still without the slightest sound, Ka-Zar swung himself upward, climbed hand over hand up the opposite side of the tree trunk.

Squatting on the lowest bough, he peered downward. What a keen pleasure it would be to drop, screeching, into the midst of these stupid Oman! Or to let the roar of the lion blast from his throat, causing them to scatter pellmell in all directions!

But the fate of a kingdom was at stake and this was no time to indulge in such heroics.

From the farthermost tip of the branch on which he squatted, there was but a short space to the dense forest growth beyond. Moving on his belly like a great snake, Ka-Zar worked his way out toward the end of the limb. There, clutching the branches, drawing his body back like an archer's bow, he let go. There was a breathless moment as he hurtled through empty air. Then his outstretched hands brushed foliage, caught a projecting tree branch and he swung up into a tall baobab.

HE KEPT TO the trees. Like Chaka the ape he swung easily from branch to branch, traveling as swiftly as if he had been on the ground below. With a long, gliding swing he proceeded toward the heart of the jungle.

He paused at last in the dense foliage of a towering daboukra. Filling his lungs, spreading his brawny shoulders, he set the forest trembling with the stentorian roar of the lion.

A hush fell over the jungle as in fear and terror of that dreaded sound, all smaller animals scurried to cover. For a long moment the wilderness lay dark and silent under the slanting rays of the slender, sickle moon, that rode above the rim of the cliffs. Ka-Zar cocked his head to one side and waited.

Then it came—drifting to him on the warm wind—the echoing rumble of Zar's answering call. Satisfied, Ka-Zar awaited the coming of his brother.

He had not long to wait. A faint breeze stirred the leaves, bringing with it a familiar, pungent scent. Then thirty paces away the undergrowth parted and a great tawny shape materialized on the forest floor.

With a low rumble of welcome in his throat, Ka-Zar dropped lightly down from his perch. Whining greetings were exchanged by these strange blood brothers.

"Trouble has come to these Oman," said Zar in guttural growls.

Ka-Zar nodded. "True, wise one," he answered. "But it shall soon be ended. Ka-Zar goes to slay the evil ones who have caused it. The fat black Om and the skinny white one, whose eyes are like those of Pindar the eagle. Nay," he corrected himself, "not Pindar—but Kru the vulture."

Golden gleams danced the depths of Zar's eyes. "No longer will Zar lie low in the forest," he said. "He goes with his brother."

Ka-Zar looked at his faithful friend and a burden lifted from his weary heart. When he had summoned the lion, he had hoped to hear those very words. So be it. Just they two—against enemies whose number was legion. No more of this Oman's warfare—they would fight like the jungle animals that they were.

There was no need to express his gratitude. He fingered the haft of the knife at his belt and said simply: "Come."

On soundless feet and padded paws, side by side, they traveled swiftly over the jungle floor toward the subterranean caverns under the cliffs. Their path paralleled the road that the people of Khalli had hewed through the forest. To their keen ears came the sound of much traffic across it now. Occasionally they caught glimpses of twinkling lights through the trees. Always fearful of the encroaching forest after nightfall, the blacks moved now in the safety of numbers and the light of flaring torches.

MAN AND LION came at length to the last, dense clump of mangroves near the opening in the cliffs. There they crouched and waited, watching from slitted eyes for their opportunity to proceed further. Several times groups of slaves hurried past them, happily unaware of two pairs of glowing eyes that watched their movements from the nearby undergrowth. But in the jungle patience is as important as courage and not by the slightest sound did Ka-Zar or Zar betray their presence.

Their chance came at last. The open space between them and

the cliffs was, for a brief interlude, empty of all but the gauzy light of the moon. Slipping from cover, they glided soundlessly across it, plunged abruptly into the darkness that brooded over the shores of the vast, subterranean lake.

As his most likely objective, Ka-Zar determined to go first to the Temple of Pthos. Zar voiced no question, fell obediently into place at his heels. Each time the glow of a torch illumined their path, they paused to make sure that no eyes were watching before they exposed themselves in the light. Several times they had to fall swiftly back into shadowy recesses, as parties of blacks came noisily along the muddy bank.

Without mishap they reached the spot where they must turn off to go to the temple. For some inexplicable reason Zar halted, hesitated. Ka-Zar, frowned, looked questioningly at the lion. Then, as though drawn by some irresistible force, his eyes searched farther on. He froze in his tracks.

A figure emerged from a tunnel mouth some distance ahead. A sputtering flare was in its upraised hand and the flickering light illumined the obese form directly below it. There was no mistaking that monstrous, repellent creature. Ka-Zar's breath caught in his throat; Zar's lips curled back in a soundless snarl. It was Seti—the High Priest of Pthos.

Seti saw them at the same moment. His eyes bulged, his puffy cheeks turned an ashen gray. With a shrill wail of terror he clutched the torch tighter, turned and plunged back into the mouth of the tunnel.

Silently Ka-Zar and Zar bounded forward in hot pursuit. In a series of long leaps they gained the opening of the passage. Plunging in they raced after their quarry. They could hear his frightened yelps as he. ran deeper and deeper into the bowels of the earth.

Ka-Zar's brain whirled. Though Seti's first scream had apparently raised no alarm, he realized that they must get the High Priest and silence him. For if the blacks once learned that he and Zar were in the heart of their stronghold, they would never escape. The slaves knew every twist and turning in this maze of passageways, but to Ka-Zar they were still strange, a menace and trap.

Though fear had lent wings to Seti's feet, his short stumpy legs were no match for theirs. They rounded a bend—slithered to a sudden bait. There before them stood Seti, at the edge of a bubbling pool. The torch was still clutched in his hand and his face was a mask of stark terror. When he saw the glittering knife in Ka-Zar's hand and the massive lion who crouched by Ka-Zar's side, his lips worked like soft rubber. A stream of saliva trickled from one corner of his mouth, then it opened and once more his paralyzed throat let a single shriek escape it.

HE TURNED TO flee again, tripped over a stone, plunged headlong forward. The torch flew from his hand, struck the ground and shattered in a burst of spitting embers. In the ensuing darkness there came a mighty splash. Then the hairs at the back of Ka-Zar's neck bristled and in his ears rang the most awful cry he had ever heard—a mournful wail that rose to a high crescendo, died there in an ominous gurgle.

Sheathing his knife, he leaped forward, snatched up the fallen torch, blew upon its smouldering tip. It burst into flame again and holding it high, he stepped toward the pool.

The waters slapped and frothed against the sides. With his free hand outstretched, Ka-Zar waited for Seti's head to bob up again. Behind him, Zar whined.

But gradually the tossing waters subsided—and the High Priest failed to reappear. Ka-Zar was silent. There was awe in his heart as he knelt by the pool. For some reason he felt no exultation that one of his hated enemies had met his death.

He became aware of a faint, acrid odor. He wrinkled his nostrils. He sniffed, raised his eyes about him. Then he lowered his head a trifle more over the bubbling pool.

The unpleasant odor was stronger—it emanated from the water. A vague thought that eluded him disturbed Ka-Zar's brain. He dipped a little of the water up in his palm, touched his tongue to the liquid.

It burned like fire at the contact. With a gesture of revulsion he spilled the water from his hand, wiped his palm on his belt. He was very sober as he rose to his feet, turned silently to the crouching lion. For that vague thought had crystallized in his brain—he knew now that this was the poison spring—these were the terrible waters of the Cup of Pthos.

It took much to shake the stout heart of Ka-Zar, king of the jungle. But his step was a trifle unsteady as he led Zar back down the tunnel through which they had come.

CHAPTER XXI

THE SECRET TUNNEL

BUT AN ENEMY is an enemy. And an enemy dead is not a matter to brood about, but to forget. By the time they emerged once more on the bank of the lake, Ka-Zar's step was again springy and his mind busy with other matters.

Seti was disposed of. There yet remained Zut, the more important of that ungodly pair. Again Ka-Zar headed for the Temple of Pthos in search of the counselor.

Now that he had cast aside the customs of men and become an animal again, Fortune once more smiled upon him. He and Zar met no one as they strode down the long passageway, came at last to the bronze door of the temple. Thrusting it cautiously inward, Ka-Zar peered first into the great dim chamber beyond. Only the low snarl of the chained leopard greeted him. With a low growl to Zar to follow, he stepped inside, let the lion enter and then shut the massive portal behind him.

At the sight of the crouching black form near the wall, the long hairs on the back of the lion's neck rose to a stiff ruff. The tuft at the tip of his tail switched. His lips pulled back from his fangs. Confronted now by two such formidable enemies, N'Jagi quivered down his supple length. His fear was greater than his hate as he spat. But Ka-Zar was not concerned with the old feud between them, right now. He dropped a hand on Zar's head and the low growl that rumbled in the lion's throat subsided.

Turning their backs on the captive beast, they surveyed the

dim reaches of the temple. Ka-Zar saw with keen disappoint-ment that except for the presence of the leopard, they were alone. The remains of the idol still lay where they had fallen on the night when he had toppled the grinning image from its throne. It was highly probable that during the bloody war that had broken out immediately after, no one had even entered the temple.

Zar moved forward, sniffing. Cautiously he climbed up the dais, nosed curiously about in the wreckage. Ka-Zar turned, wondering where next to seek for Zut. The death of Seti ac-complished nothing unless he sent the scheming counsellor to join his fat-faced accomplice.

He had almost reached the door when a low whine from Zar spun him around. He looked up to see Zar sinking from sight!

He bounded forward but even as he leaped up the steps of the dais, Zar leaped back to safety. Together they stared down at something so unbelievable that for a moment both doubted the evidence of their eyes.

On the very spot where the base of the huge idol had stood, a square block of stone had tilted downward. Cautiously Ka-Zar stooped, found that it took all his strength to thrust it back yet further. It was a cleverly concealed trap-door and judging from the way its rusted hinges squeaked, it had been many, many years since it had last been opened.

At first he wondered vaguely why, when Zut had concealed himself in the idol, he had not fallen through. Then he realized that it had been the tremendous weight of the lion that had caused the trap to drop. Quite possibly—he did not know that he guessed the truth—even the all-knowing Zut had never suspected its existence.

Together he and Zar peered dawn the opening. In the dim light all they could make out was a flight of cut stone steps leading down into the blackness.

With a thoughtful frown wrinkling his brow, Ka-Zar squat-ted at the edge of the aperture and considered. Though their presence in the underground caverns was not yet suspected, there was still a good chance that they would be caught before they could get out of the catacombs. He had to find Zut—true. But he did not have the faintest idea where to look for him and somehow, this gaping hole had a growing fascination for him.

He looked at Zar, voiced his indecision in a low whine.

Calmly Zar answered. "Zar goes where his brother goes."

KA-ZAR WAITED FOR no more. Dropping lithely over the edge of the hole, he landed on the stone steps. Zar followed.

There was a bronze ring on the under side of the slab. Lest the secret trap door be discovered while they were below, Ka-Zar closed it behind them. He braced his legs on the steps, but it took all his mighty strength to raise the block of stone to the level of the platform above.

With the closing of the aperture, they were left in utter blackness. Feeling their way cautiously they descended the flight of steps. Down—down—down....

Then abruptly they struck a level earth floor. Feeling about with his outstretched hands, Ka-Zar found that they stood in a narrow, low tunnel. He hesitated but a moment. It made small difference whether they turned right or left. At random, he chose the left.

The passage was very narrow and so low that he had to stoop well over, as he moved cautiously forward. Even his jungle-trained eyes could not see his hand before him in the abysmal blackness. If any crawling dangers lurked in the tunnel, he and Zar would be struck before they sensed their peril.

But nothing stirred or moved. Mere not even the drip of water broke the profound stillness. Apparently all living creatures shunned these lowest depths.

The passage twisted and turned like a snake, straightened out again, then at last began a gradual ascent. Were Ka-Zar's eyes deceiving him? Or was the blackness a shade lighter?

A few moments later he knew that he was right. The Stygian gloom gave way gradually to a dim twilight, which in turn brightened with every step. And at last up ahead was light—a diffused bluish radiance that could only be the effulgence of the moon!

They broke into a run, came to an abrupt halt at the end of the tunnel. They were standing at the bottom of a sheer shaft. But unlike the precipitous hole down which they had first tumbled from the upper earth, this shaft was scalable! Steps had been cut into the rock walls—a long flight of stairs that wound round and round clear up to the level of the world above.

Here was the end of Ka-Zar's long search for an outlet from the lost kingdom! By sheer accident Zar had discovered a long-forgotten, secret exit. The way to freedom—the way back to their dearly-beloved jungle—was clear before them.

With a single, joyous leap Zar gained the fifth step, looked back eagerly for Ka-Zar to follow. But the bronzed giant did not move.

With an impatient growl, Zar urged him to come. To his bewilderment, Ka-Zar sadly shook his head.

"No." The single guttural syllable rumbled in his throat. "Go back to the forest, O mighty Zar. Your faithful mate, your stalwart sons, your jungle people wait anxiously for your coming.

"Ka-Zar will follow. But first there is work to be done. Ka-Zar has given his word and Ka-Zar must not break faith."

Zar crouched on the step, whined.

"Go," repeated Ka-Zar. "Soon Ka-Zar will be free to follow. He will find Nono also—we must not desert the silly one."

Zar whined again. His eyes turned up longingly toward the patch of midnight sky far above.

With heavy heart Ka-Zar raised a bronzed arm in farewell salute, then turned abruptly on his heel.

But before he had taken three strides back into the dim tunnel, the massive form of Zar fell silently into place again at his heels.

Ka-Zar's heart was choked by an emotion that could not be expressed in words. With a low cry he dropped to his knees beside the great lion, clenched his hands in the shaggy mane and laid his cheek against the tawny fur. Then with a lighter heart, he sprang once more to his feet and started back at a long, swinging stride.

HE DID NOT stop until they stood once more under the trap-door that opened into the Temple of Pthos. Before them the mysterious tunnel went yet farther.

Ka-Zar leaned over and spoke gutturally into the ear of the lion. "To go back as we have come is dangerous. Many Oman stir in the caves. Already we have found the way out of this evil place. Shall Ka-Zar go now in the other direction, to see what lies there?"

Zar's answer was simple and given without a second's hesitation—a single growl of assent.

And so the two set forth down the tunnel. As before, the passageway wound and twisted, turned back on itself, veered off again at a tangent. Even the keen sense of direction that was a heritage of these jungle creatures failed them. There was neither moon nor star nor breath of air to tell them where they went, only blackness hemmed in on both sides by walls of rock.

This time they traveled longer than it had taken them to find the shaft at the opposite end. They traveled until Zar's paws grew tender from the rough floor, until Ka-Zar began to wonder whether the passage was truly endless.

Always, though, they maintained their caution. Zar felt his foothold at every step, lest a pitfall send him hurtling downward. Ka-Zar kept one hand on the wall at his side, the other thrust out before him.

Then abruptly the floor of the tunnel sloped steeply upward— up, up, a hundred paces until Ka-Zar was halted by a blank wall.

Groping about him in the impenetrable gloom, he discovered a trap-door, like the one that opened into the temple, directly above his head. The roof of the passage here was very low and without difficulty he located the metal ring in its center.

He growled softly to Zar. "Here is another entrance made long ago by the Oman. Whither it leads, Ka-Zar does not knew. What waits on the other side—danger—death—a trap—Ka-Zar cannot tell. But he shall soon know!"

Zar's only answer was to crouch back on his powerful haunches. They would leap out together—face whatever fate awaited them on the far side of that block of stone.

Ka-Zar grasped the bronze ring with both hands, gritted his teeth and with all the strength at his command, pulled it downward. The slab yielded slowly at first, its rusty hinges protesting. Then as Ka-Zar heaved again, it dropped, disclosing a square aperture.

With an agile spring, his hand ready at the hilt of his knife, he leaped through the opening. Fangs bared, ears flattened back against his skull, Zar vaulted up beside him.

For a moment both stared blankly about them, blinking their eyes in the light of the moon after their long hours in the absolute darkness below. Nothing moved or stirred. Then suddenly Ka-Zar flung back his head and laughed.

He recognized this place—it was a little-used blind alley that ran directly back of Tamiris' palace.

CHAPTER XXII

PLAN OF CAMPAIGN

L **EAVING ZAR TO** wait for him, Ka-Zar sped swiftly through the deserted halls of the palace on his way to the Queen's apartments.

For the second time that night he pushed through the heavy door without the formality of announcing his coming. On his entrance, Tamiris whirled from the balcony, where she had been brooding over her beleaguered city.

Then with a little, glad cry she recognized the bronzed figure in the doorway and with hands outstretched she ran to meet him.

Without thinking, Ka-Zar clasped her tiny hands in his own, looked deep into her melting eyes. The Queen veiled hers at last with long lashes and a little breathlessly she drew away.

"Ka-Zar!" she breathed with a long drawn sigh of relief. "Merciful Isis has heard my prayer and has answered it. You return safely once more to Khalli. You have succeeded?"

"By half," said Ka-Zar. "The fat-bellied Seti is dead—a victim to his own well of poison—to the bitter waters of his own god."

Tamiris' eyes lit up with exultation, then clouded over. "And Zut—you found him not?"

Ka-Zar shook his head. "No. But Ka-Zar had discovered something else. Ka-Zar has a plan that may yet defeat the hordes of blacks and save your city, O Tamiris."

"Speak," she said urgently. "My life—nay, that means nothing—my kingdom is in your hands."

Swiftly Ka-Zar told her of the secret tunnel he had stumbled on; how it led from the very wall of the palace beneath them to the spot in the Temple of Pthos where the fallen idol had stood.

"From the state of this passage," continued Ka-Zar, "no man knows of its existence. Not even the all-knowing Zut, for many, many moons have passed since it has last been used."

"And your plan?" continued Tamiris eagerly, impatient for him to continue.

"A simple one," answered Ka-Zar. "At the head of a hundred of your picked men, Ka-Zar will lead the way through the tunnel. Then while Ankhamen makes a great show of fight from the walls of the city, we will fall upon Zut and his warriors from the rear in a surprise attack.

"In the instant we strike, Ankhamen is to throw open the gate and sally forth with his men. Thus, caught between our two forces, Zut's slaves will be dazed and will fall easy victim to our spears and swords." He drew himself up to his full height. "Ka-Zar will see that Zut escapes him not a second time."

Tamiris' eyes were alight with a new hope—and with something else, too—when he had finished.

"Well conceived, O mighty Ka-Zar," she exclaimed. "It shall be done as you say. The pick of my men shall follow you." With an eager step she crossed the room to a gilded cord that hung by her bed. She jerked it twice and somewhere deep in the palace a brazen gong clanged. Then she returned and stood by Ka-Zar's side. All her old arrogance had deserted her. With bowed head she stood before him, humble, meek.

"True, I have prayed to the goddess Isis that Khalli might be saved," she murmured. "But I have prayed more you be spared the evil fortunes of war. Oh Ka-Zar...."

But Ka-Zar was not to know then the confession that was in her heart. A heavy fist sounded on the portal. At a word from Tamiris the door opened and Ankhamen strode into the room. For a moment he stared with open-eyed amazement at Ka-Zar, then made a low obeisance before the Queen.

"Rise, faithful Ankhamen," said Tamiris. "And behold in Ka-Zar the saviour of Khalli. He has a plan conceived by the gods. And something in my heart tells me that it will not fail."

CHAPTER XXIII

THE BATTLE AND WHAT FOLLOWED

AN HOUR LATER, Ka-Zar and Zar once more descended down the sheer black slope of the tunnel. But this time they were not alone. In single file a hundred soldiers followed them. Flares lighted the way but though they were deep in the bowels of the earth, Ka-Zar took no further chances. Silence was the strict order. And the tunnel stirred only to the shuffle of many feet and the occasional clink of metal.

When they emerged from the dim temple, Fortune still favored the jungle god. There were no warriors to be seen and only a few hags, terrified at the sight of Ka-Zar, the mighty lion and the file of armed men, scurried for their holes and stayed quaking in them.

And so by what seemed a miracle they made their way through the jungle and came at last within sight of their enemies, without a single alarm having been raised.

For a long hour, tense, alert, every sense and perception on trigger edge, Ka-Zar crouched low in the dense tangle of forest that encroached on the clearing surrounding the beleaguered ramparts of Khalli. Resting on the ground before him was a ponderous, two-bladed sword. By his side crouched the faithful Zar, the hairs of his mane standing stiff and erect. Behind his back, already over their first fear of the great beast, lay a hundred of Tamiris' most trusted warriors.

They had been hand-picked by Ankhamen himself. And before following Ka-Zar into the secret tunnel, each man had sworn that for him there would be no retreat that night.

Now they waited, impatient, eager for the final conflict while the moon slipped slowly down the western sky.

Before them, in the open clearing before the city, Zut's men still stormed about the walls. With each long day, of the fruitless seige their blood lust had increased. They were a mob, a pack of hungry wolves closing in for the kill.

The sweat of impatience standing out on his brow, even though the air was chill, Ka-Zar watched as the pale moon dipped at last behind the surrounding cliffs. An instant later, as if unseen hands were pulling it, a carpet of dark shadow raced out from the walls and engulfed his hiding place and his men.

With a long, pent-up sigh of relief he snatched up his sword and rose swiftly to his feet. As one, the men behind him rose with him. Zar was already bellying forward to the edge of the jungle wall.

With the jungle giant in the lead, the raiding party edged cautiously forward a few feet until they stood on the very edge of the clearing. There was grim resolution in every man's eye as he silently picked out his first victim. Muscles bulged, bellies tautened.

Ka-Zar turned to his men and issued his last order. "At the call of the lion, break a long pace from the jungle into the open—let go your spears in a single volley—then close with swinging sword."

The men nodded. Ka-Zar turned back once more to the clearing, saw that Zar's mighty back was already arched for the spring. His tawny eyes became flecked with steel. A great joy was in his heart. First he would save the Queen and her lost city, then with Zar at his side and Nono on his shoulder, he would traverse for the last time the underground passageways— to freedom. To freedom and his jungle domain.

With a sudden exultant movement he flung back his head. His chest expanded to the full and the rumbling roar of the lion crashed from his lips. With the cry still rattling in his throat he leaped forward. Behind him, with the hoarse shouting of a thousand men instead of a meager hundred, his men followed after him.

A SHRILL WAIL of alarm went up from the slaves at the sudden, unexpected onslaught. And as they turned to face the new danger that threatened them, the air became suddenly alive with hungry, steel-tipped spears.

Not a spear was wasted. Every one found its mark. The charge of the slaves was checked in confusion. And as the blacks recoiled before the slashing advance of Ka-Zar and his men, Ankhamen threw open the gate of the City and at the head of his men sallied forth.

The maneuver was executed with neatness and dispatch. Caught between two lines of charging steel the slaves were thrown into a panic. The only explanation they had for this sudden attack on their rear was that Pthos, their god of darkness, had deserted them—that Isis had prevailed.

And then over the din and clatter of battle, Ka-Zar heard the voice of Zut. The counsellor had earlier, during the lull in the fighting when Ka-Zar had made his secret sally out of Khalli, gone from the caves to the battle-front. He had come only to exhort his black horde to victory, planning a thundering assault on the city on the morrow. Now he had been trapped with his men and his shrill voice rose in a frantic effort to lash them on.

In vain.

Even the will of their leader could not help them now.

Ka-Zar's pulses leaped as he finally made out the gaunt form of his enemy, striking out blindly at friend and foe alike in a sudden panic as he realized that defeat was inevitable. He plunged heedlessly in that direction, his great sword flashing death to right and left, with Zar dealing terror beside him.

But many men were between Ka-Zar and the man he wanted so desperately to reach. Zut saw him coming from a distance, saw the huge lion that sent the blacks shrieking in all directions.

The blood turned to water in Zut's veins. His craven heart almost stopped beating. Then in mad panic he burst through the ranks of the slaves and with his tattered robes whipping about his skinny legs, plunged headlong into the forest and headed toward the distant caves.

Ka-Zar saw him disappear—voiced his fury, not in the language of Khalli but in a guttural snarl to Zar.

Together they redoubled their savage onslaught, working their way toward the point where Zut had vanished. Their path was a bloody one. Blacks screamed and died before Ka-Zar's flashing sword; met a fearful fate before the sabre claws and dripping fangs of the mighty Zar. It was the presence of the massive lion, as much as anything else, that accounted for the rout.

They were free of the milling press at last. With low growls rumbling in their throats, the mighty brothers of the jungle plunged into the underbrush that fringed the forest. Ka-Zar took to the trees, swinging in long flights from bough to bough to keep pace with the charging lion below. He had a keen intuition that Zut was fleeing to but one place—the Temple of Pthos. It seemed fitting and proper, fore-ordained that the denouement between them should take place in that dim vaulted chamber, amid the ruins of the image of the god.

Whether the hate in his heart had sharpened his senses, or whether it was merely the suggestion of his own mind, Ka-Zar thought he could still catch the hated scent of Zut on the sultry air. But the fleeing counsellor had had a fair start and mortal fear had lent wings to his feet.

They caught no sight of him as they burst from the jungle, raced to the opening in the cliffs and headed up the shore of the lake. But when they turned at last into the tunnel that led to the temple, there was no doubt about the scent that assailed their nostrils. A powerful odor is given off by beast—or man— in the grip of mortal fear. Both jungle-man and lion caught the scent, realized its significance. Already the taste of victory was theirs and they made the passage reverberate to their roars.

THE BRONZE DOOR of the temple was closed but with a reckless courage, Ka-Zar flung it open and the pair bounded across the threshold.

Just inside the portal they slid to a sudden halt.

On the opposite side of the vast chamber stood Zut, his face ashen-gray and his eyes haggard. Crouched at his feet was N'Jagi and Zut's hand was on the leopard's chain.

Ka-Zar's intuition had led him to the right place.

The hand of the treacherous counsellor had never known weapons. He flinched now at the sight of Ka-Zar's blood-stained sword. In his mad panic he had come to the one friend he had in Khalli—the one creature who would lay down his life to defend him.

Leopard and lion faced each other across the dim stretch that separated them. Then the shrill scream of N'Jagi and the challenging roar of Zar blended in a blast that made the very walls tremble. Ka-Zar dropped a hand to his friend's neck, restrained him.

"A fitting combat," he shouted to Zut. "Ka-Zar against Zut—my brother against yours. A kingdom for the victors! Death for the vanquished! Loose the leopard, O Zut!"

Already the ring of triumph was in his voice. Zut heard it and his bloodless lips could not answer. Instead, he fumbled with the chain, snapped open the glittering link that joined N'Jagi's collar. He pointed a trembling, bony finger at the bronzed giant and the tawny lion in the doorway. A thin trickle of saliva drooled from the corner of his mouth as he urged the beast forward.

"Slay them!" he mumbled. "For long years Zut has fed and nursed you. Now defend your master!"

N'Jagi's ears flattened against his skull. His lips pulled back from his teeth and his emerald eyes glared malevolently. With a single lithe bound he sprang to the middle of the temple, stopped in a crouch.

Near the portal Zar and Ka-Zar tensed. For a moment not a sound broke the stillness but their hoarse breathing. N'Jagi snarled—a low, strangled sound that started deep down in his throat. He glared at the pair in the doorway. And fear crept into his glittering orbs.

Once before he had fought with the two-legged one—had been at the point of death. New beside him stood N'Jagi's hereditary enemy—the most enormous lion he had ever seen! For a moment the devils of hate battled with the fear in N'Jagi's black heart. Then suddenly he realized that his enemies stood between him and the door. The vague notion that he was trapped was too much for him. An eerie whine came from his throat.

Zut, too, was in the grip of a terrible fear. In a sudden desperation he stepped forward, cried out to N'Jagi: "Fall upon them! Rend them with your claws! Tear them with your fangs!"

The hairs along the leopard's spine quivered. The tip of his tail lashed back and forth. With a hunted look in his green eyes he glanced first at Ka-Zar and the lion, then at the frightened man who egged him on.

Suddenly a red film dimmed his eyes. The fact that Zut was his master was wiped from his animal brain. Zut's shrill voice was hateful in his ears. A blind fury, such as he had never known, filled his heart. With a hideous scream he gathered his haunches under him and sprang—sprang straight at his paralyzed master!

TOO LATE ZUT flung up his hands in horror. Too late he stumbled backward. The black fury was upon him—ripping, clawing, snarling. And this time the scream of the leopard blended with another sound—a quavering cry of mortal anguish. Claws of pointed steel dug deep into Zut's vitals; N'Jagi's foetid breath was hot on his face as he crashed to the ground.

For a moment Ka-Zar forgot their own hatred of these two, as they stared at the bloody spectacle. The smell, the taste of blood sent N'Jagi berserk. He clawed the lifeless body of his protector until nothing remained but a torn thing of mangled flesh and tattered rags.

Then suddenly his flat black head came up and he spat in the direction of the doorway. His fear was gone, now. It was not courage, either, but sheer madness that made him spring across the temple.

With a rumbling growl, Zar bounded out from under Ka-Zar's hand. Like a tawny fury he met the leopard's charge with one of his own.

And Ka-Zar, clutching his knife, stayed his own hand to watch the most magnificent spectacle of the jungle—Zar, aroused, terrible in all his might.

Leopard and lion met in mid-air and the crushing shock of the impact sent them both sprawling But neither loosed his hold and they rolled over and over, slashing, clawing, ripping.

N'Jagi fought for his life. And Zar—to bold the supremacy with which he reigned over all the beasts of the wilderness. The lion was heavier, but the lithe black leopard was faster.

Breathing fast, his nostrils flared, his tawny eyes gleaming, Ka-Zar watched the death struggle between the two great beasts. He could not have taken a hand if he wished, for it was almost impossible to distinguish friend from foe in that whirling mass of black and tawny fur. He knew, also, that Zar would hold it a deadly insult if he interfered.

Back and forth they battled across the width of the temple. And now a trail of crimson spattered their wake.

Then suddenly a piercing screech echoed in the vaulted chamber. It died abruptly. A massive tawny body rose. Ka-Zar could see Zar's jaws still clamped about the throat of his enemy. The great lion shook the limp black body beneath him from side to side. Then his jaws relaxed their grip and the leopard lay still—never to move again.

Slowly, majestically, Zar turned to face his brother in the doorway. His regal head came up and it seemed strangely fitting that the Temple of Pthos, with the shattered idol of its god, with the body of its unholy guardian lifeless on the floor, should echo to the defiant rumble of the jungle lord's kill.

CHAPTER XXIV

FREEDOM

BY THE TIME Ka-Zar and Zar reached the battle-ground, the fighting was over. A few warriors still harassed groups of fleeing blacks, but most of the slaves had long since fled into the wilderness or scurried into caverns in the cliffs.

The triumphant Egyptians lined the ramparts of the tiered city, clustered about the gates that were now thrown wide. They greeted the appearance of Ka-Zar and the lion with a concerted cheer that made the valley ring.

The stately figure of Ankhamen moved up as they neared the gate.

"You have done your part well," Ka-Zar told him. "You have struck straight and true and Ka-Zar is proud to call you comrade."

Ankhamen bowed low. "I could ask for no greater reward than the words my leader has just spoken," he answered gravely. "Fain would I sing your praises, O mighty Ka-Zar. But I must not delay you. The Queen anxiously awaits your coming in the palace."

It was a procession of state that escorted Ka-Zar and the great lion up through the city. All the way was lined with the inhabitants of Khalli, who had thronged out to see their bronzed god. Ka-Zar could not restrain the ghost of a bitter smile as he remembered that he had first entered the city in chains. By his side Zar padded majestically along, proudly aloof to the cheers of these Oman whom he would always despise.

Their escort left them at the gates of the palace. There were

439

pleased smiles and sly winks exchanged behind their backs as alone the pair made their way to the apartments of the Queen.

Again Tamiris had decked herself out in all her most resplendent raiment. This time she was sheathed in white like an alabaster statue, glittering with gems and swirling feathers. The breath caught in Ka-Zar's throat as he entered the room and she rose to meet him.

She took one step forward—then stopped. She stiffened as she saw the great tawny lion who stood at Ka-Zar's side.

It was a tribute to her courageous heart that she neither moved nor cried out at the sight of Zar, for this was the first time that she had ever been near such a terrifying beast. "Fear not my brother," cried Ka-Zar, stepping to meet her. "Fear nothing again. Zut is dead—slain by his own hideous guardian of the Temple of Pthos. Ka-Zar has given you back your throne."

Tamiris stretched out her hands. Her cheeks were flushed, her eyes starry. "And Tamiris lays it at your feet, O mighty lord of the jungle," she said huskily. "All my pride has crumbled to ashes. I see that in your eyes that I have longed to see there—and that is enough. You do not speak—so I do it for you. Come to me, Ka-Zar!"

She let her hands drop to her sides, palms turned forward. It was an eloquent gesture. Her regal head tilted back, her scarlet lips parted, her firm breast high, she offered herself to him.

Ka-Zar felt strangely awed, humbled. He had a mad impulse to fling himself before her, bury his hot face in the folds of her snowy draperies, kiss her tiny sandaled feet.

Surely no ordinary mortal would have hesitated. But then, Ka-Zar was no ordinary mortal.

WITH A COURTLY gesture that he had never been taught, he dropped to one knee and bowed his head.

"Gracious Queen," he said mournfully, "Ka-Zar could find no greater happiness than to stay forever by your side. But his heart is heavy within him. There is a duty that calls."

A spasm of pain crossed Tamiris' face. Her cheeks paled, but slowly she nodded. She was a daughter of the Ptolemies and she knew the stern demand of duty.

Ka-Zar looked appealingly up at her. "The kingdom of Tamiris is once more safe," he explained. "But how fares Ka-Zar's jungle domain? He must return there to see, to make sure that peace and quiet reign over the wilderness." He rose to his feet, took her tiny hands in his own and looked into her eyes with such burning depths in his own that she quivered under his stare. "But Ka-Zar shall return," he said simply.

Once more Ka-Zar, with Nono atop his shoulder and Zar beside him, stood at the base of the steep shaft that led from the secret tunnel to the world above. And this time, as Zar bounded joyfully up the steps hewn in the rocky walls, his brother followed eagerly in his wake.

With exultant hearts they emerged, stood for a moment to drink in the precious draught of freedom. The immense blue bowl of the sky was high and cloudless above them. A dim speck in the azure vastness, Kru the vulture sailed on motionless pinions. A vagrant breeze stirred the long locks of Ka-Zar's hair, brought to his nostrils mingled odors of the distant places through which it traveled—the perfume of flowers, the rushes that edged a lake, the damp scent of the jungle. He inhaled deeply, filled his mighty lungs.

Nono chattered with delight. Zar raised his massive head and gave vent to a joyous roar.

They had come out on the side of a bare, rock-strewn bank. Above them the earth rose sheer toward the top of the tumbled, inaccessible cliffs that hemmed in the lost valley. Zar swung his head slowly from side to side, his amber eyes narrowed. Then with a leap, he bounded up the face of the bank.

His hind leg dislodged a heavy stone. It tore loose from its moorings, rolled over and over with swiftly-increasing momentum. Earth and pebbles followed it in a sliding rush—that increased in volume with every yard.

Ka-Zar whirled, cried out. Zar's legs were already going out from under him. He struggled to escape the landslide that he had created, dug in deep with his claws as with an ominous rumble the whole face of the bank came crashing downward.

Ka-Zar gained safety with a series of mighty leaps. Zar slid for some distance on the crest of the landslide, then with a last desperate effort, managed to bound clear of the falling earth.

The air was suddenly obscured by fine particles of heavy dust. The trio choked, coughed as the stuff got into their nostrils.

At last it gradually subsided and the air cleared again. And as it did, a low cry of dismay broke from Ka-Zar's lips.

The shaft from which they had just come—the opening to the secret tunnel—was no longer visible! With a whine he leaped back to the place where he had stood a few moments before, pawed wildly at the earth. But to no avail. The secret entrance and exit of the lost kingdom was sealed—closed forever!

THE VISION OF the Queen Tamiris, as he had last seen her, rose up before Ka-Zar's eye. With the keenest anguish he realized that never would he see her again. Bravely she would wait for him to return. And then when at last she learned about the sealing of the tunnel, she would go back to her lonely throne.

With haunted eyes he turned to look at Zar. And the lion instinctively averted his head.

Swift, keen suspicion flashed to Ka-Zar's brain. Zar had not been able to understand the words that he and Tamiris had exchanged at their parting. But the wise lion's eyes were keen— he would have read their words in their eloquent eyes.

Had Zar done this an purpose? Had Zar started this land-slide—risking his own life—so that his brother would not leave the jungle to return to Khalli? A terrible rage flared in Ka-Zar's breast.

He knew that he had guessed the truth.

Then slowly his wrath died within him. Perhaps, after all, Zar was right. The wilderness was his home. Quite probably the frail hands of a woman—even such a glorious creature as Tamiris—would fail to hold him in the confines of the sunken valley.

His shoulders squared. The sun gleamed on his bronzed body as he drew himself erect. The gentle fingers of the breeze touched his cheek, played with his hair. With a precious memory, but no sorrow in his heart he turned toward the direction of his jungle home and with a single guttural growl to Zar, said: "Come."

Freedom was his—freedom not only of body but of spirit—as with a glad rumble deep in his throat, Zar fell into place at his side and the trio headed for home.

CPSIA information can be obtained at www.ICGtesting.com
Printed in the USA
BVOW06s2338070416

443465BV00019B/138/P